DATE DUE

PRINTED IN U.S.A.

SOMETHING ABOUT THE AUTHOR®

Something about
the Author *was named
an "Outstanding
Reference Source"
the highest honor given
by the American
Library Association
Reference and Adult
Services Division.*

ISSN 0276-816X

R

SOMETHING ABOUT THE AUTHOR®

Facts and Pictures about Authors and Illustrators of Books for Young People

EDITED BY
DIANE TELGEN

VOLUME 72

Gale Research Inc. • DETROIT • WASHINGTON, D.C. • LONDON

STAFF

Editor: Diane Telgen

Associate Editor: Elizabeth A. Des Chenes

Senior Editor: James G. Lesniak

Sketchwriters: Marilyn K. Basel, Sonia Benson, Carol Brennan, Joanna Brod, Victoria France Charabati, Bruce Ching, Kathleen J. Edgar, Marie Ellavich, Norma R. Fryatt, David M. Galens, Anne Janette Johnson, Denise E. Kasinec, Jane M. Kelly, Sharon Malinowski, Margaret Mazurkiewicz, Mark F. Mikula, Tom Pendergast, Cornelia A. Pernik, Nancy Rampson, Susan M. Reicha, Jean W. Ross, Mary K. Ruby, Michael D. Senecal, Pamela L. Shelton, Kenneth R. Shepherd, Deborah A. Stanley, and Polly A. Vedder

Research Manager: Victoria B. Cariappa
Research Supervisor: Mary Rose Bonk
Editorial Associates: Reginald A. Carlton, Clare Collins, Andrew Guy Malonis, and Norma Sawaya
Editorial Assistants: Mike Avolio, Patricia Bowen, Rachel A. Dixon, Shirley Gates, Sharon McGilvray, and Devra M. Sladics

Margaret A. Chamberlain, *Picture Permissions Supervisor*
Pamela A. Hayes, *Permissions Associate*
Amy Lynn Emrich, Karla Kulkis, Keith Reed, Nancy Rattenbury, *Permissions Assistants*

Production Director: Mary Beth Trimper
External Production Assistant: Shanna P. Heilveil
Art Director: Cynthia Baldwin
Keyliners: Nick Jakubiak, C. J. Jonik, and Yolanda Latham

 This book is printed on acid-free paper that meets the minimum requirements of American National Standard for Information Sciences—Permanence Paper for Printed Library Materials, ANSI Z39.48-1984.

Library of Congress Catalog Card Number 72-27107

ISBN 0-8103-2282-X ISSN 0276-816X

Printed in the United States of America.

Published simultaneously in the United Kingdom by Gale Research International Limited
(An affiliated company of Gale Research Inc.)

10 9 8 7 6 5 4 3 2 1

Contents

Introduction

Something about the Author (*SATA*) is an ongoing reference series that deals with the lives and works of authors and illustrators of children's books. *SATA* includes not only well-known authors and illustrators whose books are widely read, but also those less prominent people whose works are just coming to be recognized. This series is often the only readily available information source on emerging writers or artists. You'll find *SATA* informative and entertaining whether you are a student, a librarian, an English teacher, a parent, or simply an adult who enjoys children's literature for its own sake.

What's Inside SATA

SATA provides detailed information about authors and illustrators who span the full time range of children's literature, from early figures like John Newbery and L. Frank Baum to contemporary figures like Judy Blume and Richard Peck. Authors in the series represent primarily English-speaking countries, particularly the United States, Canada, and the United Kingdom. Also included, however, are authors from around the world whose works are available in English translation. The writings represented in *SATA* include those created intentionally for children and young adults as well as those written for a general audience and known to interest younger readers. These writings cover the entire spectrum of children's literature, including picture books, humor, folk and fairy tales, animal stories, mystery and adventure, science fiction and fantasy, historical fiction, poetry and nonsense verse, drama, biography, and nonfiction.

Obituaries are also included in *SATA* and are intended not only as death notices but as concise views of people's lives and work. Additionally, each edition features newly revised and updated entries for a selection of *SATA* listees who remain of interest to today's readers and who have been active enough to require extensive revision of their earlier biographies.

Two Convenient Indexes

In response to suggestions from librarians, *SATA* indexes no longer appear in each volume, but are included in alternate (odd-numbered) volumes of the series, beginning with Volume 57.

SATA continues to include two indexes that cumulate with each alternate volume: the Illustrations Index, arranged by the name of the illustrator, gives the number of the volume and page where the illustrator's work appears in the current volume as well as all preceding volumes in the series; the Author Index gives the number of the volume in which a person's Biographical Sketch or Obituary appears in the current volume as well as all preceding volumes in the series.

The Author Index also includes references to authors and illustrators who appear in Gale's *Yesterday's Authors of Books for Children, Children's Literature Review,* and the *Something about the Author Autobiography Series.*

Easy-to-Use Entry Format

Whether you're already familiar with the *SATA* series or just getting acquainted, you will want to be aware of the kind of information that an entry provides. In every *SATA* entry the editors attempt to give as complete a picture of the person's life and work as possible. A typical entry in *SATA* includes the following clearly labeled information sections:

- *PERSONAL:* date and place of birth and death, parents' names and occupations, name of spouse, date of marriage, and names of children, educational institutions attended, degrees received, religious and political affiliations, hobbies and other interests.

- *ADDRESSES:* complete home, office, and agent's address.

- *CAREER:* name of employer, position, and dates for each career post; military service.

- *MEMBER:* memberships and offices held in professional and civic organizations.

- *AWARDS, HONORS:* literary and professional awards received.

- *WRITINGS:* title-by-title chronological bibliography of books written and/or illustrated, listed by genre when known; lists of other notable publications, such as plays, screenplays, and periodical contributions.

- *ADAPTATIONS:* a list of films, television programs, plays, and other media which have been adapted from the author's work.

- *WORK IN PROGRESS:* description of projects in progress.

- *SIDELIGHTS:* a biographical portrait of the author's development, either directly from the person—and often written specifically for the *SATA* entry—or gathered from diaries, letters, interviews, or other published sources.

- *FOR MORE INFORMATION SEE:* references for further reading.

- *EXTENSIVE ILLUSTRATIONS:* photographs, movie stills, manuscript samples, book covers, and other interesting visual materials supplement the text.

How a SATA Entry Is Compiled

A *SATA* entry progresses through a series of steps. If the biographee is living, the *SATA* editors try to secure information directly from him or her through a questionnaire. From the information that the biographee supplies, the editors prepare an entry, filling in any essential missing details with research and/or telephone interviews. When necessary, the author or illustrator is sent a copy of the entry to check for accuracy and completeness.

If the biographee is deceased or cannot be reached by questionnaire, the *SATA* editors examine a wide variety of published sources to gather information for an entry. Biographical and bibliographic sources are consulted, as are book reviews, feature articles, published interviews, and material sometimes obtained from the biographee's family, publishers, agent, or other associates. Entries compiled entirely from secondary sources are marked with an asterisk (*).

We Welcome Your Suggestions

We invite you to examine the entire *SATA* series, starting with this volume. Please write and tell us if we can make *SATA* even more helpful to you. Send comments and suggestions to: The Editor, *Something about the Author*, Gale Research Inc., 835 Penobscot Bldg., Detroit, Michigan 48226.

Acknowledgments

Grateful acknowledgment is made to the following publishers, authors, and artists whose works appear in this volume.

CATHERINE CORLEY ANDERSON. Illustration by Catherine Corley Anderson from her *Puppet Boy.* Children's Activities, 1950. Reprinted by permission of Catherine Corley Anderson./ Jacket of *John F. Kennedy: Young People's President,* by Catherine Corley Anderson. Copyright © 1991 by Lerner Publications Co. Front cover photograph courtesy of the Minnesota-Democratic-Farmer-Labor Party Central Committee. Reprinted by permission of Lerner Publications Co./ Photograph courtesy of Catherine Corley Anderson.

CHERITH BALDRY. Cover of *A Rush of Golden Wings,* by Cherith Baldry. Copyright © 1991 by Cherith Baldry. Cover art by Michael Carroll. Reprinted by permission of Good News Publishers/Crossway Books, 1300 Crescent Street, Wheaton, IL 60187./ Photograph courtesy of Cherith Baldry.

NINA BAWDEN. Jacket of *Kept in the Dark,* by Nina Bawden. Copyright © 1982 by Nina Bawden. Jacket illustration copyright © 1982 by James Nazz. All rights reserved. Reprinted by Lothrop, Lee, and Shepard Books, a division of William Morrow & Company, Inc./ Jacket of *The Finding,* by Nina Bawden. Jacket illustration copyright © 1985 by Catherine Stock. Reprinted by permission of Lothrop, Lee, and Shepard Books, a division of William Morrow & Company, Inc./ Cover of *Squib,* by Nina Bawden. Copyright © 1971 by Nina Bawden. Cover illustration by Gerry Contreras. Reprinted by permission of HarperCollins Publishers./ Jacket of *The Peppermint Pig,* by Nina Bawden. Copyright © 1975 by Nina Bawden. Jacket painting by Charles Lilly. Reprinted by permission of HarperCollins Publishers./ Photograph courtesy of Nina Bawden.

MARGARET BINGLEY. Cover of *Deadtime Story,* by Margaret Bingley. Cover copyright © by Popular Library. Reprinted by permission of Popular Library./ Photograph courtesy of Margaret Bingley.

DAVID BIRCHMAN. Jacket of *Brother Billy Bronto's Bygone Blues Band,* by David F. Birchman. Jacket illustration copyright © 1992 by John O'Brien. Reprinted by permission of Lothrop, Lee, and Shepard Books, a division of William Morrow & Company, Inc./ Photograph courtesy of David Birchman.

GARY BLACKWOOD. Photograph courtesy of Gary Blackwood. Cover of *Beyond the Door,* by Gary Blackwood. Reprinted by permission of Atheneum Publishers, an imprint of Macmillan Publishing Co.

CANDY DAWSON BOYD. Jacket of *Breadsticks and Blessing Places,* by Candy Dawson Boyd. Copyright © 1985 by Macmillan Publishing Company, a division of Macmillan, Inc. Jacket copyright © 1985 by Jerry Pinkney. Reprinted by permission of Jerry Pinkney./ Cover of *Circle of Gold,* by Candy Dawson Boyd. Cover painting by Charles Lilly. Reprinted by permission of Scholastic, Inc./ Cover of *Charlie Pippin,* by Candy Dawson Boyd. Puffin Books, 1988. Copyright © 1987 by Candy Dawson Boyd. Cover illustration by Cornelius Van Wright, copyright © 1987 by Macmillan Publishing Company. Reprinted by permission of Cornelius Van Wright./ Photograph courtesy of Candy Dawson Boyd.

ROBBIE BRANSCUM. Jacket of *Old Blue Tilley,* by Robbie Branscum. Macmillan Publishing Company, 1991. Copyright © 1991 by Macmillan Publishing Company, a division of Macmillan, Inc. Copyright © 1991 by Ted Lewin. Jacket design by REM studio. Reprinted by permission of Ted Lewin./ Photograph by Ted Beilby and Rick Eissler.

BRUCE BROOKS. Jacket of *The Moves Make the Man,* by Bruce Brooks. Jacket art copyright © 1984 by Wayne Winfield. Jacket copyright © 1984 by Harper & Row, Publishers, Inc. Reprinted by permission of HarperCollins Publishers./ Cover of *Midnight Hour Encores,* by Bruce Brooks. Harper Keypoint, 1988. Copyright © 1986 by Bruce Brooks. Cover art copyright © 1988 by Michael Deas. Cover copyright © 1988 by Harper & Row, Publishers, Inc. Reprinted by permission of HarperCollins Publishers./ Jacket of *No Kidding,* by Bruce Brooks. Jacket art copyright © 1989 by Fred Marcellino. Jacket copyright © 1989 by Harper & Row, Publishers, Inc. Reprinted by permission of HarperCollins Publishers./ Jacket of *Everywhere,* by Bruce Brooks. Jacket art copyright © 1990 by Kam Mak. Jacket Copyright © 1990 by Harper & Row, Publishers, Inc. Reprinted by permission of HarperCollins Publishers.

ASHLEY BRYAN. Illustrations from *Beat the Story-Drum, Pum-Pum,* retold by Ashley Bryan. Atheneum, 1987. Copyright © 1980 by Ashley Bryan. Illustrations by Ashley Bryan. Reprinted with the permission of Atheneum Publishers, an imprint of Macmillan Publishing Company./ Illustration from *The Dancing Granny,* by Ashley Bryan. Copyright © 1977 by Ashley Bryan. Reprinted with the permission of Atheneum Publishers, an imprint of Macmillan Publishing Company./ Photograph by Matthew Wysocki.

R. E. C. BURRELL. Photograph courtesy of R. E. C. Burrell.

RICHARD & JUDY DOCKREY YOUNG. Photograph courtesy of Richard and Judy Dockrey Young.

something about the author

ANDERSON, C. C.
See ANDERSON, Catherine Corley

*   *   *

ANDERSON, Catherine Corley 1909-
(C. C. Anderson, Catherine C. Anderson, Mrs. Melvin Anderson, Cora Lee, Coralie)

PERSONAL: Born March 21, 1909, in Chicago, IL; daughter of Gaynor Joseph (a book publisher) and Anna (a schoolteacher; maiden name, Higgins) Corley; married Melvin Anderson (a police lieutenant), January 15, 1930 (deceased); children: Judy (Mrs. Earl Oquist), Charles. *Education:* Attended University of Chicago, 1930-33; School of the Art Institute of Chicago, B.A.E., 1933; attended St. Xavier College, 1933-34, and Northwestern University, 1934. *Politics:* Moderate liberal. *Religion:* Roman Catholic. *Hobbies and other interests:* Puppetry, live theater, painting, drawing, illustrating.

ADDRESSES: Home—3513 Vanderbilt Ct., Garland, TX 75043.

CAREER: Mercy High School, Chicago, IL, art teacher, 1934-35; Chicago Park District, Chicago, artcraft instructor, 1935-42; free-lance writer and illustrator, 1942—. Scott, Foresman (publisher), free-lance editor of school readers, 1944-46. Chicago Marionette Company, cofounder, 1932-85. Council of Catholic Women, study club leader, 1960-85; National Museum of Women in the Arts, charter member.

MEMBER: Children's Reading Round Table (Chicago branch; secretary, 1956-57; vice president and program chair, 1957-58; president, 1958-59), Puppeteers of America, Art Institute Alumni Association, St. Louis Puppet Guild.

AWARDS, HONORS: Poetry prizes from Poets Club of Chicago and Catholic Poetry Society, both c. 1960, and National Federation of State Poetry Societies, 1968.

CATHERINE CORLEY ANDERSON

"Puppet Boy," a tale set in Portugal, is just one of hundreds of stories Anderson has written for children's magazines. (Illustration by the author.)

WRITINGS:

Officer O'Malley on the Job, illustrations by Chauncey Maltman, Albert Whitman, 1954.
Sister Beatrice Goes to Bat, Bruce Publishing, 1958.
Sister Beatrice Goes West, self-illustrated, Bruce Publishing, 1961.
Sister Beatrice and the Mission Mystery, self-illustrated, Bruce Publishing, 1963.
John F. Kennedy: Young People's President, Lerner Publications, 1991.

Author of "Busy Bee Fun Books," under name Catherine C. Anderson, Child Life, c. 1952-53. Contributor of hundreds of stories, articles, plays, poems, songs, and illustrations, sometimes under names C. C. Anderson, Mrs. Melvin Anderson, Coralie, and Cora Lee, to magazines, including *Chicago Tribune Magazine, Childcraft, Children's Activities, Highlights for Children, JR, Junior Trails,* and *Writer.*

WORK IN PROGRESS: Aladdin and His Wonderful Book, a musical comedy for children; *On with the Puppet Show,* a complete book on puppetry.

SIDELIGHTS: Catherine Corley Anderson told *SATA:* "I'm sure having the kind of parents I had aided me in developing my interest in art and reading and writing. My mother was a schoolteacher before she was married (in those days a teacher had to resign when she got married). She taught me to read long before I went to

school. She was a wonderful poet, far ahead of her time in style. She took me to the library when I was five, and she let me select my own books. My father brought home books from the publishing company he worked for, such as James Fenimore Cooper's 'Leatherstocking Tales,' Charles Dickens, *The Scarlet Pimpernel* by Baroness Emmuska Orczy, *The Legend of Sleepy Hollow* by Washington Irving, and many others.

"I was the oldest of four children in a very happy home. I often think how lucky I was and am. We didn't have a great many luxuries, but we had a comfortable frame home in a far south suburb of Chicago, Illinois. Most all the homes were of wood, with large back yards, middling-size front yards, and luxurious old trees that met to form green cool tunnels over the street in the summertime. We had a park two blocks away, where we had ice skating in the winter, baseball and football games in the summer and fall, Fourth of July picnics, and band concerts. We also had a library, which we visited every two days, winter and summer. An inside municipal swimming pool was only three or four blocks away. Girls used it on alternate days with boys.

"One of our great treats at home was to listen to our mother and father at the piano some evenings, often with a small group of friends, singing and playing all the popular songs of the day. My mother had a beautiful alto voice, and my father was a bass. They played the piano together, not very professionally, but it sounded good to us. My father sang with the First Chapter of the Barbershop Quartet Singers of America.

"I was also lucky in my choice of husband. When we met I was attending the Art Institute of Chicago and he was studying music at the Cosmopolitan College of Music a couple of blocks away. Although Mel had to give up his music career, he never gave up his music, and it was a source of delight to us both. He helped in my writing by getting me library books and in learning puppetry so he could work with me on that. We had a wonderful marriage.

"All my life, writing and art seemed to go hand in hand. I started when I was very young. My parents sent me to a Saturday class in oil painting when I was eight years old. It was at a girls' boarding school, but I and several of my schoolmates from St. Margaret School, a few blocks away, were recommended by our grade-school teacher. We enjoyed those classes a great deal and continued them all through grade school.

"My favorite subject was English composition all through grammar school and high school. In high school I won a city-wide short story contest for students in public and parochial schools. That settled it for me. I was not going to be a teacher, I was going to be a writer

CATHERINE CORLEY ANDERSON

Anderson's interest in John F. Kennedy stems back to a speech she heard him make in 1956.

and artist. I enrolled at the Chicago Art Institute, and I wound up teaching—but teaching art, which I enjoyed.

"Somehow writing always became a part of whatever I was doing. I began writing for children when my son, Charles, was a baby, and my poetry was appearing regularly in newspaper columns.

"Since much of my school life was spent in Catholic schools, it was natural that three of my books featured a peppy, athletic nun, Sister Beatrice. Officer O'Malley was another natural, since my husband became a police officer in Chicago, and I had made a thorough study of the job. I became interested in John F. Kennedy when I heard him on radio making the nominating speech for Adlai Stevenson for president in 1956. I kept a file on him from that time on. After his assassination in 1963 I wrote and talked to many people who knew him, traveled to cities including Brookline, Massachusetts, Brooklyn, New York, Washington, D.C., and Dallas, Texas, and read about fifty books as well as magazine articles and newspapers from all over."

*   *   *

ANDERSON, Catherine C.
See ANDERSON, Catherine Corley

*   *   *

ANDERSON, Mrs. Melvin
See ANDERSON, Catherine Corley

*   *   *

AVERILL, Esther (Holden) 1902-1992
(John Domino)

OBITUARY NOTICE—See index for *SATA* sketch: Born July 24, 1902, in Bridgeport, CT; died May 12, 1992. Publisher, illustrator, and author. A children's book author and publisher, Averill is remembered for her "Cat Club" series of picture books, the first of which, *The Cat Club,* featured a little black cat with a red scarf named Jenny Linsky. After moving to Paris in 1925, Averill began her publishing career in 1931 by establishing the Domino Press, which specialized in children's picture books. Three years later, she returned to the United States and launched the Domino Press, New York. Averill also illustrated much of her own work, including *Jenny's First Party, Jenny's Moonlight Adventure, When Jenny Lost Her Scarf,* and *The Fire Cat.* In addition, she wrote one book, *Fable of a Proud Poppy,* under the pseudonym John Domino.

OBITUARIES AND OTHER SOURCES:

BOOKS

The Writers Directory: 1992-1994, St. James Press, 1991.

PERIODICALS

School Library Journal, July, 1992, p. 16.

B

BALDRY, Cherith 1947-

PERSONAL: Born April 3, 1947, in Lancaster, England; daughter of William (a factory foreman) and Evelyn Annie (a homemaker; maiden name, Dixon) Baker; married Peter James Baldry (a scientist), September 3, 1971; children: William, Adam. *Education:* University of Manchester, B.A. (with honors), 1969; St. Anne's College, Oxford, B.Litt., 1973; Aberdeen Teacher Training College, teaching certificate, 1974. *Religion:* Church of England.

ADDRESSES: Home—12 Wraylands Dr., Reigate, Surrey, England RH2 OLG. *Office*—Priory School, Bolters Lane, Banstead, Surrey, England SM7 2AJ.

CAREER: Jewish High School for Girls, Manchester, England, teacher of English, 1971-73; St. Margaret's School for Girls, Aberdeen, Scotland, teacher of English, speech, and drama, 1975; Fourah Bay College, Freetown, Sierra Leone, lecturer in English literature, 1976-79; Tandridge School District, Surrey, England, teacher of adult education English, 1980-81; Associated Examining Board of Guildford, Surrey, England, assistant examiner, 1980—, moderator of General Certificate of Secondary Education English literature, 1987—; Surrey County Council, Surrey, supply teacher, 1985-86; Stowford College, Sutton, Surrey, teacher of English literature, 1986-88; Priory School, Banstead, Surrey, teacher of English and librarian, 1988—; Cambridge Board, Cambridge, England, assistant examiner of English, 1989—.

MEMBER: Fellowship of Christian Writers (committee member, 1991—), British Science Fiction Association.

AWARDS, HONORS: First prize, *London Calling* magazine competition, 1988, for short story "Happiness Inc."; Nottingham and Notts Drama Association Award, 1991, for *Achilles His Armour.*

CHERITH BALDRY

WRITINGS:

JUVENILE FICTION

The Book and the Phoenix ("Stories of the Six Worlds" series), illustrated by Vic Mitchell, Kingsway, 1989, published as *A Rush of Golden Wings,* Crossway, 1991.

Hostage of the Sea ("Stories of the Six Worlds" series), illustrated by Mitchell, Kingsway, 1990.

The Carpenter's Apprentice ("Stories of the Six Worlds" series), Kingsway, 1992.
The Other Side of the Mountains, Kingsway, in press.

PLAYS

Where Late the Sweet Birds Sang (one-act), produced at Merstham in Surrey, England, published in *Triad 74: A Fine Selection of One-Act Plays,* New Playwrights' Network, 1989.
Achilles His Armour (one-act; produced at Long Eaton in Nottinghamshire, England, 1991), Nottingham and Notts Drama Association, 1991.
House Arrest, New Playwrights' Network, in press.

Also author of play *Out of Darkness.*

OTHER

A Students' Guide to 'The Silver Box' by John Galsworthy, Graham Brash (Singapore), 1989.
Questions and Answers on 'The Merchant of Venice', Graham Brash, in press.

Author of *God and the Little Green Men* in *Vector 163.* Contributor of short stories to periodicals, including *Surrey Mirror, Vector,* and *Xenos.*

WORK IN PROGRESS: Another children's book; an adult science fiction novel.

SIDELIGHTS: Cherith Baldry told *SATA:* "I can't remember a time when I didn't write; certainly, I have memories of doing so as a very small child. My grandfather was a wonderful storyteller, and so making up stories always seemed a natural thing to do. It's only quite recently that I realized not everyone has characters walking around in their head.

"I also became interested in science fiction from a very early age, mainly through sneaking a look at my father's library books. I didn't understand them—they were aimed at adults anyway—but I'll never forget the sensation of something excitingly unusual. Although I started reading children's science fiction as well, in those days it was mostly adventure stories in space suits, and, with a few exceptions, it didn't capture the imagination in the same way.

"When I started writing seriously for publication, I wrote some science fiction, and an Arthurian novel, and quite a lot of detective fiction, all unpublished. I still have an ambition to publish a detective story of the classic puzzle type.

"In all this early material, I never thought of myself as a Christian writer. Although I've always been a Christian, writing a novel about my faith seemed far too difficult an undertaking. Then I began a science fiction novel about a group of people living in a very restricted society, who were gradually going to wake up to the possibilities of freedom and personal commitment. I realized that if I was going to write this book honestly, they had to wake up spiritually as well, and so, terrified, I introduced a Christian theme.

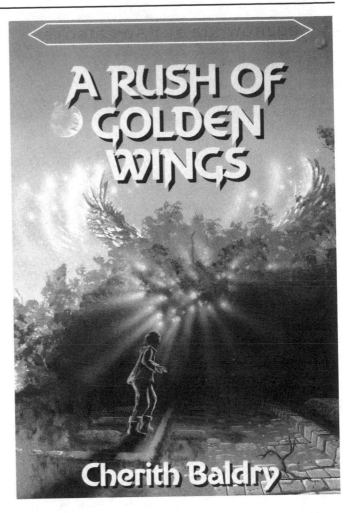

One of Baldry's "Stories of the Six Worlds" series, *A Rush of Golden Wings* recounts a young boy's adventures after he discovers the only copy of the Bible that exists on his world. (Cover illustration by Michael Carroll.)

"This book was rejected by a couple of publishers, and then I went with my husband to Sierra Leone, where we worked for four years, and though I continued to write, difficulties with postage meant that I submitted very little work for publication.

"Back in England I dusted off the Christian book and tried it again, this time with specifically Christian publishers, and once again it was rejected, for perfectly valid reasons, but enough interest was shown to make me realize that I had to write another Christian book. I also began to realize that I could write for older children.

"I had no ideas whatsoever, except that I wanted the book to be science fiction and that I felt more comfortable dealing with Christian themes in a symbolic way. Then I had the idea—while standing outside Foyle's book shop at the top of the Charing Cross Road in London—of using one of the medieval symbols of Christ: what about a phoenix? Going home on the train I was simmering away, and by the time I reached home I had the outline of the plot and the main characters of what eventually became *The Book and the Phoenix,* published in the United States as *A Rush of Golden Wings.*

"Even before *Phoenix* was accepted for publication, I wanted to write another book using the same basic background of the 'Six Worlds.' For a long time I had had the idea of writing a book about the developing friendship between two very different young men, but although I had ideas for incidents that would build up the relationship, the story had no basic direction; it was impossible to write it. Seeing it as another 'Six Worlds' book gave it that direction, and *Hostage of the Sea* came into being. After Kingsway accepted these books, they asked for another in the series, [which led to] *The Carpenter's Apprentice.*

"At the same time, I was writing plays. I have always had an interest in drama, and at various times of my life I have taught drama, and acted in and produced amateur theater. On the whole my plays have been neither science fiction nor Christian, since I find it difficult to write in either area for the stage. However, a recent play, *Out of Darkness,* which was written for the Canterbury Cathedral Drama Awards, is both Christian and science fiction. It was placed on the short list and is being considered for publication. Meanwhile, an earlier play, *Achilles His Armour,* which draws on the myths and legends that have also influenced my science fiction, won an award and was performed last summer.

"My ambitions for the immediate future are to go on writing the 'Six Worlds' series and perhaps other Christian fiction. I would very much like to write adult Christian fantasy. I should also like to move into secular writing, not out of any sense of dissatisfaction, but because I would like to bring a Christian viewpoint into a wider area."

*   *   *

BAWDEN, Nina (Mary Mabey) 1925-

PERSONAL: Born January 19, 1925, in London, England; daughter of Charles and Ellalaine Ursula May (Cushing) Mabey; married Austen Steven Kark (an executive for British Broadcasting Corp.), 1954; children: (prior marriage) Nicholas Bawden (deceased), Robert Humphrey Felix Bawden; (current marriage) Perdita Emily Helena Kark. *Education:* Somerville College, Oxford, B.A., 1946, M.A., 1951; additional graduate study at Salzburg Seminar in American Studies, 1960. *Hobbies and other interests:* Traveling, reading, garden croquet.

ADDRESSES: Home—22 Noel Rd., London N1 8HA, England. *Agent*—Curtis Brown, Ltd., 575 Madison Ave., New York, NY 10022.

CAREER: Writer, 1952—. Assistant, Town and Country Planning Associates, 1946-47; Justice of the Peace, Surrey, England, 1968-76.

MEMBER: PEN, Royal Society of Literature (fellow), Society of Women Writers and Journalists (president), Authors Lending and Copywright Society, Lansdowne, Ski Club of Great Britain.

AWARDS, HONORS: Carnegie commendation, 1973, for *Carrie's War; Guardian* Award for children's fiction, 1975, for *The Peppermint Pig; Yorkshire Post* Novel of the Year Award, 1977, for *Afternoon of a Good Woman;* Parents' Choice citation, 1982, and Edgar Allan Poe award nomination, 1983, both for *Kept in the Dark;* Parents' Choice citation, 1985, for *The Finding;* Booker Prize nomination, 1987, for *Circles of Deceit;* Parents' Choice citation, 1992, for *Humbug.*

WRITINGS:

JUVENILES

The Secret Passage, Gollancz, 1963, published as *The House of Secrets,* Lippincott, 1964.
On the Run, Gollancz, 1964, published as *Three on the Run,* Lippincott, 1965.
The White Horse Gang, Lippincott, 1966.
The Witch's Daughter, Lippincott, 1966.
A Handful of Thieves, Lippincott, 1967.
The Runaway Summer, Lippincott, 1969.
Squib, Lippincott, 1971.
Carrie's War, Lippincott, 1973.
The Peppermint Pig, Lippincott, 1975.
Rebel on a Rock, Lippincott, 1978.

NINA BAWDEN

The Robbers, Lothrop, 1979.

(Adaptor) *William Tell,* illustrated by Pascale Allamand, Lothrop, 1981.

Kept in the Dark, Lothrop, 1982.

St. Francis of Assisi (nonfiction), Lothrop, 1983.

The Finding, Lothrop, 1985.

Princess Alice, Deutsch, 1985.

Henry, Lothrop, 1988 (published in England as *Keeping Henry,* Gollancz, 1988).

The Outside Child, Lothrop, 1989.

Humbug, illustrated by Ian Newsham, Clarion, 1992.

ADULT NOVELS

Eyes of Green, Morrow, 1953 (published in England as *Who Calls the Tune,* Collins, 1953).

The Odd Flamingo, Collins, 1954.

Change Here for Babylon, Collins, 1955.

The Solitary Child, Collins, 1956, Lancer, 1966.

Devil by the Sea, Collins, 1957, Lippincott, 1959, abridged edition for children, Lippincott, 1976.

Glass Slippers Always Pinch, Lippincott, 1960 (published in England as *Just Like a Lady,* Longmans, Green, 1960).

In Honour Bound, Longmans, Green, 1961.

Tortoise by Candlelight, Harper, 1963.

Under the Skin, Harper, 1964.

A Little Love, a Little Learning, Longmans, Green, 1965, Harper, 1966.

A Woman of My Age, Harper, 1967.

The Grain of Truth, Harper, 1968.

The Birds on the Trees, Longmans, Green, 1970, Harper, 1971.

Anna Apparent, Harper, 1972.

George beneath a Paper Moon, Harper, 1974.

Afternoon of a Good Woman, Harper, 1976.

Familiar Passions, Morrow, 1979.

Walking Naked, St. Martin's, 1981.

The Ice House, St. Martin's, 1983.

Circles of Deceit, St. Martin's, 1987.

OTHER

Contributor to *Evening Standard* and *Daily Telegraph* newspapers; contributor of essays and interviews to books and periodicals on children's literature.

ADAPTATIONS: Many of Bawden's children's stories have been adapted for television in Great Britain. A four-part adaptation of *Carrie's War* was shown on American Public Broadcasting in May, 1981; an adaptation of *The Finding* was broadcast in 1990 as part of the Public Broadcasting System's "Wonderworks" series.

SIDELIGHTS: "When someone takes time to count, Nina Bawden's body of work will be seen as the remarkable achievement it is," writes Margaret Meek in the *School Librarian.* Bawden, a native of London, has written fiction of every sort—mysteries, gothic romances, and novels of manners for adults, as well as more than a dozen adventure-mystery works for children. She had been publishing for ten years before she wrote her first children's book, but in the last three decades her work for children and young adults has kept pace with her novels aimed at a mature audience.

Bawden's talent for portraying family relationships is highlighted in her novel about an adopted boy who inherits a fortune from an elderly neighbor who believes he is a long-lost relative. (Cover illustration by Catherine Stock.)

Children's Book Review contributor Margot Petts notes that in her children's books, Bawden "has an unerring ear and eye for the subtleties in relationships between children in a group—each one is a detailed portrait of a living, breathing human being, freckles an' all."

Bawden's books for young adults most commonly have realistic settings and plots drawn from daily life. Her characters may have vivid imaginations and indulge in fantasies, but often the world intrudes in ways that reveal life's unfairness and unpredictability. In *Children's Literature in Education,* Nicholas Tucker cites Bawden for books "both wise and immensely entertaining." The critic adds: "[Her] characters are constantly made to recognize that most things don't work out easily 'like something in a book' .... If Nina Bawden's young characters get into trouble with the police, however noble their motives, there is no twinkle-eyed Inspector to bail them out and promise to come to tea next day. Instead, it's the real works: police station, worried parents and horrible embarrassment. When a crook is caught, it's usually a messy unheroic business, leaving you feeling sick in the stomach." Bawden's earliest children's work offered detailed, mystery-laden plots

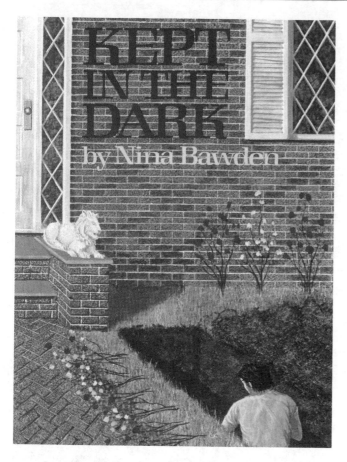

The author branched out from adult mysteries into suspenseful books for children, such as this tale about a sinister guest who menaces a secretive family. (Cover illustration by James Nazz.)

with moments of pace and excitement. Her more recent books highlight the personalities of the characters themselves, and how they relate to adults and other children.

Bawden was born in London and spent her earliest years in the suburbs of that city. Her father was a marine engineer who was often on a ship out at sea, but she and her younger brother enjoyed a conventional middle-class lifestyle with their mother. In *British Children's Authors*, Bawden states that she began writing when she was quite young, completing a novel by the time she was eight years old. She also wrote plays for her toy theater "and an epic poem in blank verse about a beautiful orphan with curly golden hair—my own was straight and dark."

World War II intruded upon the household as it did amongst all Londoners. Bawden and her brother were among the hundreds of children who were tagged like suitcases and sent by rail to safer parts of the country. The two youngsters relocated first to a mining village in South Wales and then later moved to a more congenial farm in Shropshire. The circumstances of the evacuation forced the children to live with a variety of host families, some of whom offered very little hospitality.

Summers spent on the Shropshire farm were the favorite times for Bawden. She learned to drive a tractor and to care for farm animals. She even organized a group of Italian prisoners of war who were sent out to help with the hard labor in the fields. When she was seventeen she returned to London to finish school, even though the city was still under attack. She graduated from high school there and attended Somerville College, Oxford, earning a bachelor's degree in 1946 and a master's degree in 1951. She studied politics, economics, and philosophy.

After graduating from Oxford the young woman married H. W. Bawden. The union was short but produced two sons. In 1954 she married Austen Kark, a Controller of the British Broadcasting Corporation. By that time she had begun to publish novels under her first married name, Nina Bawden, and she retained the name professionally. *Dictionary of Literary Biography* essayist Gerda Seaman describes Bawden's earliest fiction as "thrillers with a nice edge of menace." Works such as *Eyes of Green, The Odd Flamingo,* and *Change Here for Babylon* are almost standard thrillers, and *The Solitary Child* is a gothic romance. Bawden struck a change of pace with her 1957 novel *Devil by the Sea,* the first to feature children in important roles.

Devil by the Sea, which has since been adapted for a young adult audience, tells the story of Hilary, an imaginative youngster who becomes fascinated with a dim-witted derelict. As her interest in the man draws her closer to him, Hilary narrowly escapes becoming another victim of his murderous impulses. Seaman notes that this pivotal book introduces a theme that is present in much of Bawden's work for children: "that there is a world which is childhood's end, a world where 'other people are not to be relied upon ... promises can be broken; loyalty abandoned.'"

It was some six years after *Devil by the Sea* that Bawden made the decision to write a novel specifically for children. She accepted the challenge of her own growing children, who asked her to write something for them, and she soon discovered that she liked writing for young audiences very much. A number of works soon appeared from her pen, including *The House of Secrets,* a mystery about a passage into a run-down cellar, and *The White Horse Gang,* a tale of three close friends in a wooded countryside. Bawden also drew notice for *Squib,* a story in which four children face real danger to discover the identity of a helpless street urchin.

The best known of Bawden's children's books are two based most closely on her own experiences. *Carrie's War* tells the story of a brother and sister who are evacuated to Wales during the Second World War. The children are left in the care of grumpy Councillor Evans, whose rules are even more oppressive than his personality. Eventually Carrie and her brother learn to cope with and even to pity Mr. Evans, as Aidan Chambers notes in *Horn Book.* "By the end," Chambers writes, "we've learned, as has Carrie, to understand, if not to feel affection for, the man. He could so easily have been a stock villain, the heavy of the piece. He becomes a person; and Carrie, he, and Nick develop three-dimensional relationships. Everyone has grown in the process—including the reader."

Another Bawden favorite is her 1975 *Guardian* Award-winning novel, *The Peppermint Pig*. Once again the story focuses on uprooted children, suddenly made dependent upon relatives in a Norfolk country town. The children make a pet of Johnnie, a runt pig, but their affection for the animal cannot save its life during a time of ill fortune. *School Library Journal* contributor Jane Abramson calls *The Peppermint Pig* "an uncommonly good family album whose portraits stand out in remarkably sharp focus."

For some years now Bawden has been alternating between adult and juvenile fiction, turning out a novel a year. In *British Children's Authors,* Cornelia Jones and Olivia R. Way note that the author feels that writing for children should be the same as writing for adults: "the

One of Bawden's best-known works, *The Peppermint Pig* details how a cherished pet changes the lives of a London family forced to move in with country relatives. (Cover illustration by Charles Lilly.)

Convinced that a homeless boy is the brother she thought drowned years before, Kate faces danger to discover the truth. (Cover illustration by Gerry Contreras.)

books should present life honestly, with happiness and sadness, with excitement and discovery, but also with such negatives as poverty and loneliness. And so, she [writes], not with any age group in mind, but just to write an appealing story."

Bawden admits in the same publication that she actually enjoys writing for children more than writing for adults. "When boys and girls enjoy my books," she said, "it makes me want to write more. It's marvelous when they write and tell me they like my stories, and take the trouble to say what they like and why they like it. It's the most rewarding thing that can happen to a writer."

WORKS CITED:

Abramson, Jane, *School Library Journal,* February, 1975, p. 43.

Chambers, Aidan, "Nina Bawden—Storyteller Argent, Children's Writer Proper," *Horn Book,* June, 1974, pp. 265-68.

Dictionary of Literary Biography, Volume 14: *British Novelists since 1960,* Gale, 1983, pp. 77-86.

Jones, Cornelia and Olivia R. Way, *British Children's Authors,* American Library Association, 1976, pp. 41-48.

Meek, Margaret, *School Librarian,* September, 1973, pp. 259-60.

Petts, Margot, *Children's Book Review,* September, 1971, pp. 121-22.

Tucker, Nicholas, "Getting Used to Things as They Are: Nina Bawden as a Children's Novelist," *Children's Literature in Education,* number 13, 1974, pp. 35-44.

FOR MORE INFORMATION SEE:

BOOKS

Children's Literature Review, Volume 2, Gale, 1976.

PERIODICALS

Children's Literature in Education, fall, 1988.
Horn Book, February, 1980.*

* * *

BINGLEY, Margaret (Jane) 1947-
(Margaret Kirby)

PERSONAL: Born June 17, 1947, in Sutton, Surrey, England; daughter of Lionel Lewis (a senior civil servant) and Audrey Ethel Jane (Penfold) Kirby; married Alan Bradley Bingley (managing director of a publishing distribution center), December, 1977; children: Alexander Russell. *Education:* Rickards Lodge Secretarial College, Wimbledon, certificate of distinction, 1965. *Politics:* "Not interested." *Religion:* Church of England. *Hobbies and other interests:* Opera, cinema, reading.

ADDRESSES: *Home and office*—1 Hall Dr., Grantham, Lincolnshire NG31 9LB, England. *Agent*—Maggie Noach, 21 Redan St., London WL4 0AB, England.

CAREER: British Broadcasting Corporation (BBC), London, England, secretary, 1964-67; Heinemann Group of Publishers, Lower Kingswood, Tadworth, Surrey, England, secretary, 1967-72; writer, 1978—.

MARGARET BINGLEY

Grantham Initiative for Terminal Support Care (GIFTS), trustee, 1990—.

MEMBER: National Trust, Royal Opera House (Covent Garden), Grantham Writers Circle, Belton Woods Golf and Country Club.

WRITINGS:

The Devil's Child, Piatkus, 1983, Warner Books, 1987.
Such Good Neighbours, Piatkus, 1984.
The Waiting Darkness, Piatkus, 1984.
Children of the Night, Piatkus, 1985, Warner Books, 1989.
After Alice Died, Piatkus, 1986, Warner Books, 1989.
Change of Circumstances, Severn House, 1986.
The Unquiet Dead, Piatkus, 1987.
In Sickness and in Wealth, Severn House, 1987, Magna, 1988.
Seeds of Evil, Piatkus, 1988, Carrol & Graf, 1989.
(Under pseudonym Margaret Kirby) *Betrayal,* Piatkus, 1989.
Deadtime Story, Warner Books, 1990.
Village of Satan, Piatkus, 1990.
Gateway to Hell, Piatkus, 1991.

Also author of *A Song of Death.* Contributor of short stories to periodicals. Some of Bingley's works have been published in Germany, France, Holland, and Greece.

WORK IN PROGRESS: Working on a "true crime book"; researching the effect of undisclosed child abuse on the victim when he or she reaches adulthood and attempts normal relationships.

SIDELIGHTS: Margaret Bingley told *SATA:* "My English teacher, Miss Carter, always encouraged me in creative writing, spotting a talent no one else ever noticed! I originally would have liked to be a journalist but settled for very enjoyable work in other areas of creativity. When my son was born he was physically exhausting and scarcely ever slept, but mentally I was extremely bored and decided to try my hand at writing a book, something I could do at home. It's probably no coincidence that my first published novel, *The Devil's Child,* concerns a difficult small boy! Most of my books concern the paranormal, and feature children very strongly. This is because I find the total amorality and self-centeredness of the small child fascinating, as are society's desperate attempts to 'civilize' these intriguing individuals. I try to set these novels in very normal backgrounds and then slightly twist them from the norm, which to my mind is more frightening than blood and gore!

"The research for *Seeds of Evil* was extensive as I needed to know everything possible about test-tube babies. The lack of controls over the donor fathers that I uncovered was very disturbing. As far as possible I like all my plots to be factually accurate. After *Village of Satan* I was even contacted by a member of a coven, so obviously they believed I knew what I was writing about!

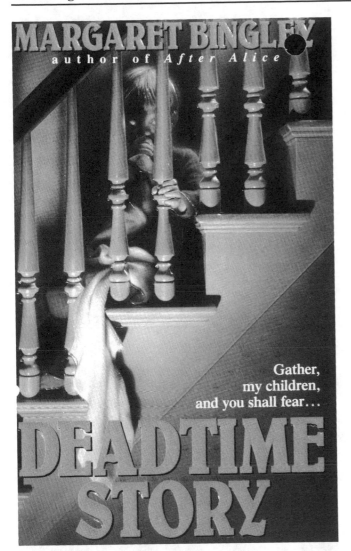

MARGARET BINGLEY
author of *After Alice*

Gather,
my children,
and you shall fear...

DEADTIME
STORY

Bingley's novels of the supernatural have "normal" backgrounds and often feature young children.

"I do not set out to write for children. Indeed as far as I know my books are enjoyed equally by adults. All I try to do is write a book that will keep people turning the pages.

"My success in America has really delighted me, giving me the opportunity to reach a far larger readership. Film rights to *The Waiting Darkness* have also been sold, and if anything comes of that then a new audience will become aware of my writing. And for an 'ordinary' (i.e. not famous in any other walk of life) author such breaks are extremely important.

"I've actually been writing for twelve years now, and I still love it. It gets harder, as each book must be 'better' than the last, but the thrill of receiving the new book in its final form never diminishes. As long as you have determination, self-discipline, and are willing to accept criticism, then if you want to write go ahead and start. It's the only way, and if you don't try you'll never know what you could have accomplished."

BIRCHMAN, David 1949-

PERSONAL: Born September 24, 1949, in Tacoma, WA; son of Fred (an air force mechanic) and Florine (a homemaker; maiden name, Beaulieu) Birchman; married Diane Lynn Turcott (a music teacher), June, 1977; children: Cole, Genevieve. *Education:* Attended University of Washington, 1968-71; studied in France, 1969-70; Western Washington State College (now Western Washington University), B.A., 1972; Reed College, M.A., 1977. *Politics:* "Democratic Socialist/Green."

ADDRESSES: Home—2196 Greenpark Ct., Thousand Oaks, CA 91362.

CAREER: Clatskanie High School, Clatskanie, OR, English teacher, 1977-78; instructor, writer, and computer consultant for aerospace firms in California and Saudi Arabia, 1981—; Moorpark College, Moorpark, CA, part-time English instructor, 1981—; writer.

MEMBER: Society of Children's Book Writers.

WRITINGS:

Victorious Paints the Great Balloon, illustrated by Johnathan Hunt, Bradbury, 1991.
Brother Billy Bronto's Bygone Blues Band, illustrated by John O'Brien, Lothrop, 1992.

DAVID BIRCHMAN

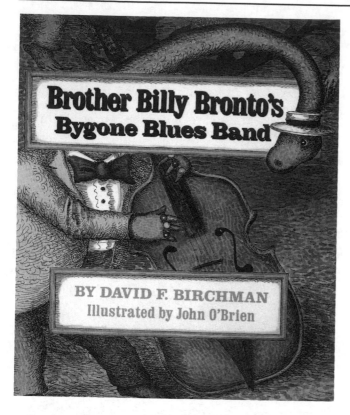

Great reptiles make music and rhythm in Birchman's second book for children. (Cover illustration by John O'Brien.)

WORK IN PROGRESS: The Raggley Scraggly, No Soap, No Scrub Girl, Jigsaw Jackson, and *A Green Horn Blowing,* all for Lothrop; *Tale of Tulips, A Tale of Onions,* for Four Winds Press.

SIDELIGHTS: David Birchman told *SATA:* "I grew up on a small farm outside of Battle Ground, Washington, in the shadow of Mt. St. Helens. It seemed back then that most of life went to chores. The summers were spent picking strawberries, raspberries, blackcaps, and string beans to earn money for school clothes. My father would take us down to the J. C. Penney's just before school started each year to get my three brothers, sister, and me outfitted. All the boys got new Oxfords. Even today when I imagine Santa Claus or God, I imagine him with the face of J. C. Penney.

"When I was twelve my father died, so I was left half wild and unsupervised at a fairly early age. Fortunately, I was always more prone to discovery than criminality.

"Our old house was bedlam, so I took every opportunity I could to hide out behind the wood stove in the basement with a good thick adventure book. Anything illustrated by N. C. Wyeth would do. My brothers, sister, and I were also fond of Carl Sandburg's *Rootaba-ga Stories* and a particular version of the Paul Bunyon Tales illustrated by Rockwell Kent (I sure wish I could find that book again).

"I write slowly and half by ear. The lines in a successful children's story always have an internal rhythm which carries the reader along. Usually, when an effort of mine goes flat it's because I haven't been listening."

*   *   *

BLACKWOOD, Gary L. 1945-

PERSONAL: Born October 23, 1945, in Meadville, PA; son of William Roy (a mechanic) and Susie (Stallsmith) Blackwood; married Judith McPeak, 1971 (divorced, 1973); married Jean Ann Lantzy (a librarian), 1974; children: Gareth, Giles, Tegan. *Education:* Grove City College, B.A., 1967. *Politics:* Libertarian. *Religion:* "No organized religion."

ADDRESSES: Home and office—Route 3, Box 290A, Carthage, MO 64836.

CAREER: Worked as an advertising copywriter in Cleveland, OH, 1967-68, and Ithaca, NY, 1974-75; a bookstore clerk in Cleveland, 1970-73, Medford, OR, 1976-77, and Rolla, MO, 1977-80; and a library assistant in Rolla, 1980-83; free-lance writer, 1984—; Missouri Southern State College, Joplin, instructor in playwriting, 1989—. *Military service:* U.S. Army, 1968-70; became sergeant.

AWARDS, HONORS: The Dying Sun was named a best young adult novel by Friends of American Writers, 1989.

GARY L. BLACKWOOD

WRITINGS:

The Lion and the Unicorn, Eagle Books, 1983.
Wild Timothy, Atheneum, 1987.
The Dying Sun, Atheneum, 1989.
Beyond the Door, Atheneum, 1991.

WORK IN PROGRESS: Attack of the Mushroom People, a play, for Players Press; *Futures*, a play; *Thoreau*, a one-man show; and *Come On In, The Water's over Your Head*, a musical play.

SIDELIGHTS: Gary L. Blackwood told *SATA:* "I didn't set out to be a children's writer as such; I just wanted to be a writer, for as long as I can remember. I always loved books—not just reading them, but the sight and the feel and the smell of them. They were like small, self-contained worlds for me, portable ones that I could enter and leave at will.

"The real world interested me, too. I spent a lot of my childhood roaming through my neighbors' fields and woods, and I'm sure this is where Timothy's adventures in *Wild Timothy* spring from. Though I'm not free to spend quite as much of my time outdoors now, I'm still very concerned about nature and its possible fate, as anyone who reads *The Dying Sun* and *Beyond the Door* can surely guess.

"For someone who has *always* wanted to be a writer, it took me a dismayingly long time to reach the point where others considered me one. I did sell a few short stories early on, beginning in college, actually, and had a musical play produced regionally in 1971, but then I turned my efforts to books. I wrote nine of them over a period of sixteen years and self-published one of them before I finally sold one to a major publisher. One of those nine, *Beyond the Door*, has since seen print, and another, the very first one I wrote, has metamorphosed into a young adult book.

"As far as themes in my work go, I don't think I've actively tried to explore any particular theme—in fact, I teach my playwriting students that situation and character come first, and theme arises from these—but a couple of concerns keep popping up in my work like old friends, or perhaps old enemies, and they're the same concerns that run through my own life. The main one is that we humans have lost touch with the rest of nature; in fact, we've tried to set ourselves above and apart from it with all our technology and luxuries that we've come to think of as necessities. I think it's good for people to discover, as Timothy and James and Scott do, what are 'the true means and necessaries of life,' to use Thoreau's words.

"The result of this loss of touch with the rest of the natural world is that we treat it very cavalierly, using it for our own ends as if it were all put there just to gratify us.

"Most of the forms of entertainment we have tend to promote this way of life and this way of thinking. In spite of the fact that we have to cut down trees to make

Blackwood's concern for the environment and his belief that man has lost touch with the natural world are topics that crop up in many of his books. (Cover painting from *Beyond the Door*.)

them, only books seem to offer any real alternatives and have any real lasting value, which is one of the reasons I'm glad to be able to say I write them. Let's face it, I'm not in it for the money."

*   *   *

BLAIR, Walter 1900-1992

OBITUARY NOTICE—See index for *SATA* sketch: Born April 21, 1900, in Spokane, WA; died June 29, 1992, in Chicago, IL. Educator, editor, and author. Blair, who taught English at the University of Chicago for more than thirty-five years, is recognized as one of the first American scholars to appraise humor academically, and his 1937 study, *Native American Humor: 1800-1900,* is still considered the archetypal work in the field. The first recipient of the Mark Twain Circle's Distinguished Scholar Award, Blair edited several critical editions on Twain, wrote *Mark Twain and "Huck Finn": 1855-1873,* and coauthored *The Art of Huckleberry Finn.* His admiration of oral stories developed into an interest in folklore in graduate school and led him to publish *Tall Tale America: A Legendary History of Our Humorous Heroes,* a collection of oral and written narratives which has proven to be popular with both children and adults.

OBITUARIES AND OTHER SOURCES:

BOOKS

Authors of Books for Young People, 3rd edition, Scarecrow, 1990.

PERIODICALS

Chicago Tribune, June 30, 1992, section 1, p. 10.
New York Times, July 1, 1992, p. A21.

* * *

BOYD, Candy Dawson 1946-

PERSONAL: Full name is Marguerite Dawson Boyd; born August 8, 1946, in Chicago, IL; daughter of Julian Dawson and Mary Ruth Ridley. *Education:* Northeastern Illinois State University, B.A., 1967; University of California, Berkeley, M.A., 1978, Ph.D., 1982.

ADDRESSES: Home—1416 Madrone Way, San Pablo, CA 94806. *Office*—St. Mary's College of California, School of Education, Box 4350, Morgana, CA 94575.

CAREER: Overton Elementary School, Chicago, IL, teacher, 1968-71; Longfellow School, Berkeley, CA, teacher, 1971-73; University of California, Berkeley, extension instructor in the language arts, 1972-79; Berkeley Unified School District, Berkeley, district teacher trainer in reading and communication skills, 1973-76; St. Mary's College of California, Morgana, extension instructor in language arts, 1972-79, lecturer, 1975, assistant professor, 1976-87, tenured associate professor, 1983-91, professor of education, 1991—, director of reading leadership and teacher effectiveness programs, 1976-87, director of elementary education, 1983-88.

MEMBER: International Reading Association, American Educational Research Association, California Reading Association.

AWARDS, HONORS: Circle of Gold was named a notable children's trade book in the field of social studies by the National Council for the Social Studies and the Children's Book Council in 1984, and a Coretta Scott King Award Honor Book by the American Library Association in 1985; *Breadsticks and Blessing Places* was selected for the Children's Books of the Year List by the Child Study Children's Book Committee at Bank Street College; *Charlie Pippin* was nominated for the Mark Twain Award and the Dorothy Canfield Fisher Children's Book Award, 1988, and was selected by the International Reading Association and Children's Book Council for the Children's Choices for 1988 List, and by the Oklahoma Library Association for the Oklahoma Sequoyah Children's Book Award Master List, 1989.

Boyd received the Outstanding Bay Area Woman Award, 1986; Outstanding Person in Mount Diablo Unified School District, Black Educators Association,

CANDY DAWSON BOYD

1988; The Author's Hall of Fame Certificate of Appreciation for literary and artistic contributions to the field of literature for children and adults, San Francisco Reading Association and Santa Clara Reading Association, 1989; Celebrate Literacy Award for exemplary service in the promotion of literacy, International Reading Association and the San Francisco Reading Association, 1991; Distinguished Achievement Award, National Women's Political Caucus, San Francisco Chapter, 1991; and she was the first recipient of the St. Mary's College of California Professor of the Year Award, 1992.

WRITINGS:

Circle of Gold, Scholastic, 1984.
Breadsticks and Blessing Places, Macmillan, 1985, published as *Forever Friends,* Viking, 1986.
Charlie Pippin, Macmillan, 1987.
Chevrolet Saturday, Macmillan, 1992.

Also contributor of articles and essays to professional journals. Reviewer of children's literature for the *Los Angeles Times* and *San Francisco Chronicle.*

WORK IN PROGRESS: The Strategy Approach to Teaching Reading and *Concept-Based Curriculum;* three picture books; academic research on ability-based reading groups.

SIDELIGHTS: Candy Dawson Boyd's empathy and respect for children are unmistakable foundations to her work as a professor of education and an award-winning children's writer. A former teacher of children of many ethnic and cultural backgrounds, Boyd strives to provide "her children" (by which she means her students and her readers) with the kind of rich cultural knowledge she derived from her own childhood in an African-American family. In an interview with *SATA*, Boyd remarked that throughout her life she has been strengthened by the stories she heard as a child about the determination and fortitude of her family and ancestors. As a writer for children and young adults she provides the positive message she once took from those stories, the message "that you make it. It's going to be hard and tough and it's not fair," she told *SATA*, "but you make it."

As a child, Boyd had no desire to grow up to become a teacher or a children's writer. Although her mother and grandmother had both been teachers, Boyd wanted the glamour of being a jazz singer or an actress. In fact, she told *SATA*, "I didn't particularly like kids, and the thought of spending all day with them ...! I remember thinking that I wouldn't be able to wear my make up or play my music or have fun or do anything! It seemed terrible to me." She came across an obstacle to her dream of becoming a jazz singer when she joined the junior choir in high school and discovered she was tone deaf. She pursued acting in college and, although she received leading roles in plays and encouragement from teachers, she says that racial attitudes interfered with the possibility of a successful career. As a light-skinned African American she found she was too light to get parts as a black woman and unlikely to get roles playing white women. Fortunately, Boyd had many other interests.

As a child, Boyd read *The Moved Outers,* a story by Florence Crandall Means about a Japanese-American girl who lived in California during World War II, when the government placed many Americans of Japanese descent in internment camps. Boyd explained the book's profound effect on her to *SATA*. In the story, "one day the girl and her family were just moved out and put into a camp. Everything was taken away from them because they were Japanese. I was just hysterical. How could they do this to her? How could they come, these soldiers, and just take a family away and take all their stuff? I remember running to my mother screaming, 'They didn't do this—it didn't happen, did it?' I remember my mother telling me 'yes.' And after that I was different. That was when I became a political child. Of course, I was aware of what it meant to be black; racism was always a part of life. With that, plus what happened in this book, something totally changed inside. I lost my innocence and trust about how protected you were as a citizen of this country."

While still in high school, disturbing social events motivated Boyd to take her first step into the world of political activism. Her high school's neighborhood, a section of Chicago where middle-class black families were beginning to settle, was threatened by a corrupt real estate practice called blockbusting. Blockbusters were people who convinced white property owners that their houses were losing value because minority families were moving into their neighborhoods. Capitalizing on the fear that they themselves inspired, the blockbusters bought homes at low prices and then sold them for large profits. Boyd told *SATA:* "I organized another black girl, a Jewish girl, and a white Protestant girl, and we went around and visited with two hundred white families one summer to try to convince them to stay. We were there when the blockbusters called. They would say, 'A family of niggers just bought the house two houses down from you. You just lost two thousand dollars on your house— you better hurry up and sell it.' And of course these were the same people that controlled certain real estate companies."

Boyd remained active in college, organizing other students in the civil rights movement, sending food and clothing to African Americans in the South, establishing the Negro History Club at her school, and creating a coffee shop where speakers could lead discussions on contemporary issues at the college. Eventually, these activities superseded her schoolwork. Boyd quit school and went to work as a field staff organizer with Martin Luther King, Jr.'s Southern Christian Leadership Conference. She worked for over a year in both the North and the South, but the violent deaths of movement leaders such as Medgar Evers, the Kennedys, and Martin Luther King, Jr., left Boyd so emotionally devastated that, she told *SATA*, "it was like going into a dungeon." She returned to college, this time to pursue a degree in education, continuing to participate in the civil rights movement with activist Jessie Jackson in the teacher's division of Operation PUSH (People United to Save Humanity).

After college, Boyd worked for several years as an elementary school teacher in her own predominantly black Chicago neighborhood. Although external circumstances had forced her out of the civil rights movement and into teaching, she found that she was able to pursue her social ideals in the classroom. "I was a militant teacher," Boyd told *SATA*. "I knew that being black and poor meant life was going to be a lot harder for my students, and I wanted them to have as much opportunity as possible." Boyd demanded that the black national anthem be played in school and organized marches for beautifying the neighborhood. In her way, she "adopted" her students, playing a role in their lives that her own mother had played in hers. "My mama was determined to give us what she called 'culture,'" Boyd told *SATA*. "We would go to museums and art institutes and we would go to see plays at the Goodman Theater. There wasn't a lot of money so we would sit in Orchestra Hall in Chicago at the very top. Mama said this culture would help us make it in the world. So that's what I did with my kids [Boyd's students]. Some of my children had never seen Lake Michigan. So we would meet by the liquor store on Saturdays and we would go downtown to the Goodman Theater and we took a Greyhound bus tour of Chicago. They became my children, and I wanted them."

Boyd moved to Berkeley, California, in 1971, where, she told *SATA,* "I ended up teaching children who weren't black: Asian children and Latino children and Caucasian children and children from India and all over the world." Seeking reading material for her students, Boyd found a disturbing lack of children's books from the diverse cultural backgrounds that comprised her classroom. "I got absolutely enraged when I went out and I looked at the atrocity of the books out there. I couldn't even find decent books for some of the white ethnic groups that I had. I wanted material, good books, strong books, books that had very interesting characters and ordinary stories. But I never saw children of color in realistic fiction depicted as children whose culture, embedded within them as a part of who they were, came out in ways that were ordinary and regular. That enraged me and I decided to become a writer."

The strength of Boyd's feelings about the value of multicultural readings for children probably goes back to her own childhood. An avid reader as a child, Boyd remembers few books by African Americans, but from her family and her teachers she learned much about her heritage. "Chicago schools were segregated, so I got stories at school about Africa and its kingdoms. But the

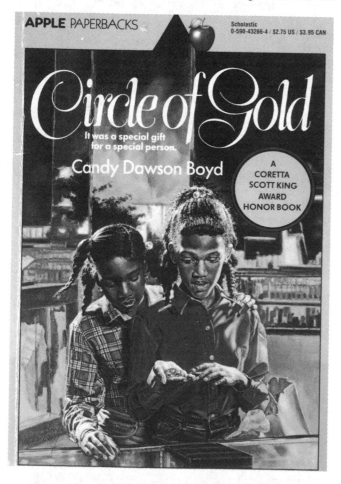

The author's determination to create books that spoke to multicultural students led to her first novel about Mattie's efforts to purchase a special gift for Mother's Day. (Cover illustration by Charles Lilly.)

stories I got at home were the ones that were more powerful because they were about the things that happened to family members and how we had survived and prevailed.

"My father is a very proud, brilliant black man, which is—has been for me—an unbelievable tragedy. He fought. He did not accept racism of any kind and it's a wonder that he's not dead, but he isn't. His pride, his spirit, his refusal to buckle under all the things that happened to him affected me. My mother's determination to have a family and to keep it together affected me." Boyd also learned a lot simply by living in her neighborhood as a child. "It was all black, but it wasn't a ghetto even though there was terrible segregation. I saw it as a neighborhood; my dentists and my doctors were black and lawyers were black, and there was a woman down the street who was nosy and watched all the children and told on them. I mean, my world was just overwhelmingly rich. My world was full of laughter and full of sadness and tragedy and things that were terribly scary but it was *rich* with stories.

"One of the people that influenced me through the stories I heard about him was my father's father—my grandfather. He was a thoracic surgeon. I found out, not that long ago, that Northwestern University admitted my grandfather based on his unbelievably high test scores. It was only when he arrived that they found out he was black. By then he had been admitted. He was full of determination and brilliance, and yet this was a man I remember as being very quiet and reserved. I remember a story about how he wasn't allowed to do an internship because he was black and he wasn't allowed to practice in a white hospital. So he did his work in Budapest and Vienna because those were two of the top areas in the world for thoracic surgery. And I remember a story about Granddaddy only having, for a period of time, two pairs of underwear, and how he washed one and he wore one. That's what got me through gauntlets like the Ph.D. program at U.C. Berkeley."

Boyd's childhood experiences of family, school, and neighborhood made some of the stereotypical literature written by whites about blacks repellent to her. "That's something I have fought other writers about," she told *SATA.* "You don't have the right to write about my people when you don't know anything about them. You don't have the right to portray neighborhoods as full of gangs, with no fathers. The statistics show that that is not true. Although more neighborhoods are like that now because of crack [cocaine], at the same time there are lots of families that go to work and kids that go to work and try to make it every day." Boyd has received letters from readers confirming her view that not enough literature has depicted normal African-American life. "I've had white kids write to me and say, 'I didn't know that black kids had feelings like me.' My attitude was, How could you know? You don't live in a country that lets that happen. And if a book could reach you in that kind of way, then ... wow!"

The story of a young girl's struggle to deal with the death of her best friend, *Breadsticks and Blessing Places* was based on Boyd's own experiences and served as a goodbye to the childhood friend she lost. (Cover illustration by Jerry Pinkney.)

When Boyd decided to become a writer, she told *SATA*, "I spent the first two years reading all the books written for children in the Berkeley Public Library—from A to Z, fiction and nonfiction—because I wanted to see what was out there and what wasn't there. I also did research and took two courses at the University of California, Berkeley, on writing for children. I wrote manuscripts that my teachers thought were good, but for nine years I was rejected by publishing companies." One of the manuscripts Boyd sent to many publishers was *Breadsticks and Blessing Places*, a book that, Boyd told *SATA*, was "very, very important" to her.

Breadsticks and Blessing Places is the story of Toni, a twelve-year-old girl whose parents want to send her to a prestigious prep school. Toni, who has difficulties with math in her present school, fears disappointing her parents. She also struggles with two friends who are very different from one another and don't always get along. When one of them, the carefree Susan, is killed by a drunk driver, Toni is inconsolable. The novel follows her slow and painful route toward recovery from this trauma. A reviewer of *Breadsticks and Blessing Places* for the *Bulletin of the Center for Children's Books*

commented: "Boyd deals fully and candidly with a child's reaction to the death of a close friend as well as to other aspects of the maturation process that are universal." The critic added that the story is presented "with insight and compassion."

Boyd told *SATA* that publishers who rejected *Breadsticks and Blessing Places* said it was "relentless" on the subject of death. She wrote the book based on her own childhood experience. Her best friend died when she was in the fourth grade, and Boyd felt that she had never really said goodbye to her. *Breadsticks and Blessing Places* was written as a goodbye to her friend but also as an effort to help children who have experienced a loss to work out their own feelings. To write the book, Boyd conducted two years of research on grief as experienced by children. "In that period of research," she told *SATA*, "I learned that children grieve deeply over a long period of time and that the rituals that adults use at wakes and funerals don't work for children." Boyd wanted her book to respect children's emotions and give them a safe forum. "I call my books a safe place. Children are complex. They have very strong, meaningful ideas and questions about the world that they live in. They have strong emotions that persist, and I think that there should be a genre of books that they read that respect that. A kid wrote me and said, 'I never had anybody I really loved die, but I know that if I did, your book would help me.' That means the book is a safe place for him to go with those feelings."

Boyd's first published novel was the award-winning *Circle of Gold*, the story of Mattie Benson, a young girl on a quest to buy a gold pin for her mother. Mattie's father has died prior to the opening of the story, leaving her mother to support Mattie and her twin brother by working long hours at a factory and managing the apartment building in which they live. Mattie works hard to help out at home, but her mother is tired and unhappy and shows more irritation than love for her daughter. Mattie, already suffering the loss of her father, feels she is losing her mother as well. In school, a mean-spirited girl named Angel accuses Mattie of stealing her bracelet and, although Mattie is not punished, she is treated like a thief by her teacher and her peers. Against these harsh and daunting odds, Mattie's quest to buy the expensive pin—the circle of gold—for her mother vividly symbolizes her love of her family and her determination to make things right again.

Boyd's 1987 book, *Charlie Pippin*, again explores family relationships that have become troubled due to outside circumstances. Charlie is an energetic and curious eleven-year-old girl with unusual entrepreneurial skills. Despite her very good intentions, Charlie has difficulty following her school's disciplinary code. At home, she has difficulty with her father, a Vietnam War veteran who is embittered, isolated, and unwilling to discuss his experience except by defending the war. Charlie, trying to better understand her father, undertakes a report on the Vietnam War for her social studies class. In her research she finds a newspaper clipping about her father and two of his friends who were killed in action during the war. Asking her grandparents and her mother about the article, Charlie learns that her father was a war hero and, before his experience in Vietnam, a man of dreams and joy.

Charlie's father is not pleased with her choice of report topics, or the trouble that her extracurricular business dealings have caused at school, but Charlie's spirit is invincible. She deceives her parents and convinces a favorite uncle to take her to Washington, D.C., to see the Vietnam Veteran's War Memorial. There she acquires rubbings from the wall of the names of her father's dead friends. On her return, Charlie provokes her father to honestly confront the anguish of his past—an anguish that has broken down some of the family's lines of communication. Sybil Steinberg wrote in her *Publishers Weekly* review of *Charlie Pippin:* "A strong black protagonist makes this a rare YA book; the finesse with which Boyd ties its many themes into a very moving, unified whole turns this into a stellar offering."

In Boyd's novels, families, although loving, are besieged with real problems. Parents often inadvertently impose

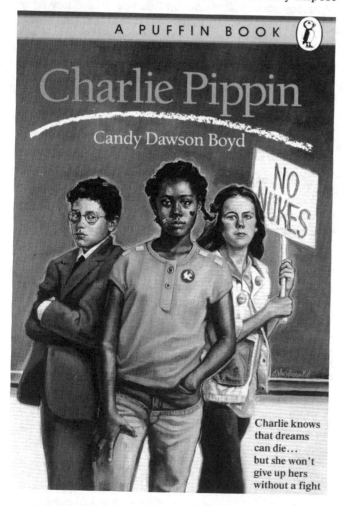

A PUFFIN BOOK

Charlie Pippin

Candy Dawson Boyd

NO NUKES

Charlie knows that dreams can die... but she won't give up hers without a fight

Charlie comes into conflict with her father, an embittered Vietnam veteran, over her defiance of school rules and her insistence in understanding his war experiences. (Cover illustration by Cornelius Van Wright.)

a cynicism—brought about by the injustice and grief they have encountered—upon children who are better able to maintain dreams and an idealistic approach to life. The young protagonists of Boyd's novels strive for a place in the world of their family as well as the world at large, despite the harshness they witness. Through youthful endeavors to set things right, the stories conclude optimistically. Boyd told *SATA:* "I refuse to have losers as characters. I hate the words 'coping' and 'adjusting.' In my families there is always a possibility of renewal."

Just as the family in Boyd's books represents both a source of turmoil and hope for a better world, school is a crucial and beneficial, if imperfect, environment for her young characters. "School is a major part of what happens to the child," the author told *SATA.* "As a teacher I know school, and I know what a large part of a child's life it is. School is one of the places where children can have an opportunity to grow outside of the family—to find parts of themselves that they may not be able to find inside the family." In *Charlie Pippin,* for example, the young protagonist's vitality and ingenuity frequently conflict with her school's rigid discipline code. "As a teacher and then a teacher educator," Boyd commented, "I've met principals and seen discipline codes like that one. The thought of a character like Charlie being caught in the system like that was just irresistible." Charlie genuinely tries to keep her record at school clean, and she takes advantage of the opportunity that is presented to her in her social studies class to pursue her interest in Vietnam. By researching and working with fellow classmates, Charlie finds that although her view of the war opposes her father's view, it is nevertheless an informed and well considered outlook. But, driven by a nature that is creative, curious, and optimistic, Charlie is far from being a perfect student. "She has to live in this world," Boyd said. "But I wouldn't want my life caught in the middle of a discipline code. In all my books I've been wrestling with dilemmas children encounter that come from the decisions adults make."

Boyd acknowledges that she is a little like each of her protagonists. Like Charlie, she has worked on both sides of the rules that govern her life and career. After completing her doctorate in education, she began teaching education at St. Mary's College of California, where she was named the first Professor of the Year in 1992. She has become renowned for her devotion to training teachers and developing systems that help young people become enthusiastic readers. Even so, she maintains an independent spirit that is full of humor, indignation at hypocrisy and injustice, and even a sense of mischief. "If you have the spirit," Boyd told *SATA,* "even when you grow up you move from one discipline code to another. Even a role is a discipline code—like being a full professor. You're supposed to act in a certain way. Well, to me that's stupid. Many times I won't do it. Sometimes I don't do it just because I like the shock value of not doing it. But I also won't act the role because the role is only a part of who I am, not the definition of who I am. My books are much more a definition of who I am than that degree is."

Both her books and her teaching have won Boyd many distinguished awards. "My dreams of being famous were satisfied when I was still a child," Boyd told *SATA*. "Yes, I'm honored when I receive an award, but often the decision [to grant her an award] is political, and I don't know how these decisions are made. Not knowing, I take it all with less ego." The idealism that Boyd has exhibited since her own childhood now hinges on her profound belief in children. "I still have hope," she told *SATA*. "I have a lot invested in the children. Not much of my hope lies with adults. If books help children, or give them a safe place to go, then that's the biggest reward for writing."

WORKS CITED:

Boyd, Candy Dawson, telephone interview with Sonia Benson for *Something about the Author*, conducted May 27, 1992.
Review of *Breadsticks and Blessing Places, Bulletin of the Center for Children's Books*, July-August, 1985.
Steinberg, Sybil, review of *Charlie Pippin, Publishers Weekly*, April 10, 1987, p. 96.

FOR MORE INFORMATION SEE:

PERIODICALS

Bulletin of the Center for Children's Books, May, 1987.
Publishers Weekly, June 7, 1985, p. 81.
School Library Journal, September, 1985, p. 142; April, 1987, p. 92; November, 1988, p. 53.
Voice of Youth Advocates, February, 1986, p. 382; October, 1987.

—*Sketch by Sonia Benson*

*   *   *

BRANSCUM, Robbie 1937-

PERSONAL: Born June 17, 1937, near Big Flat, AR; daughter of Donnie H. (a farmer) and Blanch (Balitine) Tilly; married Duane Branscum, c. 1952 (divorced, 1969); married Lesli J. Carrico, July 15, 1975 (divorced); children: Deborah. *Hobbies and other interests:* Reading, gardening, cooking.

ADDRESSES: Home—Eufaula, OK.

CAREER: Farmer; author of children's books.

AWARDS, HONORS: Friends of American Writers Award, 1977, for *Toby, Granny and George;* outstanding book of the year citations, *New York Times,* 1977, for *The Saving of P.S.,* 1978, for *To the Tune of a Hickory Stick,* and 1982, for *The Murder of Hound Dog Bates: A Novel; Johnny May* was named "Best of the Best 1966-1978" by *School Library Journal* in 1979; Edgar Allan Poe Award, 1983, for *The Murder of Hound Dog Bates: A Novel.*

WRITINGS:

FOR CHILDREN

Me and Jim Luke, Doubleday, 1971.
Johnny May, Doubleday, 1975.
The Three Wars of Billy Joe Treat, McGraw, 1975.
Toby, Granny, and George, illustrated by Glen Rounds, Doubleday, 1976.
The Saving of P.S., Doubleday, 1977.
Three Buckets of Daylight, Lothrop, 1978.
To the Tune of a Hickory Stick, Doubleday, 1978.
The Ugliest Boy, illustrated by Michael Eagle, Lothrop, 1978.
For Love of Jody, Lothrop, 1978.
Toby Alone, Doubleday, 1978.
Toby and Johnny Joe, Doubleday, 1978.
The Murder of Hound Dog Bates: A Novel, Viking, 1982.
Spud Tackett and the Angel of Doom, Viking, 1983.
Cheater and Flitter Dick: A Novel, Viking, 1983.
The Adventures of Johnny May, illustrated by Deborah Howland, Harper, 1984.
The Girl, Harper, 1986.
Johnny May Grows Up, illustrated by Bob Marstall, Harper, 1987.
Cameo Rose, Harper, 1989.
Old Blue Tilley, Macmillan, 1991.

SIDELIGHTS: Reared amid poverty on small farms in Arkansas, Robbie Branscum later used her childhood experiences as background material for her popular novels for children and teenagers. Evoking a sense of authentic rurality through her characters' unrefined, distinct dialogue, Branscum has written some twenty books detailing youngsters' struggles to overcome difficult times and situations. Branscum displays "a convincing picture of rural life ... and a heavy hand with dialect and idiom," noted a *Bulletin of the Center for Children's Books* reviewer of the author's 1984 book

ROBBIE BRANSCUM

The Adventures of Johnny May. Winner of several book awards, Branscum has also received critical recognition for her ability to discuss with candor and sensitivity uncomfortable subjects that affect the lives of her characters. For example, *School Library Journal* reviewer Heide Piehler lauded Branscum's 1986 novel *The Girl,* which concerns sexual and physical mistreatment. Describing the book as a story of "abuse, neglect, and emotional isolation," Piehler also proclaimed it a tale "of human endurance, love, and hope in a seemingly hopeless setting."

Branscum was born on June 17, 1937, near Big Flat, Arkansas. A farmer's daughter, she remembers feeling abandoned at the age of four when her father died and she and her four siblings were sent by their mother to live on their grandparents' small farm in an even more rural area in the state. Desperately poor, Branscum lived without benefit of modern conveniences—such as indoor plumbing and electricity—laboring hard with her chores. She developed a penchant for words in her youth, memorizing new terms as fast as she could. "Our house was papered in newspapers (as all the other folks' homes around there were)," she once told *Something about the Author (SATA).* "I read every room in the house, standing on chairs to read the ceiling and sometimes standing on my head where the papers had been pasted upside down." She continued, "I went to a small, one-room schoolhouse at a time when the eighth grade was as high as a person aimed. I can remember the mental hunger for books; a book was something to cherish, to be read again and again."

After an eight-year separation, Branscum and her siblings rejoined their mother, moving to Colorado against their grandparents' wishes. Although the future author renewed her zest for learning, she ceased school after the seventh grade, opting to marry a slightly older Duane Branscum when she was fifteen. She also pursued her interest in words while in her teens, writing poetry and songs. After one child and more than fifteen years of wedlock, the Branscum marriage ended in divorce because, as the author told *SATA,* "both of us [were] too young to make a marriage work." In 1971, nearly two years after the dissolution, Branscum saw the publication of her first children's book, *Me and Jim Luke,* a tale delving into the lives of white, rural Southerners. As she furthered her career and writing talents, she began a series of stories in 1975 about a young girl growing up in a rustic region of Arkansas. In the first installment, entitled *Johnny May* after its protagonist, a ten-year-old suspects that the man courting her aunt has killed his first four wives. Interwoven with Johnny May's fervor to reveal the man's true nature is the story of the girl's sexual awakening after an innocent skinnydipping with her friend Aron.

The sequel *The Adventures of Johnny May,* published nearly ten years after the first, charts the experiences of the character, now eleven, as she must provide for her ailing grandparents. The third book, 1987's *Johnny May Grows Up,* details the thirteen-year-old's fear of losing Aron's love and her attempts to improve her physical appearance and receive a quality education. Some critics lauded the humor in the Johnny May stories, while others called them vivid, suspenseful, and fast-paced. "Add Johnny May to the list of favorite characters that young readers can grow up with," declared a *Horn Book* contributor in an evaluation of the third book. The reviewer added that Branscum's story "makes welcome reading."

Branscum again used the Arkansas backwoods as the setting for a series of coming-of-age adventures when she began chronicling the life of a girl named Toby. In each of the stories the protagonist is met with a number of difficulties and uses her positive spirit to rise above the challenges. The first book, 1976's *Toby, Granny, and George,* finds the thirteen-year-old doubting her parentage and investigating a mysterious shooting. In the sequel *Toby Alone,* the girl fights to retain her boyfriend's affections and adjusts to the death of her grandmother. The third volume, *Toby and Johnny Joe,* follows the heroine as she marries, experiences sex for the first time, and faces the loss of her unborn child and possibly her husband, who has gone off to war. In general the "Toby" tales received a warm reception. Various commentators praised the author's development of her characters, particularly the maturing of Toby. A *Horn Book* reviewer noted that *Toby, Granny, and George,* for example, features a female protagonist who is "remarkable and winning," while a *Kirkus Reviews* contributor judged her "as rugged and matter-of-fact as her hand-me-down bib overalls." Other critics applauded the third Toby story for its fresh perspective, including a *School Library Journal* writer who deemed the book an "original blend of mystery, humor, and homeliness."

Hardship and suspense also mark Branscum's 1978 award-winning book, *To the Tune of a Hickory Stick.* Again incorporating memories from her childhood days in the rural South, the author relates the saga of a brother and sister who, after their father's death, are sent to live with their aunt and uncle on a farm in the Arkansas hills. The children's mother, in order to support her offspring, has taken a job some distance away not realizing that the money she sends is being misused by the siblings' greedy keepers. While the duo work hard for what little food they receive, they are often victims of abuse lashed out by their uncle. To escape mistreatment, the pair seek refuge in a schoolhouse, abandoned for the season. The siblings are eventually cared for by their understanding teacher until their mother, presumed dead, surfaces. Branscum's use of dialogue and her straightforward handling of the subject of puberty were praised by a *Horn Book* contributor. "The basic plot of children triumphing over adversity," the commentator added, "gives the first-person narrative the appeal of the universally popular orphan story." A *Kirkus Review* writer called the author's chronicle "perky as usual," and a critic for *School Library Journal* termed Branscum's "characters ... earthy and tough when necessary."

Branscum has also been commended for her realistic characterizations in books like *The Murder of Hound Dog Bates*—the story of a thirteen-year-old boy who lives with his three single aunts on their Arkansas farm. The tale, which focuses on the lad as he discovers his beloved dog has been slain one hot summer afternoon, finds the boy suspecting that his aunts were behind the dastardly deed. Presuming he is next to be killed, he begins to investigate why his aunts have never wed and eventually teams with an ex-cop who is looking to remarry, possibly one of the aunts. As the case unfolds, however, the boy not only uncovers the true killer's identity but comes to respect his aunts. "Colloquial imagery and dialogue convey the regional setting, but the tone suggests ... a time recalled," noted a writer for *Horn Book.* Calling the book "a genuine pleasure to read," *New York Times Book Review*'s Anne Jordan claimed Branscum's use of a rural setting reveals "the wit needed by the dirt farmers in their needless battle to survive."

Branscum's 1991 novel, *Old Blue Tilley,* concerns a fourteen-year-old orphan boy who has been cared for by a preacher named Blue Tilley. Detailing the duo's experiences as they visit local folks while enroute to a revival meeting, the book shows how the boy determines to collect his inheritance, kept from him by greedy relatives, and gain his independence. While some critics found fault with Branscum's neatly resolved ending, they nevertheless praised her portrayal of her young protagonist. Describing *Old Blue Tilley* as "a carefully detailed tribute to a region and its people—a people often ridiculed or ignored," *Booklist* reviewer Randy Meyer claimed that the book's worthiness is evidenced in the author's depiction "of a unique way of life."

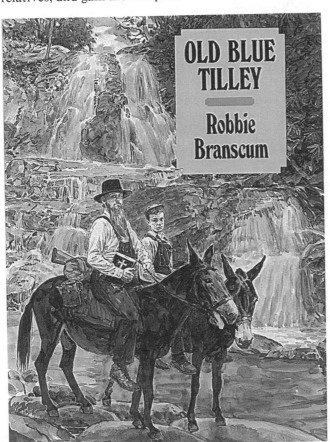

Branscum's *Old Blue Tilley* chronicles the adventures of a young orphan and a preacher en route to a revival meeting. (Cover illustration by Ted Lewin.)

WORKS CITED:

Review of *The Adventures of Johnny May, Bulletin of the Center for Children's Books,* September, 1985.

Review of *Johnny May Grows Up, Horn Book,* November, 1987, p. 736.

Jordan, Anne, review of *The Murder of Hound Dog Bates, New York Times Book Review,* October 3, 1982, p. 30.

Meyer, Randy, review of *Old Blue Tilley, Booklist,* March 1, 1991, p. 1383.

Review of *The Murder of Hound Dog Bates, Horn Book,* December, 1982, p. 647.

Piehler, Heide, review of *The Girl, School Library Journal,* October, 1986, p. 98.

Review of *Toby, Granny, and George, Horn Book,* October, 1976, p. 498.

Review of *Toby, Granny, and George, Kirkus Reviews,* May 1, 1976, p. 533.

Review of *Toby, Granny, and George, School Library Journal,* October, 1976, p. 98.

Review of *To the Tune of a Hickory Stick, Horn Book,* December, 1978, pp. 638-39.

Review of *To the Tune of a Hickory Stick, Kirkus Reviews,* October 15, 1978, p. 1138.

Review of *To the Tune of a Hickory Stick, School Library Journal,* December, 1978, p. 50.

FOR MORE INFORMATION SEE:

PERIODICALS

Bulletin of the Center for Children's Books, December, 1979; January, 1980; September, 1983; March, 1985, p. 121; December, 1986, p. 62; November, 1987, p. 43; March, 1988; April, 1991, p. 185.

Horn Book, October, 1979.

Publishers Weekly, November 19, 1982, p. 77; February 11, 1983.

School Library Journal, April, 1975, p. 50.*

—*Sketch by Kathleen J. Edgar*

*   *   *

BRESLOW, Maurice Allen 1935-

PERSONAL: Born May 25, 1935, in Boston, MA; son of Max and Freda (Tatelbaim) Breslow; married Margaret Joan Cheesman (a singer and voice teacher), December 31, 1980; children: Max, Miriam. *Education:* Cornell University, B.A., 1956; Tufts University, M.A., 1960; Yale University, D.F.A., 1972.

ADDRESSES: Home—Cedarpoint Farm, R.R.1, Seeley's Bay, Ontario, Canada K0H 2N0. *Office*—Department of Drama, Queen's University, Kingston, Ontario, Canada K7L 3N6.

CAREER: Writer. Schoolteacher until 1966; Studio Arena Theater, Buffalo, NY, director, 1966-67; Long Wharf Theater, New Haven, CT, associate artistic director, 1968-70; affiliated with Bennington College, Bennington, VT, 1970-72; Queen's University, Kingston, 1973—, became associate professor of drama. Judge, Playwright's Showcase Playwriting Competition. *Military service:* U.S. Army, 1957-59; became captain; U.S. Army Reserve, 1959-64.

MEMBER: Playwrights Canada, Association for Canadian Theatre History, Actors Equity Association.

WRITINGS:

PLAYS; JUVENILE

Pinocchio (produced in New Haven at Long Wharf Theater, 1969), Playwrights Canada, 1982.
Silver Bird and Scarlet Feather (produced at Long Wharf Theater, 1970), Playwrights Canada, 1982.
When the World Was Young (produced in Bennington at Bennington College, 1971), Playwrights Canada, 1982.

PLAYS; ADULT

Adam and Eve and After (produced at Long Wharf Theater, 1968), Playwrights Canada, 1982.
The Flying Doctor, produced at Long Wharf Theater, 1969.
The Odyssey (produced in Toronto, Ontario, at Inner Stage, 1983), Playwrights Canada, 1983.

Also contributor to periodicals, including *Queen's Quarterly* and *Reader's Digest.*

SIDELIGHTS: Maurice Breslow once commented: "My plays are of two types: children's plays and adult plays, often motivated by historical subjects. My short stories are largely autobiographical, or concerned with individuals under difficult circumstances. My articles are about theater, the arts, and baseball."

*   *   *

BROOKS, Bruce 1950-

PERSONAL: Born September 23, 1950, in Washington, DC; son of Donald D. Brooks and Lelia Colleen Collins; married Penelope Winslow, June 17, 1978; children: Alexander. *Education:* University of North Carolina at Chapel Hill, B.A., 1972; University of Iowa, M.F.A, 1982. *Politics:* "Certainly." *Religion:* "Lapsed Baptist." *Hobbies and other interests:* Music, nature study, sports, reading.

ADDRESSES: Home and office—11208 Legato Way, Silver Spring, MD 20901.

CAREER: Writer. Has worked variously as a letterpress printer, newspaper and magazine reporter, and teacher.

AWARDS, HONORS: The Moves Make the Man was named a best book of 1984 by *School Library Journal,* a notable children's book by the American Library Association (ALA), and a notable book of the year by the *New York Times,* 1984, and received a *Boston Globe-Horn Book* Award and Newbery Honor from the ALA, both 1985; *Midnight Hour Encores* was named a best book of 1986 by *School Library Journal,* a best book for young adults in 1986 by the ALA, a *Horn Book* Fanfare Honor List book in 1987, a teacher's choice by the National Council of Teachers of English in 1987, a young adult choice by the International Reading Association in 1988, and an ALA/*Booklist* best of the 1980s book for young adults; *No Kidding* was named a best book for young adults by the ALA, an ALA/*Booklist* young adult editor's choice, a best book by *School Library Journal,* and a notable children's trade book in social studies; *Everywhere* was named a notable children's book by the ALA and a best book by *School Library Journal.*

WRITINGS:

FICTION

The Moves Make the Man, Harper, 1984.
Midnight Hour Encores, Harper, 1986.
No Kidding, Harper, 1989.
Everywhere, HarperCollins, 1990.
What Hearts, HarperCollins, 1992.

NONFICTION

On the Wing: The Life of Birds from Feathers to Flight Scribner, 1989.
Predator, Farrar, Straus, 1991.
Nature by Design, Farrar, Straus, 1991.

BRUCE BROOKS

SIDELIGHTS: The author of nonfiction, novels, and stories, Bruce Brooks is an award-winning and versatile writer. Brooks's novels *The Moves Make the Man, Midnight Hour Encores, No Kidding,* and *Everywhere,* have been described by reviewers as intelligent and thought-provoking. Christine McDonnell, writing in *Horn Book,* praised the "strong voice, unusual characters, and powerful emotional ties" exhibited in Brooks's stories. *Publishers Weekly* contributor Leonard Marcus was equally enthusiastic, deeming the author's works "impassioned, [and] often psychologically complex." Critical attention to these aspects of his work pleases Brooks who, in an interview with *Authors & Artists for Young Adults* (*AAYA*), remarked, "We are capable as readers of a wild and intricate world of thought and response and feeling—things going on in different layers at the same time. I hope to write books that involve all those layers of the thinking and feeling in my reader."

Although Brooks has tried to avoid the confinement of labels such as "children's author," in his interview with Marcus the author admitted that his first four fictional works have adolescent protagonists "because my own childhood is still something I am very much wondering about." After his parents divorced when he was six years old, Brooks shuttled back and forth between homes in Washington, D.C. and North Carolina. The locations and the families contrasted; Brooks told *AAYA* that he faced the demands of adapting to life both with his father's "smaller, urban-oriented family" and the "larger Southern clan" on his mother's side. In addition the author attended various schools and was often forced to move in the middle of the year. Although originally somewhat shy, Brooks drew on his strengths to adapt to his itinerant existence. He recalled, "I never really had the chance to patiently develop a long-term relationship with kids, so I was always having to grab what I could and make friends fast. Because of that I think I overcame my shyness and was a very vivacious kid. I was always a good talker, was always a funny storyteller, was always a good mimic—language for me was a fascinating tool. I discovered that I could really be myself in words."

In his interview with *AAYA* Brooks described how moving between the North and South and lacking permanent roots in either location affected him. "Belonging to both worlds but not belonging completely to either was really an experience that made me an observer and a student of social situations; it made me learn how to apply myself to people and activities and to figure out how to belong, after figuring out which natural parts of me belonged and which parts did not." Yet this upbringing also lent itself to a certain amount of alienation. The author continued: "I could never really relax and just say 'Ah, this is me, I'm among my peers.' I was never among my peers. I was always somewhat different from everyone else. I was always the Yankee kid in the South, and when I went back to the North I was always the Southern kid. It led me to simply be very watchful."

THE MOVES MAKE THE MAN
Bruce Brooks

Brooks's experiences growing up in both the North and the South provide the backdrop for his Newbery Honor Book *The Moves Make the Man,* the story of an interracial friendship between two lonely young basketball lovers. (Cover illustration by Wayne Winfield.)

This tendency to observe and listen provided source material for Brooks when he began writing fiction. For example, during the 1950s and '60s the author's moves between the North and South allowed him a unique perspective on the burgeoning civil rights movement. Brooks was accustomed to racially mixed schools in Washington, D.C. However, in North Carolina he attended all-white schools and witnessed segregation—the enforced separation of black Americans from white in housing, education, and social situations—that was especially prevalent in the southern and border states. Brooks joined his mother's extended family in North Carolina in the wake of the 1954 landmark case *Brown v. Board of Education of Topeka,* which pronounced segregated schools inherently unequal. The ensuing movement to break down the barriers of racial discrimination—a process first enacted in public schools—was called integration, but despite the program, racial separation and tension remained prevalent.

This entrenched system of racial inequality is the background for Brooks's first book, *The Moves Make the Man.* The novel is set in North Carolina of the 1950s and chronicles the budding interracial friendship of two boys, Jerome and Bix. The boys discover that their racial differences prove less important than their common personality traits. Both loners, they frequent a secluded basketball court where Jerome teaches Bix how to play the game. Through this activity, Jerome learns about his new friend's unfortunate domestic situation. Bix's confidence and happiness has eroded since his mother suffered a nervous breakdown and entered the hospital. In addition, his stepfather refuses to take Bix to see her. Determined to visit his mother, Bix proposes a deal to his stepfather. If Bix beats him at a game of one-on-one, they will go to the hospital. Although Bix wins and invites Jerome along for the ensuing trip, the reunion is not what Bix had expected and he runs away from home, leaving Jerome alone to sort out the jarring events.

The Moves Make the Man earned enthusiastic critical response; it was named a Newbery honor book and won a *Boston Globe-Horn Book* Award. Yet Brooks confessed that such praise was not as heady as might be expected for a first-time novelist. At the times the awards were bestowed, the author explained to *AAYA,* "I hadn't written a word of fiction in three years. I'd been working out the story on my second book, *Midnight Hour Encores,* for three years mentally, but I had not written anything because I was too busy earning a living and I had a new child. So when the awards came, I felt like a hypocrite. Here everybody was saying 'Oh, brilliant new writer' and I didn't *feel* like a *writer.*" Nonetheless, Brooks's success afforded him new career opportunities; he decided to quit his job and write full-time.

For Brook's next, and equally successful, venture, he produced *Midnight Hour Encores,* a story narrated by Sibilance (Sib for short), a sixteen-year-old musical prodigy. Sib, whose parents separated after her birth, lives with her father, Taxi, in Washington D.C., and has never met her mother. The self-absorbed Sib, one of the top-ranked cello players in the world, is wrapped up in her practices, competitions, and concerts, and is preparing to attend the prestigious Juilliard School of Music in New York City. While searching for a mentor after her cello teacher dies, Sib discovers that a brilliant but reclusive player may accept a teaching post at a new music school in California. Under the guise of visiting her mother who also lives in the state, Sib travels to California to audition for the institution. Taxi drives her there, afraid all the while that his daughter will leave him. Sib initially considers Taxi's fears unfounded, but after an enjoyable and educational stay with her mother, she gradually becomes aware of what her father means to her. *Midnight Hour Encores* ends as Sib decides what school to attend and, consequently, which parent to live with.

Midnight Hour Encores was favorably received by critics. Deeming the work "another terrific book" for Brooks, *Washington Post Book World* contributor Katherine Paterson acknowledged the welcome com-...of the novel. "This is a book the reader will have ...round with, poke into, and tell in his own

Author of the Newbery Honor Book
THE MOVES MAKE THE MAN
Bruce Brooks
Midnight Hour Encores

Musical prodigy Sibilance T. Spooner travels cross-country in search of her mother and a musical mentor and ends up learning about the nature of independence and parental love in Brooks's second novel. (Cover illustration by Michael Deas.)

accents," Paterson insisted. Although several reviews of the book focused on the novel's coming-of-age slant, Brooks remarked in *AAYA* that "to me *Midnight Hour Encores* is about being a father. I wrote that book in the year after my son was born. The most important thing in my life was being a father.... My curiosity about the future—of what you get when you invest certain things in the very early days of your child's life—inspired my imagination to come up with those characters and that story."

Brooks's 1989 literary enterprise, *No Kidding,* again tackles a sophisticated topic. Set in twenty-first century Washington D.C., *No Kidding* presents a bleak environment in which alcoholics compose the majority of the population. Society is overwhelmed by this problem and schools have curriculum geared specifically toward alcoholics' offspring, more commonly referred to as AOs. The fourteen-year-old protagonist, an AO named Sam, has been forced to assume adult-level responsibility in his fatherless home. He previously committed his mother to a rehabilitation program and placed his younger brother, Ollie, with foster parents. Now that his mother's stint is completed, Sam must decide whether to reunite the family. Complicating Sam's decision is the knowledge that his mother may revert to her old behavior and that Ollie, who is unaware of her alcoholism, may experience emotional problems. At book's end, however, Sam's mother manipulates events to generate the outcome, giving Sam the chance to assume the role of a child once again. Elizabeth S. Watson, writing in *Horn Book,* remarked that "Brooks is a fine writer," and although she found some of the issues perplexing for young readers, she conceded that "Brooks has created a wonderful vehicle for discussion."

In 1990 Brooks published a short novel titled *Everywhere.* In this book, a nameless young protagonist frets about his beloved grandfather who has suffered a heart attack and is near death. As the boy keeps a vigil, a local nurse arrives with her nephew, Dooley, who suggests killing an animal in a soul-switching ceremony to save

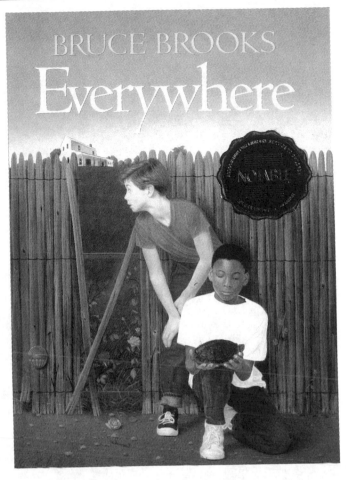

A short novel comprising a young boy's vigil over his sick grandfather, *Everywhere* explores complex issues of mortality and ethics. (Cover illustration by Kam Mak.)

Set in a bleak future in which alcoholism has devastated the population, *No Kidding* depicts the efforts of a fourteen-year-old who has assumed responsibility for his family in the absence of his recovering mother. (Cover illustration by Fred Marcellino.)

the grandfather. During the course of the story, the boy ponders his grandfather's fate, his own mortality, and the ethics of taking one life to save another. Recognizing both the accessibility and complex issues in *Everywhere,* *Horn Book* contributor Nancy Vasilakis deemed the work a "masterly novella" and added that "Brooks's precise use of language is a tour de force."

Brooks is also the author of several nonfiction works, including *On the Wing: The Life of Birds from Feathers to Flight.* In his *Publishers Weekly* interview with Marcus, the author commented that he wrote *On the Wing* because "by explaining why [birds] have the equipment they do ... we can begin to understand their behavior while still enjoying that wonderful sense of difference." Brooks added two more works about facets of animal life to his corpus with his 1991 publications *Predator* and *Nature by Design.* Reviewers admired the colorful photographs in both books and praised the author for his grasp of his subjects and for injecting humor into the narratives.

With each of his literary endeavors Brooks has shown his versatility. The opportunity for variety pleases the author, who concluded in *AAYA:* "One of the nice things about being a writer is also the biggest challenge about being a writer: you're always going to be a beginner as soon as you finish something. You wrap up one book and immediately you are a rookie again because you've never written your next book. You start all over and you're fresh and you're challenged and you're green, and you don't yet know how to solve all the problems that are going to come up. You're going to have to gain wisdom and technique as you write, so that you can take care of these new challenges. It's a constantly refreshing recurrence of being a beginner. That keeps me from being goal oriented. My goal is to be able to write my next book. That's it."

WORKS CITED:

Authors & Artists for Young Adults, Volume 8, Gale, 1992, pp. 17-24.

Marcus, Leonard, interview with Bruce Brooks for *Publishers Weekly,* July 29, 1990, pp. 214-215.

McDonnell, Christine, "New Voices, New Visions: Bruce Brooks," *Horn Book,* March/April, 1987, pp. 188-190.

Paterson, Katherine, "Heart Strings and Other Attachments," *Washington Post Book World,* November 9, 1986, p. 17.

Vasilakis, Nancy, review of *Everywhere, Horn Book,* January, 1991, pp. 72-73.

Watson, Elizabeth S., review of *No Kidding, Horn Book,* July, 1989, p. 486.

FOR MORE INFORMATION SEE:

PERIODICALS

Horn Book, January/February, 1986, pp. 38-40.
New York Times Book Review, January 4, 1987, p. 33; June 25, 1989, p. 30.

* * *

BRYAN, Ashley F. 1923-

PERSONAL: Born July 13, 1923, in New York, NY. *Education:* Earned degrees from Cooper Union Art School and Columbia University.

ADDRESSES: Office—Department of Art, Dartmouth College, Hanover, NH 03755.

CAREER: Reteller and illustrator of books for children; professor emeritus of art and visual studies at Dartmouth College. *Military service:* U.S. Army, World War II.

AWARDS, HONORS: Parents Choice Award, 1980, and Coretta Scott King Book Award, 1981, for illustrating *Beat the Story-Drum, Pum-Pum;* Coretta Scott King Honor Book citations, 1983, for illustrating *I'm Going to Sing: Black American Spirituals,* 1986, for writing *Lion and the Ostrich Chicks and Other African Folk*

ASHLEY F. BRYAN

Tales, 1988, for illustrating *What a Morning! The Christmas Story in Black Spirituals,* and 1992, for illustrating *All Night, All Day: A Child's First Book of African American Spirituals;* Parents' Choice citation, 1992, for *Sing to the Sun.*

WRITINGS:

RETELLER; SELF-ILLUSTRATED

The Ox of the Wonderful Horns and Other African Folktales, Atheneum, 1971.
The Adventures of Aku; or, How it Came about That We Shall Always See Okra the Cat Lying on a Velvet Cushion while Okraman the Dog Sleeps among the Ashes, Atheneum, 1976.
The Dancing Granny, Macmillan, 1977.
Beat the Story-Drum, Pum-Pum (Nigerian folk tales), Atheneum, 1980.
The Cat's Purr, Atheneum, 1985.
Lion and the Ostrich Chicks and Other African Folk Tales, Atheneum, 1986.
Sh-Ko and His Eight Wicked Brothers, Macmillan, 1988.
Turtle Knows Your Name, Macmillan, 1989.

ILLUSTRATOR

Rabindranath Tagore, *Moon, for What Do You Wait?* (poems), edited by Richard Lewis, Atheneum, 1967.
Mari Evans, *Jim Flying High* (juvenile), Doubleday, 1979.
Susan Cooper, *Jethro and the Jumbie* (juvenile), Atheneum, 1979.
John Langstaff, editor, *What a Morning! The Christmas Story in Black Spirituals,* Macmillan, 1987.

OTHER

(Compiler; self-illustrated) *Black American Spirituals,* Volume 1: *Walk Together Children,* Atheneum, 1974, Volume 2: *I'm Going to Sing,* Macmillan, 1982.
(Compiler and author of introduction) Paul Laurence Dunbar, *I Greet the Dawn: Poems,* Atheneum, 1978.
(Self-illustrated) *All Night, All Day: A Child's First Book of Spirituals,* Macmillan, 1991.
(Self-illustrated) *Sing to the Sun* (poems), HarperCollins, 1992.

ADAPTATIONS: The Dancing Granny and Other African Tales was recorded by Bryan for Caedmon.

SIDELIGHTS: Ashley Bryan's own paintings and drawings grace the pages of his unique versions of traditional African and West Indian folktales and spirituals. "In my work as a black American artist," he commented in an interview with Sylvia and Kenneth Marantz for *Horn Book,* "it is the African root that nourishes whatever other world culture I may draw upon." Bryan has traveled to African countries such as Uganda and Kenya, but he has found that American libraries are a rich source of tribal tales. The multitalented Bryan is also known to audiences throughout the United States for his resonating poetry readings and lectures on black American poets.

Bryan brings traditional African folktales to life in his self-illustrated retellings, such as the myth "How Animals Got Their Tails" from *Beat the Story-Drum, Pum-Pum.*

Although Bryan grew up in rough sections of the Bronx, he fortunately embarked on a productive path early in life. "I learned from kindergarten that drawing and painting were the toughest assets I had to offer my community," Bryan stated in *Illustrators of Children's Books: 1967-76.* When an enterprising teacher introduced his class to book production, "I was author, illustrator, editor, publisher, and binder" of that first hand-stitched ABC book, recalled Bryan in his *Horn Book* interview. "Rave reviews" from the Bryan family encouraged him to generate countless original volumes.

Bryan continued to enjoy the support of family, friends, and teachers for his artistic abilities throughout his school years. This support, matched with the artist's internal drive and enthusiasm, led to higher studies at Cooper Union Art School. After serving in the Army during World War II, Bryan returned to finish the program at Cooper Union and then went on to earn a degree in philosophy at Columbia University. While there, he also enrolled in a bookbinding course. Again finding himself in his element, Bryan generated thirty to forty bound books—about ten times the volume of his classmates.

When Bryan later opened a studio back in the Bronx, he was visited one day by Atheneum editor Jean Karl. At that time Bryan was in the process of illustrating his first professional book, *Fabliaux,* for Pantheon. The meeting with Karl was fortuitous: she sent Bryan a contract for drawings to accompany single-line poems by Indian poet Rabindranath Tagore, collected under the title *Moon, for What Do You Wait?* The artist told Sylvia and Kenneth Marantz what followed: "Later she asked if she could use some of my illustrations for a book of African tales. I said, 'You bet! But I don't like the way they are written.' She said, 'Tell them in your own way, Ashley.'" Bryan followed Karl's advice and continued to write and illustrate with her support, even after she went into semiretirement. "As soon as I do one book, she is immediately encouraging me to do another," he added.

The first book resulting from this encouragement was a collection of five stories called *The Ox of the Wonderful Horns and Other African Folktales,* illustrated by Bryan in a distinctive painted style resembling woodcutting. *The Dancing Granny,* published in 1977, evolved from an Ashanti story collected in Antigua in the West Indies, the area from which Bryan's parents emigrated. In his *Horn Book* interview, Bryan described how he became inspired by a visit from his grandmother when she was in her seventies: "She picked up the latest dance steps from the great-grandchildren and outdanced them all! I drew upon that." Bryan used a brushpainting technique he borrowed from the Japanese to create a sense of movement in his illustrations.

In *The Cat's Purr,* which originated in the Antilles, Bryan unearthed a tale with an unexpected twist. When

Bryan's own septuagenarian grandmother inspired his illustrations for the Ashanti tale *The Dancing Granny.*

Cat inherits the miniature family drum, Rat *must* play it, despite Cat's wishes to the contrary. "Rat's trickery gives the story a nice bit of dramatic tension, and the notion of the tiny drum as the reason cats purr today will amuse young listeners or readers with its novelty," predicted Denise M. Wilms in *Booklist.* Bryan showed his versatility with the sepia line illustrations for this text, which have a "casual quality that makes one think of an artist's sketch pad of personal jottings," noted DonnaRae McCann and Olga Richard in a *Wilson Library Bulletin* review.

During the 1800s, anthropologists and missionaries translated tribal stories into English, though they sought to preserve the languages more than the tales. Bryan begins with these materials and makes them his own, as he described in *Illustrators of Children's Books:* "I take the skeletal story motifs from the scholarly collections and use every resource of my background and experience to flesh them out and bring them alive." In all of his books, Bryan endeavors to impart the oral tradition of "texture and vitality and drama—the back and forth play of teller and audience of the oral setting," he explained to Sylvia and Kenneth Marantz. "I try things that will give a vitality of surface, a textural feeling, a possibility of vocal play to the prose of my stories. So I take risks in my books. I do a lot of things that people writing prose generally do not do: close rhythms, rhyme, onomatopoeia, alliteration, interior rhyme," he continued. Bryan recommends that stories and poetry be "read aloud, for the reader to understand the relationship between sound, spirit, and meaning," according to Alice K. Swinger in *Language Arts.* "Then, when the materials are read silently, the reader will receive more benefit because the sound and the spirit will already have been felt in the muscles and heard in the ears."

Bryan has also found success with his collections of black American spirituals. For example, *Walk Together Children* "is as sweet and varied a collection of black spirituals as one could hope to find for children," praised Virginia Hamilton in the *New York Times Book Review.* Bryan's interest in music reaches back to his childhood, when family and friends sang together on Sunday afternoons. Included among the twenty-four spirituals are the classics "Go Down Moses" and "Swing Low, Sweet Chariot." Bryan's accompanying black-and-white illustrations "surge with compassion and raw life," lauded Neil Millar in the *Christian Science Monitor. I'm Going To Sing,* published in 1982, is the critically acclaimed companion volume to *Walk Together Children.*

But not all of Bryan's working hours are spent creating books, which he does primarily in the evenings. His days are devoted to painting in a studio on an island off the coast of Maine, which he made his permanent residence after he became professor emeritus at Dartmouth College. Since the 1940s Bryan had painted and exhibited his works on the island during the summer, with plans to live there year-round one day. In his interview with Sylvia and Kenneth Marantz, Bryan described his approach to painting: "I work with oils on

An artist from an early age, Bryan's work ranges through various media, including this intricate wood-cut illustration of the story "Hen and Frog" from *Beat the Story-Drum, Pum-Pum.*

canvas, outdoors, in the spirit of the impressionists. But I don't work from the essential feeling of light at a specific time; I work from a sense of rhythm." And while he used to prefer to depict scenes from the seashore, the artist has been fascinated by the garden and other areas around his home over the past decade or so. "I paint from changing patterns of color, as flowers bloom and fade, against the background of the fields stretching down to the ocean," revealed Bryan.

The dynamic artist began sharing his knowledge of painting and drawing as a teacher at Queens College in Brooklyn, but he was also able to reach younger children at various institutions in the New York City area, such as the Brooklyn Museum and Dalton School. "I love to teach children, especially those under twelve, and participate in their development both as artists and as people," Bryan noted in *Fifth Book of Junior Authors and Illustrators.* And even though Bryan no longer teaches art at Darmouth College, he still enriches people's lives through the use of another vehicle. He explained to Sylvia and Kenneth Marantz: "Through my programs in black culture I'm trying to push past the resistances and the stereotypes and open audiences to feelings that can change, or be included in, their lives. The same energies are still being called upon."

A man of many talents, Bryan continues to mesmerize audiences throughout the United States with poetry readings and storytelling sessions. Back in his studio on the island off the coast of Maine, he paints the changing forms in the garden and illustrates the compelling spirituals and tales he retells in a rhythmic written form. As Ethel L. Heins put it in *Horn Book,* "Ashley Bryan is a humane, articulate man who links ethnicity to universal culture."

WORKS CITED:

Bryan, Ashley, essay in *Fifth Book of Junior Authors and Illustrators,* Wilson, 1983, pp. 57-59.

Hamilton, Virginia, "Walk Together Children: Black American Spirituals," *New York Times Book Review,* November 3, 1974, pp. 28-9.

Heins, Ethel L., *Horn Book,* March/April, 1989.

Kingman, Lee, *Illustrators of Children's Books, 1967-76,* Horn Book, 1978.

Marantz, Sylvia and Kenneth, "Interview with Ashley Bryan," *Horn Book,* March/April 1988, pp. 173-179.

McCann, DonnaRae, and Olga Richard, review of *The Cat's Purr, Wilson Library Bulletin,* February, 1986, p. 45.

Millar, Neil, "Songs of Lands and Seasons," *Christian Science Monitor,* November 6, 1974, p. 14.

Swinger, Alice K., "Profile: Ashley Bryan," *Language Arts,* Volume 61, No. 3, March, 1984, pp. 305-311.

Wilms, Denise M., "The Cat's Purr," *Booklist,* Volume 81, No. 16, April 15, 1985, p. 1189.

FOR MORE INFORMATION SEE:

BOOKS

Children's Literature Review, Volume 18, Gale, 1989.

PERIODICALS

Ms., December, 1974.
New York Times Book Review, December, 1987.
Scientific American, December, 1980.

OTHER

Meet Ashley Bryan: Storyteller, Artist, Writer (videocassette), American School Publications, 1991.*

*   *   *

BURRELL, R(oy) E(ric) C(harles) 1923-

PERSONAL: Born July 25, 1923, in Ilford, Essex, England; son of Percival Charles (a laborer) and Ellen Blanche Camy (a housewife; maiden name, Parmenter) Burrell; married Joyce Nora Riche (a teacher), April 16, 1949; children: Jillian Laura Davies. *Education:* Borough Road College, teaching certificate, 1949. *Hobbies and other interests:* Bridge, crossword puzzles (both solving and setting), drawing cartoons, reading, walking, board games, and visiting churches.

ADDRESSES: Office—c/o Oxford University Press, Walton St., Oxford, England, OX2 6DP.

R. E. C. BURRELL

CAREER: International Stores Office, London, England, clerk, 1939-42; teacher at various schools, 1949-79. *Military service:* Royal Navy pilot, 1942-46, served in Europe during D-Day invasion; received various campaign medals.

WRITINGS:

(And co-illustrator) *The Early Days of Man,* Wheaton, 1965, revised edition, McGraw-Hill, 1968.
The Romans and Their World, Wheaton, 1970.
The Romans in Britain, Wheaton, 1971.
England: 1750, Wheaton, 1980.
Food from the Fields, Wheaton, 1980.
What Are You Wearing?, Wheaton, 1980.
Travel and Transport by Muscle Power, Wheaton, 1980.
Travel and Transport by Machine Before 1914, Wheaton, 1980.
Travel and Transport in Modern Times, Wheaton, 1980.
Villains and Violence, Wheaton, 1980.
The Invaders, Chancellor, 1980.
The Middle Ages, Chancellor, 1980.
The Tudors and the Stuarts, Chancellor, 1980.
The Oxford Children's History, Volume 1, *Earliest Times to the Last Stuarts,* Oxford University Press, 1983.
On the Threshold of History, Oxford University Press, 1988.
The Greeks, Oxford University Press, 1989.
The Romans, Oxford University Press, 1991.

Also author of two plays broadcast on BBC: *A Look Back from Retirement* and *Napoleon.*

WORK IN PROGRESS: The Aztecs for Steck-Vaughn; a dictionary of sea terms; *A Thesaurus of Things.*

SIDELIGHTS: "I always thought I would write books from the age of about nine," R.E.C. Burrell told *Something about the Author (SATA).* "My friend and I took turns coming out on top in junior high school exams and wondered what we should do with this ability. Both swore we'd write one day—I don't know if he ever did!

"My motive for writing as an adult was triggered by the new girlfriend of an acquaintance who, in the course of conversation, admitted that she was a private secretary to the bosses of a publishing company. I foolishly said something to the effect that most publishers produced books which were not terribly suitable for school use, in spite of their avowed aim of doing just that." Burrell's remark prompted a challenge from the woman, which he accepted by writing a book of his own. The result, a long novel with British archeology as a theme, was turned down by seventeen publishers before one finally suggested he "forget the fiction and write a straightforward account of the early history of mankind." Encouraged, Burrell wrote the book while he and a friend worked on illustrations for it.

"Since that time," Burrell told *SATA,* "I have written two books about the Romans and a series on the origins of the Industrial Revolution. All of these were written to assist me in my job as head of the history department at a West London comprehensive school."

*   *   *

BUTLER, M. Christina 1934-

PERSONAL: Born December 11, 1934, in Scarborough, North Yorkshire, England; daughter of Harold Cautley (a hotel proprietor and engineer) and Mabel (Manners) Tutill; married William Anthony Butler (a political agent), August 23, 1958; children: Katharyn Charlotte, Frances Emma. *Education:* Attended St. Joseph's Convent. *Politics:* Conservative. *Religion:* Church of England. *Hobbies and other interests:* Music, swimming, walking, travel, reading.

ADDRESSES: Home—West Bank, Wold Newton Hall, Driffield, North Humberside YO25 0YF, England.

CAREER: Leeds General Infirmary, Leeds, England, state-registered nurse, 1953-57; Halifax Infirmary, Sheffield, England, worked in Outpatient's Casualty Department, 1958-60, district nursing sister, 1960-65. Playgroup supervisor, 1973-76; preschool nursery supervisor, 1977-84, 1987. Served on various village committees; Governor of local primary school, 1973-77, 1989—.

MEMBER: Fine Arts Society (local representative of national volunteers), local church committee-member.

M. CHRISTINA BUTLER

WRITINGS:

Can I Live With You?, illustrated by Meg Rutherford, Macdonald Picture Books, published as *Can I Stay with You?*, Dial, 1988.

Too Many Eggs, illustrated by Rutherford, David Godine, 1988.

Where Are My Bananas?, Macdonald Picture Books, 1989.

Stanley in the Dark, illustrated by Rutherford, Simon & Schuster, 1990.

Picnic Pandemonium, illustrated by Rutherford, George Stevens, 1991.

The Dinosaur's Egg, Simon & Schuster, 1992.

Bear Drops In on Mole, in press.

Also author of children's serials and short stories for local radio.

WORK IN PROGRESS: Picture-book text and outline layout; "Working on a play for five-to-eight-year-olds—to be performed by an adult cast."

SIDELIGHTS: Author M. Christina Butler was born in Scarborough, a seaside resort in North Yorkshire, England. While she was still a small child, her family moved to a small village, and her rural surroundings provided her with memories that she would later draw upon in writing her books for young children. "At a time when farming embraced a rich variety of activities that young people could take part in, I was fortunate enough to have a farmer's daughter as my best friend," she recalled for *SATA*. "From the age of about eight years old, weekends and holidays were spent on the farm. There was so much to do. We devised our own games—had secret codes, maps, and dens. Our constant companions were dogs and horses." Spending most of her time out-of-doors didn't leave Butler much time for reading when she was young, although she recalls being

read to by her mother. The stories of Hans Christian Andersen were among her favorites: "*The Little Match Girl* ... never failed to have us both in tears long before the end," remembered Butler.

"I loved art but was never drawn to long essay writing," Butler admitted, adding "I was, however, extremely happy at school." When she turned eighteen, her family agreed that she should obtain training in a useful occupation, so Butler enrolled in Leeds General Infirmary in West Yorkshire, where she obtained her state registration as a nurse after four years of study. In the year following graduation she married William Anthony Butler. It was her husband's busy career that prompted her to begin her own career as an author. "As my husband was often attending evening meetings, [I] began writing children's stories. For years I wrote for local radio; short stories and serials, but always cherished the hope of being published," Butler explained. The many hours she spent reading aloud after the birth of her two daughters were followed by several years spent working with other children as the supervisor of a nursery school. Butler became familiar with the wide variety of books available for young children and grew interested in the idea of writing children's picture books. In 1987, her first book was published. Designed as a novelty picture book, *Can I Stay With You?* is the story of a little bird who tries to find a new home after he accidentally falls out of the family nest. *Too Many Eggs*

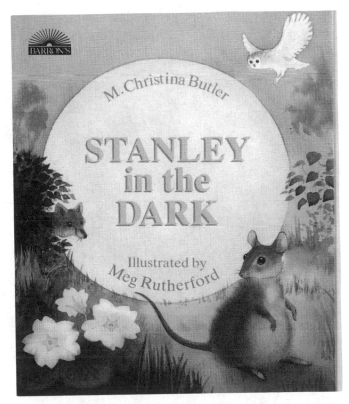

An innocent young mouse sets out at night to capture the great big "cheese" he sees in a tree in Butler's *Stanley in the Dark.* **(Cover illustration by Meg Rutherford.)**

followed in 1988, *Where Are My Bananas?* in 1989, and *Stanley in the Dark* in 1990.

"The picture book format is my ideal medium. With an interest in art—and not being particularly disposed to writing long tracts of text—I find the combination of moving the story on in the pictures and with a minimum of words fascinating." Several of Butlers's characters are based on people that she knew during her childhood spent on the farm. "Mrs. Bear in *Too Many Eggs* is my farming friend's mother—the best cook in the world who never used a recipe in her life. The mouse in *Stanley in the Dark* is a memory of long walks over the field in the dark to fasten the poultry houses, surrounded by the sounds and shadows of the night, some rather scary."

"To be able to write stories for young children that captivate, stimulate, entertain, and inform in an humorous way and leave them wanting more is my overriding ambition," Butler told *SATA*. "There is something very special about a group of wide-eyed four-year-olds listening intently to a story."

FOR MORE INFORMATION SEE:

PERIODICALS

Horn Book, July, 1990, p. 36.
School Library Journal, February, 1989, p. 66.
Times Educational Supplement, March 11, 1988, p. 24; March 29, 1991, p. 23.

C

CHAPPELL, Audrey 1954-

PERSONAL: Born January 31, 1954, in Norwich, Norfolk, England; daughter of James Stanley (a teacher) and Margaret Saunders (a teacher) Chappell. Education: Attended Norwich City College; Furzedown College of Education, education certificate, 1975.

ADDRESSES: Home—"The Old Forge," Berghapton, Mill Rd., Norwich NR15 1BQ, England; 54 Fisher House, Copenhagen St., London N1 0JE, England.

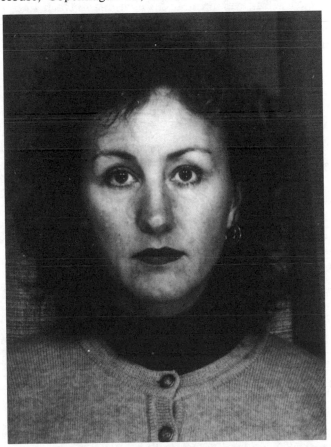

AUDREY CHAPPELL

CAREER: Islington school, London, preschool teacher, 1976-83; Haringey school, London, preschool teacher, 1984-91.

WRITINGS:

A Surprise for Oliver, Blackie Children's Books, 1989.
An Outing for Oliver, Blackie Children's Books, 1990.

SIDELIGHTS: Audrey Chappell told SATA: "I've always enjoyed writing, and love reading and books generally. Working with young children provides many incidents worthy of inclusion in a story, and with an illustrator as a friend I have been lucky enough to create two so far. Children love being read these stories and so many others, and I love reading to them."

* * *

CHMIELARZ, Sharon 1940-

PERSONAL: Surname is pronounced "schmee-lars"; born December 20, 1940, in Mobridge, SD; daughter of Theodore (a switchboard operator) and Ella Grace Clara (a homemaker, teacher, and clerk; maiden name, Pewe) Grenz; married Tad Chmielarz (a teacher), June 27, 1964. Education: University of Minnesota, B.S., M.A. Politics: "I tend to be liberal." Religion: "Brought up Christian."

ADDRESSES: Home and office—Minneapolis, MN.

CAREER: Orono School District, Long Lake, MN, teacher, 1962—; writer.

MEMBER: Loft Place for Literature and the Arts, Twin Cities.

AWARDS, HONORS: Minnesota Voices Award; Minnesota State Arts Board Grant.

WRITINGS:

POETRY
Different Arrangements, New Rivers Press, 1980.

SHARON CHMIELARZ

But I Won't Go Out in a Boat, New Rivers Press, 1990.

PICTURE BOOKS

Pied Piper of Hamelin, Stemmer House, 1990.
End of Winter, Crown, 1992.
Down at Angel's, Houghton, in press.

Contributor of poems to anthologies; contributor of stories and poems to *Cricket* and *Children's Magic Window.*

WORK IN PROGRESS: Researching the lives of "brilliant women" for a book of narrative and lyric poetry.

SIDELIGHTS: Sharon Chmielarz told *SATA:* "Something magic happened in my rather undistinguished life just at the point when I was ready for it: I began to write. Here's how it came about. I had been a foreign language teacher for years when budgets for such frivolities began to be cut. To insure having a paycheck I decided to pick up a degree in English. This included, of course, taking many literature classes.

"The class that worked best into my schedule was on the poetry of [American author Wystan Hugh] Auden and [British author] Dylan Thomas. I can still hear the professor reigning, 'Since everyone likes the poetry of Dylan Thomas we will do him last.' I had never heard of either, but I battled the afternoon traffic in to the

University, and slowly, within the walls of a gray classroom, I fell in love with the poetry of Auden. Where had I been all my life?

"My spring elective that year was a writing workshop. It's good there was no manuscript requirement since I never would have passed it, but I was lucky again, and I entered a very small section (ten people) led by a fine teacher-poet: Thomas McGrath. Thus my writing career was launched.

"It became painfully obvious that although I was the oldest student in the class, I was the least prepared. I didn't know any technique and I'd hardly read any poetry in my life—not to the degree that you must if you're going to write it. Since then I've read tons, taken many classes in writing, and attended many workshops, the biggest being Bread Loaf Writers' Conference. I look back to that time in my career (development?) with happiness and envy at my innocence. Bread Loaf to me was 'gaga' land, the Hollywood of the writing colonies. Turn any corner and you might run into a major poet or novelist. Although I had enrolled as a poet, I attended lectures by Nancy Willard—poet, children's writer and novelist—and knew in my heart I wanted at some point to write children's literature, too.

"Those were my beginnings, with thanks to many teachers and writing groups. I continue to teach since I can hardly afford to support myself on the income I receive from writing, but I look forward to the day when I can totally devote my time to writing. That desire remains constant and comes from an inner feeling of rightness which I can't deny, martyr, or rationalize away.

"The writing course with Thomas McGrath was in 1978 or 1979. When I asked him on the last day of class how I could continue to improve he said, 'Read and write.' It remains some of the best advice I've had. I've never especially enjoyed the poetry of Dylan Thomas, but I've been lucky to have had two books of poetry and two picture books published, and another on the way from Houghton Mifflin. If I never had anything published again I would continue writing as the thing I want to do to pursue what little I know about life. But I hope the years ahead hold more book contracts for me."

* * *

CLIFFORD, Rachel Mark
See LEWIS, Brenda Ralph

* * *

COLE, Brock 1938-

PERSONAL: Born May 29, 1938, in Charlotte, MI; married; wife's name, Susan (a classical studies professor). *Education:* Kenyon College, B.A.; University of Minnesota, Ph.D.

ADDRESSES: Home—158 Lombard Ave., Oak Park, IL 60302.

CAREER: University of Minnesota, instructor in English composition; University of Wisconsin, instructor in philosophy, until 1975; writer and illustrator, 1975—.

AWARDS, HONORS: Juvenile Award, Friends of American Writers, 1980, for *The King at the Door;* California Young Reader Medal, California Reading Association, 1985, and Young Readers' Choice Award, Pacific Northwest Library Association, both for *The Indian in the Cupboard,* which was also named a *New York Times* outstanding book, 1981; Smarties "Grand Prix" for children's books, Book Trust, 1985, for *Gaffer Samson's Luck;* Parent's Choice Award, Parent's Choice Foundation, 1986, for *The Giant's Toe;* Carl Sandburg Award, Friends of Chicago Public Library, 1988, for *The Goats,* which was also named a *New York Times* notable book, an American Library Association (ALA) best book for young adults, and an ALA notable book, all 1987.

WRITINGS:

JUVENILE; SELF-ILLUSTRATED

The King at the Door, Doubleday, 1979.
No More Baths, Doubleday, 1980.
Nothing but a Pig, Doubleday, 1981.
The Winter Wren, Farrar, Straus, 1984.
The Giant's Toe, Farrar, Straus, 1986.
Alpha and the Dirty Baby, Farrar, Straus, 1991.

OTHER

(Illustrator) Lynne Reid Banks, *The Indian in the Cupboard,* Avon, 1980.
(Illustrator) Jill Paton Walsh, *Gaffer Samson's Luck,* Farrar, Straus, 1984.
The Goats (young adult novel), Farrar, Straus, 1987.
Celine (young adult novel), Farrar, Straus, 1989.

BROCK COLE

SIDELIGHTS: Brock Cole had already established himself as an award-winning illustrator and author of children's picture books when he wrote his highly acclaimed young adult novel *The Goats* in 1987. Just as critics had praised the richness of detail and expressiveness of the illustrations in his early work, many applauded the depth of insight and subtle evocation of complex emotions in his later novels. Cole's successful change in genre reflects a versatility he has demonstrated throughout his career. From teaching college philosophy in the early 1970s, he turned to creating picture books that range from jocular humor to drama, from satire to allegory, and from fairy tale to spoof. His novels exhibit realism and emotional depth as well as allegorical motifs and incisive humor. In whatever form, his works generally present an intricate portrait of human nature that a child can "enjoy first and ponder later," according to *Wilson Library Bulletin* contributor Patty Campbell.

Cole was born in the small town of Charlotte, Michigan, in 1938. Although his family moved often, he remembers Charlotte fondly as "a place where a six year old could wander into the feed mill or the auto body shop and watch men work without being chased out," he commented in *Junior Literary Guild.* Throughout the family's migrations in the Midwest, reading at the local library was one of the stable pleasures in Cole's childhood. After graduating from high school in Royal Oak, Michigan, Cole majored in English at Kenyon College in Ohio. He considered becoming a writer, but turned to teaching instead, first as a freshman English instructor at the University of Minnesota, where he attended graduate school, and then as a philosophy professor at the University of Wisconsin.

In 1975 Cole, his wife Susan, and their two sons moved to Illinois, where Susan began a job as a professor of classical studies at the University of Illinois. Cole was tired of teaching and decided to pursue his interest in writing. Realizing that his stories would need illustration, he took on the challenge of becoming an artist as well as an author. With no prior training in art, he taught himself the techniques of illustration by studying the works of major illustrators and trying to imitate their style. Since 1975 he has been working full-time at writing and illustrating with impressive results.

Cole's first picture book, *The King at the Door,* is perhaps his most traditional and pointedly moralistic story, presenting themes that recur in various forms in many of his works. Set in times past, the tale begins when the King, dressed in a beggar's rags, knocks at the door of an inn. The chore-boy, Little Baggit, informs the innkeeper of the King's requests for food and drink, but the disbelieving innkeeper spitefully offers the stranger only dishwater and the dog's scraps. Little Baggit's youthful purity enables him to see the real identity of the disguised visitor. He gives up his own bread and ale to the King, and is well-rewarded the next day when the royal coach arrives for him. Like many of Cole's books, *The King at the Door* juxtaposes the perceptive powers

Alpha and the Dirty Baby, **which tells of how a girl's stoic resistance saves her parents from impish mischief, combines Cole's colorful, energetic illustrations with farcical humor.**

of innocence with the spiritual blindness of the adult social world.

Nothing but a Pig satirizes the pretensions of a social-climbing pig who scorns his real friend, a poor farmer who loves the pig for himself. The pig's social aspirations are fulfilled when he is sold to a wealthy banker. Puffed up with his own conceit and dressed in the banker's clothes, the pig is dismayed to learn that his new friend plans to butcher him for bacon. When the farmer returns to rescue him, the pig learns the meaning of friendship. *Nothing but a Pig* is full of "witty details" that enliven the moral tale, according to *New York*

Times Book Review contributor Karla Kuskin. The reviewer particularly praised Cole's illustrations of turn-of-the-century village life for "looking quite English, filled with color and clutter and always on the verge of coming apart at the picturesque seams."

Cole's other picture books are equally varied in theme and style. *No More Baths* is presented through the humorous perspective of a willful little girl who, hating baths, decides to try to clean herself in the ways that chickens, cats, and pigs do. Although she finally surrenders to a human bath, she never loses her bath-hating spirit. On a very different note, *The Winter Wren* is the allegorical tale of a young boy and his sister who travel to Winter's farm to wake Spring, doing battle with Winter all the way. Combining the humorous and the mythological approaches of his previous works, Cole's 1986 *The Giant's Toe* is a whimsical revision of the fairy tale "Jack and the Beanstalk." In this spoof, the giant cuts off his toe while gardening, and the toe comes to life as an elf-like being. This "toe" is a prankster who causes the giant to bake his hen-that-laid-the-golden-egg into a pie and throw away his golden harp. But the toe also saves the day for the giant. When an unpleasant boy named Jack mounts the beanstalk to the giant's domain there are no treasures to be found, so he goes away without further conflict. Critics applauded the originality and humor of this story as well as its funny and evocative watercolor illustrations. Luann Toth, writing for *School Library Journal*, called *The Giant's Toe* "Cole's best effort to date."

Cole's 1987 young adult novel, *The Goats,* is set in a summer camp where a cruel prank is played on a socially backward thirteen-year-old boy and a girl who has been labeled "a dog" by other campers. Both are stripped of their clothing and left on Goat Island. After

Cole's acclaimed first novel *The Goats* is a sensitive examination of how two young teens learn to trust each other despite being victimized by a cruel prank. (Cover illustration by the author.)

finding each other, the boy and girl spend several days together conspiring for survival and avoiding capture by the camp counselors. *Wilson Library Bulletin* contributor Patty Campbell raved that "from the first sentence the novel is utterly engrossing, with a satisfying rightness of phrase and event, an inevitability of character and action, and yet a constant tension of suspense."

Although the prank in *The Goats* is concocted by the campers with a rather crass adolescent notion of sexuality in mind, it results in the discovery by the boy and girl of the virtues of genuinely caring for one another. *New York Times Book Review* contributor Ron Hansen summarized that "in the few days they're on the run together [the boy and girl] acquire years of learning about cooperation and respect and the sort of intimate friendship and devotion that the happily married depend upon." After experiencing betrayal and alienation at the hands of their peers and the social world in general, the boy and girl learn to trust by reaching out to each other. Christine McDonnell wrote in a *Horn Book* article that the two "encounter what Brock Cole describes as a 'fallen world.' The cruelty of groups, insensitivity and irresponsibility of adults, crass, exploitive sex, and children's vulnerability are drawn clearly. Against them, Cole affirms the innocence and strength of his main characters." Similarly, Anita Silvey maintained in her *Horn Book* review that "*The Goats* will repel some readers and attract others," with its lack of positive adult role models and its "raw emotions." But the critic concluded that the novel's publication "signifies that we are still creating children's books that affirm the human spirit and the ability of the individual to rise above adversity."

With his 1989 novel, *Celine,* Cole demonstrates his keen sense of humor in the midst of some poignantly sad scenes, and once again reflects his attraction to innocence in a frequently corrupt world. Celine is a sixteen-year-old girl whose divorced parents are following their dreams on separate continents, leaving her with her twenty-two-year-old stepmother in a Chicago loft. Celine babysits for Jake, a seven-year-old boy whose parents are in the process of separation. In a chaotic and often absurd tangle of romantic attachments and detachments, the growing affection between Jake and Celine counteracts the desolation that adult turmoil has left to them. Several reviewers remarked that Celine's narrative perspective illuminates the book with charm and wit. An *Entertainment Weekly* critic observed, "since [Celine's] mind shoots off in daring flights of speculation at the slightest provocation, we're in for a wild, funny ride." Betsy Hearne commented in the *Bulletin of the Center for Children's Books* that Celine's "observations of adult antics, of peer idiosyncrasies, and of her own irregularities are, subtly or raucously, irreverent." Describing Cole's *The Goats* as "one of the most important books of the decade," Hearne concluded that *Celine,* "a marriage of craft and appeal so intelligent as to satisfy any standards," is a triumphant successor to Cole's debut as a novelist.

A self-taught artist, Cole learned drawing techniques by studying and imitating the works of great illustrators; he has now established his own drawing style in several children's stories. (Illustration by Cole from *Gaffer Samson's Luck* by Jill Paton Walsh.)

"I don't write with children in mind, although I care very much what they think of what I do," the author revealed in *Junior Literary Guild*. Nevertheless, he told McDonnell that "I want to make the work accessible. What I like to think of is a relationship between the book and the child without intermediaries." While works such as *The Goats* may not be appropriate for all readers, he added, "I have much more faith in children's ability and judgment than a lot of people. They turn away if they find something too scary or too burdensome." And, he concluded, he wants to provide his readers with "an honest view.... You want your books to be influential, so they enlarge a person's experience."

WORKS CITED:

Campbell, Patty, review of *The Goats, Wilson Library Bulletin,* January, 1988, p. 75.
Review of *Celine, Entertainment Weekly,* May 4, 1990, p. 114.
Cole, Brock, autobiographical sketch, *Junior Literary Guild,* September, 1979.
Hansen, Ron, "Discovering the Opposite Sex," *New York Times Book Review,* November, 8, 1987, p. 31.
Hearne, Betsy, review of *Celine, Bulletin of the Center for Children's Books,* December, 1989, pp. 75-76.

Kuskin, Karla, "The Art of Picture Books," *New York Times Book Review,* November 15, 1981, pp. 57, 60.
McDonnell, Christine, "New Voices, New Visions: Brock Cole," *Horn Book,* September/October, 1989, pp. 602-05.
Silvey, Anita, review of *The Goats, Horn Book,* January/February, 1988, p. 23.
Toth, Luann, review of *The Giant's Toe, School Library Journal,* October, 1986, p. 158.

FOR MORE INFORMATION SEE:

BOOKS

Children's Literature Review, Volume 18, Gale, 1989, pp. 81-85.

PERIODICALS

Booklist, October 15, 1979, pp. 348, 350.
Bulletin of the Center for Children's Books, December, 1979; October, 1984; July/August, 1986; October, 1987.
Kirkus Reviews, September 15, 1979, p. 1063; September 1, 1984, p. J-59.
School Library Journal, May, 1980, p. 52.*

*   *   *

CORA LEE
See ANDERSON, Catherine Corley

*   *   *

CORALIE
See ANDERSON, Catherine Corley

*   *   *

CUMBAA, Stephen 1947-

PERSONAL: Surname is pronounced *"kum* ba"; born April 8, 1947, in Brooksville, FL; son of Bill Price (a theatre manager) and Carolyn (a homemaker; maiden name, Martin) Cumbaa; married Sharron Bowie, 1972 (divorced, 1982); married Penelope Cowan (a teacher), 1987; children: Christian Anders, Alison Wynne, Emily Kersey, Madison Anne. *Education:* Lake-Sumter Community College, A.A., 1967; University of Florida, B.A., 1969, M.A., 1972, Ph.D., 1975. *Politics:* "Generally liberal." *Religion:* Christian (Protestant).

ADDRESSES: Home—194 Keyworth Ave., Ottawa, Ontario, Canada K1Y 0E9. *Office*—Canadian Museum of Nature, Ottawa, Ontario, Canada K1P 6P4.

CAREER: National Research Council, Ottawa, Ontario, postdoctoral fellow, 1975-77; Canadian Museum of Nature, Ottawa, zooarchaeologist, 1977-80, head of zooarchaeological identification centre, 1981-86, assistant director of collections and research, 1987-90, research scientist, 1991—. Young Men's Christian Association (Y.M.C.A.) and Young Women's Christian Association (Y.W.C.A.), adult fitness instructor, 1980-92, supervisor of early morning adult fitness, 1986-90.

STEPHEN CUMBAA

MEMBER: Society of Vertebrate Paleontology, Ontario Archaeological Society (chapter president, 1987-88).

AWARDS, HONORS: Ripley P. Bullen Medal, best student paper in anthropology, Florida State Museum.

WRITINGS:

The Bones Book and Skeleton, Workman Publishing, 1991.

Also editor of Lake-Sumter Community College newspaper, 1966-67.

WORK IN PROGRESS: Popular science articles for museum newsletter; research on Cretaceous period fossil fishes.

SIDELIGHTS: Stephen Cumbaa told *SATA:* "I was born in Brooksville, Florida, the nearest town with a hospital to Inverness, where my parents lived. My earliest memories, though, are of Leesburg, another small town in central Florida and the place I still think of as 'home.' My parents liked the peace and quiet of the country, and my brothers and I grew up exploring the lakeshore and the swamps at every spare moment. We always knew where to find the largest alligators, the greatest variety of snakes, or the meanest snapping turtle. Remarkably, we all survived with fingers and toes intact and with a first-hand knowledge and appreciation of nature.

"My dad wouldn't allow a television in the house until I was twelve, and for that I'm grateful. I was (and still am)

an avid reader and took home stacks of books from the public library for those frequent days when it rained or when we were temporarily banned from our careers as explorers due to a slight 'misunderstanding' of the limits, or perhaps too accurate an understanding of the results, of our last foray into the wilderness.

"My passion for bones came in those early years. My parents were very supportive of my collecting efforts, and I brought home and kept bones of fish, turtles, snakes, birds, raccoons, opossums, and all sorts of creatures we stumbled across in the woods and swamps. The intricacy of the structure was easy to appreciate, and the identity as well as the 'architecture'—the form and function of the bones—were mysteries and satisfying puzzles to solve. Museum visits during family vacations were requisite stops, and I never failed to learn from a trip through the exhibits. Museums were places of wonder to me: storehouses of fascinating collection, information, and expertise. I first saw human skeletons there, and was fascinated by the excavated

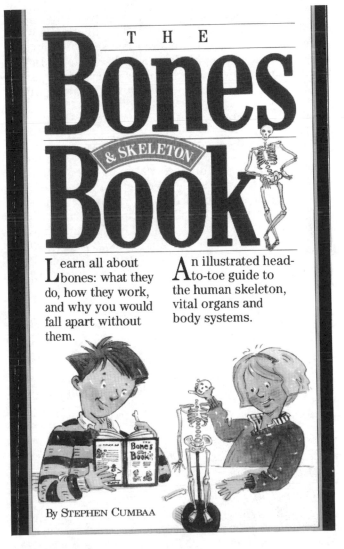

Cumbaa brings his childhood enthusiasm for investigating the wilderness and its inhabitants to his bestselling book and model guide to how the human body works. (Cover illustration by Kim La Fave.)

burials in archaeological exhibits in places like Kolomoki Mounds in Georgia and Dickson Mounds in Illinois, and how much could be learned from scientific examination of bones.

"Interests are fun, but the time came to choose a university and a career. I figured no one would ever pay me to look at bones, so I decided to follow another interest—writing—and major in journalism. That decision lasted long enough for me to reach university, where I became seduced by anthropology and archaeology, and the chance to study other cultures and other peoples, some long dead. I also eventually found out I could get paid to study bones through teaching in museums, and that was the clincher. I feel sorry for people who don't really enjoy what they do in life.

"I've always liked to write and credit my English teachers in grades seven through twelve for making words fun. They gave me a strong background, a lot of encouragement, and developed in me a sense of self-confidence in written and oral expression. Most of the writing I do now is for other scientists—literary is hardly the word for it—but I thoroughly enjoy the chance to make science fun and interesting for kids, and hope *The Bones Book* is a good example. Having children of my own has given me a renewed perspective on the fun, trials, and tribulations of growing up."

* * *

CURRY, Ann (Gabrielle) 1934-

PERSONAL: Born July 19, 1934, in Lancashire, England; daughter of Edward Michael (an interior decorator) and Mary Elizabeth Maloney; married Michael J. Curry (a school principal), December 30, 1954; children: Joanna, Georgina, Carmel, Louisa, Simon, Marie, Gemma, Antony, Felicity, Gabrielle. *Education:* University of Kent at Canterbury, B.A. (with honors), 1978; postgraduate certificate in education from Christ Church College, 1980. *Religion:* Roman Catholic.

ADDRESSES: Home—1 Island Wall, Whitstable, Kent CT5 1EP, England.

CAREER: St. Vincent's School, Whitstable, Kent, England, special education boarding school teacher and company secretary, 1979-86; writer. Affiliated with *Blind Persons' Talking Newspaper,* 1982—.

WRITINGS:

The Book of Brendan, Macmillan (London), 1989, Holiday House, 1990.

WORK IN PROGRESS: Dr. Titus Marvel, a sequel to *The Book of Brendan; Cooper's Croft,* an adventure featuring children protagonists in an old house helping to prevent a theft; and *Green Magic,* a book about strange happenings in a country park.

SIDELIGHTS: Ann Curry told *SATA:* "Although I am fifty-seven, my career in writing is only just beginning. I

married young and had my large family of ten children, so I led a very busy life at home until my youngest daughter was five years old in 1975. At that time I decided to further my education. I had been to a good school and matriculated at a decent standard, so my local university accepted me for a degree course in English literature. I graduated in 1978 and did a further year's study to gain a postgraduate certificate in education. I had always taken an interest in my husband's work with difficult boys. During the whole of our married life we had lived in schoolhouses attached to boarding schools for this type of boy. So, when I qualified, I joined him in his work, helping with both administration and the teaching of English and drama.

"The boys we dealt with were all from the London area and all had serious educational and behavioural problems, and were from severely deprived backgrounds. We found that drama was particularly good in helping them to enjoy education and achieve some measure of success. We had difficulty in finding appropriate material, so began to produce our own. We wrote plays, musicals and film scripts, tailored to suit their interests and capabilities. We enjoyed ourselves very much and so did our boys. Although we were amateurs we produced well-presented and creditable performances for our local public. This was how I really began to write, even though in my years at home I had had occasional poems

ANN CURRY

published and an odd short children's story in local papers.

"However, in 1986 our school, along with many others of its kind, closed down owing to changes in government policy. My husband and I took early retirement. It was then I decided to write a children's novel and *The Book of Brendan* was the result. Needless to say, I was delighted when it was accepted by Macmillan in 1988 and subsequently published in 1989. Its further acceptance by Holiday House was very exciting. At that stage one imagines that, having surmounted the initial hurdle of publication—especially in America also!—the rest will follow. It doesn't! Although my American publisher declared it to be 'beautifully written,' and it received some good reviews, it hasn't sold well at all. I comfort myself with the reason that, since the publication of the paperback has been delayed, a hardcover by an unknown writer is too expensive to attract many customers.

"I am still determined to carry on writing and submitting manuscripts. The sequel to the Brendan story is 'doing the rounds' and so is *Cooper's Croft,* an adventure story which does not go into the realms of fantasy. I am now working on *Green Magic,* a fantasy set in a country park. I am using animal characters as well as humans, who pit their wits against the mischief-making Puck, who has returned to the English countryside. They are eventually helped by the archetypal figure of the Green Man.

"I try to write because I enjoy the actual process of working out a story and deciding upon the rhetoric of its presentation to the reader. I have found that, so far, I prefer to write for the child in the nine-to-twelve age group, rather than for the younger child or teenager. They are old enough to want a 'long' story and yet still young enough to enjoy fantasy and high adventure without love interest. The teenagers I know all tend to read adult fiction anyway, especially since from age fourteen they study adult literature for examination purposes.

"I like to research my background carefully before I begin a story. With *The Book of Brendan* it was Anglo-Saxon times, and for *Dr. Titus Marvel,* early eighteenth-century history. Probably because I'm a teacher, even small historical inaccuracies annoy me in books for children. For my present story I have been reading up the Green Man archetype, as found in folklore and religious art from earliest times. Since my eldest son is an environmental biologist who works in a country park, I have been able to spend time there and consult an expert as well.

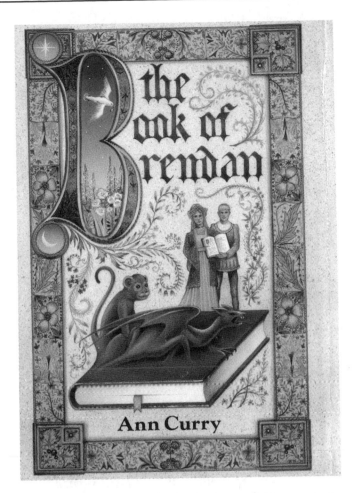

A young student at an abbey enlists the aid of a magical book and the legendary King Arthur to defeat the evil designs of a power-mad magician in Curry's first book. (Cover illustration by Alun Hood.)

"I think that I ought to add that the thing I feel most strongly about is the treatment of children. I've spent all of my adult life looking after children, my own and pupils. I now have lots of grandchildren and still do quite a lot of private tuition. I am very angry when children are not treated with respect, and I feel that this respect should be reflected in the books which are written for them."

FOR MORE INFORMATION SEE:

PERIODICALS

School Library Journal, May, 1990, pp. 103-104.
Voice of Youth Advocates, October, 1990, p. 226.

D

DARROLL, Sally
    See ODGERS, Sally Farrell

* * *

DAVIS, Leslie
    See GUCCIONE, Leslie Davis

* * *

DAY, Edward C. 1932-

PERSONAL: Born May 7, 1932, in Boston, MA; son of Edward Joseph (an Episcopal minister) and Mary Lillian (a homemaker; maiden name, Crocker) Day; married Caroline Foster, September 10, 1960 (divorced); married Joanna Butts (a production editor), July 8, 1988; children: Jeffrey Laurence, Alexander Follansbee. *Education:* Harvard University, A.B., 1953. *Politics:* Democrat. *Religion:* None.

ADDRESSES: Home and office—12 Jay St., Montpelier, VT 05602. *Agent*—(adult books) Harvey Klinger, Inc., 301 West 53rd St., New York, NY 10019; (children's books) Andrea Brown, P. O. Box 429, El Granada, CA 94018-0429.

CAREER: Harvard University Press, Cambridge, MA, began as assistant sales manager, became advertising manager, 1957-69; Itek Corporation, Lexington, MA, public relations representative, 1969-70; Bates College, Lewiston, ME, part-time staff writer, 1970-72; Bath Art Shop and Gallery, Bath, ME, owner and operator, 1973-74; Whitcoulls Publishers, Christchurch, New Zealand, assistant publishing manager, 1974-77; Alaska Northwest Publishing Company, Edmonds, WA, associate editor, 1977-78; Whitcoulls Publishers, assistant publishing manager, 1979-80; Summer Street Studios, Rockport, ME, landscape photographer, 1980-83; *WoodenBoat,* Brooklin, ME, merchandise manager, 1983-85; Colby College, Waterville, ME, development writer and director of corporate and foundation relations, 1985-90; free-lance writer, 1990—. Member of executive committee, Greater Boston Committee for a Sane Nuclear

Policy, 1957-60; delegate to Maine State Democratic Convention. *Military service:* U.S. Coast Guard Reserve, 1954-57; became lieutenant.

AWARDS, HONORS: Reading Magic Award, *Parenting,* 1989, and International Reading Association Teachers' Choices, 1990, both for *John Tabor's Ride*.

WRITINGS:

John Tabor's Ride, illustrated by Dirk Zimmer, Knopf, 1989.

Coauthor with wife, Joanna B. Day, of travel articles.

WORK IN PROGRESS: A historical novel; children's books; research on canal and railroad history in the United States and England; research on Canada's provincial parks.

SIDELIGHTS: In his children's book *John Tabor's Ride,* Edward C. Day describes the trials at sea of a young, mid-1800s seaman named John Tabor. Day, who is a retired Coast Guard lieutenant, based his book on the real-life stories of sailor John Tabor found in J. Ross Browne's *Etchings of a Whaling Cruise.* In Day's book, Tabor constantly complains of his weariness of being out at sea until one night when an old, dwarf-like mariner takes Tabor on a sea voyage around the world on a whale. This experience cures Tabor of his crankiness, and he becomes one of the crew's most cheerful sailors.

Day once commented: "Book publishers must turn away from awarding multi-million-dollar advances to a handful of best-selling authors and provide more support for new and 'lesser' authors, if the industry is to be healthy. To award a twenty-million-dollar contract to an author and have it turned down is obscene!"

De HAVEN, Tom 1949-

PERSONAL: Born May 4, 1949, in Bayonne, NJ; son of Clarence Richard and Margaret Elizabeth (O'Hare) De Haven; married Santa Sergio (an artist), June 26, 1971; children: Jessie Ann, Kate Marie. *Education:* Rutgers University, B.A., 1971; Bowling Green University, M.F.A., 1973. *Hobbies and other interests:* Comics.

ADDRESSES: Home—13918 Sagewood Trace, Midlothian, VA 23112. *Office*—English Dept., Hibbs Hall, Virginia Commonwealth University, Richmond, VA. *Agent*—Charles Verrill, Liz Darhansoff Agency, 1220 Park Ave., New York, NY 10128.

CAREER: Writer. Magazine Associates, New York City, managing editor, 1973-76; free-lance magazine editor, 1977-80; Hofstra University, Hempstead, NY, adjunct professsor of creative writing, 1981-87; Rutgers University, New Brunswick, NJ, assistant professor of American Studies, 1987-90; Virginia Commonwealth University, Richmond, associate professor of American Studies/creative writing, 1990—.

MEMBER: PEN, Authors Guild, Poets and Writers.

AWARDS, HONORS: Fellowships from National Endowment for the Arts, 1979 and 1986, and New Jersey State Council on the Arts, 1980.

WRITINGS.

Freaks' Amour, Morrow, 1978.
Jersey Luck, Harper, 1980.
Funny Papers, Viking, 1985.
Necromancer, Volume I (graphic fantasy novel; adapted from the novel by William Gibson), edited by David Harris, illustrated by Bruce Jensen, Epic Comics, 1989.
Walker of Worlds: Chronicle of the King's Tramp, Book I (fantasy novel), Doubleday/Foundation, 1990.
Pixie Meat, illustrated by Gary Panter and Charles Burns, Water Row Press, 1990.
The End-of-Everything Man: Chronicle of the King's Tramp, Book II (fantasy novel), Doubleday/Foundation, 1991.
The Last Human: Chronicle of the Kings' Tramp, Book III (fantasy novel), Bantam, 1992.

YOUNG ADULT NOVELS

U.S.S.A., illustrated by Ralph Reese, Avon, 1987.
Joe Gosh, Walker Millennium, 1988.

COLLECTIONS

Sunburn Lake: A Trilogy (novellas; contains *Clap Hands! Here Comes Charley, He's All Mine,* and *Where We'll Never Grow Old*), Viking, 1988.

Contributor to periodicals, including *Raw, New Virginia Review,* and *Entertainment Weekly.*

ADAPTATIONS: Portions of *Freaks' Amour* were adapted by artist Gary Painter in the comic strip *Young Lust;*

TOM De HAVEN

Jersey Luck was optioned by Susan Seidelman for Philly Dog Productions.

SIDELIGHTS: Tom De Haven is best known for his highly imaginative fiction featuring odd—and often bizarre—characters and situations. Many of his novels, such as *Freaks' Amour* and *Where We'll Never Grow Old* deal with the aftermath of man-made catastrophes; others, including *Clap Hands!* concern themselves with more intimate tragedies involving love and marriage. De Haven has also produced writings for younger audiences: *U.S.S.A., Joe Gosh,* and the "Walker of Worlds" series. *U.S.S.A.* is set in a near future in which the American government is replaced by a repressive military regime. For seventeen-year-old Eddie Ludlow, this means the loss of friends, family, and long-held personal freedoms. Norma Klein, writing in the *Los Angeles Times,* noted that while *U.S.S.A.* "has its heart in the right place," the novel suffers from "much of the same dogmatism, oppression and prejudice it purportedly seeks to attack." A reviewer for *Kliatt* was less critical, calling the book's premise "thought-provoking."

Joe Gosh tells the story of a jobless muscleman who falls in love with a mobster's daughter. After junk mail begins to materialize above his television set, Gosh finds himself in a series of adventures involving a transference machine, thieving zombies, and game-playing robots. "Definitely for the fun-loving," claimed Don D'Ammassa in *S.F. Chronicle.* D'Ammassa added that, due to its mix of satire and humor, the book is "unlike anything else I have seen written for this age group." De Haven's unique brand of humor is also evident in the "Walker of Worlds" series. As monsters and bizarre characters begin to appear on Earth, journalist and recovering amnesiac Pete Musik finds himself in a deadly battle with the two men who originally stole his

THE BESTSELLING FANTASY SERIES CONTINUES!
CHRONICLES OF THE KING'S TRAMP ✦ BOOK 2
THE END-OF-EVERYTHING MAN
TOM DE HAVEN

De Haven's unique brand of humor infuses his fantasy series about a universal war between good and evil that finds Earth one of the battlegrounds. (Cover illustration by Kevin Johnson.)

memory. A *Publishers Weekly* reviewer called *Walker of Worlds* an "inventive tale" marked by "horror, humor and a passel of plot twists." And John Clute, writing in the *Los Angeles Times Book Review,* found the novel flawed but still written "brilliantly at points."

WORKS CITED:

D'Ammassa, Don, review of *Joe Gosh, S.F. Chronicle,* August, 1988, p. 53.
Klein, Norma, review of *U.S.S.A., Los Angeles Times,* March 7, 1987.
Review of *U.S.S.A., Kliatt,* April, 1987, p. 8.
Review of *Walker of Worlds, Los Angeles Times Book Review,* July 29, 1990.
Review of *Walker of Worlds, Publishers Weekly,* June 8, 1990, pp. 49-50.

FOR MORE INFORMATION SEE:

PERIODICALS

New Yorker, March 8, 1985.
New York Times Book Review, March 17, 1985.
Village Voice, November 1, 1988.

* * *

DERESKE, Jo 1947-

PERSONAL: Born October 1, 1947, in Ludington, MI; daughter of John (an electrician) and June (a homemaker; maiden name, Zemke) Dereske; married Kip Winsett (a salesman), September 12, 1987; children: Karen Marie, Erik Jon. *Education:* Western Michigan University, B.A., 1969, M.L.S., 1971.

ADDRESSES: Home—1240 St. Paul, Bellingham, WA 98226. *Agent*—Susan Schulman, 454 West 44th St., New York, NY 10036.

CAREER: Western Washington University, Bellingham, interlibrary loan librarian, 1978-1988. Corridor Information Services (a research company), owner-operator, 1983-87.

AWARDS, HONORS: Glom Gloom was nominated for the William Allen White Children's Book Award, 1985; Artist Trust grant for research on novel in progress, 1989; Dorothy Canfield Fisher Children's Award nomination, 1989, and South Carolina Children's Book Award, 1991-92, both for *The Lone Sentinel.*

WRITINGS:

Glom Gloom, Atheneum, 1985.
The Lone Sentinel (Junior Library Guild Book Club selection), Atheneum, 1989.
My Cousin, the Poodle, Atheneum, 1991.

Also contributor of adult short stories, articles and other free-lance writing to periodicals.

WORK IN PROGRESS: Adult novel about Lithuanians (which was awarded an Artist Trust Grant); a young adult fantasy about the Spanish flu epidemic of 1918-1919.

SIDELIGHTS: "I grew up in Walhalla, Michigan, a small village with a population less than three hundred," Jo Dereske told *Something About the Author* (SATA). "We were surrounded by the Manistee National Forest and several lakes we could bike to. The Pere Marquette River remains one of my all-time favorite places. For the first three years of my education, I attended a one-room school with twenty-one other students in eight grades. Being able to listen to what all those other grades were learning gave me a curiosity and excitement (and impatience!) with education. When I wasn't outside, I spent as much time as I could reading. Everyone in my family—and there were seven of us—was referred to as a 'reader.' We kept so many books that even our kitchen

JO DERESKE

cupboards doubled as bookcases. During the summer, the bookmobile made a regular stop in our driveway.

"I can't recall a time when I didn't want to be a writer. As soon as I learned to read I realized that through words I could visit another land, another planet, even inside someone's head. It seemed like magic! As a writer, I especially enjoy fantasy and science fiction because although we must remain true to ourselves, there are no limits to what can happen in the worlds we create.

"It wasn't until I left my very rural area for college that I met a 'real live' writer and discovered that writers weren't exotic creatures but hard-working people who sometimes struggled mightily finding just the right way to share their stories with their readers.

"I'm convinced that everything a writer sees or does, no matter how happy, sorrowful, or trivial, ends up in that 'noodle soup' that a writer draws from for books or stories.

"When I write, I'm never certain how a story will end. Even when I begin with a plan, when my characters become so real that I can *see* them, they tend to take *me* along with them on their adventures. I'm always anxious to find out exactly how everything is going to turn out in the end.

"*Glom Gloom* began as a short story for my two children when we lived in Scotland for a winter. Our home was a wee stone cottage surrounded by a low stone wall. There was a small forest nearby where the children loved to play and pretend magical stories. It wasn't until four years later that I turned that short story into a book and I think I was very influenced by our months in Scotland. I'm frequently asked if the Bulkings are really tall or the Weeuns are really small and why I made the largest creatures the good folks, when giants are usually evil. I think the tall/small question can only be answered by the reader, but I'm a very tall person and I think I feel a natural sympathy for oversized people.

"The plot for *The Lone Sentinel* was actually hatched on an automobile cross-country trip with my two children and my mother. In the plains states, we passed tall steel towers in the midst of the prairies. These towering, graceful structures, probably radio relay towers, dominated the landscape. When we passed one particularly remote tower, my son, looking wistfully out the car window, said, 'Look at that lone sentinel.'

"That statement began to cook in my head and I grabbed my notebook (which I always carry with me) and began sketching out the plot of Erik, who along with his father, mans the remote Lone Sentinel outpost on the planet Azure. When his father is killed, Erik tries to keep it a secret so he won't be removed from the Lone Sentinel, the only home he's ever known.

"Writing *My Cousin, the Poodle* was sheer fun. It's very loosely based on my eccentric aunt and uncle and their horrendously spoiled poodle, Terry Berry. I placed the story in 1955 because I believe life was a little less controlled—and safer—then and some of the escapades Tommy and Barbara share with Uncle Rupert and Aunt Tofelia and Terry Berry wouldn't be possible today."

*   *   *

DEVONS, Sonia 1974-

PERSONAL: Born October 12, 1974, in London, England; daughter of David Jon (a patent agent) and Catherine Stone (a landscape gardener; maiden name, Bates) Devons. *Education:* Currently attending Kingston College of Further Education.

ADDRESSES: c/o Blackie & Son Ltd., 7 Leicester Pl. London WC2H 7BP, England.

CAREER: Author.

WRITINGS:

Shut the Gate!, illustrated by Shoo Rayner, Blackie & Son, 1990.

SIDELIGHTS: Sonia Devons's *Shut the Gate!* shows what can happen when a child forgets his mother's admonishment to close the gate behind him as he goes out for a walk. Young John leaves the gates to the family farm open and then must retrieve the animals that follow him out. Said *School Library Journal* reviewer JoAnn Rees, "This didactic story is simple enough for two-year-olds, although John appears to be a preadolescent, right down to his Walkman."

WORKS CITED:

Rees, JoAnn, review of *Shut the Gate!, School Library Journal,* March, 1991, p. 170.

FOR MORE INFORMATION SEE:

PERIODICALS

School Librarian, November, 1990, p. 142.

* * *

DIGBY, Anne 1935-

PERSONAL: Born January 7, 1935, in Kingston-upon-Thames, England; married Alan Davidson (a writer); children: one son and three daughters. *Education:* Attended North London Collegiate School. *Religion:* Church of England. *Hobbies and other interests:* Painting, drawing, playing tennis, Third World issues.

ADDRESSES: Home and office—Coombe House, Packers Hill, Holwell, Sherborne, Dorset DT9 5LN, England.

CAREER: Amalgamated Press, London, editor and writer, 1951-56; freelance writer and journalist, 1957-62, 1965—. Oxfam, Oxford, England, chief press officer, 1962-65. Lecturer to school children on writing; cofounder of community village school, 1981.

MEMBER: Society of Women Writers and Journalists, West Country Writers Association, Cambridge Book Association.

WRITINGS:

A Horse Called September, Dennis Dobson, 1976, St. Martin's, 1982.
The Quicksilver Horse, Granada, 1979, St. Martin's, 1982.
The Big Swim of the Summer, Dennis Dobson, 1979.
The Ghostbusters Storybook, Scholastic Inc., 1984.
Roland Rat, Hippo, 1987.
Indiana Jones and the Last Crusade Storybook, Scholastic Inc., 1989.

"TREBIZON" SERIES

First Term at Trebizon, W. H. Allen, 1978, illustrated by Gavin Rowe, Granada, 1980.
Second Term at Trebizon, W. H. Allen, 1979, illustrated by Rowe, Granada, 1980.
Summer Term at Trebizon, W. H. Allen, 1979, illustrated by Rowe, Granada, 1980.
Boy Trouble at Trebizon, Granada, 1980, illustrated by Rowe, 1981.
More Trouble at Trebizon, illustrated by Rowe, Granada, 1981.
The Tennis Term at Trebizon, illustrated by Rowe, Granada, 1981.
Summer Camp at Trebizon, illustrated by Rowe, Granada, 1982.
Into the Fourth at Trebizon, illustrated by Rowe, Granada, 1982.
The Hockey Term at Trebizon, illustrated by Paul Wright, Granada, 1984.
Fourth Year Triumphs at Trebizon, illustrated by Robert Hales, Granada, 1985.
The Ghostly Term at Trebizon, Chivers Press, 1990.
Fifth Year Friendships at Trebizon, Chivers Press, 1990.

"ME, JILL ROBINSON" SERIES

Me, Jill Robinson and the Television Quiz, Granada, 1983.
Me, Jill Robinson and the Seaside Mystery, Granada, 1983.
Me, Jill Robinson and the Christmas Pantomime, Granada, 1983.
Me, Jill Robinson and the School Camp Adventure, Granada, 1984.
Me, Jill Robinson and the Perdou Painting, Granada, 1984.
Me, Jill Robinson and the Stepping Stones Mystery, Granada, 1985.

"THREE R DETECTIVES" SERIES

Three R Detectives and the Milk Bottle Mystery, illustrated by Anthony Lewis, Piccadilly Press, 1991.
Three R Detectives and the Mystery of Missing Footprints, illustrated by Lewis, Piccadilly Press, 1992.

ANNE DIGBY

Digby recounts the fun and adventures of everyday schoolchildren in her "Jug Valley Juniors" series. (Cover illustration by David Kearney.)

"JUG VALLEY JUNIORS" SERIES

Boys V Girls at Jug Valley Juniors, illustrated by Piers Sanford, Puffin, 1992.

Headmaster's Ghost at Jug Valley Juniors, illustrated by Sanford, Puffin, 1992.

Hand Up! at Jug Valley Juniors, illustrated by Sanford, Puffin, 1992.

The Photofit Mystery at Jug Valley Juniors, illustrated by Sanford, Puffin, 1992.

Poison Pen at Jug Valley Juniors, illustrated by Sanford, Puffin, 1993.

The Magic Man at Jug Valley Juniors, illustrated by Sanford, Puffin, 1993.

Contributor of short stories to children's periodicals, including *Girl.* Regular contributor to *Gemini News Service* on Third World issues.

WORK IN PROGRESS: Mocks and Romances at Trebizon, and *Some Summer Goodbyes at Trebizon*

SIDELIGHTS: British writer and journalist Anne Digby is the author of several series of books that have established her reputation as a popular children's novelist. Beginning with *First Term at Trebizon,* published in 1978 as the first of the "Trebizon" books, Digby involves her readers in the continuing adventures of girls at an English boarding school. The "Me, Jill Robinson," "Three R Detectives," and "Jug Valley Juniors" series weave mystery and excitement into the day-to-day experiences of likeable young characters to create a sense of fun and adventure for Digby's middle-grade audience.

A prolific writer, Digby recalls keeping a journal as far back as she can remember. As she told *SATA:* "I've been an obsessive writer since childhood, winning a national poetry competition at the age of nine." Her creative talent caught the notice of a school-friend's father who was impressed by some of her stories and drawings. At age sixteen he offered her a position as editorial trainee at his company, Amalgamated Press, the British publishing house credited with producing the first comic book, *Comic Cuts,* in 1892. Digby worked at A. P. through the '50s and early '60s, first as a staff editor and writer and later as a freelance writer. As she told *SATA,* she has always been grateful for the opportunity to work at Amalgamated Press and "catch the afterglow of the golden age of British comics."

Writing comic books is a tougher job than people might think, according to Digby. "Working for a kind of 'fun factory' dedicated to producing a constant flow of ideas and stories designed to thrill, amuse, entice and entertain children could be quite gruelling at times, requiring an endless input of wit, invention and originality," she

Digby's popular "Trebizon" series details the ups and downs of life at an all-girls' boarding school in West England. (Illustration from Digby's *More Trouble at Trebizon* by Gavin Rowe.)

recalls of her time spent at Amalgamated Press. "Little wonder that only the most talented survived. But we were proud to be treading in the footsteps of such all-time greats as P. G. Wodehouse, who began his career writing serials for an A. P. weekly boys' paper, and Roald Dahl, whose 1957 short story for an A. P. magazine was later developed into *Danny, Champion of the World.* It was a good writing school."

"After these halcyon days of extended childhood I reluctantly grew up, gained maturity, wrote about serious adult matters and reared four children of my own from whom I gained new and deeper insights into childhood," she recalled, "but it was only a matter of time before the child in me lurking below the surface bubbled up and the full-length children's books started to pour forth." Digby's first novel, published in 1976, was *A Horse Called September.* Probably among the best-known of her work in the United States, it is a story about the friendship between two girls and their shared love for a horse named September. When one girl is given a better mount by her father and goes off to a prestigious equestrian boarding school to learn show-jumping, the friendship dwindles, along with her affection for September. The girl left at home deals with her loneliness by transferring her attention to September; she rescues the horse from the glue factory, works him into top form, and together they win the grand prize at the horse show.

A Horse Called September was followed by both another horse story, *The Quicksilver Horse* about life in a Gypsy circus, and *The Big Swim of the Summer* before Digby began the series' of novels for which she is best known. Her "Trebizon" books introduce readers to a girl from London who travels to West England to attend Trebizon, an academy for young women. The friendships, problems, and adventures that she encounters while growing up at boarding school provide entertaining reading in the many "Trebizon" volumes, including *Boy Trouble at Trebizon* and *Fourth Year Triumphs at Trebizon.* Juliet Townsend praised Digby in an article for *The Spectator* as "one of the very few people still writing about life in a girls' boarding school." Commenting on the popularity of the "Trebizon" series, Townsend added that the stories are "fast-moving and readable." The "Me, Jill Robinson" series features one of Digby's most popular characters, Jill Robinson as she adjusts to her family's move to a new town, makes new friends, and encounters new responsibilities such as looking after her mischievous younger brother. Although the "Trebizon" and "Me, Jill Robinson" books have not yet been introduced to American readers, Digby's series are popular throughout much of the English-speaking world, and have been translated for young readers in many countries, including Denmark, France, Germany, Greece, Holland, Japan, and Spain. Even so, Digby has noticed something curious about the letters she has received from her readers: "I do get fan letters for the 'Trebizon' series from the U.S., so maybe copies sneak in somehow."

WORKS CITED:

Townsend, Juliet, "The Happiest Days of Their Lives," in *The Spectator,* June 2, 1990, pp. 33-34.

FOR MORE INFORMATION SEE:

PERIODICALS

Voice of Youth Advocates, February, 1983, p. 35.

*   *   *

DOHERTY, Berlie 1943-

PERSONAL: Surname is pronounced "*Doh*-er-ty"; born November 6, 1943, in Liverpool, England; daughter of Walter Alfred (a railway clerk) and Peggy (Brunton) Hollingsworth; married Gerard Adrian Doherty, 1966; children: Janna, Tim, Sally. *Education:* University of Durham, B.A. (with honors), 1964; University of Liverpool, postgraduate certificate in social science, 1965; University of Sheffield, postgraduate certificate in education, 1978. *Hobbies and other interests:* Opera, ballet, music of all kinds, singing, theatre, walking in the countryside.

ADDRESSES: Home—38 Banner Cross Road, Sheffield, York S11 9HR, England. *Agent*—Gina Pollinger, 222 Old Brompton Road, London, England.

CAREER: Leicestershire Child Care Services, Leicester, England, social worker, 1966-67; homemaker, 1967-78; English teacher in Sheffield, England, 1978-80; schools broadcaster for British Broadcasting Corporation (BBC)-Radio Sheffield, 1980-82; full-time writer, 1983—. Writer-in-residence at various schools and libraries. Chair of Arvon Foundation at Lumb Bank, 1989—; member of Yorkshire Arts Literature Panel, 1988-90.

MEMBER: Writers Guild of Great Britain, Northern Association of Writers in Education (deputy chair, 1988-89), Arvon Foundation.

AWARDS, HONORS: Carnegie Medal, British Library Association, 1986, Burnley/National Provincial Children's Book of the Year Award, 1987, and *Boston Globe-Horn Book* Honor Award, 1988, all for *Granny Was a Buffer Girl;* award from Television and Film Awards, New York, 1988, for "White Peak Farm"; Carnegie Medal, 1991, for *Dear Nobody.*

WRITINGS:

FOR CHILDREN

Tilly Mint Tales, illustrated by Thelma Lambert, Methuen, 1984.
Paddiwak and Cosy, illustrated by Teresa O'Brien, Methuen, 1988, Dial, 1989.
Tilly Mint and the Dodo (also see below), illustrated by Janna Doherty, Methuen, 1989.
Snowy, illustrated by Keith Bowen, HarperCollins, 1992.

BERLIE DOHERTY

FOR YOUNG ADULTS

How Green You Are! (short stories; also see below), illustrated by Elaine McGregor Turney, Methuen, 1982.

The Making of Fingers Finnigan (short stories), illustrated by John Haysom, Methuen, 1983.

White Peak Farm (also see below), Methuen, 1984, Orchard, 1990.

Children of Winter (also see below), illustrated by Ian Newsham, Methuen, 1985.

Granny Was a Buffer Girl (also see below), Methuen, 1986, Orchard, 1988.

Tough Luck, Hamish Hamilton, 1988.

Spellhorn, Hamish Hamilton, 1989.

Dear Nobody, Hamish Hamilton, 1991.

Walking on Air (poetry), illustrated by J. Doherty, HarperCollins, 1993.

FOR ADULTS

Requiem (adult novel; also see below), M. Joseph, 1991.

TELEVISION AND RADIO PLAYS

The Drowned Village, BBC-Radio 4, 1980.

Requiem, BBC-Radio 4, 1982.

The White Bird of Peace, BBC-Radio 4, 1983.

A Case for Probation (also see below), BBC-Radio 4, 1983.

Miss Elizabeth, BBC-Radio 4, 1984.

Fuzzball, BBC-TV, 1985.

Sacrifice, BBC-Radio 4, 1985.

The Mouse and His Child (adapted from Russell Hoban's work of the same title), BBC-Radio 4, 1986.

White Peak Farm (serial), BBC-TV, 1988.

Dream of Unicorns, BBC-Radio 4, 1988.

Children of Winter, BBC-Radio 4, 1988.

Granny Was a Buffer Girl, BBC-Radio 4, 1990.

There's a Valley in Spain, BBC-Radio 4, 1990.

Dear Nobody, BBC-Radio 5, 1993.

STAGE PLAYS

Smells and Spells (two-act), produced in Sheffield, England, 1978.

Howard's Field (one-act), produced in Sheffield, 1979.

A Growing Girl's Story (one-act), produced in Hartlepool, England, 1980.

The Amazing Journey of Jazz O'Neil, produced in Hull, England, 1984.

Rock 'n' Roll Is Here to Stay (one-act), produced in Sheffield, 1984.

Return to the Ebro (one-act), produced in Manchester, England, 1986.

Tilly Mint and the Dodo, produced in Doncaster, England, 1986.

A Case for Probation, published in *Studio Scripts,* edited by David Self, Hutchinson, 1986.

How Green You Are!, published in *Drama I,* edited by John Foster, Macmillan, 1987.

Matthew, Come Home, published in *Drama 2,* edited by Foster, Macmillan, 1987.

Tribute to Tom, published in *Drama 3,* edited by Foster, Macmillan, 1988.

Home, published in *Stage Write,* edited by Gervase Phinn, Unwin Hyman, 1988.

Memories (one-act), produced in Halifax, England, 1992.

Who Wants Gold (two-act), produced in Newcastle-under-Lyme, England, c. 1993.

Work represented in anthologies, including *School Poems,* Oxford University Press, 1986, and *Best Short Stories, 1989.* Contributor to magazines and newspapers, including *Arts Yorkshire, Times Educational Supplement, Stand,* and *Critical Quarterly.* Author of numerous series for local radio.

ADAPTATIONS: Several of Doherty's works have been adapted onto audio-cassette by Chivers Press, including *Granny Was a Buffer Girl,* 1988, and *Tilly Mint Tales,* 1991.

WORK IN PROGRESS: Walking on Air, a book of poetry for younger children; a storybook for beginning readers for Walker Books; *The Vinegar Jar,* a novel for adults.

SIDELIGHTS: Award-winning British author Berlie Doherty has written books for children of all ages, from picture books such as *Snowy* and *Paddiwak and Cosy* to short story collections for older readers. Probably best known for the novels she writes for young adults, Doherty has been consistently praised by critics for her realistic characters and the vivid settings in which she places them. Two of her most popular novels, *Granny Was a Buffer Girl* and *Dear Nobody,* were honored as outstanding works for children by receiving the British Library Association's prestigious Carnegie Medal. Doherty is also the author of numerous plays for radio, stage, and television that have been performed by theater groups in her native England and produced by the British Broadcasting Corporation (BBC). Her popularity as an author for young people lies in the realism with which she portrays both the pleasures and sorrows which befall her young protagonists as they experience growing into adulthood.

Doherty was born on November 6, 1943, in Liverpool, England, but moved with her family to a small seaside village when she was four years old. Her family's strong Irish-Catholic background led to her enrollment at a secondary-level convent school. While there, she developed a great enthusiasm for the study of English, inspired in part by her father's example. "When I was a child I remember my father writing," Doherty told an interviewer for *SATA.* "He loved writing poetry and short stories so it was always a very familiar and comforting thing to see him typing away on the typewriter in the corner of the room." The stories she wrote eventually came to the notice of an exceptional English teacher during one of her last years at school: "[She was] a brilliant woman who influenced me greatly," recalled Doherty. "One of the wonderful things she did for me when I was about sixteen was to take me to her house and show me her study which was lined with books, and say, 'Take home as many of these as you want, and when you finish with them, bring them back and take some more.' It was a fantastic introduction to literature for me." Doherty left her teacher's house armed with volumes of works by American and Irish playwrights. "I'd never really read a play—I'd never even *seen* a play before—but maybe it was through her influence that I decided to take those [books] . . . I was bowled over by them. Later I got into poetry too."

Once she was introduced to literature, Doherty never stopped reading. Among her favorite books as an older child were *Heidi* by Johanna Spyri, *Little Women* by Louisa May Alcott, *Swallows and Amazons* by Arthur Ransome, Francis Hodgson Burnett's *The Secret Garden,* and *Nicholas Nicklby* and *David Copperfield,* two novels by Charles Dickens. But even as a child of five Doherty had known she wanted to be a writer. "I don't know what I thought a writer was or did, but Dad used to tell me bed-time stories every night, and I can remember thinking at a very early age that that's what I'd like to do; I'd like to make up stories for people to read at bed-time. It seemed then a very simple thing to do. It doesn't seem so simple now."

After graduating from convent school, Doherty enrolled at the University of Durham and received a degree in English in 1964. She continued on with her studies, obtaining a post-graduate certificate in social science from the University of Liverpool a year later. After marrying Gerard Doherty in 1966, she worked for a year

with Leicester Child Care Services as a child care officer before leaving to start a family in 1967. During the years that followed, while she was at home raising her three children, Janna, Tim, and Sally, Doherty found time to obtain an additional post-graduate certificate, this time in education, from the University of Sheffield. In 1978, when her children were old enough to allow her to return to work, Doherty got a job teaching school in Sheffield. It was during the time she spent in the classroom that she was inspired to resume her writing for young children. In 1980, Doherty left the classroom to take a position with BBC-Radio Sheffield as a schools radio broadcaster. She was delighted when one of her radio plays, *The Drowned Village,* was produced by BBC-Radio 4 in 1980. She was also pleased to find that several of her stage plays were being produced in the Sheffield area.

In 1982, Doherty published her first children's novel, *How Green You Are!,* a collection of short-story episodes originally broadcast on radio. Characteristic of all her writing, Doherty weaves elements of her own childhood into the background of many of her stories. As she told *SATA:* "Writers do tend to write about what they know. In my writing for children, I would say that my own childhood is very, very much explored in the first two books that I wrote, *How Green You Are!,* and *The Making of Fingers Finnigan.*" Taking as their setting the same small town on Britain's west coast where Doherty lived as a small girl, both these collections of short-story episodes are based on recollection from her past. Then Doherty imbues those memories with what she calls "let's pretend"—the author lets her imagination take hold to craft the actual into an entertaining tale. In *How Green You Are!,* all the stories feature Bee, Julie, Kevin, and Marie, four average teenagers who live near each other in a small seaside town. Their friends, relatives, acquaintances, and the events surrounding them at home and at school provide the subjects for stories that range from funny to sad. Bee entertains a Russian violinist who is defecting to the West; Marie receives a pet monkey for her birthday but then loses it after the animal develops rabies and is shot by the police; and Kevin and a friend are caught in the tide while boating and must be rescued. Reviewer A. Thatcher notes in a review for *Junior Bookshelf* that the stories contain "all the sadness, stress and problems of real life—strikes, death, illness, as well as the happier events." *The Making of Fingers Finnigan* continues the adventures of these young people. They become civic-minded and attempt to save the old community swimming pool; meanwhile, Julie's mischievous younger brother, Robert, becomes locked in the movie theater only to be rescued by Fingers Finnigan, a small-time crook.

As the mother of three small children, finding enough time to both work full-time and write two novels was difficult. "I was bringing up my children on my own and I was working full-time and my writing time used to be late at night or early in the morning," Doherty recalled. When her first two books had been accepted for publication, she decided to leave her job as a teacher and embark upon a career as a full-time author. In 1984,

Doherty's *White Peak Farm* was originally written as a radio serial; for publication she transformed the series about a Derbyshire farm family into a collection of interrelated stories. (Cover illustration by Diane Paterson.)

her first year spent writing full-time, Doherty published both *White Peak Farm,* a young adult novel, and *Tilly Mint Tales,* a fantasy book for younger children. Similar in format to her two previous novels, *White Peak Farm* is a collection of ten interwoven stories about events in rural Derbyshire. Jeanie, the young narrator, describes events occurring within her unusual family, with friends and neighbors, and the rituals of farm life, all the while drawing the reader into the struggle of young people as they break from the traditions of an older generation, from family, and from the rural community where their roots are in search of their individuality. Critic Maggie Freeman describes the novel in *Twentieth-Century Children's Writers:* "The first two stories are gentle, with the dying grandmother setting the underlying theme.... Then the father begins to dominate. His hatred, loneliness and bad temper 'divided him from the rest of us and from each other.' Theirs is a 'house of secrets,' of strong suppressed emotions, each person living in their own world." Freeman goes on to praise *White Peak Farm,* calling it "Doherty's greatest commitment to her characters and their setting."

Originally broadcast as a series of radio stories for younger children, *Tilly Mint Tales* is a group of stories about a little girl who is carried off on a series of magical, dreamlike adventures whenever her babysitter, old Mrs. Hardcastle, falls asleep. *Junior Bookshelf* critic E. Colwell praises the book as "an encouragement to children to use their imagination and so make their own magic, a timely stimulus in these days when children rely so much on passive viewing of television." In the book's sequel, *Tilly Mint and the Dodo,* Doherty brings issues such as animal extinction and conservation into her story. Tilly Mint obtains a very large, old egg from the loveable Mrs. Hardcastle. Out is hatched a wise dodo-bird who transports the young girl to the land of yesterday. Tilly Mint comes face to face with the process of animal extinction through her friendship with Dodo, and although the book contains an important lesson about the importance of conservation, Doherty imparts her message to her young audience with humor and a delicate touch. Reviewer John Mole comments in the *Times Literary Supplement* that Doherty "instructs by pleasing, and knows that the wisdom lies in the delight." *Tilly Mint and the Dodo* is also unique in that it was a collaboration between Doherty and her daughter, Janna, who provided the illustrations. Janna went on to eventually illustrate her mother's first poetry collection, *Walking on Air.*

Because her early writing was originally commissioned for radio, much of Doherty's works take the form of episodes. In her books, each of these episodes serves as chapters linked together through shared characters and settings. Both *White Peak Farm* and *Granny Was a Buffer Girl* showcase Doherty's ability to write engaging vignettes: "Every chapter had to be of a particular length and I liked the idea of the chapter having a unity of it's own, a focus, so that if somebody forgot to listen to the next episode ... it wouldn't really matter because of the kind of fulfillment in that particular episode," she explained to *SATA.*

Granny Was a Buffer Girl, one of Doherty's most popular books and the winner of several notable awards, was published in 1986. The novel focuses on Jess, a young woman preparing to leave her hometown of Sheffield, England, to go abroad for a year of study in Paris, France. When three generations of family members gather together to wish Jess well before her departure, her relative's reminisces recall those sometimes bittersweet events that will always unite these people together in a common heritage. Grandpa Albert's life as a steel worker; Grandma Dorothy's job operating the buffing wheel that polished silverplate cutlery; Grandma Bridie and Grandpa Jack's courage in defying the religious differences of their own parents when they fall in love; Jess's own parents' courage in dealing with the handicap and premature death of her older brother Danny: Doherty's portrayal of the small moments that connect individuals has been repeatedly praised as a poignant distillation of humanity. Helen Pain, in *Books for Keeps,* asserted that "the reader cannot help but be drawn into these vital and homely stories, with their mix of humor and heartfelt sadness.... Here is a highly memorable insight into family life."

Winner of the prestigious Carnegie Medal, *Granny Was a Buffer Girl* presents the quietly courageous lives of three generations of a British family as they deal with the pains of everyday life. (Cover illustration by Toby Gawing.)

As with her other novels, Doherty adapted *Granny Was a Buffer Girl* into a radio play that aired on BBC-Radio 4. Radio is her favorite medium "because the writer can go anywhere and so can the listener. The world inside your head is perhaps the greatest—it is obviously the greatest imaginative world there is ... as long as the language is strong enough and vivid enough that you're going to take your reader with you, you're going to invoke an emotional response and you're going to create the color."

Doherty's belief in the power of spoken language over words printed on a page was intensified through her working on her fantasy novel, *Spellhorn,* with young children at a school for the blind, where she saw first hand the capacity of language to inspire creativity. Because of this, she has worked with children in ways that extend well beyond just essay-writing in her residencies with students in and around Sheffield. "I think more than anything else I want to teach them the joy of writing," Doherty told *SATA.* "I'm not really interested in the end product .... I don't expect them to become novelists, short-story writers, poets, playwrights in the short time that I'm with them. What I want from them is an absolute delight in language and ideas." Doherty encourages her young students to explore different

literary genres, opening up new worlds of possibilities. "I think that it is very important with new writers that they explore the different ways of writing. I think that the language that is used in poetry, for instance, can only help the kind of language they'll use in their prose writing. The dialogue that they need for their plays will help the dialogue that they need for their short stories."

In addition to inspiring her young students, Doherty has used her experiences with children as the basis for many of her own stories. For example, soon after publishing *Granny was a Buffer Girl,* she was serving as writer-in-residence at a school in Doncaster, England. She recounts the experience that inspired the book *Tough Luck* in the *Times Educational Supplement:* "When I suggested to 3P, a lively class of [thirteen- and fourteen-year-olds] at Hall Cross Comprehensive school in Doncaster, that I'd like to write a book with them, they responded with enthusiasm.... I established the pattern of the project by dividing the class into random groups of five or six and taking the first group off to a quiet room to talk. I used a tape recorder, and we talked about home and school, hobbies, boyfriends, girlfriends, hates, pets, etc.... I had no idea what would actually be written down, but was searching for something from within their own experience to start me off.... We wrote sample chapters in class; I left them with strings of questions to consider; every week we compared notes. Our small group sessions were invaluable; we talked our way through problem scenes; they offered me lively challenges and criticisms.... Many, many hours have gone into the writing of *Tough Luck,* but those first eleven or so in the mobile classroom in the snowy school yard, when 3P gave me so much of themselves, are the life-blood of the book."

With more recent novels such as *Tough Luck* and the Carnegie Medal-winning *Dear Nobody,* Doherty has adopted a more traditional novel format. In *Dear Nobody* in particular, the structure serves a very specific purpose—it is divided into nine chapters, one for each month of the young woman's pregnancy. Dealing with the sensitive subject of teenage pregnancy, Doherty wanted to structure the book to reflect not only the point of view of Helen, the unborn child's mother, but of Chris, the father, as well. "I didn't want it to be a piece of romantic fiction," Doherty told *SATA.* "I wanted to look seriously and genuinely at love because that's a major part of what being a teenager is about." In a series of letters to her child—the "Dear Nobody" of the title—Helen expresses the feelings of fear, astonishment, and bewilderment a young mother-to-be. Both Chris's narrative and Helen's letters also explore the feelings of their parents and grandparents—all those who contributed to the support of Helen and Chris throughout the nine-months leading up to the birth of their baby. Although Helen and Chris end up parting company during the story, as Doherty notes, "They never totally separate ... its a journey towards their own parents. It's a way for them to find out as much as they can about their own parents—to come to an understanding about what *parenthood* means."

Dear Nobody
BERLIE DOHERTY
1992 CARNEGIE MEDAL WINNER

Divided into nine chapters—one for each month of a teenager's pregnancy—*Dear Nobody* examines the viewpoints not only of a future mother and father but of their parents as well. (Cover illustration by Paterson.)

Her growing popularity as a children's author has made it increasingly difficult for Doherty to find time in her busy schedule to keep up with putting her story ideas down on paper. She finds that writing late at night is the most productive time to work; both the growing volume of mail she receives from readers and the "business" of being a writer takes up her daytime hours. "I never sit down and say 'I'm going to write today,' take an empty sheet of paper and see what happens. That's not the way I can work at all. If I don't have something absolutely fizzing and buzzing inside me it just won't work. There is no point, so I don't even try until I'm so full of the story that it's just got to be written down." Unlike her prolific outpouring of novels, stories, and plays for young readers, *Requiem,* her first adult novel, took a long time finding its way onto the page. Doherty finally published the novel in 1991, and once remarked that "all the time I was writing my children's books, *Requiem* was growing stronger in my head till at last I felt ready to sit down and write it. It feels as if everything I've written has been a preparation for *Requiem.*"

What advice does Doherty give to young people aspiring to be authors? "Well, I wouldn't tell them to start sending their stories off to publishers at age fifteen or sixteen," she told *SATA.* "I'd tell them just to write and write and to love writing. To write about anything and everything. To keep a notebook, to make writing part of their daily life whether or not they call it a diary or a journal. To just pour everything out, to keep going back to things. To take an idea that they've written about and bring it out again and rework it—never to think of something as being finished."

WORKS CITED:

Doherty, Berlie, "Snowy Story," in *Times Educational Supplement,* February 13, 1987, p. 48.

Doherty, Berlie, in an interview for *Something about the Author,* July, 1992.

Colwell, E., *The Junior Bookshelf,* December, 1984, p. 254.

Fox, Geoff, *Times Educational Supplement,* September 7, 1984, p. 29.

Freeman, Maggie, "Berlie Doherty" in *Twentieth-Century Children's Writers,* 3rd edition, St. James Press, 1989, pp. 292-293.

Mole, John, "A Friend Lost, a Lesson Learnt," *Times Literary Supplement,* December 16, 1988, p. 1406.

Pain, Helen, "Carnegie and Greenaway: The 1986 Winners," in *Books for Keeps,* July, 1987, p. 11.

FOR MORE INFORMATION SEE:

BOOKS

Children's Literature Review, Volume 21, Gale, 1990.

PERIODICALS

Growing Point, May, 1985.
Horn Book, May/June, 1988.
Junior Bookshelf, August, 1982; December, 1983.
School Librarian, September, 1982; December, 1984.
Times Educational Supplement, January 18, 1985; November 11, 1988.
Times Literary Supplement, December 16-22, 1988.

*   *   *

DOMINO, John
See AVERILL, Esther (Holden)

*   *   *

DONOVAN, John 1928-1992

PERSONAL: Born in Lynn, MA, 1928; died of cancer April 29, 1992, in New York, NY. *Education:* Graduated from William and Mary College; received law degree from University of Virginia.

CAREER: Writer. Children's Book Council, New York City, president, 1967-1992. International Board on Books for Young People (IBBY), executive director of U.S. National Section, 1967-1987, treasurer, 1986-1990, chairman of Congress Programme Committee, 1990. Worked as teacher of English, as examiner in U.S. Copyright Office, and was affiliated with St. Martin's Press.

JOHN DONOVAN

AWARDS, HONORS: Horn Book honor list citation, Children's Book of the Year citation, Child Study Association of America, and *Book World*'s Children's Spring Book Festival honor book citation, both 1969, all for *I'll Get There, It Better Be Worth the Trip; School Library Journal*'s Best Book citation, and *New York Times* Outstanding Book of the Year citation, both 1971, and National Book Award, Children's Book category, 1972, all for *Wild in the World;* Children's Book of the Year citation, Child Study Association of America, 1976, for *Family;* Children's Reading Roundtable Award, Children's Reading Roundtable of Chicago, 1983; Jella Lepman Medal (for IBBY program development), IBBY, 1991.

WRITINGS:

JUVENILE

The Little Orange Book, illustrated by Mauro Caputo, Morrow, 1961.
I'll Get There, It Better Be Worth the Trip, Harper, 1969.
Wild in the World, Harper, 1971.
Remove Protective Coating a Little at a Time, Harper, 1973.
Good Old James, illustrated by James Stevenson, Harper, 1974.
Family: A Novel, Harper, 1976.

OTHER

Riverside Drive (adult play), produced in New York City, 1964.

Contributor of articles to periodicals, including *Publishers Weekly, Wilson Library Bulletin, Horn Book,* and *School Library Journal.*

ADAPTATIONS: Film rights for *I'll Get There, It Better Be Worth the Trip* were sold in 1973.

SIDELIGHTS: Books by John Donovan, who was executive director of the Children's Book Council from 1967 until his death in 1992, have presented topics such as adolescent homosexuality, alcoholism, and coping with death. Though some critics feel that this material may not be suitable for all readers in Donovan's intended young audience, they believe he approached sensitive topics with compassion. His central theme—the coldness of people toward animals, nature, and each other—was developed in characters who find themselves cut off from others by events or by choice. Davy Ross of *I'll Get There, It Better Be Worth the Trip,* John Gridley of *Wild in the World,* and the elderly hero of *Good Old James* presented this theme from the human viewpoint. The escaped laboratory monkeys in the novel *Family* criticized human insensitivity indirectly. Their cooperation and commitment to mutual survival stands in sharp contrast to the behavior of the supposedly superior humans around them. With these books, Donovan became known as a writer who was not afraid to present challenging topics to young readers.

Davy of *I'll Get There, It Better Be Worth the Trip,* rejected by divorced parents, shares his life with a dog, a grandmother, and his alcoholic mother. Later in the story he has a brief sexual experience with a classmate at a private school in New York. Donovan's treatment of their encounter showed how boys without female partners are sometimes drawn to each other during a time of sexual discovery. The implication that incidental homosexual experience can be a natural part of growing up was welcome to some critics and offensive to others. Martha Bacon declared in the *Atlantic* that the book might disturb young readers who are otherwise unconcerned about sexuality. In contrast to Bacon's warning, Paul Heins wrote in *Horn Book,* "The novel makes skillful use of the elements of divorce, alcoholism, adolescence, school friendships, and death to portray a boy at a crucial time in his life and derives its effective power from the protagonist's frankness and intelligence."

Davy's open expressions about living with difficult adults accounted for the book's ability to keep the reader interested. His description of their faults gives his story emotional power. For example, he is "mercilessly honest" about his mother's mood swings, finally summing up, "I can never tell whether she is going to be my big buddy or a regular witch." His unusually intense interest in his dog, and his isolation after the deaths of both his animal companion and the one adult who respected him, bring Donovan's theme of man's essential aloneness into the spotlight.

The main character of *Wild in the World* is the youngest member of his family and its last remaining survivor. The story begins by explaining how the other twelve members of the family have died. John's inadvertent role in the deaths of his parents, a brother, and a sister partly explains his emotional distance from everyone he knows. When a stray dog wanders into his home, however, a new friendship begins, and he names it Son. After nursing Son back to health following a rattlesnake bite, John gradually becomes able to express his feelings about the lost family. He teaches the dog some simple tricks and naively plans to find a place for both of them in the world by joining a circus. When death intervenes, however, Donovan brings the novel to an emotionally moving close. June Jordan, writing in the *New York Times Book Review,* found the book too bleak to be suitable for adolescents who look to books for "reassurance" during times of loss. On the other hand, for its treatment of the subjects of commitment and grief, Barbara Wersba said in the *New York Times Book Review,* "This novel is more suited to contemporary children than almost any kind of literature I can think of."

Remove Protective Coating a Little at a Time also developed the theme of communication breakdown between an adolescent and the adults he loves. John Rowe Townsend commented in the *New York Times Book Review,* "In *I'll Get There, It Better Be Worth the Trip* and again in this new book, Donovan seems concerned with a special kind of isolation that is often felt by young people in our time. This is the state of noncommunication resulting from the failure of the parental generation to say anything to the young. (It is misleading to see it as the refusal of the young to listen.) We now have an uneasy void where, in less 'advanced' societies, there would be a whole web of intimate relationships and a great handing-down of essential advice and information." Harry, the young man in *Remove Protective Coating a Little at a Time,* receives this kind of knowledge from a 72-year-old bag lady whose home is in a condemned apartment building. His parents, young teens themselves when he was conceived, are so enclosed in their own "protective" coverings that they hardly communicate with each other, let alone with their son. The affection that grows between the boy and the derelict, their uninhibited discussions about sex, and his grief when she can no longer be found, all bring him into a world where meaningful communication is finally possible. Like his other characters, however, Harry sometimes questions whether the journey from childhood to adulthood is worth the trip.

Donovan's next book showed that lack of meaningful communication with others is not a problem exclusive to adolescence. *Good Old James* looks in on the loneliness of a retired man who finds that his large home, his former occupation, and a new generation no longer serve to meet his emotional needs. Noticing a housefly in a hotel room, he sets out some crumbs for it. This book "is for adults and kids to share," Louise Armstrong wrote in the *New York Times Book Review.* Children see a story about a man and his pet, while older readers see the loneliness of advanced age.

In *Family,* a group of apes escape from a university laboratory to form a family group. In sharp contrast to the lack of commitment and affection displayed by the human characters, their sense of community with members of their own species eventually leads them back to an uncertain fate among the captive apes. Telling the story from the animals' point of view allowed Donovan to criticize many aspects of human behavior in the twentieth century. For example, the narrator observes that when humans move into a place, they change it to serve their purposes, while animals in tune with their surroundings simply accept nature as it is. Other thought-provoking challenges in the book include the narrator's explanations of animal feeling, ranging from appreciation of the beauty of a sunset to feelings of anger and guilt. The implied condemnation of the people who exploit the animals for the sake of their experiments or kill them for sport is balanced by the presence of a kind young man who helps the escaped primates to find food. The apes' ability to hope for a better future is also a challenge; when they return to the laboratory, their hope is that mankind as a race, and the humane facet of human nature, is not lost.

As executive director of the Children's Book Council, Donovan expressed his concerns about the future of children's books in an age where profitability was a deciding factor in publishing. Children's books will survive, he predicted in an article for *Publishers Weekly;* however, books with limited appeal, such as translations of children's books from other countries, are less sure of finding publishers. Even if these books must be produced at a cost to the publisher, Donovan stressed "they *must* be published unless American children's books are to be so parochial as to deny that the rest of the world exists." New talents also deserve to be published, he believed.

In a similar article, Donovan invited children's book publishers to meet several challenges. One challenge was to present a variety of materials to young readers. "A child's world can be fact-filled; a visual one; a retreat from reality into stories of another time, or a coming to grips with reality through stories of another time or of today; a world of language in which words can give children and the people who work with children insights they might not dare to articulate unless they had read a certain poem," he declared in *Publishers Weekly.* Another challenge is to learn how best to introduce new books to people who work with children. "Now is a good time for trade publishers to work far more closely with the educational community," he recommended. "When one compares all the new American children's books with the books published in most other countries, it almost takes one's breath away to think of the classroom revolution our books could effect if only we were more successful in letting teachers know their potential."

WORKS CITED:

Armstrong, Louise, review of *Good Old James, New York Times Book Review,* May 4, 1975, p. 40.

Bacon, Martha, review of *I'll Get There, It Better Be Worth the Trip, Atlantic Monthly,* December, 1969, p. 150.

Donovan, John, *I'll Get There, It Better Be Worth the Trip,* Harper, 1969.

Donovan, "Observations about Children's Book Week," *Publishers Weekly,* November 9, 1970, pp. 31-33.

Donovan, "Will Children's Books Survive?," *Publishers Weekly,* February 24, 1975, pp. 62-63.

Heins, Paul, review of *I'll Get There, It Better Be Worth the Trip, Horn Book,* August, 1969, pp. 415-16.

Jordan, June, " . . . or just another horror story, told in monotone?," *New York Times Book Review,* September 12, 1971, part 2, p. 8.

Wersba, Barbara, "For Young Readers: One of the Most Moving Books Ever Written for Children," *New York Times Book Review,* September 12, 1971, part 2, p. 8.

FOR MORE INFORMATION SEE:

BOOKS

Children's Literature Review, Volume 3, Gale, 1978, pp. 139-143.

Contemporary Literary Criticism, Volume 35, Gale, 1985, pp. 51-56.

Twentieth-Century Children's Writers, St. Martin's, 1978, 2nd edition, 1983, pp. 294-295.

PERIODICALS

Commonweal, May 23, 1969, p. 300.
Horn Book, June, 1968, pp. 302-306.
Library Journal, May 15, 1969, p. 2111.
New York Times Book Review, May 4, 1969, part 2, p. 8; May 17, 1976, p. 14.
Psychology Today, September, 1975.
Publishers Weekly, October 9, 1961; May 4, 1975, p. 40; April 26, 1976.
School Library Journal, November, 1977, pp. 22-26.
Variety, January 31, 1973.
Washington Post Book World, May 4, 1969, p. 4.
Wilson Library Bulletin, January, 1969, pp. 432-37; October, 1974, pp. 144-45.

OBITUARIES:

PERIODICALS

Publishers Weekly, May 11, 1992, p. 16.*

*   *   *

DUNNE, Jeanette 1952-

PERSONAL: Born in June, 1952, in Carrick-on-Shannon, Ireland; daughter of Alan and Attracta (a publican; maiden name, Ryan) Dunne; married Oliver Burke (a banker), June 17, 1978 (died, 1992); children: Alan, Laura. *Education:* National College of Art and Design, degree (with honors), 1975. *Religion:* Roman Catholic.

ADDRESSES: Home—Summer-hill, Carrick-on-Shannon, County Leitrim, Ireland.

CAREER: Illustrator. Radio-Television Ireland, Dublin, graphic designer, 1975-80. Bosco preschool, illustrator and graphic designer for children's programs.

AWARDS, HONORS: Peter Owens Award for animation, 1974, for television commercial "Keep Ireland Beautiful"; received commendations from the Irish Book Design Awards, 1982, for *The Fairy Isle of Coosanure,* and 1986, for *The Uninvited Guest; Run Swift, Run Free* received the Irish Book Awards Medal, 1987, and was a White Raven selection of the Irish Children's Book Trust, International Youth Library, Munich, 1988; *Run with the Wind* was named a Bisto Book of the Decade, 1980-90.

ILLUSTRATOR:

Curriculum Development Unit, *The Celtic Way of Life,* O'Brien Educational, 1976.

Curriculum Development Unit, *Ulster Cycle,* O'Brien Educational, 1976.

Liam O'Flaherty, *The Wilderness* (novel), Wolfhound Press, 1978.

Peter Tremayne, *Irish Masters of Fantasy,* Wolfhound Press, 1979.

Frank Egan, *The Fairy Isle of Coosanure,* Wolfhound Press, 1982.

Mullen, *Sea Wolves from the North,* Wolfhound Press, 1983.

Egan, *The Uninvited Guest,* Wolfhound Press, 1986.

Jack Scoltock, *Quest of the Royal Twines,* Wolfhound Press, 1988.

Cormac MacRaois, *Battle below Giltspur,* Wolfhound Press, 1988.

MacRaois, *Dance of the Midnight Fire,* Wolfhound Press, 1989.

JEANNETTE DUNNE

Dunne's early fascination for comics and drawing led to career in illustration. (Illustration by Dunne from *Lightning over Giltspur*, by Cormac MacRaois.)

Scoltock, *Badger-Beano and the Magic Mushroom*, Wolfhound Press, 1990.

MacRaois, *Lightning over Giltspur*, Wolfhound Press, 1991.

"WILDLIFE" SERIES, BY TOM McCAUGHREN

Run with the Wind, Wolfhound Press, 1983.
Run to Earth, Wolfhound Press, 1984.
Run Swift, Run Free, Wolfhound Press, 1986.
Run to the Ark, Wolfhound Press, 1991.

Also illustrator of *On Foot: Exploring the Wilderness in Dublin and Wicklow*, by Christopher Moriarity, Wolfhound Press; and *Our Way of Life: Heritage, Wildlife, Countryside, People*, Wolfhound Press, 1990.

SIDELIGHTS: Jeanette Dunne told *SATA:* "I have been drawing since I could hold a pencil. When, as a child, I discovered comics and developed a fascination for this particular art form, my academic studies took second place. Having graduated from art college in 1975, I started my career in T.V. as a graphic designer, where I spent six happy years. Having left television to start a family, my main body of work has been in book illustration, specializing in children's books. I feel that's where my future lies."

E

EARLY, Margaret 1951-

PERSONAL: Born April 10, 1951, in Coff's Harbour, New South Wales, Australia; daughter of Victor Maynard (a medical practitioner) and Patricia (an artist; maiden name, Bosanquet) Early; married Micheal Farrell (an artist), March 6, 1992. *Education:* Sydney University, B.A., 1972; attended Shillito Design School, 1973-76, and St. Martin's School of Art, 1977-78.

ADDRESSES: Home—Cardet Village, Gard 30350, France. *Agent*—Walter McVitty, M/S 956 41-57 Mill Hill Rd., Montville 4560, Australia.

CAREER: Artist and illustrator of children's books in Sydney, Australia, 1978-85, in France and Ireland, 1986—.

EXHIBITIONS: Group exhibitions at the Royal Overseas League, London, England, and Edinburgh, Scotland, both 1978; Blaxland Gallery, Sydney, Australia, 1979; *Sydney Morning Herald* Heritage Exhibition, University of New South Wales, 1980 and 1981; University of New South Wales Invitation Exhibition, Sydney, 1982, 1983, and 1985; Blake Prize Exhibition, Sydney, 1982 and 1983; Coolangatta Winter Festival Exhibition, Queensland, Australia, 1982 and 1983; Cowra Art Exhibition, New South Wales, 1982; Macquarie University Exhibition, Sydney, 1982; Faber-Castell Drawing Exhibition, Sydney, 1983; "Les Oreades" Gallery, Toulouse, France, 1984; Prix International d'Art de Monte Carlo, Monaco, 1984, 1985, 1986, and 1989; Galway Arts Festival, Ireland, 1987; Union Feminine Artistique et Culturelle Salons Internationaux, Japan, 1988, Turkey and Cyprus, 1992. Solo shows at the Arts Council, Sydney, 1976; Holdsworth Gallery, Sydney, 1981, 1983, 1986, 1988, and 1991; Cintra House Galleries, Brisbane, Queensland, 1984; and Galerie L'Angle Aigu, Brussels, Belgium, 1987.

AWARDS, HONORS: Early's paintings have won several awards, including First prize, Cowra Art Exhibition, 1982; Calted Prize, Cowra Art Exhibition, 1982; and first prize, Coolangatta Winter Festival, 1982; Chil-

MARGARET EARLY

dren's Book of the Year Honour Book, Children's Book Council of Australia, 1992, for *William Tell.*

ILLUSTRATOR:

Ali Baba and the 40 Thieves, retold by Walter McVitty, Walter McVitty, 1988.
(And reteller) *William Tell,* Walter McVitty, 1991.
(And reteller) *Sleeping Beauty,* Walter McVitty, in press.

Work represented in collections at University of New South Wales and the Cowra Council.

A Japanese edition of *Ali Baba and the 40 Thieves* has been printed.

WORK IN PROGRESS: An exhibition in Brisbane, Australia.

SIDELIGHTS: Margaret Early told *SATA:* "I'm an artist turned illustrator and have only two books to my name. How I came to turn to illustration was a result of listening to a radio interview on the Australian Broadcasting Corporation (ABC) network. I was then living in Sydney and in the process of completing a year's work for an exhibition of paintings for the Holdsworth Galleries in Sydney. The interview I was listening to was with my publisher, Walter McVitty, who had just started publishing his first book and was talking about wanting to get quality back into children's books.

"I telephoned him and arranged to show him the paintings ready for exhibition—subjects from medieval history such as figures going to Canterbury, plus a couple of Persian stories, notably 'Sohrab and Rustum' treated like a Persian miniature. He called a couple of weeks later and asked me if I was interested in doing *Ali Baba*—he would retell the story if I could do the fourteen illustrations.

"After completing the first two illustrations we signed a contract and I left for Europe the next day. The following twelve illustrations for me are a travelling diary of the next seven months. The next two illustrations were done in a very cheap hotel room in Paris, painted at the standard small table one finds in such hotels. The following four illustrations were done over the next couple of months in the Ardeche in the southern central part of France. Here I worked with a tray on my knees as the house was very spartan. I then left for Ireland. The next two illustrations were done in Dublin. We were staying with a doctor friend and so I now had the marble dining-room table to paint on. The last of the illustrations plus the borders were painted in a house we rented in Connemara on the west coast of Ireland. The work was then posted to my publisher in Australia." Commenting on sources for her illustrations,

Illustration from "WILLIAM TELL"

Early's background in painting historical scenes has resulted in illustrations for retellings of famous legends and fairy tales, including this piece from *William Tell*.

the author stated that "for *Ali Baba and the Forty Thieves* the greatest influence was Persian miniatures."

Early's next book was a retelling of *William Tell*. She recalled for *SATA*: "[The year after *Ali Baba*] I went to Switzerland to visit my cousin. Her boss commissioned me to do a painting of mythical Swiss folk hero William Tell and so while there I spent time doing research into Swiss medieval art and read the play by eighteenth-century writer Johann von Schiller. Shortly after this my Australian publisher visited me in France and asked me if I'd like to choose the second book as he'd chosen *Ali Baba*. My obvious choice was *William Tell*. The book was executed in my home in the south of France plus a three-month visit to Dublin. Living in France has been wonderful for the study of medieval art which was the reference material for the book. The fourteen illustrations were completed after twelve months.

"I've now started on a third book, *The Sleeping Beauty*, and for this I've been studying French paintings of the seventeenth and eighteenth centuries. It will be at least a year before it's completed."

*   *   *

ECKERT, Horst 1931-
(Janosch)

PERSONAL: Born March 11, 1931, in Zaborze, Germany (now Poland); son of Johann (a shopkeeper) and Hildegard E. (Glodny) Eckert. *Education:* Attended gymnasium in Zaborze, 1940-43, and textile design school in Krefeld, Germany, 1947-49. *Religion:* None.

ADDRESSES: Munich, Germany.

CAREER: Author and illustrator of children's books. Once worked as an industrial designer. *Exhibitions:* Wilhelm-Busch-Museum, Germany, 1980; Stadt-und Schiffahrtsmuseum Kiel, Germany, 1981; Stadtgeschichtliche Museen Nuernberg, Duererhaus, Germany, 1981.

AWARDS, HONORS: Hans Christian Andersen highly commended illustrator, German Federal Republic, 1972; German Children's Book Prize Honor List.

WRITINGS:

FOR ADULTS

(With Wolfgang Menz) *Absatzplanung und Verkaufssteuerung in der Druckindustrie: ein Leitfaden* (nonfiction), Graphische Gewerbe, 1973.

UNDER PSEUDONYM JANOSCH; FOR ADULTS

Cholonek; oder, Der liebe Gott aus Lehm (adult novel; title means "Cholonek, or, the God of Clay"), Bitter, 1970.
Sacharin im Salat (novel), Guetersloh, 1975.
Sandstrand (novel), Beltz, 1979.

UNDER PSEUDONYM JANOSCH; FOR CHILDREN

The Magic Auto, illustrations by Caroline Sommer, Crown, 1971 (originally published as *Das Regenauto,* Ellermann, 1969).
Autos Autos viel Autos, illustrations by Friedrich Kohlsaat, Beltz, 1971.

UNDER PSEUDONYM JANOSCH; FOR CHILDREN; SELF-ILLUSTRATED; IN ENGLISH TRANSLATION

The Yellow Auto Named Ferdinand, Carolrhoda, 1973 (originally published as *Das Auto hier heisst Ferdinand,* Deutscher Buecherbund, 1965).
Just One Apple, Walck, 1966 (originally published as *Das Apfelmaennchen,* Parabel, 1965).
Tonight at Nine, Walck, 1967 (originally published as *Heute um neune hinter der Scheune,* Parabel, 1965).
Has Anyone Seen Paul? Who Will Be He?: A Story and Counting Rhymes, translation by Margaret Green, Dobson, 1969 (originally published as *Rate mal, wer suchen muss,* Parabel, 1966, Austrian and Swiss editions published as *Rat einmal, wer suchen muss,* Domino, 1966).
Joshua and the Magic Fiddle, World Publishing, 1968 (originally published as *Der Josa mit der Zauberfiedel,* Parabel, 1967).
Mr. Wuzzle, adaptation and translation by Judy Lester, Longman, 1969 (originally published as *Herr Wuzzel und sein Karussell,* Parabel, 1968, Swiss edition published as *Herr Wuzzel und sein Zauber-Karussell,* Globi-Verlag, 1968).
Luke Caraway: Master Magician or Indian Chief, translation by Anthea Bell, Andersen, 1977 (originally

HORST ECKERT

published as *Lukas Kuemmel, Zauberkuenstler*, Paulus, 1968).

Bollerbam, translation by Refna Wilkin, Walck, 1969 (originally published as *Boellerbam und der Vogel*, Middelhauve, 1968).

Dear Snowman, World Publishing, 1970, published in England as *Oh, Dear, Snowman!*, Dobson, 1972 (originally published as *Ach lieber Schneemann*, Parabel, 1969).

The Thieves and the Raven, translation by Elizabeth Shub, Macmillan, 1970 (originally published as *3 Raeuber und 1 Rabenkoenig*, Parabel, 1969).

Leon the Magic Flea; or, The Lion Hunt in Upper Fimmel, translation by A. Bell, Abelard-Schuman, 1974 (originally published as *Leo Zauberfloh; oder, Die Loewenjagd in Oberfimmel*, Bitter, 1970).

The Crocodile Who Wouldn't Be King, Putnam, 1971 (originally published as *Komm nach Iglau Krokodil*, Parabel, 1970).

Not Quite as Grimm, translation by Patricia Crampton, Abelard-Schuman, 1974 (originally published as *Janosch erzaehlt Grimm's Maerchen und zeichnet fuer Kinder von heute; fuenfzig ausgewaehlte Maerchen*, Beltz & Gelberg, 1972).

One-Eye, Ginger, and Lefty, Dobson, 1972.

I Am a Great Big Hairy Bear, translation by James Dobson, Dobson, 1973 (originally published as *Ich bin ein grosser Zottelbaer*, Parabel, 1972).

Tales of the Lying Nutcracker, translation from the German by Erika Hyams, Abelard-Schuman, 1973.

Time for Bed, Dobson, 1973.

Zampano's Performing Bear, translation by J. Dobson, Dobson, 1976 (originally published as *Baerenzirkus Zampano*, Parabel, 1975).

The Trip to Panama, translation by A. Bell, Andersen, 1978, Little, Brown, 1981 (originally published as *Oh, wie schoen ist Panama*, Beltz & Gelberg, 1976).

The Big Janosch Book of Fun and Verse, translation by A. Bell, Andersen, 1980 (originally published as *Das grosse Janosch Buch: Geschicten und Bilder*, Beltz & Gelberg, 1976).

Crafty Caspar and His Good Old Granny, translation by J. Dobson, Dobson, 1979 (originally published as *Kasper Loeffel und seine gute Oma*, Parabel, 1977).

Hey Presto! You're a Bear!, translation by Klaus Flugge, Little, Brown, 1980 (originally published as *Ich sag, du bist ein Baer*, Beltz & Gelberg, 1977).

The Rain Car, translation from the German by J. Dobson, Dobson, 1978.

The Treasure-Hunting Trip, translation from the German by A. Bell, Andersen, 1980.

A Letter for Tiger, Andersen, 1981.

Animal Antics, in Words and Pictures, translation by A. Bell, Andersen Press, 1982 (originally published as *Leben der Thiere*).

See You in the Morning!, translation from the German by A. Bell, Methuen, 1983.

The Higher and Higher House, translation from the German by A. Bell, Methuen, 1984.

The Cricket and the Mole, translation by Elizabeth D. Crawford, Bradbury Press, 1987 (originally published as *Die Fiedelgrille und der Maulwurf*, Diogenes, 1985).

"I'll Make You Well, Tiger," Said the Bear, translation by Elisabeth Muhlemann, Adama Books, 1985, published in England as *Little Tiger, Get Well Soon!*, Andersen, 1986 (originally published as *Ich mach dich gesund, sagte der Baer*).

The Old Man and the Bear, Bradbury Press, 1987 (originally published as *Der Alte Mann und der Baer*).

Also author and illustrator of *The Curious Tale of Hare and Hedgehog*, 1988, *Hello, Little Pig*, 1988, and *The Little Hare Book*, 1988.

UNDER PSEUDONYM JANOSCH; FOR CHILDREN; SELF-ILLUSTRATED; UNTRANSLATED WORKS

Historia de Valek, el caballo, Editorial Lumen, 1963.

Valek y Jarosch, Editorial Lumen, 1963.

Onkel Poppoff kann auf Baeume fliegen, Domino, 1964.

Leo Zauberfloh; oder, Wer andern eine Grube graebt, Domino, 1966.

Poppoff und Piezke, Parabel, 1966.

Hannes Strohkopp und der unsichtbare Indianer, Parabel, 1966.

Schlafe, lieber Hampelmann, Parabel, 1967.

Rabenkoenig Muckelbass, Domino, 1967.

Wir haben einen Hund zu Haus, Parabel, 1968.

Der Maeuse-Sheriff: Luegengeschicten aus dem Wilden Westen, erlogen von einer Maus, Bitter, 1969.

Flieg Vogel, flieg, Parabel, 1971.

Loewe spring durch den Ring, Parabel, 1971.

Ene bene Bimmelbahn, Parabel, 1971.

Lari Fari Mogelzahn; jeden Abend eine Geschichte, Beltz & Gelberg, 1971.

Bilder und Gedichte fuer Kinder, Westermann, 1972.

Schulfiebel 1, Westermann, 1972.

Wohin Rast die Feuerwehr, [Munich], 1972.

Familie Schmidt, Rowohlt, 1974.

Hottentotten gruene Motten, Rowohlt, 1974.

Das starke Auto Ferdinand, Parabel, 1976.

Die Globeriks, Globi-Verlag, 1976.

Die Loewenreise, Beltz & Gelberg, 1976.

Die Maus hat rote Struempfe an Beltz, Beltz & Gelberg, 1978.

Ein Mann ein Kahn die Maus das Haus, Parabel, 1978.

Das kleine Hasenbuch, Parabel, 1978.

Schnuddelbuddel sagt gutnacht, Parabel, 1978.

Traumstunde fuer Siebenschlaefer, Beltz & Gelberg, 1978.

Das grosse Panama-Album, Beltz & Gelberg, 1984.

Herr Korbes will Klein Huehnchen kuessen, Diogenes, 1984.

Schimanski; die Kraft der inneren Maus, Diogenes, 1989.

Also author and illustrator of numerous other juvenile books, including *Ich male einen Bauernhof*, Parabel.

ILLUSTRATOR; UNDER PSEUDONYM JANOSCH; IN ENGLISH TRANSLATION

Mischa Damjan (pseudonym), *The Magic Paintbrush*, Walck, 1967 (originally published as *Filipo und sein Wunderpinsel*, Nord-Sued, 1967).

Eckert, who illustrates under the name Janosch, is well-known for his animated, carefree drawings, such as this scene from Anne K. Rose's *How Does a Czar Eat Potatoes?*

Jack Prelutzky, *Lazy Blackbird, and Other Verses,* Macmillan, 1969.

Hans Baumann, *Gatalop the Wonderful Ball,* Walck, 1971 (originally published as *Der wunderbare Ball Kadalupp,* Betz, 1969).

Anne K. Rose, *How Does a Czar Eat Potatoes?,* Lothrop, 1973.

Yuri Koval, *A Pig in a Poke,* translation from the Russian, Abelard-Schuman, 1975.

ILLUSTRATOR; UNDER PSEUDONYM JANOSCH; UNTRANSLATED WORKS

Jozef Wilkon, *Die Loewenkinder,* Middelhauve, 1968.

Hans-Joachim Gelberg, *Die Stadt der Kinder,* Bitter, 1969.

Herbert Heckmann, *Geschicten vom Loeffelchen,* Middelhauve, 1970.

Beverly Cleary, *Die Maus auf dem Motorrad,* Union, 1972.

B. Cleary, *Mauserich Ralf Haut ab,* Union, 1972.

Walter D. Edmonds, *Das Mausehaus,* Loewes, 1972.

Paul Maar, *Kikerikiste,* Deutscher Taschenbuch, 1973.

James Kruss, *Der Kleine Flax,* Oetinger, 1975.

Bombo, Parabel, 1978.

Bombo kann alles, Parabel, 1978.

Wasja kauft den Hund im Sack, Thienemann, 1978.

Der Weihnachtsstern, Oetinger, 1978.

Kaese Kaese, Mosaik, 1978.

Christine Noestlinger, *Einer,* Beltz & Gelberg, 1980.

Herbert Rosendorfer, *Die Herberge zum irdischen Paradies: ein Plaeydoyer fuer das unsterbliche Wirtschaus,* Etcetera, 1982.

Also illustrator of *Bonko,* by H. Baumann, 1972, *Yosi ve-khinor ha-kesamim,* by Tzvi Rozen, 1972, and *Die lustigen Abenteur des Kasperl larifari,* by Franz-Graf von Pocci, 1972. An exhibition catalog of Janosch's illustrations entitled *Janosch: Gemalde and Grafik* was published by Merlin, 1980.

SIDELIGHTS: Horst Eckert has written and illustrated over seventy books under the name Janosch, and his books are familiar to children all over the world through their translations from German into many different languages. Most of his books are populated by animals, and the animated expressions and carefree antics of the author's bears, pigs, and other creatures delight young children. Eckert was highly commended for his skills as an illustrator by the Hans Christian Andersen jury in 1972 for the body of his work, but his popularity can best be measured by the over half a million copies of his books that have sold worldwide.

Eckert was born in 1931 in the Polish town of Zaborze, which was under German rule until after World War II. He attended school until he was thirteen, when he left to work in a blacksmith's shop and later in different factories. In 1953 he tried to study at the Academy of Art in Munich, Germany, but in his autobiographical sketch for *Fourth Book of Junior Authors and Illustrators* he says, "I had to leave the academy. I had no talent." Eckert stayed on in Munich, living on the little money he earned doing odd jobs. A chance conversation gave him the idea to write a children's book, but he had no success until he wrote his seventh book, which sold ninety thousand copies. From that point on he has made his living writing and illustrating his own children's books and illustrating books for other authors. "And now I succeed too in painting," he comments in his autobiographical sketch. "I have had many exhibitions, and it doesn't matter so much whether the pictures are all sold every time because now I don't need money. But to be a painter—that was what I wanted to become when it began."

Naomi Lewis, writing in the *Observer*, called *The Big Janosch Book of Fun and Verse* (originally *Das grosse Janosch Buch*) "the nursery book of the season." The volume contains hundreds of illustrations, numerous poems and fables, and even some mini-novels; all contain a lesson, though none are overtly moralistic.

Hey Presto! You're a Bear! (originally *Ich sag, du bist ein Baer*) is a picture-book fantasy in which a young boy discovers that he has the power to turn people into any animal he wants by saying "Hey Presto!" The story resembles Dr. Seuss's *The Cat in the Hat*, but in Eckert's version the young boy's parents join in the game, and parent and child alike enjoy the playful fantasy.

WORKS CITED:

Fourth Book of Junior Authors and Illustrators, H. W. Wilson, 1978, pp. 196-97.
Lewis, Naomi, "Poetry, Fable, Song," *Observer*, December 7, 1980.

FOR MORE INFORMATION SEE:

PERIODICALS

Library Journal, September 15, 1967, p. 110; September 1, 1970.
National Observer, November 4, 1968.
New York Times, November 3, 1968.
New York Times Book Review, May 22, 1966; November 7, 1971.
Observer, July 19, 1987.
School Library Journal, February, 1981, pp. 57-58; October, 1981, p. 130; August, 1987, p. 70.
Times Literary Supplement, April 12, 1969; July 2, 1970; April 6, 1973; June 15, 1973, p. 687.*

F

FARRELL, Sally
See ODGERS, Sally Farrell

* * *

FINE, Anne 1947-

PERSONAL: Born December 7, 1947, in Leicester, England; daughter of Brian (a chief scientific experimental officer) and Mary Laker; married Kit Fine (a university professor), 1968; children: two daughters. *Education:* University of Warwick, B.A. (with honors), 1968.

ADDRESSES: Home—County Durham, England. *Agent*—Murray Pollinger, 222 Old Brompton Rd., London SW5 0BZ, England.

CAREER: English teacher at Cardinal Wiseman Girls' Secondary School, 1968-70; Oxford Committee for Famine Relief, Oxford, England, assistant information officer, 1970-71; Saughton Jail, Edinburgh, Scotland, teacher, 1971-72; free-lance writer, 1973—. Volunteer for Amnesty International.

AWARDS, HONORS: Guardian/Kestrel Award nominations, 1978, for *The Summer-House Loon,* and 1987, for *Madame Doubtfire;* Scottish Arts Council Book Award, 1986, for *The Killjoy; Observer* Prize for Teenage Fiction nomination, 1987, for *Madame Doubtfire;* Smarties (6-8) Award, 1989, for *Bill's New Frock; Guardian* Award for Children's Fiction, 1989, and Carnegie Medal, 1990, both for *Goggle Eyes;* Children's Author of the Year, British Book Awards, 1990.

WRITINGS:

FICTION FOR CHILDREN

The Summer-House Loon, Methuen, 1978, Crowell, 1979.
The Other, Darker Ned, Methuen, 1979.
The Stone Menagerie, Methuen, 1980.
Round behind the Ice-House, Methuen, 1981.
The Granny Project, Farrar, Straus, 1983.

Scaredy-Cat, illustrated by Vanessa Julian-Ottie, Heinemann, 1985.
Anneli the Art Hater, Methuen, 1986.
Madame Doubtfire, Hamish Hamilton, 1987, published as *Alias Madame Doubtfire,* Little, Brown, 1988.
Crummy Mummy and Me, illustrated by David Higham, Deutsch, 1988.
A Pack of Liars, Hamish Hamilton, 1988.
My War with Goggle Eyes, Little, Brown, 1989 (published in England as *Goggle Eyes,* Hamish Hamilton, 1989).
Stranger Danger?, illustrated by Jean Baylis, Hamish Hamilton, 1989.
Bill's New Frock, illustrated by Philippe Dupasquier, Methuen, 1989.
A Sudden Puff of Glittering Smoke, illustrated by Adriano Gon, Picadilly Press, 1989.
Only a Show, illustrated by Valerie Littlewood, Hamish Hamilton, 1990.

ANNE FINE

A Sudden Swirl of Icy Wind, illustrated by Higham, Picadilly Press, 1990.

The Country Pancake, illustrated by Dupasquier, Methuen, 1990.

Poor Monty, illustrated by Clara Vulliamy, Clarion Books, 1991.

A Sudden Glow of Gold, Picadilly Press, 1991.

The Book of the Banshee, Hamish Hamilton, 1991.

The Worst Child I Ever Had, illustrated by Vulliamy, Hamish Hamilton, 1991.

Design-A-Pram, Heinemann, 1991.

The Genie Trilogy (contains *A Sudden Puff of Glittering Smoke, A Sudden Swirl of Icy Wind,* and *A Sudden Glow of Gold*), Mammoth, 1992.

The Angel of Nitshill Road, illustrated by K. Aldous, Methuen, 1992.

OTHER

The Granny Project (play; based on her story), Collins, 1986.

The Killjoy (adult novel), Bantam (London), 1986, Mysterious Press, 1987.

Taking the Devil's Advice (adult novel), Viking, 1990.

Also author of radio play *The Captain's Court Case,* 1987. Contributor of short stories to periodicals.

ADAPTATIONS: Goggle-Eyes was produced on cassette by Chivers Sound & Vision, 1992.

SIDELIGHTS: In such children's books as *The Summer-House Loon, Alias Madame Doubtfire,* and *My War with Goggle-Eyes,* novelist Anne Fine brings a keen comic insight to bear on family problems. "I was brought up in the country, in a family of five girls, including one set of triplets," Fine once related. "My husband was brought up in a family of six boys, including twins. Family relationships have always interested me and it is with the close members of their families that the characters in my books are either getting, or not getting, along."

Fine had a love of books and reading from an early age. "As the story was always told, the local education authority took pity on my mother and let her pack me off to Highlands Road Infant School two years earlier than usual," the author related in her *Something about the Author Autobiography Series* (*SAAS*) essay. "I was three. And so it is that I can truthfully claim that, apart from stepping off that log into the duckweed, I have no memory at all of a time when I couldn't read." As a result of entering school early, Fine was ahead of her class and was allowed to spend time reading. "I'd read everything in all the classrooms. There was no school library. And so I was allowed to scour the shelves in the headmistress's office for things to read.... And nobody ever came to hurry me or fetch me back. Yes, it was my first library."

Writing became a favorite activity as well, the author continued in her *SAAS* essay. "What I loved writing were stories, and I was lucky here.... When I was young, we were allowed to fly in English. 'Write an

Fine sensitively explores family relationships in both novels and picture books, including this story of young Monty's attempts to get his busy mother, a doctor, to notice he is sick. (Cover illustration by Clara Vulliamy.)

essay,' they'd tell us. 'At least three sides—and I *mean* that, Shirley. No talking. You've got till break. Now just shut up and get on with it.' They'd chalk some titles—any old titles—up on the board.... Oh, bliss! You'd have to be halfway to being an idiot, frankly, not to be able to twist at least one of the titles into something you could write about."

But while the young Fine found writing an enjoyable activity that came easily to her, she didn't harbor ambitions to be an author. "Did I know I was going to be a writer?" Fine related in *SAAS.* "Not at the start.... The earliest I know the idea must have surfaced was when, in secondary school, when I was about twelve, a strange thing happened. Miss Sinton was teaching us English. I think she was probably fed up with us already. Certainly she'd made us pull our desks apart from one another, dished out some written work, and was pacing up and down between the desks, hushing and scolding, and pointing out mistakes. It was no time to start causing trouble.... I must really have wanted to know, to pick that time to stick my arm out like a traffic cop, stopping her in her tracks, and ask her outright: 'Could *I* be a writer?' She looked down her nose at the arm that prevented her from sweeping past. Hastily I drew it back. Then she looked down her nose at me. But I persisted. 'Could I?' And, cross as she was with the whole pack of us, she gave me an answer, and I'll always be grateful for that. She wasn't too friendly about it. But she was straight. 'Oh, yes,' she said. '*You could.*'"

Nevertheless, Fine didn't begin writing until after college. "I started the first on an impulse," she explained in her autobiographical essay. "Clinically depressed, and kept from the library by a snowstorm, I waited till the baby fell asleep, then snatched up a pencil and began to write. It came out fast and easily, far more so than anything I've written since. And it was a sunny book. A lot of what I've written since is comedy, but usually it has a black edge. That first book was truly light in spirit. When I look back at the bleak, miserable creature who sat down to write it, I can hardly believe that she was me, and that she wrote a book like that."

In that first book, *The Summer-House Loon,* Fine presents teenager Ione Muffet, the daughter of a blind college professor who is sometimes oblivious to her. The novel portrays a single, farcical day in Ione's life as she attempts to match her father's secretary with an intelligent yet fumbling graduate student. Calling the novel "original and engaging..., mischievous, inventive and very funny," *Times Literary Supplement* writer Peter Hollindale praises Fine for "a fine emotional delicacy which sensitively captures, among all the comic upheaval, the passionate solitude of adolescence." *The Summer-House Loon* is "not just a funny book, although it is certainly that," Marcus Crouch of *Junior Bookshelf* likewise comments. "Here is a book with deep understanding, wisdom and compassion. It tosses the reader between laughter and tears with expert dexterity."

A sequel, *The Other, Darker Ned,* finds Ione organizing a charity benefit for famine victims. "Through [Ione's] observations of other people" in both these works, Margery Fisher comments in *Growing Point,* "we have that delighted sense of recognition which comes in reading novels whose characters burst noisily and eccentrically out of the pages." While these books "are not for everyone, requiring a certain amount of sophistication," Anthea Bell remarks in *Twentieth-Century Children's Writers,* for readers "in command of that sophistication they are stylishly lighthearted entertainment."

Some of Fine's next novels directly examine such social issues as homelessness and care of the elderly. *The Stone Menagerie,* in which a boy discovers that a couple is living on the grounds of a mental hospital, is "devised with a strict economy of words, an acute sense of personality and a shrewd, ironic humour that once more shows Anne Fine to be one of the sharpest and humorous observers of the human condition writing today for the young," Fisher writes in *Growing Point.* And in using humor while "tackling the aged and infirm," Fine's *The Granny Project* "against all the odds contrives to be both audacious and heart-warming," Charles Fox remarks in *New Statesman.* The story of how four siblings conspire to keep their grandmother out of a nursing home by making her care a school assignment, *The Granny Project* is "mordantly funny, ruthlessly honest, yet compassionate in its concern," Nancy C. Hammond notes in *Horn Book.*

The author brings a farcical tone to the serious subject of divorce in this lively tale of how a divorced father's attempts to see more of his children turn into a riotous masquerade.

Alias Madame Doubtfire brings a more farcical approach to a serious theme, this time the breaking up of a family. "Novels about divorce for children are rarely funny," Roger Sutton observes in the *Bulletin of the Center for Children's Books,* but Fine's work "will have readers laughing from the first page." To gain more time with his children, out-of-work actor Daniel poses as Madame Doubtfire, a supremely capable housekeeper, and gets a job in his ex-wife Miranda's household. Miranda remains blind to her housekeeper's identity while the children quickly catch on, leading to several amusing incidents. But "beneath the farce, the story deals with a serious subject," Mark Geller states in *New York Times Book Review:* "the pain children experience when their parents divorce and then keep on battling." "The comedy of disguise allows the author to skate over the sexual hates and impulses inherent in the situation without lessening the candour of her insights into the irreconcilable feelings of both adults and children," Fisher concludes. "Readers of the teenage novel, weary of perfunctory blue-prints of reality, should be thankful to Anne Fine for giving them such nourishing food for thought within an entertaining piece of fiction."

Crummy Mummy and Me and *A Pack of Liars* "are two more books whose prime intent is to make young people laugh," Chris Powling of the *Times Educational Supple-*

ment observes. "Both exploit the standard comic techniques of taking a familiar situation, turning it on its head, and shaking it vigorously to see what giggles and insights fall into the reader's lap." *A Pack of Liars* recounts how a school assignment to write to a pen pal turns into a mystery of sorts, while *Crummy Mummy and Me* presents a role-reversal in the relationship between an irresponsible mother and her capable daughter. "Details of the plots, though neatly worked out, may sometimes seem a little farfetched in the abstract," Bell notes; "in practice, however, the sheer comic verve of the writing carries them off." Powling agrees, commenting that "once again the narrative shamelessly favours ingenuity over plausibility on the pretty safe assumption that a reader can't complain effectively while grinning broadly." Both books, the critic concludes, "offer welcome confirmation that humour is closer to humanity than apostles of high seriousness care to admit."

In *My War with Goggle-Eyes*, Fine offers yet another "comic yet perceptive look at life after marriage," Ilene Cooper states in *Booklist*. From the opening, in which young Kitty relates to a schoolmate how her mother's boyfriend "Goggle-Eyes" came into her life, "to the happy-ever-after-maybe ending, Fine conveys a story about relationships filled with humor that does not ridicule and sensitivity that is not cloying," Susan

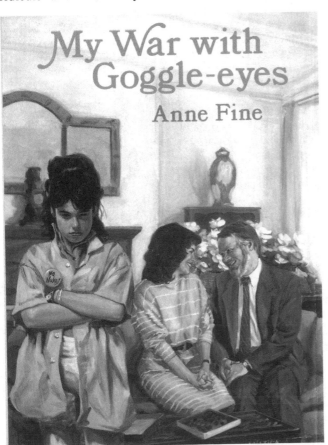

A young girl must learn to adjust to her divorced mother's new boyfriend—a man she finds completely repulsive—in Fine's *My War with Goggle-eyes*. (Cover illustration by Rick Mujica.)

Schuller comments in *School Library Journal*. In showing how Kitty gradually learns to accept her mother's new relationship, "Anne Fine writes some of the funniest—and truest—family fight scenes to be found," Sutton observes in *Bulletin of the Center for Children's Books*. The result is "a book that is thoroughly delightful to read," Schuller concludes.

The author once commented: "I find I write mostly about that period during which the stability of childhood, when almost all decisions are made by others, is giving way to a wider world. A sense of the need for a sort of personal elbow-room is developing, and people outside the family seem to be showing other ways to go. Growing through to a full autonomy is, for anyone, a long and doggy business and for some, more sabotaged than others by their nature or upbringing, it can seem impossible. I try to show that the battle through the chaos and confusions is worthwhile and can, at times, be seen as very funny." And in *SAAS*, Fine summarized her feelings about the power of fiction: "It changes people, and it changes lives. When we are young, we read about the miller's daughter spinning her straw to gold. And that, I believe, is the writer's great privilege. We only gain from letting our childhoods echo down the years, and we're allowed to spend our lifetimes spinning straw."

WORKS CITED:

Bell, Anthea, "Anne Fine," *Twentieth-Century Children's Writers,* 3rd edition, St. James Press, 1989, pp. 336-337.

Cooper, Ilene, review of *My War with Goggle-Eyes, Booklist,* April 15, 1989, p. 1465.

Crouch, Marcus, review of *The Summer-House Loon, Junior Bookshelf,* August, 1978, pp. 202-203.

Fine, Anne, essay in *Something about the Author Autobiography Series,* Volume 15, Gale, 1993.

Fisher, Margery, review of *The Stone Menagerie, Growing Point,* September, 1980, p. 3756.

Fisher, review of *Madame Doubtfire, Growing Point,* September, 1987, p. 4858.

Fisher, review of *The Summer-House Loon* and *The Other, Darker Ned, Growing Point,* May, 1990, pp. 5343-44.

Fox, Charles, "Beyond Tact," *New Statesman,* December 2, 1983, p. 26.

Geller, Mark, review of *Alias Madame Doubtfire, New York Times Book Review,* May 1, 1988, p. 34.

Hammond, Nancy C., review of *The Granny Project, Horn Book,* October, 1983, p. 573.

Hollindale, Peter, "Teenage Tensions," *Times Literary Supplement,* July 7, 1978, p. 767.

Powling, Chris, "Relative Values," *Times Educational Supplement,* June 3, 1988, p. 49.

Schuller, Susan, review of *My War with Goggle-Eyes, School Library Journal,* May, 1989, p. 104.

Sutton, Roger, review of *Alias Madame Doubtfire, Bulletin of the Center for Children's Books,* April, 1988, p. 155.

Sutton, review of *My War with Goggle-Eyes, Bulletin of the Center for Children's Books,* May, 1989, p. 222.

FOR MORE INFORMATION SEE:

BOOKS

Children's Literature Review, Volume 25, Gale, 1991.

PERIODICALS

Growing Point, September, 1988.
New York Times, March 27, 1987, p. 21.
Spectator, July 4, 1987.
Times Literary Supplement, November 20, 1981.
Wilson Library Bulletin, February, 1990.

*   *   *

FLEISCHMAN, Paul 1952-

PERSONAL: Born September 5, 1952, in Monterey, CA; son of Albert Sidney (a children's author) and Beth (Taylor) Fleischman; married Becky Mojica (a nurse), December 15, 1978; children: Seth, Dana. *Education:* Attended University of California, Berkeley, 1970-72; University of New Mexico, B.A., 1977.

ADDRESSES: Home—855 Marino Pines, Pacific Grove, CA 93950.

CAREER: Author. Worked variously as a bagel baker, bookstore clerk, and proofreader.

MEMBER: Authors Guild, Society of Children's Book Writers.

AWARDS, HONORS: Silver Medal, Commonwealth Club of California, Golden Kite honor book, Society of Children's Book Writers, and *New York Times* outstanding book citation, all 1980, all for *The Half-a-Moon Inn;* Newbery honor book, American Library Association (ALA), 1983, for *Graven Images: Three Stories;* Golden Kite honor book, Society of Children's Book Writers, and Parents' Choice Award, Parents'

PAUL FLEISCHMAN

Choice Foundation, both 1983, both for *Path of the Pale Horse; Boston Globe-Horn Book* Award honor book, best books for young adults nomination, ALA, both 1988, and Newbery Medal, ALA, 1989, all for *Joyful Noise: Poems for Two Voices; Boston Globe-Horn Book* Award honor book, 1990, and ALA notable book, 1991, both for *Saturnalia;* Golden Kite Honor Book, 1992, for *The Borning Room.*

WRITINGS:

JUVENILE BOOKS

The Birthday Tree, illustrated by Marcia Sewall, Harper, 1979.
The Half-a-Moon Inn, illustrated by Kathy Jacobi, Harper, 1980.
Graven Images: Three Stories, illustrated by Andrew Glass, Harper, 1982.
The Animal Hedge (picture book), illustrated by Lydia Dabcovich, Dutton, 1983.
Path of the Pale Horse, Harper, 1983.
Phoebe Danger, Detective, in the Case of the Two-Minute Cough, illustrated by Margot Apple, Houghton, 1983.
Finzel the Farsighted, illustrated by Sewall, Dutton, 1983.
Coming-and-Going Men: Four Tales, illustrated by Randy Gaul, Harper, 1985.
I Am Phoenix: Poems for Two Voices, illustrated by Ken Nutt, Harper, 1985.
Rear-View Mirrors, Harper, 1986.
Rondo in C, illustrated by Janet Wentworth, Harper, 1988.
Joyful Noise: Poems for Two Voices, illustrated by Eric Beddows, Harper, 1988.
Saturnalia, Harper, 1990.
Shadow Play (picture book), illustrated by Beddows, Harper, 1990.
The Borning Room, HarperCollins, 1991.
Time Train, illustrated by Claire Ewart, HarperCollins, 1991.
Townsend's Warbler (nonfiction), HarperCollins, 1992.

OTHER

Contributor to various journals and magazines.

SIDELIGHTS: Paul Fleischman's writings encompass a variety of genres, from picture books and poetry to eerie tales and young adult novels, but all are unified by his intense attention to sound. Claiming he would be a musician if he had talent, Fleischman fills his works with musical words instead. He enhances his historic, mysterious tales and lyrical poetry with his sensual use of language, utilizing such writing techniques as alliteration and rhythm. And out of this language emerge intricate psychological and moral stories in which characters exhibit powerful emotional needs and make revealing discoveries about themselves and each other. "Fleischman establishes a storyteller's hold on his audience; they can put themselves in his hands with the assurance that they won't be disappointed," maintains a *Kirkus Reviews* contributor.

Growing up among books and music helped form Fleischman's distinct, lyrical style—which appears in his nonfiction, picture books, and verse collections such as *I Am Phoenix: Poems for Two Voices*. (Cover illustration by Ken Nutt.)

Fleischman first learned the importance of sound in stories from his father, Sid Fleischman, who also writes children's books. While growing up in Santa Monica, California, Fleischman would gather with the rest of his family to hear the chapters of his father's books as he completed them. "As well as being a good writer, he's an excellent reader," explains Fleischman in the *Fifth Book of Junior Authors*. "The sense of beginning communicated by the rhythm of an opening sentence, the feeling of closing inherent in a chapter's last line were unmistakable. His books brim with the pleasures to be found in the sounds of speech: dialect, forgotten turns of phrase, wonderful names for characters." Music itself became a major influence when Fleischman discovered the classical masters while in high school. He spent hours in the public library listening to such artists as Beethoven, Bach, and Brahms, learning how to shape his writing from what he heard.

Shortly after graduating from the University of New Mexico, Fleischman presented his father with a story he had written. The elder Fleischman recounted his reaction in *Horn Book*: "I read the pages with growing amazement. This was not a story written with the telltale creaks and groans of the beginner. It was a skilled handling of a difficult subject, the uncanny relationship between a boy and an apple tree planted in celebration of his birth. It was a bravura performance." Nevertheless, Fleischman's father was somewhat perplexed by his son's seemingly sudden blossoming: "How had Paul learned to stage manage his scenes, to fine tune the story tensions, to bring the characters to life?" Sid Fleischman then realized that his son, a "lightning-quick study," had been learning from his father all his life: "I simply hadn't noticed it."

Fleischman's fascination with the past, where he often sets his books, was also passed on to him from his father. "Like my father," comments Fleischman in the *Fifth Book of Junior Authors*, "I'm attracted to the past. From him I learned the joys of research: digging up old names, old words, old facts about how people dressed, what they ate, how they worked." Fleischman's two short story collections, *Graven Images: Three Stories* and *Coming-and-Going Men: Four Tales*, reflect this interest. Linked together by the dominant image of a sculpted figure, the stories in *Graven Images* are powerful and mysterious narratives that include everything from a comical love story to the tale of a sculptor commissioned by a disagreeable ghost. "Unusual in our day," asserts *Horn Book* contributor Ethel L. Heins, Fleischman's "timeless, elegant, figurative prose is fashioned with fluency and skill."

In *Coming-and-Going Men* Fleischman uses a central location, New Canaan, Vermont, to connect his stories of four travelling men. The men are salesmen or showmen, and each, while leaving a lasting impression on at least one of the inhabitants of New Canaan, is deeply affected by their visit to the town. A *Bulletin of the Center for Children's Books* contributor points out, "Period details (the year is 1800) are convincing, the language and the concepts of the characters are appropriate for the time and place, and the writing style is honed and polished in a book that is enjoyable almost as much for its style as for its story." And a *Kirkus Reviews* contributor concludes that "one can easily imagine Fleischman himself a coming-and-going man, fabricating his way through his storybook Early America and enthralling the populace with his illusionist's wordcraft." The author told the true story of a traveling man in the 1992 nonfiction book *Townsend's Warbler*, an account of two nineteenth-century naturalists whose trek across America is played against the migrations of an unnamed species of bird.

Fleischman pays particular attention to the crafting of his words in his two poetry collections, *I Am Phoenix: Poems for Two Voices* and *Joyful Noise: Poems for Two Voices*. Both works are designed to be read aloud by two alternating voices, and Fleischman's celebration of sound is evident throughout. The first collection, *I Am Phoenix*, extols a variety of birds, whereas the second, *Joyful Noise*, focuses on the diverse inhabitants of the insect world. "Fleischman steps imaginatively inside each insect and in fine, free verse gives that creature's own point of view on its unique qualities, life cycle, and

JOYFUL NOISE

Poems for Two Voices

PAUL FLEISCHMAN

illustrated by Eric Beddows

Designed to be read aloud by two alternating voices, Fleischman's Newbery Award-winner *Joyful Noise* imaginatively details the inhabitants of the insect world in verse. (Cover illustration by Eric Beddows.)

habits," describes Carolyn Phelan in *Booklist*. Although Katha Pollitt, writing in the *New York Times Book Review*, maintains that the "words and images" in *Joyful Noise* "are sometimes surprisingly flat and prosaic," Mary M. Burns claims in *Horn Book*: "The imagery throughout the volume is as remarkable as the technique: memorable but never intrusive, again because the words seem exactly right for the particular voice.... Each selection is a gem, polished perfection. If Paul Fleischman never wrote another book, his reputation would remain secure with this one."

With *Shadow Play*, a picture book published in 1990, Fleischman continues his rhythmic writing and combines elements of the past and the present. The book tells the story of a young brother and sister at a county fair. Having only a limited amount of money, they decide to exchange it for admission into a small theater where a shadow play of *Beauty and the Beast* is to be presented. The play takes an unexpected turn when a fierce bull storms into the story, but a young girl is able to tame him with her gentleness. After the show is over, the children and the reader are invited backstage and learn that one man alone made all the shadows. "The

grittiness of the relatively modern carnival is contrasted with the refined and graceful shadow play, set in an earlier, more elegant time," points out Arthur Yorinks in the *New York Times Book Review*. "This is what a picture book is meant to be—words, pictures, rhythm, pacing, all woven together to tell a complete story."

Although Fleischman sees the actual story being told as the most important element of his work, he derives the most pleasure out of the actual writing of it. "If I can please my readers' ears while telling my tale, such that a listener who knew no English would enjoy it read aloud purely for its music, so much the better," writes Fleischman in *Horn Book*. "Since I think the sense of my stories out in some detail before I put them into words, the spontaneous, joyful, serendipitous, and most satisfying side of writing for me is trying to do exactly that: moving this clause to take advantage of that rhyme, finding a four-syllable word for *slender,* playing with the length of sentences. Giving the sense a sound."

WORKS CITED:

Burns, Mary M., review of *Joyful Noise: Poems for Two Voices, Horn Book,* May-June, 1988, pp. 366-67.
Fleischman, Paul, essay in *Fifth Book of Junior Authors and Illustrators,* edited by Sally Holmes Holtze, H. W. Wilson, 1983, pp. 114-16.
Fleischman, Paul, "Sound and Sense," *Horn Book,* September-October, 1986, pp. 551-55.
Fleischman, Sid, "Paul Fleischman," *Horn Book,* July, 1989, pp. 452-455.
Heins, Ethel L., review of *Graven Images: Three Stories, Horn Book,* December, 1982, p. 656.
Phelan, Carolyn, review of *Joyful Noise: Poems for Two Voices, Booklist,* February 15, 1988, p. 1000.

The author combines the vitality and clamor of the carnival with the silent beauty of silhouettes in *Shadow Play*. (Cover illustration by Beddows.)

Pollitt, Katha, review of *Joyful Noise: Poems for Two Voices, New York Times Book Review,* March 26, 1989.
Review of *Coming-and-Going Men: Four Tales, Bulletin of the Center for Children's Books,* September, 1985.
Review of *Coming-and-Going Men: Four Tales, Kirkus Reviews,* May 15, 1985, pp. J32-J33.
Review of *Graven Images, Kirkus Reviews,* August 15, 1982, p. 937.
Yorinks, Arthur, "Backstage Secrets," *New York Times Book Review,* November 11, 1990, p. 52.

FOR MORE INFORMATION SEE:

BOOKS

Chevalier, Tracy, editor, *Twentieth-Century Children's Writers,* 3rd edition, St. James Press, 1989, pp. 349-50.
Children's Literature Review, Volume 20, Gale, 1990, pp. 63-70.

PERIODICALS

Booklist, June 15, 1980, p. 1531; June 1, 1983, p. 1275.
Bulletin of the Center for Children's Books, March, 1983, pp. 125-26; January, 1984; October, 1985, p. 26; April, 1986; February, 1988, p. 115.
Horn Book, June, 1980, p. 294; June, 1983, p. 289; May-June, 1986, pp. 329-30; September-October, 1988, p. 614; July, 1989, pp. 452-55; May-June, 1990, pp. 337-38; January-February, 1991, pp. 63-64.
Kirkus Reviews, May 15, 1979, p. 573; April 1, 1983, pp. 375-76; September 1, 1983, pp. J147-J148; December 15, 1987, p. 1732; September 15, 1988, p. 145.
New York Times, December 3, 1990.
New York Times Book Review, April 27, 1980, pp. 45, 67; November 28, 1982, p. 24; March 4, 1984, p. 31; September 8, 1985, p. 35; September 30, 1990, p. 39.
New York Times Magazine, November 28, 1982.
Publishers Weekly, February 25, 1983, p. 88; September 30, 1988, pp. 67-68; February 1, 1991, p. 81; March 29, 1991, p. 94.
School Library Journal, September, 1979, p. 110; May, 1983, p. 92; December, 1983, p. 65; November, 1985, p. 84; May, 1986, pp. 102-03; February, 1988, p. 79; May, 1988, pp. 48-49; November, 1988, p. 86.
Voice of Youth Advocates, June, 1986, p. 78; August, 1988, p. 145; June, 1990, p. 102.
Washington Post Book World, May 8, 1983, pp. 15, 18; August 12, 1990, p. 8; March 24, 1991, p. 12.

*   *   *

FRITZ, Jean (Guttery) 1915-

PERSONAL: Born November 16, 1915, in Hankow, China; daughter of Arthur Minton (a minister and YMCA missionary) and Myrtle (Chaney) Guttery; married Michael Fritz, November 1, 1941; children: David, Andrea. *Education:* Wheaton College, A.B., 1937; study at Columbia University.

ADDRESSES: Home—50 Bellewood Ave., Dobbs Ferry, NY 10522. *Agent*—Gina MacCoby Literary Agency, 1123 Broadway, Suite 1010, New York, NY 10010.

CAREER: Author of historical biographies and novels for young people. Silver Burdett Co., New York City, research assistant, 1937-41; Dobbs Ferry Library, Dobbs Ferry, NY, children's librarian, 1955-57; Jean Fritz Writers' Workshops, Katonah, NY, founder and instructor, 1962-70; Board of Co-operative Educational Service, Westchester County, NY, teacher, 1971-73; Appalachian State University, Boone, NC, faculty member, summers, 1980-82. Lecturer.

AWARDS, HONORS: New York Times outstanding book of the year citations, 1973, for *And Then What Happened, Paul Revere?,* 1974, for *Why Don't You Get a Horse, Sam Adams?,* 1975, for *Where Was Patrick Henry on the 29th of May?,* 1976, for *What's the Big Idea, Ben Franklin?,* 1981, for *Traitor: The Case of Benedict Arnold,* and 1982, for *Homesick: My Own Story; Boston Globe-Horn Book* honor book citations, 1974, for *And Then What Happened, Paul Revere?,* 1976, for *Will You Sign Here, John Hancock?,* and 1980, for *Stonewall;* named outstanding Pennsylvania author, Pennsylvania School Library Association, 1978; Honor Award for Nonfiction, Children's Book Guild, 1978, for the "body of her creative writing," and 1979; American Book Award nomination, 1980, for *Where Do You Think You're Going, Christopher Columbus?,* and 1981,

JEAN FRITZ

for *Traitor: The Case of Benedict Arnold;* LL.D., Washington and Jefferson College, 1982, Wheaton College, 1987; Child Study Award and Christopher Award, both 1982, Newbery Honor Book Award, American Book Award, and *Boston Globe-Horn Book* honor book, all 1983, all for *Homesick: My Own Story; Boston Globe-Horn Book* Nonfiction Award, 1984, for *The Double Life of Pocahontas,* and 1990, for *The Great Little Madison;* Regina Award, 1985; Laura Ingalls Wilder Award, 1986; Orbis Pictus Award, National Council of English Teachers, 1989, for *The Great Little Madison;* Knickerbocker Award for Juvenile literature, 1992; many of Fritz's books have been named notable books by the American Library Association.

WRITINGS:

FOR CHILDREN

Bunny Hopwell's First Spring, illustrated by Rachel Dixon, Wonder Books, 1954.

Help Mr. Willy Nilly, illustrated by Jean Tamburine, Treasure Books, 1954.

Fish Head, illustrated by Marc Simont, Coward, 1954.

Hurrah for Jonathan!, illustrated by Violet La Mont, A. Whitman, 1955.

121 Pudding Street, illustrated by Sofia, Coward, 1955.

Growing Up, illustrated by Elizabeth Webbe, Rand McNally, 1956.

Fritz is noted for her ability to take historical figures and events and bring them to life. (Cover illustration by Enrico Arno.)

The Late Spring, illustrated by Erik Blegvad, Coward, 1957.

The Cabin Faced West, illustrated by Feodor Rojankovsky, Coward, 1958.

(With Tom Club) *Champion Dog, Prince Tom,* illustrated by Ernest Hart, Coward, 1958.

The Animals of Doctor Schweitzer, illustrated by Douglas Howland, Coward, 1958.

How to Read a Rabbit, illustrated by Leonard Shortall, Coward, 1959.

Brady, illustrated by Lynd Ward, Coward, 1960.

Tap, Tap Lion, 1, 2, 3, illustrated by Shortall, Coward, 1962.

San Francisco, illustrated by Emil Weiss, Rand McNally, 1962.

I, Adam, illustrated by Peter Burchard, Coward, 1963.

Magic to Burn, illustrated by Beth Krush and Joe Krush, Coward, 1964.

Surprise Party (reader), illustrated by George Wiggins, Initial Teaching Alphabet Publications, 1965.

The Train (reader), illustrated by Jean Simpson, Grosset, 1965.

Early Thunder, illustrated by Ward, Coward, 1967.

George Washington's Breakfast, illustrated by Paul Galdone, Coward, 1969.

And Then What Happened, Paul Revere?, illustrated by Margot Tomes, Coward, 1973.

Why Don't You Get a Horse, Sam Adams?, illustrated by Trina Schart Hyman, Coward, 1974.

Where Was Patrick Henry on the 29th of May?, illustrated by Tomes, Coward, 1975.

Who's That Stopping on Plymouth Rock?, illustrated by J. B. Handelsman, Coward, 1975.

Will You Sign Here, John Hancock?, illustrated by Hyman, Coward, 1976.

What's the Big Idea, Ben Franklin?, illustrated by Tomes, Coward, 1976.

The Secret Diary of Jeb and Abigail: Growing Up in America, 1776-1783, illustrated by Kenneth Bald and Neil Boyle, Reader's Digest Association, 1976.

Can't You Make Them Behave, King George?, illustrated by Tomie de Paola, Coward, 1977.

Brendan the Navigator, illustrated by Enrico Amo, Coward, 1979.

Stonewall, illustrated by Stephen Gammell, Putnam, 1979.

Where Do You Think You're Going, Christopher Columbus?, illustrated by Tomes, Putnam, 1980.

The Man Who Loved Books, illustrated by Hyman, Putnam, 1981.

Traitor: The Case of Benedict Arnold, illustrated by John Andrew, Putnam, 1981.

Back to Early Cape Cod, Acorn Press, 1981.

The Good Giants and the Bad Pukwudgies (folktales), illustrated by de Paola, Putnam, 1982.

Homesick: My Own Story, illustrated by Tomes, Putnam, 1982.

The Double Life of Pocahontas, illustrated by Ed Young, Putnam, 1983.

China Homecoming, illustrated with photographs by Mike Fritz, Putnam, 1985.

Make Way for Sam Houston!, illustrated by Elise Primavera, Putnam, 1986.

Shh! We're Writing the Constitution, illustrated by de
  Paola, Putnam, 1987.
China's Long March: 6000 Miles of Danger, illustrated
  by Yang Zhr Cheng, Putnam, 1988.
The Great Little Madison, Putnam, 1989.
Bully for You, Teddy Roosevelt!, Putnam, 1991.
George Washington's Mother, illustrated by DyAnne
  DiSalvo-Ryan, Putnam, 1992.
(With Katherine Paterson, Fredrick & Patricia McKis-
  sack, Margaret Mahy, and Jamake Highwater) *The
  World in 1492,* illustrations by Stefano Vitale, Holt,
  1992.

OTHER

*Cast for a Revolution: Some American Friends and
  Enemies, 1728-1814* (adult biography), Houghton,
  1972.
(Contributor) William Zinsser, editor, *Worlds of Child-
  hood: The Art and Craft of Writing for Children,*
  Houghton, 1990.

Book reviewer, *San Francisco Chronicle,* 1941-43, and
New York Times, 1970—. Contributor of short stories to
periodicals, including *Seventeen, Redbook,* and *New
Yorker.*

Fritz's papers are housed in a permanent collection in
the Children's Literature Collection at the University of
Oregon, Eugene, and included in the Kerland Collection
at the University of Minnesota, and in a collection at the
University of Southern Mississippi.

ADAPTATIONS: Fritz's writings have been recorded on
audio cassette.

SIDELIGHTS: Jean Fritz is generally acknowledged as
being one of the best authors of historical biographies
written for young people. Although many of these
biographies are studies of American Revolutionary War
figures (including George Washington, Paul Revere,
Samuel Adams, and John Hancock), Fritz has also
published books on such people as Christopher Columbus, King George the Third, Pocahontas, St. Brendan
the Navigator, and Thomas Jonathon "Stonewall" Jackson. In 1978, Fritz was given the Children's Book
Guild's Honor Award for Nonfiction, paying tribute to
the "body of her creative writing."

Fritz has attributed her love of writing to the fact that
her childhood was most unusual and she needed an
outlet to record her thoughts and feelings. Fritz spent
the first thirteen years of her life in China because her
parents were doing missionary work. An only child,
Fritz often felt lonely and out of place in China. Writing
became her "private place, where no one could come,"
she recalls in a *Publishers Weekly* interview.

At an early age, Fritz told her parents she wanted to
become a writer and began keeping a journal. According
to O. Mell Busbin in *Dictionary of Literary Biography,*
this journal "at first consisted primarily of quotes from
books and poems she was reading but which soon
expanded into more than just a collection of comments

As an American growing up outside the United States,
Fritz became fascinated with patriotic heroes such as
George Washington. (Cover illustration by Paul
Galdone.)

on life by great writers; it became a place for her to
articulate her feelings about people and life. Years later
she drew upon it in her writings for children."

While living in China and separated from their homeland, Fritz's parents spoke glowingly of their memories
of the United States. Fritz listened to these stories with
intense interest, forming strong emotional bonds to
America. "I think it is because I was so far away that I
developed a homesickness that made me want to
embrace not just a given part of America at a given time
but the whole of it," Fritz writes in an article for *Horn
Book.* "No one is more patriotic than the one separated
from his country; no one is as eager to find roots as the
person who has been uprooted."

In addition to reminiscing about life in the United
States, Fritz's father frequently told her fascinating
stories about American heroes, especially his favorite,
Woodrow Wilson. In her award winning and critically
acclaimed biographies, Fritz seems to combine her keen
curiosity with American heroes and her appreciation for
this fine country to create books that are both fascinating to read and educational.

Critics have marvelled at the fact that a Fritz biography
consistently delivers a well-crafted, realistic, thoroughly

researched, and frequently witty look at the characters that have shaped and influenced our history. For example, in her *Language Arts* review of *Traitor: The Case of Benedict Arnold,* Ruth M. Stein notes that Fritz's "books exemplify criteria for good biographies—accuracy, interest, relevance to our times, and insight into the person, the period, and contemporaries.... However cozy the style and informal the writing, the scholarship is solid, yet unobtrusive. Primary and secondary material are woven so neatly into the narrative, you scarcely notice the internal documentation.... She manages to clarify her protagonist and the positions he took, even though she cannot be accused of remaining unbiased." And Georgess McHargue remarks in the *New York Times Book Review* that "Jean Fritz has what amounts to perfect pitch when writing history or biography for young people."

Fritz's talent for making her characters come to life is one of the major reasons for her popularity with readers and critics alike. As Busbin states in *Dictionary of Literary Biography:* "In her biographies Fritz attempts to get at the truth of the individual through his likes, dislikes, worries, joys, successes, failures. In each case she reveals the humanity of the individual, presenting his life as revealed in his diary, letters, and other original sources. Through her humorous style she paints a full, believable picture of each individual, using specific, exact language and precise detail. She refuses to create fictional dialogue for the characters in her biographies; the only conversation found in these books is that

Fritz often uses diaries, letters, and other original sources to enliven her historical biographies. (Cover illustration by Trina Schart Hyman.)

which she has discovered in letters, diaries, journals, and other original sources, which she draws upon plentifully." "I like being a detective, a treasure hunter, an eavesdropper," Fritz reveals to Richard Ammon in a profile for *Language Arts.* "I look for personalitites whose lives make good stories. I like complicated people, persons who possessed contradictions or who have interesting quirks."

In the *Los Angeles Times Book Review,* Barbara Karlin cites the reasons she feels Fritz's historical character studies are so well-received. Karlin explains in a review of *And Then What Happened, Paul Revere?, What's the Big Idea, Ben Franklin?,* and *Where Was Patrick Henry on the 29th of May?* that Fritz's "style is original for this type of book and is what makes these books so attractive to young readers—a friendly, almost chatty delivery, accessible and human subjects. They have foibles and frailties, neuroses and warts. She includes the kind of personal anecdotes and facts that kids find fascinating. Studying American history was never so much fun." And in an article on Fritz's *Homesick: My Own Story,* James A. Michener reports in the *New York Times Book Review* that what impresses him most is "the felicitous way in which Mrs. Fritz uses children's language and conveys the attitudes of a faraway land and period."

Fritz once shared her thoughts on the reasons behind her books' popularity with *CA:* "I think young people of almost any age or ability read biographies for the same reason that adults do—or would if they could find what they what. We all seek insight into the human condition, and it is helpful to find familiar threads running through the lives of others, however famous. We need to know more people in all circumstances and times so we can pursue our private, never-to-be-fulfilled quest to find out what life is all about. In actual experience we are able to see so few lives in the round and to follow them closely from beginning to end. I, for one, need to possess a certain number of relatively whole lives in the long span of history."

Fritz is also widely recognized for her juvenile novels, many of which (like her biographies) are set in colonial America at the time of the Revolutionary War. Most critics find that these books are written in the same clear, easy to read, informative style as her biographies. Fritz's research for these novels has been called extraordinary, and reviewers note that she has a habit of turning up new facts about familiar historical happenings. As a result, her work is often called refreshing and innovative; as Zena Sutherland, writing in the *Bulletin of the Center for Children's Books* observes, "Jean Fritz really has an approach to history that is unique; she makes it fun." And finally, Faith McNulty reflects in the *New Yorker* that "it is a rare writer who can recapture the intense feelings and bittersweet flavor of childhood as honestly and convincingly as Jean Fritz."

Fritz sums up her feelings on writing about America's past in her biographies and novels in this manner: "My interest in writing about American history stemmed originally, I think, from a subconscious desire to find

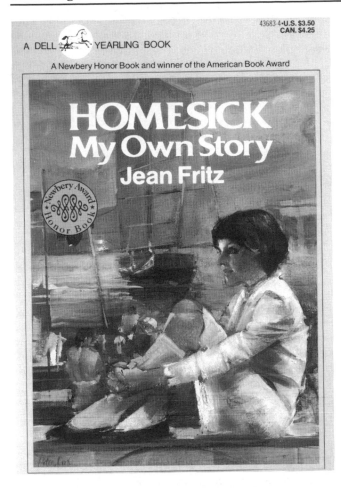

The author earned a Newbery Honor citation for her recollections of life in China and her journey to a "homeland" she had never seen.

roots. I lived in China until I was thirteen, hearing constant talk about 'home' (meaning America), but since I had never been 'home,' I felt like a girl without a country. I have put down roots quite firmly by now, but in the process I have discovered the joys of research and am probably hooked. I eavesdrop on the past to satisfy my own curiosity, but if I can surprise children into believing history, I will be happy, especially if they find, as I do, that truth is stranger (and often funnier) than fiction."

WORKS CITED:

Ammon, Richard, "Profile: Jean Fritz," *Language Arts,* March, 1983, pp. 365-69.

Busbin, O. Mell, *Dictionary of Literary Biography,* Volume 52: *American Writers for Children since 1960: Fiction,* Gale, 1986.

Horn Book, October, 1967.

Karlin, Barbara, review of *And Then What Happened, Paul Revere?, What's the Big Idea, Ben Franklin?,* and *Where Was Patrick Henry on the 29th of May?, Los Angeles Times Book Review,* July 25, 1982, p. 9.

McHargue, Georgess, "Early Explorers," *New York Times Book Review,* November 9, 1980, pp. 60-1.

McNulty, Faith, review of *Homesick: My Own Story, New Yorker,* December 6, 1982.

Mitchener, James A., "China Childhood," *New York Times Book Review,* November 14, 1982, pp. 41, 57.

Stein, Ruth M., review of *Traitor: The Case of Benedict Arnold, Language Arts,* September, 1982, p. 605.

Sutherland, Zena, review of *Where Was Patrick Henry on the 29th of May?, Bulletin of the Center for Children's Books,* November, 1975, p. 44.

FOR MORE INFORMATION SEE:

BOOKS

Children's Literature Review, Gale, Volume 2, 1976, Volume 14, 1988.

Hostetler, Elizabeth Ann Rumer, *Jean Fritz: A Critical Biography,* University of Toledo, 1981.

Norton, Donna E., *Through the Eyes of a Child: An Introduction to Children's Literature,* 2nd edition, Merrill, 1987.

Something about the Author Autobiography Series, Volume 2, Gale, 1986.

PERIODICALS

Bulletin of the Center for Children's Books, March, 1961; March, 1974; July/August, 1982.

Catholic Library World, July/August, 1985.

Early Years, February, 1982.

Five Owls, May/June, 1987.

Horn Book, October, 1967; January/February, 1985; July/August, 1986.

Language Arts, February, 1977; April, 1980.

Publishers Weekly, July 24, 1981.

San Francisco Chronicle, April 3, 1985.

School Library Journal, November, 1967.

Top of the News, June, 1976.

G

GAGE, Wilson
See STEELE, Mary Q(uintard Govan)

*   *   *

GARNET, A. H.
See SLOTE, Alfred

*   *   *

GELMAN, Amy 1961-

PERSONAL: Born August 18, 1961, in New York, NY; daughter of David (a journalist) and Elaine (a nurse practitioner; maiden name, Rodkinson) Gelman; married Eric Haugesag (a lighting technician), September 16, 1990. *Education:* Barnard College, B.A., 1983; attended University of Texas at Austin, 1984-86. *Politics:* "Left of center."

CAREER: Linguistics Research Center, University of Texas at Austin, researcher, 1984-88; Twin/Tone Records, Minneapolis, MN, director of publicity and marketing, 1986-88; Lerner Publications/Carolrhoda Books, Minneapolis, editor and foreign rights manager, 1988—; free-lance writer and translator, 1988—.

WRITINGS:

New York, Lerner Publications, 1992.
Connecticut, Lerner Publications, 1992.

TRANSLATOR

Fanny Joly and Brigitte Boucher, *Marceau Bonappetit,* illustrated by Agnes Mathieu, Carolrhoda, 1989.
Siegfried Aust, *Flight! Free as a Bird,* illustrated by Hans Poppel, Lerner Publications, 1991.
Aust, *Communication! News Travels Fast,* illustrated by Rolf Rettich, Lerner Publications, 1991.
Aust, *Lenses! Take a Closer Look,* illustrated by Helge Nyncke, Lerner Publications, 1991.
Wolfgang Epple, *Clocks! How Time Flies,* illustrated by Poppel, Lerner Publications, 1991.
Epple, *Barn Owls,* illustrated by Manfred Rogl, Carolrhoda, 1992.

Elvig Hansen, *Guinea Pigs,* self-illustrated, Carolrhoda, 1992.

WORK IN PROGRESS: "I am currently working on two young adult novels, one on 'female bonding' and the other on white involvement in the civil rights era in the early 1960s; researching personal histories from the civil rights era."

*   *   *

GIBBONS, Gail (Gretchen) 1944-

PERSONAL: Born August 1, 1944, in Oak Park, IL; daughter of Harry George (a tool and die designer) and Grace (Johnson) Ortmann; married Glenn Gibbons, June 25, 1966 (died May 20, 1972); married Kent Ancliffe (a builder), March 23, 1976; children: (stepchildren) Rebecca, Eric. *Education:* University of Illinois, B.F.A., 1967.

GAIL GIBBONS

New England's coastal islands and villages—where the author sometimes resides—have provided the material for several works, including this book about seasonal living on an island. (Illustration by the author from *Surrounded by Sea.*)

ADDRESSES: Home—Corinth, VT 05039. *Office*—Goose Green, Corinth, VT 05039. *Agent*—Florence Alexander, 80 Park Ave., New York, NY 10017.

CAREER: Free-lance writer and illustrator of children's books, 1975—. WCIA-Television, Champaign, IL, artist, 1967-69; WMAQ-TV, Chicago, IL, promotions and animation artist, 1969; Bob Hower Agency, Chicago, staff artist, 1969-70; WNBC-Television, House of Animation, New York, NY, staff artist, 1970-76; United Press International, New York City, free-lance artist, 1977—.

AWARDS, HONORS: New York City Art Director Club award, 1979, for *The Missing Maple Syrup Sap Mystery;* American Institute of Graphic Arts award, 1979, for the *Clocks and How They Go;* National Science Teachers Association/Children's Book Council Award, 1980, for *Locks and Keys,* and 1982, for *Tool Book;* certificate of appreciation from U.S. Postmaster General, 1982, for *The Post Office Book: Mail and How It Moves;* American Library Association Notable Book award, 1983, for *Cars and How They Go,* and 1985, for *The Milk Makers; Washington Post* Children's Book Guild Award, 1987, for contribution to nonfiction children's literature.

WRITINGS:

SELF-ILLUSTRATED NONFICTION CHILDREN'S BOOKS

Willy and His Wheel Wagon, (Junior Literary Guild selection), Prentice-Hall, 1975.
Salvador and Mister Sam: A Guide to Parakeet Care, Prentice-Hall, 1976.
Things to Make and Do for Halloween, F. Watts, 1976.
Things to Make and Do for Columbus Day, F. Watts, 1977.
Things to Make and Do for Your Birthday, F. Watts, 1978.
The Missing Maple Syrup Sap Mystery, Warne, 1979.
Clocks and How They Go, Crowell, 1979.
Locks and Keys, Crowell, 1980.
The Too Great Bread Bake Book, Warne, 1980.
Trucks, Crowell, 1981.
The Magnificent Morris Mouse Clubhouse, F. Watts, 1981.
Tool Book, Holiday House, 1982.
The Post Office Book: Mail and How It Moves, Crowell, 1982.
Christmas Time, Holiday House, 1982.
Boat Book, Holiday House, 1983.
Paper, Paper, Everywhere, Harcourt, 1983.
Thanksgiving Day, Holiday House, 1983.

New Road!, Crowell, 1983.
Sun Up, Sun Down, Harcourt, 1983.
Department Store, Crowell, 1984.
Fire! Fire!, Crowell, 1984.
Halloween, Holiday House, 1984.
The Seasons of Arnold's Apple Tree, Harcourt, 1984.
Tunnels, Holiday House, 1984.
Check It Out! The Book about Libraries, Harcourt, 1985.
Lights! Camera! Action! How a Movie Is Made, Crowell, 1985.
Fill It Up! All about Service Stations, Crowell, 1985.
The Milk Makers, Macmillan/Collier, 1985.
Playgrounds, Holiday House, 1985.
Flying, Holiday House, 1986.
From Path to Highway: The Story of the Boston Post Road, Crowell, 1986.
Happy Birthday!, Holiday House, 1986.
Up Goes the Skyscraper!, Four Winds, 1986.
Valentine's Day, Holiday House, 1986.
Deadline! From News to Newspaper, Crowell, 1987.
Dinosaurs, Holiday House, 1987.
The Pottery Place, Harcourt, 1987.
Trains, Holiday House, 1987.
Weather Forecasting, Four Winds, 1987.
Zoo, Crowell, 1987.
Dinosaurs, Dragonflies and Diamonds: All about Natural History Museums, Four Winds, 1988.
Farming, Holiday House, 1988.
Prehistoric Animals, Holiday House, 1988.
Sunken Treasure, Crowell, 1988.
Catch the Wind! All about Kites, Little, Brown, 1989.
Easter, Holiday House, 1989.
Marge's Diner, Crowell, 1989.
Monarch Butterfly, Holiday House, 1989.
Beacons of Light: Lighthouses, Morrow, 1990.
Weather Words and What They Mean, Holiday House, 1990.
How a House Is Built, Holiday House, 1990.
The Puffins Are Back!, HarperCollins, 1991.
From Seed to Plant, Holiday House, 1991.
Surrounded by Sea: Life on a New England Fishing Island, Little. Brown, 1991.
Whales, Holiday House, 1991.
The Great St. Lawrence Seaway, Morrow, 1992.
Sharks, Holiday House, 1992.
Recycle! A Handbook for Kids, Little, Brown, 1992.
Say Woof!: The Day of a Country Veterinarian, Macmillan, 1992.
Stargazers, Holiday House, 1992.

ILLUSTRATOR

Yolen, Jane, *Rounds about Rounds*, F. Watts, 1977.
Judith Enderle, *Good Junk*, Dandelion Press, 1979.
Catherine Chase, *Hot & Cold*, Dandelion Press, 1979.
Chase, *My Balloon*, Dandelion Press, 1979.
Chase, *Pete, the Wet Pet*, Dandelion Press, 1979.
Chase, *The Mouse at the Show*, Dandelion Press, 1980.
Cole, Joanna, *Cars and How They Go*, Crowell, 1983.
Asch, Frank, *Baby in the Box*, Holiday House, 1989.

ADAPTATIONS: Christmas Time, Dinosaurs, and *Check It Out! The Book about Libraries* have been made into filmstrips and cassettes; *The Milk Makers, Check It*

Out! The Book about Libraries, Fill It Up! All about Service Stations, Lights! Camera! Action! How a Movie Is Made, and *Sunken Treasure* have all been featured on *Reading Rainbow.*

SIDELIGHTS: Gail Gibbons is an award-winning author and illustrator of nonfiction books for children that explain the stories behind objects and concepts youngsters encounter every day. Included among her book topics are newspapers, clocks, trains, various species of animals, and a range of holidays from Columbus Day to Christmas.

Born in Illinois to parents with artistic talents, Gibbons always had a need "to put words down on paper and draw and paint pictures," she once wrote in an essay for *Something about the Author Autobiography Series* (*SAAS*). "I never had to debate with myself as to what I wanted to do with my life," Gibbons recalled for *SAAS.* "The answer was always there. I wanted to be a writer and an artist."

A voracious reader as well as a prolific artist, Gibbons discovered early on that her creative talents provided her with a unique way of fulfilling her wishes. At the age of ten, when her own desire for a dog was thwarted by an apartment policy which didn't allow pets, Gibbons put together a picture book about a girl with a dog named Flip. At about the same time, she visited a Wisconsin farm with a friend and found it "the most marvelous place on earth," she recalled for *SAAS.* When

"It's there! It's really there!"
The rotting hull of a ship has been found on the ocean floor. Within the wreck lies a fabulous treasure.

Gibbons began drawing at a young age, when she would make her own "books" to help her recreate her favorite places and things. (Illustration by the author from *Sunken Treasure.*)

Gibbons brings her talent for explaining the process behind everyday enterprises to the restaurant business in her self-illustrated *Marge's Diner*.

she returned home, she missed the farm so much that she put together another book about her enjoyable experiences there. "I found myself writing and drawing pictures of what I loved and where I wanted to be. It became a form of expressing myself," she wrote.

As an adult, Gibbons continued to find satisfaction in artistic expression. After graduating with a B.F.A. from the University of Illinois art school, Gibbons found work as a graphic artist with a television station where she created sets, animation and on-air graphics. When she and her husband moved to New York a few years later, she began working for WNBC-TV on such shows as *Nightly News* and *Saturday Night Live.* It wasn't long before Gibbons, looking for a change of pace, found herself working on a children's show called *Take a Giant Step.* The children on the series were impressed with her artistic abilities and asked if she had ever done a children's book. That question ignited a spark in Gibbons' mind. "All of a sudden a lot of what I had been interested in came rushing at me," she recalled in

her *SAAS* essay. "Why don't I do a children's book?" she asked herself.

Unfortunately, Gibbons' plans were left temporarily unrealized when her husband, only twenty-eight years old, died suddenly. It took Gibbons several years before she felt ready to devote herself to her work again. When she finally did begin working, she decided to try her hand at a children's book and was pleased to meet with success on her very first try. Illustrating the concept of set theory to children learning new math, *Willy and His Wheel Wagon* was named a Junior Literary Guild selection soon after its release.

Once her writing career was well on its way, Gibbons began to feel she wanted to escape the New York lifestyle. The solution she found was to split her time between work in the city and relaxation in Provincetown, Massachusetts. It was there that she met her future husband, Kent Ancliffe, with whom she started a new life in Vermont. Their adventures in New England provided Gibbons with new ideas for children's books, including *The Missing Maple Syrup Sap Mystery,* which Gibbons wrote after she and Kent tapped thousands of sugar maple trees on their 240 acres.

While Gibbons' books were well-received, it wasn't until she began writing nonfiction books that she truly found her niche. Gibbons was led to the genre when several acquaintances mentioned the lack of visually exciting children's nonfiction on the market. When her own research confirmed these remarks, she began work on *Clocks and How They Go,* which Barbara Elleman of *Booklist* complimented for its "concisely worded text and clean line work over bold, contrasting colors." In the *Horn Book Magazine,* Ann A. Flowers called it "an admirable example of the kind of book that explains for the young reader how mechanical things work."

"Nonfiction requires a tremendous amount of research," Gibbons told *SAAS.* "I want it to be accurate and up-to-date information.... To me, researching for a book is one of my favorite parts of doing a book. I've had some wonderful experiences." Gibbons' books on paper, fire, newspapers and farming have led her to paper mills, fire stations, newsrooms, and a dairy farm. Her popularity among children, teachers, and librarians has resulted in many speaking engagements. "Some of the people I've met along the way have been very delightful and many of them I've kept in touch with over the years. I've also been able to travel to many interesting parts of the country," Gibbons told *SAAS.*

Gibbons continues to write nonfiction books about topics which interest her and her young readers. Critical praise seems to follow as each new book is published. "Hooray for Gail Gibbons!" wrote Beverly Woods in *Children's Book Review Service.* "She consistently comes up with colorful, factual and well-presented books on topics of great interest to young children." Most recently, Gibbons' purchase of a cottage on the coast of Maine spawned an interest in a neighboring lighthouse, the whales in the area, and the puffins that inhabited a nearby island. All these became topics for her books. "I must be excited about a subject enough to write about it, so I find personal interests very important in my decision making," she once told *SAAS.*

WORKS CITED:

Elleman, Barbara, review of *Clocks and How They Go, Booklist,* November 1, 1979, p. 448.
Flowers, Ann A., review of *Clocks and How They Go, Horn Book Magazine,* December, 1979, p. 676.
Gibbons, Gail, article in *Something about the Author Autobiography Series,* Volume 12, Gale, 1991, p. 71.
Woods, Beverly, review of *Fire! Fire!, Children's Book Review Service,* September, 1984, p. 2.

FOR MORE INFORMATION SEE:

PERIODICALS

Children's Literature Review, Volume 8, Gale, 1985.
Horn Book, January, 1986, p. 97.

Junior Literary Guild, March, 1984; April, 1986; September, 1986; October, 1987; March, 1988.
Publishers Weekly, February 26, 1988.
School Library Journal, March, 1987.

* * *

GIBSON, Andrew (William) 1949-

PERSONAL: Born April 27, 1949, in London, England; son of William Thorburne (a headmaster) and Elizabeth (a teacher; maiden name, Howard) Gibson; married Pamela Nary, 1977 (divorced, 1987); children: William Alexander Philip, Thomas Peter Tregarthen. *Education:* St. John's College, Oxford, B.A. (with honors), 1970.

ADDRESSES: Home—11A, Ashness Rd., London SW11 6RY, England. *Office*—Royal Holloway and Bedford New College, Egham Hill, Surrey TW20 0EX, England. *Agent*—Rosemary Canter, Jung Hall, Ltd., The Chambers, No. 504, Chelsea Harbour, London SW10 0XF, England.

CAREER: Writer. Hong Kong University, Hong Kong, lecturer in comparative literature, 1973-76; Royal Holloway and Bedford New College, Egham Hill, England, lecturer in English, 1977-90, senior lecturer in English, 1990—.

ANDREW GIBSON

WRITINGS:

JUVENILE

Ellis and the Hummick, Faber, 1989.
The Abradizil, Faber, 1990.
Jemima, Grandma, and the Great Lost Zone, Faber, 1991.
The Rollickers and Other Stories, Faber, in press.

Also author of *The Amazing Witherspoon's Amazing Circus Crew,* 1991.

OTHER

Reading Narrative Discourse, Macmillan, 1990.
Pound in Perspective, in press.

WORK IN PROGRESS: A collection of essays on the "Circle" episode in Joyce's *Ulysses;* a book about postmodernism and narrative theory.

SIDELIGHTS: Andrew Gibson spent most of his youth in Cornwall. "I ... have vivid memories of a Cornish childhood," he told *SATA.* "The green country lanes; the plant life; and, above all, the constant trips to the sea .... It was a good place to be for a child with a little imagination, and I haven't forgotten it." Young Gibson was an avid reader whose favorite authors included Robert Louis Stevenson and Rudyard Kipling. Gibson noted that these writers "became a kind of world ... which I really think I never lost. It comes back in my own books in all sorts of different ways."

Gibson was inspired to write for young people by the birth of his sons. "Having children reawoke the storyteller in me. To invent tales for my children, and to tell tales to please or comfort them, seemed natural enough, an extension of our physical relationship," he reported to *SATA.* Most of Gibson's fiction has featured fantastic themes and situations, something the author feels is lacking in much of today's literature for young audiences: "I ... tend to feel that one of the besetting vices of the English is their incessant demand for realism .... I want to see other things before children. I would like my books to make the world richer for children—as the best children's writers have usually done—rather than reflecting its poverties."

* * *

GILCHRIST, Jan Spivey 1949-

PERSONAL: Born February 15, 1949, in Chicago, IL; daughter of Charles (a minister) and Arthric (a homemaker; maiden name, Jones) Spivey; married Arthur Van Johnson (an auditor), August 1, 1970 (divorced, August, 1980); married Kelvin Keith Gilchrist (an administrator), September 5, 1983; children: (first marriage) Ronke Diarra; (second marriage) William Kelvin. *Education:* Eastern Illinois University, B.S., 1973; University of Northern Iowa, M.A., 1979; attended Hartwick College, 1985.

JAN SPIVEY GILCHRIST

ADDRESSES: Home and office—82 Graymoor Lane, Olympia Fields, IL 60461. *Agent*—Marie Brown Associates, 625 Broadway, New York, NY 10012.

CAREER: Fine artist for twenty years, exhibiting throughout North America; Chicago Board of Education, Chicago, IL, substitute teacher, 1973-76; Harvey Schools, Harvey, IL, art teacher, 1976-79; Cambridge School Department, Cambridge, MA, art teacher, 1980-81; Joliet Public Schools, Joliet, IL, art teacher, 1982-83; free-lance artist in Glenwood, IL, 1983—. Member of board of Illinois Library Association. Juried full member of Ward-Nasse Gallery.

MEMBER: Phi Delta Kappa, honorary member of Alpha Kappa Alpha.

AWARDS, HONORS: Commissions from Eastern Illinois University, 1974, and State of Illinois Families with a Future campaign, 1986-87; purchase awards, Du Sable Museum, 1983-85; Coretta Scott King Book Award (illustration), American Library Association—Social Responsibilities Round Table, 1990, for *Nathaniel Talking,* and 1992, for *Night on Neighborhood Street;* Distinguished Alumni Award, Eastern Illinois University, 1992.

WRITINGS:

SELF-ILLUSTRATED

Indigo and Moonlight Gold, Black Butterfly Children's Books, 1992.

ILLUSTRATOR

Lessie Jones Little, *Children of Long Ago* (poetry), Philomel, 1988.

Eloise Greenfield, *Nathaniel Talking* (poetry), Black Butterfly Children's Books, 1988.

Greenfield, *Big Friend, Little Friend,* Black Butterfly Children's Books, 1991.

Lucille Clifton, *Everett Anderson's Christmas Coming,* Holt, 1991.

Greenfield, *First Pink Light,* Black Butterfly Children's Books, 1991.

Greenfield, *I Make Music,* Black Butterfly Children's Books, 1991.

Greenfield, *My Daddy and I,* Black Butterfly Children's Books, 1991.

Greenfield, *My Doll, Keshia,* Black Butterfly Children's Books, 1991.

Greenfield, *Night on Neighborhood Street* (poetry), Dial Books for Young Readers, 1991.

Sharon Bell Mathis, *Red Dog Blue Fly* (poetry), Viking, 1991.

Greenfield, *Aaron and Gayla's Alphabet Book,* Black Butterfly Children's Books, 1992.

James Weldon Johnson, *Lift Every Voice and Sing,* HarperCollins, 1993.

Greenfield, *William and the Good Old Days,* HarperCollins, 1993.

Also illustrator of *Aaron and Gayla's Counting Book,* Black Butterfly Children's Books; *Sweet Baby Coming,* by Greenfield, 1993; *The Baby,* by Monica Greenfield, 1993. Work represented in permanent collections, including those owned by the Du Sable Museum and the Southside Community Art Center.

SIDELIGHTS: After illustrating *Nathaniel Talking,* a 1988 collection of poetry by Eloise Greenfield, Jan Spivey Gilchrist received both widespread critical recognition and the 1990 Coretta Scott King Book Award. In addition to collaborating with Greenfield on numerous books, Gilchrist has provided artwork for authors including Sharon Bell Mathis and Lucille Clifton. Her illustrations promote the positive representation of African Americans in children's literature with characters who interact with family and spend time with friends. She has been praised by reviewers for the effective use of light and shadow in her illustrations and for her ability to capture a wide range of emotions in her artwork.

Gilchrist was raised on the south side of Chicago in a close-knit community. She remarked in an interview with *Something about the Author* (*SATA*) that "the kids in the neighborhood played at night on porches while everybody watched the mother—whoever's porch we were sitting on, that person's mother was the mother. We played games on the sidewalks. We got into blankets and lay down on the porch. This would keep the children off the streets and in their backyards." She added, "Our family generally had more children visit than any other because each one of us had friends and my mother loved having kids around."

The porch was a very significant place for Gilchrist as a child. At a young age, she was afflicted with a bone disease that kept her from becoming involved in physical activities that might have caused her injury. When she first became aware of her handicap, she felt a sense of alienation in not being able to participate in the games that children played in front of her house. In her interview she recalled "the feeling that I had become separate from my friends—like the fun stopped at the porch and then I felt very lonely for a while with life. And then I picked up my pen and I picked up my pencil and I realized that I could do something because I had been drawing since I was little, and that didn't have to stop because I was sitting there. And people would come and sit on the porch and I would draw them."

As a child, Gilchrist copied pictures from a lavishly illustrated version of the Bible which belonged to her father, who was a minister. Among her favorite stories to interpret were accounts of the birth of Jesus Christ because they included familial images of the Virgin Mary and Joseph with the baby Jesus. Gilchrist was fascinated with babies from an early age and was grateful that many of her siblings were born in the

Gilchrist's childhood in a close-knit Chicago neighborhood is reflected in her many portraits of children at play. (Illustration by Gilchrist from *Aaron and Gayla's Alphabet Book,* by Eloise Greenfield.)

Gilchrist portrays the special relationship between a boy and his father in this scene from Eliose Greenfield's *Nathaniel Talking*.

family house because it gave her the opportunity to draw them at various stages of infancy.

Gilchrist's parents both encouraged their child's interest in art at an early age. With her father she often went to the Art Institute of Chicago and was shocked by the lack of artwork that depicted African Americans. She told *SATA:* "I thought of it as a chronological problem. I thought that we weren't 'invented' yet. Being a child, I didn't understand time and how things come about—I wanted to see the section where we were invented so I could see us. And it was a shock when I found out that there was no area in the museum where we were represented. I was in denial. I just wanted it never to happen again. When you're very little and you're surrounded by a number of people who say you are great, you are gifted, you are talented, you believe that you can do anything. So I decided that I was going to change everything. I was going to make sure that African Americans were in paintings and in books."

Gilchrist's teachers also encouraged her to develop her creative talent. In her interview, she spoke of the unique position that a child artist enjoys in a classroom environment: "When you're an artist, kids aren't jealous of you. They are proud of you; you're the artist in the class. I think in some other things like sports, there is jealousy. But with an artist, kids will say, 'This is our artist, Jan.' And teachers kind of fall in line because they don't have to worry about making the other children jealous."

Although Gilchrist was constantly reminded of her potential as an artist, her father recommended that she study for a career. Gilchrist elaborated in her interview: "My parents always thought that art was a gift; they never stopped pushing that. But my father, he would always say, 'You have to eat.'" Following his practical advice, Gilchrist continued her education in college with the intention of teaching. The decision to study was not difficult however. Throughout her early life she had motivated herself to learn. She told *SATA:* "I used to go to the library and get books that were really big and really hard because I wanted to be a scholar. And the important thing was that the books were inside of me. Somehow I thought that if I could read Geoffrey Chaucer's *Canterbury Tales,* if I could read William Shakespeare's plays, if I could read Ernest Hemingway's work, then I was a big person—that that was enough—not that someone had to hand me a degree for it."

As an undergraduate at Eastern Illinois University, Gilchrist took several art classes and admittedly made her share of mistakes. "Being young and wanting to shine, I tried to adapt myself to what was popular and at the time a lot of the work around was dishonest," she said. "With age you get more confident with yourself and you learn." After her graduation, Gilchrist conducted classes in Illinois and gained further insight from her teaching experiences into the value of honesty in art. She stated in her interview that young people have respect for "the law of the book—even if it's fiction, it's still law to them. I've learned that I cannot cheat them, I

A girl's special memories of her late mother are captured in Gilchrist's soft brushstrokes in this scene from her first self-illustrated book, *Indigo and Moonlight Gold.*

cannot lie to them in a book. I cannot negatively put in sexist or racist images. That can happen with illustrations—you can say, 'This is a neighborhood,' then you can paint something very ugly to represent a neighborhood—a stereotype. For me it's very important that I am true and honest and absent of stereotypes in my work." She added that instructors often unintentionally send mixed messages in pushing the value of books without informing their students that some stories promote negativity.

In addition to teaching, Gilchrist continued to paint; her first husband did not, however, support her artistic career. Hoping to find the encouragement that she needed to develop creatively, Gilchrist attended the University of Northern Iowa in the late 1970s and worked for a master's degree. She lived in an apartment and converted it—with the exception of her daughter's bedroom—into "a gallery." While in Iowa she benefited from working in "a secure, peaceful kind of environment" that reminded her of her tranquil childhood neighborhood. In her interview she spoke of how her upbringing has helped her to portray people affirmatively in her drawings: Gilchrist focuses on "that mother holding that child's hand crossing the street. And she has this other baby in her arm who is looking up at the stoplight. Well some people don't see that. They're looking for something negative that's happening on the other side of the street. I still gravitate toward that same positive feeling that I grew up with."

After gaining attention for her paintings for nearly twenty years, Gilchrist received the opportunity to illustrate children's books. She told *SATA* that she might have been led into the new field by critics of her paintings who often said, "'Her work is quite narrative, illustrative.' These were words that were, I guess, hints to say that this is where I belonged." Encouraged by a colleague, she went to a gathering which was attended by notable author Eloise Greenfield. Gilchrist had often read Greenfield's work to her daughter because the books promoted positive images of African Americans. In her interview she said, "You looked at Eloise Greenfield's books, and there you saw African Americans whereas other books didn't seem to have any African Americans. And the characters had lives like yours—real lives. There was a father there. And a mother. And they were doing real things that you saw on the street—they were doing normal things. When you grow up African-American, you don't often see pictures of yourself, the way you are, the way you live." When Gilchrist went to the reception, she took slides of her art as well as a picture of a little girl, which she intended to present to Greenfield as a gift. Upon seeing her work, the author suggested that Gilchrist illustrate children's books.

Two weeks later, Gilchrist received a call from the author and was asked to send art samples to Philomel, a publisher in New York. She convinced her second husband, whom she had married in 1983, that she would increase her chances of being accepted as an illustrator if she personally presented her work to

Patricia Gow, the editor in chief. With the full support of her husband, she and her family then traveled to New York together. Unfamiliar with standard procedures in showing her artwork, Gilchrist went to the publisher without setting up an appointment and begged Gow to allow her an interview. After seeing her work, the editor offered her the opportunity to illustrate *Children of Long Ago,* a book of poetry written by Eloise Greenfield's mother, Lessie Jones Little.

In her interview with *SATA* Gilchrist spoke affectionately of *Children of Long Ago,* which focuses on African Americans who lived in the early 1900s. Through her work on the project, Gilchrist became closer to her grandfather, who was able to inform her of his own experiences in the South near the turn of the century. Commenting on the illustrator's work, Lucille Clifton of the *New York Times Book Review* remarked that "the soft pastel drawings ... of people going about their activities but caught in a golden light are a perfect complement to the verses."

In 1988 Gilchrist illustrated *Nathaniel Talking,* a book of Greenfield's poetry in which an African-American boy relates his experiences and feelings while growing up. Nathaniel's manner of speaking varies throughout the book, and reviewers complimented Greenfield for her ability to write verse that is modeled after such musical forms of expression as rap and the blues. In regard to the illustrations, Mary M. Burns of *Horn Book* complimented Gilchrist for providing drawings that "match the vitality and dynamism of the text." After commending Greenfield and Gilchrist for the unified feel of their work, she stated that *Nathaniel Talking* is "a marvelous book in subject, execution, and design."

In addition to receiving critical praise for her work, Gilchrist won the Coretta Scott King Book Award for illustrating *Nathaniel Talking.* At the time that she received the award, she felt mixed emotions because her mother was fatally ill at the time. She told *SATA:* "I come from a religious background, and sometimes you don't know whether to be too happy when someone else is very sad. You don't want to be disrespectful. After I found out about the award, I was slapped back into reality—my mother was dying. My mother, she was bedridden and she was almost comatose right before she died—she was back and forth all the time. Sometimes she could look and understand me. I told her what happened and she said she was so proud of me. That meant a lot."

Gilchrist welcomed the opportunity to illustrate *Nathaniel Talking* using only black and white, even though it was risky to print a book without multicolored pictures. The project allowed her to work in pencil, the medium that she had grown accustomed to using as a child. In her interview, the illustrator remarked: "The pencil is my baby. I didn't have any chalk as a child so I made grand, grand things with the pencil. And for years I only used a number-two pencil because I didn't know anything else. I had full control over it." People often bought her other types of pencils to experiment with,

Gilchrist has had a rich and fruitful partnership with Eloise Greenfield; for her illustrations for *Nathaniel Talking,*
Gilchrist used pencil drawings to capture the feelings of an intelligent, proud, and hopeful African-American boy.

but Gilchrist rarely used them. "I put them on the other side because I couldn't do anything with them. I could do all this with a number-two which made me feel kind of good because everyone was making me out to be this great big gifted person. If they only knew how easy it was with only one pencil."

Working in pencil also kept Gilchrist from interfering with Greenfield's poetry. In her interview she related: "I was thinking this is Nathaniel talking and I don't want to mess it up with color. When I was a little girl, my mother would say, 'Baby is talking. Baby just learned how to talk. Just put yourself together and listen to children, and they will tell you what's going on. They may not be able to use all the words that we have the way we have them. But if you listen very carefully, you'll understand.' When I did the work, I wanted to make sure that I didn't interrupt any of the words of that child."

As with all of her illustration projects, Gilchrist used real people as models for the characters in *Nathaniel Talking*. Regarding Michael, the young person who inspired the title figure, Gilchrist acknowledged: "He was a little, tiny, brilliant person and he was of strong will and he knew what he wanted to do with his life. This was Nathaniel. I somehow would forget to call him Michael. His eyes were Nathaniel's, they were pure they looked directly at me when he spoke." In addition to employing models, Gilchrist often captures the emotions of her characters by examining her own face while drawing. "I look at myself in the mirror and move back a little and I can see the tension in my face," she said. "Sometimes I don't even have to look. I can feel it from inside, the tension. I can't say to a child, 'Look painful.' I have the child, but I don't have the emotion at the time because they're not actors, they're models. It sounds so corny, but what's inside of you comes out when you're working."

In her interview Gilchrist acknowledged that illustration presents different challenges from creating art for other forums: "I have the utmost regard for the author. I understand that this is not Jan's day, that I am not painting for a gallery. I am an interpreter, I am illustrating. I am reading a manuscript, taking it to heart and interpreting, so I have to have some regard for the text. There is the artist who cannot enter while you're working from the author. It has to be one thing when it's done. That child has to look at Nathaniel and hear him talking and see Nathaniel. Nathaniel can't be some little boy I decided to look grand. He has to look and feel and breathe the words. So that's the most important thing—to become one with the author."

In addition to working on *Nathaniel Talking* Gilchrist has illustrated numerous other books written by Greenfield including *Night on Neighborhood Street,* for which she won a second Coretta Scott King Award. Published in 1991, the book relates the experiences of several people living in the same community. Included are poems about a local drug dealer, a child who fears nighttime noises, and a family that has fun together before going to bed. Gilchrist said that working on *Night on Neighborhood Street* was like a returning to her own childhood environs.

First Pink Light, also released in 1991, tells the story of a father who has been away from home for a month taking care of an older relative. His son, Tyree, wants to stay awake and welcome his father home. Tyree's mother, involved in a homework assignment, provides her son with a pillow and a blanket and allows him to sit in a chair and wait for his father's return. The child falls asleep before his dad arrives home. Reviewers commended Gilchrist and Greenfield for presenting positive images of an African-American family in *First Pink Light.* Among Gilchrist's works with other authors are *Red Dog Blue Fly* by Sharon Bell Mathis, which features poems about a football team, and *Everett Anderson's Christmas Coming* by Lucille Clifton, which examines various emotions that the title character feels near the holiday season.

In her interview Gilchrist spoke of her intention when illustrating a book for young people: "I want my readers to feel that they are important. I want them to see that the work is honest, that it's very positive, and that they—when they put the book down—feel that there is hope. I think that no matter what happens in that book from the first page, to the middle, to the end—no matter what occurs—when the book is put down, there should be hope for a child to walk forward."

WORKS CITED:

Burns, Mary M., review of *Nathaniel Talking, Horn Book,* September-October, 1990, p. 613.
Clifton, Lucille, review of *Children of Long Ago, New York Times Book Review,* July 17, 1988, p. 31.
Gilchrist, Jan Spivey, telephone interview with Mark F. Mikula, August 8, 1992.

—*Sketch by Mark F. Mikula*

GILLILAND, Alexis A. 1931-

PERSONAL: Born August 10, 1931, in Bangor, ME; son of William Lester (a chemistry professor) and Lucille (a homemaker; maiden name, Cartmell) Gilliland; married wife, E. Dorothea, August 29, 1959 (died, November 27, 1991); children: Michael L., Charles D. *Education:* Purdue University, B.S., 1953; George Washington University, M.S., 1963. *Politics:* "Radical centrist." *Religion:* Jewish.

ADDRESSES: Home—4030 8th St. South, Arlington, VA 22204.

CAREER: National Bureau of Standards, Thermochemistry Branch, Washington, DC, chemist, 1956-67; General Services Administration, Standardization Division, Washington, chemist and technical writer, 1967-87. *Military service:* U.S. Army, private first class, 1954-56.

MEMBER: Science Fiction Writers of America, American Association for the Advancement of Science, Washington Science Fiction Association, Sigma Xi.

AWARDS, HONORS: John W. Campbell Award for best new writer, 1982; Hugo Award, World Science Fiction Convention, for best fan artist, 1979, 1983, 1984, 1985.

WRITINGS:

SCIENCE FICTION NOVELS

The Revolution for Rosinante, Del Rey, 1981.
Long Shot for Rosinante, Del Rey, 1981.
The Pirates of Rosinante, Del Rey, 1982.
The End of the Empire, Del Rey, 1983.
Wizenbeak, Bluejay, 1986.
The Shadow Shaia, Del Rey, 1990.
Lord of the Troll-Bats, Del Rey, 1992.

ALEXIS A. GILLILAND

CARTOONS

The Waltzing Wizard: Cartoons, Starmont, 1989.

Also author of *The Iron Law of Bureaucracy* and *Who Says Paranoia Isn't In, Anymore?* (cartoons). Also contributor of cartoons to magazines, including *Science Fiction Review, Washington Science Fiction Association Journal,* and *Webber Woman's Revenge.*

WORK IN PROGRESS: Dauvia Rising.

SIDELIGHTS: "I started writing shortly after the birth of my first son in 1963 as a way of occupying myself without going out of the house," Alexis A. Gilliland told *Something about the Author* (*SATA*). "Eventually the traditional bad first novel was finished, of which, like the curate's egg, parts were very good. The process, however, was rather enjoyable and except for being a terrible way to make a living was something I thought I'd rather enjoy doing.

"In 1979 the opportunity arose when my office was reorganized to eliminate most of my duties. Giving my work absolute first priority, I returned calls and letters with admirable promptness and made sure that all deadlines were met on time. The rest of the time I sat at my desk, writing the first draft of *The Revolution from Rosinante* on a yellow legal pad. At the end of the day, I'd go home and type up the second draft," Gilliland recalled for *SATA*.

"In 1982, my first two novels won me the Campbell Award as best new writer," he continued, "but more importantly there was a major reorganization at work, in which people in my series and grade were being fired. I had seniority and was a veteran besides, but elected to take an early retirement and become a full-time writer. The felt mood of that period, the sense of betrayal, permeates *The End of the Empire,* an excellent novel with a terrible cover.

"When I began *The End of the Empire,* it had been my intention to try a fantasy, as a way of stretching myself, but I couldn't bring myself to do it. Afterwards, having warmed up on space opera, I wrote *Wizenbeak,* whose story expanded itself more or less organically into three independent novels, with *The Shadow Shaia* and *The Lord of the Troll-Bats* rounding out what might be called an autonomous trilogy.

"In many respects, *The Lord of the Troll-Bats* was the hardest book I'd ever written. Completely at a loss to know what to do with some of my major characters, I wrote them out of the story. Big mistake. My editor had bought the other two, but unhesitatingly rejected the third, and so I had to put the major characters back in and figure out what their function was. Actually, I sat for a long time reflecting on the story and pondering what was needed and finally began a total re-write without any clear idea of where I would be going. The solutions that eventually appeared were astonishing; certainly nothing I would have imagined sitting down to outline a plot.

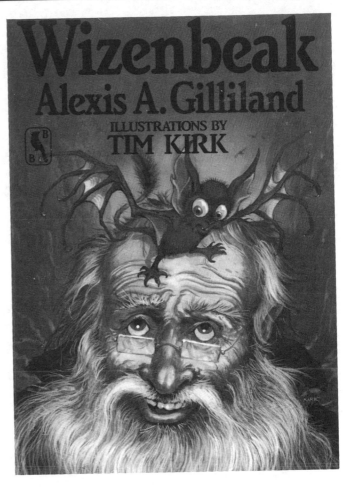

Wizenbeak, **a humorous, tangled fantasy about political intrigue in a magical kingdom, opens Gilliland's "autonomous trilogy" about the country of Cymdulock.** (Cover illustration by Tim Kirk.)

"My current project is science fiction again, life in the asteroids about a millennia hence. A lot of contemplation and research took place before I ever began writing, so that I know far more about the milieu than is convenient to tell. The seed around which my thinking crystallized was a joke: all the asteroids should be connected by a rail, so space travel would be done by trolley instead of ship. The rails are virtual instead of literal, of course, but there are any number of interesting consequences. The reader is invited to stay tuned."

In addition to his popular science fiction novels, Gilliland is also an avid cartoonist whose work regularly appears in *Science Fiction Review* and other periodicals. Gilliland, who is not above sending cartoons to the smaller "fanzines" that request them, described the typical request in a *Science Fiction Review* interview. The fanzine editors, he said, "have my address and they send it to me and sometimes I send them two or three cartoons and sometimes I'll send them a letter of comment and sometimes I say, 'Gee, this is strange,' and I don't send 'em anything."

WORKS CITED:

Phillips, Curt, interview with Gilliland in *Science Fiction Review,* winter, 1986.

*   *   *

GLIORI, Debi 1959-

PERSONAL: Surname pronounced "lee-*oh*-ree"; born February 21, 1959, in Glasgow, Scotland; daughter of Lionel (a musical instrument maker) and Josephine (a tax inspector; maiden name, McEnhill) Gliori; married George Karl Carson, August 2, 1976 (divorced, February 14, 1978); married Jesse Earl Christman (a furniture maker), June 21, 1991; children: (first marriage) Rowan Gliori; (second marriage) Benjamin Christman. *Education:* Edinburgh College of Art, B.A. (with honors), 1984, postgraduate diploma in illustration. *Politics:* "Anything or any party that is anti-war and pro-children." *Religion:* "Not affiliated with any church but I do believe in God."

ADDRESSES: Home—The Grieves Cottage, Snawdon Farm, Gifford, East Lothian EH41 4PJ, Scotland. *Agent*—Gina Pollinger, 222 Old Brompton Rd., London SW5 OB2, England.

CAREER: Free-lance illustrator, 1984—. Design consultant to Scottish Development Agency.

MEMBER: Association of Illustrators, Children's Book Group (Scotland).

WRITINGS:

SELF-ILLUSTRATED

New Big Sister, Walker/Boots, 1990.
New Big House, Walker/Boots, 1991.
My Little Bother, Walker/Boots, 1992.

DEBI GLIORI

What a Noise, Creative Edge, 1992.
When I'm Big, Walker Books, 1992.

ILLUSTRATOR

Roger McGough and Dee Reid, *Oxford Children's ABC Picture Dictionary,* Oxford University Press, 1990.
Sue Stops, *Dulcie Dando,* Deutsch, 1990.
Margaret Donaldson, *Margery Mo,* Deutsch, 1991.
Stephanie Baudet, *The Incredible Shrinking Hippo,* Hamish Hamilton, 1991.
McGough, *Oxford 123 Book of Number Rhymes,* compiled by Nicolas Tucker, Oxford University Press, 1992.
Stops, *Dulcie Dando Disco Dancer,* Scholastic, 1992.
Donaldson, *Margery Mo's Magic Island,* Scholastic, 1992.
Stops, *Dulcie Dando, Soccer Star,* H. Holt, 1992.

WORK IN PROGRESS: Illustrations for *The Lizzie Stories* by David Martin for Candlewick; four books— "wonderful stories that I'm going to illustrate by June, 1992"; a dinosaur anthology for Scholastic.

SIDELIGHTS: Debi Gliori told *SATA:* "My father still has the first book I wrote and illustrated at the tender age of four. It's a wondrously mis-spelt tale of fairies, princesses and aeroplanes that has very little in the way of 'plot,' but heaps of wobbly pictures. I always wanted to be an artist that painted and apart from a brief flirtation with wanting to be an astrophysicist at fifteen, I think that illustration has always been my goal. However, I put a spanner in my own works by getting married and having a baby at sweet seventeen, and it wasn't until my baby was up and walking and my first husband had disappeared over the western horizon that I could start at art college. Into each life some rain must fall and all that jazz. . . .

"When I finally graduated, design work poured in, and I overdid it to the point of total collapse. I'd get up at 7 a.m., cook breakfast, take my little boy to school, work 'til 5 p.m., pick him up, cook supper, play 'til 8 p.m., then work 'til about 3 a.m. Probably that's why I look like a bag-lady at the age of thirty-two.

"I kept trying to write stories, and would send them off to publishers, then leap on the postman, waiting for a reply! Eventually it all came together in 1988, when a delightful editor, Caroline Royds at Walker Books, phoned me up to say my story had made her laugh out loud, and would I like to change this and that and so *New Big Sister* was begun. By this time I'd met my husband-to-be number two and we had produced our little boy, and childbirth and such delights were very much on my mind (hence the subject matter of *New Big Sister*) as was the difficulty of having a book with the mother throwing up on the first page! Caroline is a peach of an editor, and we've worked together on all the subsequent books for Candlewick, which are first published in Britain by Walker Books.

"*My Little Bother* is about a girl who detests her pest of a baby brother, and is dedicated to my stepbrother, who

Gliori examines the imaginative turns a child's resentment of a younger sibling takes in her self-illustrated *My Little Bother.*

I now love dearly. I drew him as a frog in diapers on the dedication page, and I think he has just about forgiven me. I wrote [*My Little Bother*] one autumn on holiday with my Mum, and by the time we'd had our first cup of coffee, I had the text completed, and was asking what she thought of it over breakfast. *New Big House* is dedicated to her, because we moved so often when I was small.

"*When I'm Big* is for Sebastian Walker, the founder of Walker Books, who died tragically early in the summer of 1991. I wish he could have seen the book—he was in my thoughts constantly (and still is) as I was painting the pictures. Without his love and encouragement, I could not have made books like those above.

"I work now in a little wooden building in our garden in Scotland, looking out over the hills to the sea, but mostly looking inwards, drawing and writing for the child within. It's a very solitary occupation, very introspective, and the best books I can do are ones that teach me more about myself, where I can get under the skin of the child that I'm drawing. I love my work; I'm engaged mind and soul in the process of continually striving for better and better books. Our children are the future, their imaginations shape their world—may we help them through books to build a safe and harmonious land."

GOVE, Doris 1944-

PERSONAL: Surname rhymes with "stove"; born April 10, 1944, in Seattle, WA; daughter of Philip Babcock (a lexicographer) and Grace Edna (Potter) Gove; married Chauncey J. Mellor (a professor of German), December 11, 1977; children: Laura Grace. *Education:* MacDuffie School, 1960-62; Barnard College, Columbia University, B.A. (zoology), 1966; University of Tennessee, M.S., Ph.D. (zoology), 1978. *Politics:* "Fanatic conservationist." *Religion:* Unitarian.

ADDRESSES: Home—4204 Taliluna Avenue, Knoxville, TN 37919.

CAREER: U.S. Peace Corps, Kapsabet, Kenya, biology teacher, 1967-69; Highlands Biological Station Nature Center, Highlands, NC, summer supervisor, 1978-1984; Ijams Nature Center, Knoxville, TN, director, 1979-82; University of Tennessee, Knoxville, biology instructor, 1982-85; University of Tennessee College of Veterinary Medicine, technical writer, 1985-90.

MEMBER: Greenpeace, Sierra Club, Audubon Society, Nature Conservancy, Society for Children's Book Writers, Tennessee Citizens for Wilderness Planning.

WRITINGS:

Miracle at Egg Rock: A Puffin's Story, Down East, 1985.

(Translator, with husband, C. J. Mellor) *Foundations of Comparative Ethology,* Van Nostrand, 1985.
A Water Snake's Year, illustrated by Beverly Duncan, Atheneum, 1991.
Red-Spotted Newt, Atheneum, 1993.

WORK IN PROGRESS: Blue Tailed Skink, a biography of a common lizard; *Some Rainy Night,* a description of catching animals (toads, salamanders) for a nature center and then releasing them.

SIDELIGHTS: Doris Gove grew up on a small farm in Massachusetts—"with woods, brooks, stone walls, and overgrown fields," she recalled to *SATA.* After graduating from Barnard College in 1966, Gove spent two years with the Peace Corps in Kenya as a teacher of biology. After her return to the United States, she enrolled at the University of Tennessee to pursue an advanced degree in the study of snake and lizard behavior. Graduating in 1978, Gove went on to teach biology at the University of Tennessee and at Pellissippi State Technical Community College and also worked as a science writer and editor for the university's College of Veterinary Medicine.

Gove's interest in both conservation and biology has extended well beyond her teaching career. She has spent several summers working as a naturalist in a Tennessee park and has served as director of the University of North Carolina's Highlands Nature Center. Gove continues to share her enthusiasm for biology and the environment by writing books for children that broaden their understanding of the world of nature, as well as by visiting many schools and scout troops to talk about snakes, biology, and environmental education.

Gove's first book for children, *A Miracle at Egg Rock: A Puffin's Story,* is told from the point of view of a puffin, a seabird which frequents the rocky coastline of north-

Naturalist Gove spent nearly two summers observing the behavior of snakes near a stream in preparation for *A Water Snake's Year.* (Cover painting by Beverly Duncan from *A Water Snake's Year.*)

ern New England and Canada. The book describes the Audubon Society's successful reintroduction of puffins to an island off the coast of Maine. Gove went on to complete her second children's book several years later. "*A Water Snake's Year* follows a water snake's life on the Middle Prong of the Little River in the Great Smoky Mountains National Park," Gove told *SATA.* "The snake comes out of hibernation, finds safe places to bask in the sun, catches fish and frogs, mates, sheds her skin, escapes predators, gives birth to forty-two babies, and finally returns to hibernation." The book was based on the graduate research that Gove conducted in the Smoky Mountains: "I sat on a rock near the stream and watched snakes. I did this almost every day for two summers."

*   *   *

GREENBERG, Melanie Hope 1954-

PERSONAL: Born December 28, 1954, in New York City; daughter of Lawrence and Ruth (Gerger) Greenberg. *Education:* Attended Hunter College, 1971 and 1976. *Religion:* "Born-again pagan."

ADDRESSES: Home and office—168 Hicks St., Brooklyn, NY 11201. *Illustration agent*—Jane Feder, 305 East 24th St., New York, NY 10010.

CAREER: Freelance graphic artist, 1980-89; illustrator, author and lecturer, 1989—. Publicity Director, mem-

DORIS GOVE

MELANIE HOPE GREENBERG

ber of steering committee, and bulletin board organizer for Children's Book Illustrators Group. *Exhibitions:* Greenberg's work has been displayed at several exhibition sites, including Once Upon an Illustration, New York City; the Brooklyn Public Library; and the Washington Square Outdoor Art Exhibition, New York City.

MEMBER: Graphic Artists Guild, Society of Children's Book Writers.

AWARDS, HONORS: Greenberg's designs were chosen for United Nations Children's Fund (UNICEF) greeting cards, 1982, 1986, and 1991; *My Father's Luncheonette* was included in the American Institute of Graphic Arts book show, 1991.

WRITINGS:

SELF-ILLUSTRATED

At the Beach, Dutton, 1989.
My Father's Luncheonette, Dutton, 1991.
Celebrations: Our Jewish Holidays, Jewish Publication Society, 1991.

ILLUSTRATOR

It's My Earth Too: How I Can Help the Earth Stay Alive, June, 1992.

SIDELIGHTS: Melanie Hope Greenberg told *SATA:* "While I was growing up in the South Bronx in New York City I never dreamed that I would become a published author-illustrator. My two older sisters taught me how to read before I started to go to kindergarten. I treasured the books on my shelf. I wrote stories for school projects. My oldest sister, Barbara, a budding fashion designer, always had available paints, crayons, brushes, pencils, and paper to play with. I could sit and paint for hours on end. My friends and I created theatrical extravaganzas which we wrote and performed;

for a while in my teens I put aside the paints and pursued an acting career. I studied theater and music at Hunter College, but my favorite classes were always art history classes.

"I was in my twenties, managing a small print gallery in Manhattan, when I began to create my three-dimensional miniature watercolor paintings. Using thick opaque gouache, color pencils, and pen and ink I began to develop my own style of urban folk art. After a time I discovered that I loved painting most of all and I could easily put aside my dreams of becoming a star. My career as an artist has gone through many ups and downs in the past decade, but through it all I have created greeting cards, mugs, wrapping paper, and I am most proud of my designs selected by UNICEF and The Children with AIDS Program because my work is being used to help people around the world. I have also published illustrations for magazines, poster graphics, and a live-animated film.

"Writing and illustrating picture books gives me a splendid opportunity to express my vision of a child's-eye-world. Presenting my work to audiences of young students at the schools I visit as an artist-in-residence is

Greenberg uses her imagination to present a child's-eye view of Jewish holidays in her self-illustrated *Celebrations*.

an extremely rewarding part of my career. My presentation takes the students through a very simple step-by-step process of bookmaking: from rough idea, to sketch dummy, to the printed package. I hope I can continue to have a positive impact and inspire people everywhere, especially young people, with my artwork and my writing."

*   *   *

GREENE, Constance C(larke) 1924-

PERSONAL: Born October 27, 1924, in New York, NY; daughter of Richard W. (a newspaper editor) and Mabel (a journalist; maiden name, McElliott) Clarke; married Philip M. Greene (a radio station owner), June 8, 1946; children: Sheppard, Philippa, Stephanie, Matthew, Lucia. *Education:* Attended Skidmore College, 1942-44. *Politics:* Democrat. *Religion:* Roman Catholic.

ADDRESSES: Home—East Hampton, Long Island, NY 11937. *Agent*—Marilyn Marlow, Curtis Brown Ltd., 575 Madison Ave., New York, NY 10022.

CAREER: Associated Press, New York City, began as mail-room clerk, became reporter, 1944-46; writer, 1968—.

AWARDS, HONORS: A Girl Called Al was named a *Washington Post Book World* Spring Book Festival Honor Book, 1969, and listed as an American Institute of Graphic Arts Children's Book, 1970; *A Girl Called Al, Beat the Turtle Drum* and *The Love Letters of J. Timothy Owen* were all named American Library Association Notable Books.

WRITINGS:

A Girl Called Al, illustrated by Byron Barton, Viking, 1969.

CONSTANCE C. GREENE

Leo the Lioness, Viking, 1970.
The Good-Luck Bogie Hat, Viking, 1971.
Unmaking of Rabbit, Viking, 1972.
Isabelle the Itch, illustrated by Emily McCully, Viking, 1973.
The Ears of Louis, illustrated by Nola Langner, Viking, 1974.
I Know You, Al, illustrated by Barton, Viking, 1975.
Beat the Turtle Drum, illustrated by Donna Diamond, Viking, 1976.
Getting Nowhere, Viking, 1977.
I and Sproggy, illustrated by McCully, Viking, 1978.
Your Old Pal, Al, Viking, 1979.
Dotty's Suitcase, Viking, 1980.
Double-Dare O'Toole, Viking, 1981.
Al(exandra) the Great, Viking, 1982.
Ask Anybody, Viking, 1983.
Isabelle Shows Her Stuff, Viking, 1984.
Star Shine, Viking, 1985.
Other Plans (adult novel), St. Martin's, 1985.
The Love Letters of J. Timothy Owen, Harper, 1986.
Just Plain Al, Viking, 1986.
Isabelle and Little Orphan Frannie, Viking, 1988.
Monday I Love You, Harper, 1988.
Al's Blind Date, Viking/Kestrel, 1989.
Funny You Should Ask (short story collection), Delacorte, 1992.
Odds on Oliver, Viking, 1992.

Contributor to periodicals, including New York *Daily News.*

ADAPTATIONS: Beat the Turtle Drum was presented as "Very Good Friends" on *ABC Afternoon Special,* 1976; "Very Good Friends" and *A Girl Called Al* are available on audiocassette, both distributed by Listening Library, both 1985.

SIDELIGHTS: Since both of her parents worked for the New York *Daily News,* children's and young adult fiction writer Constance C. Greene was born with the "tools" of her trade readily accessible. "I grew up with typewriters, newspapers, books, magazines, and conversation all around," Greene related in an interview for *Authors and Artists for Young Adults (AAYA).* "So while it wasn't inevitable that I'd become a writer, that background certainly influenced me.

"My father was a long-time editor of the paper, and my mother reviewed movies for them. The *Daily News* was much more powerful in those days and had the largest circulation in the country. They didn't call themselves journalists back then; they were newspaper people. I've always thought that newspaper work was the best possible profession because it led to a very interesting life. A friend of mine whose father was a businessman said that she used to be so impressed because my family talked about all kinds of ideas and things that weren't discussed at her house."

Greene grew up in the suburbs, but her family eventually moved to the city. "I lived in Larchmont, and that was about twenty-five minutes from New York," she recalled in her *AAYA* interview. "But shortly after I turned fifteen, the *Daily News* made my father their managing editor. He began to work all night long, which was why we moved into the city. This was just before World War II, so New York City was still comparatively safe, but exciting."

Greene completed her secondary schooling in Manhattan, but then left Skidmore College after only two years. She explained to *AAYA*: "Not a serious student, I tired of wasting my time and my father's money. I really wanted to get a job in newspapers. I tried the *Sun, World Telegram,* and *Time,* but nobody would hire me. I finally asked the Associated Press [AP] if they needed help and they put me to work in the mailroom—the bottom rung of the ladder, a very lowly job, indeed. I worked nights for $16.50 a week. At midnight, I would go home by myself on the subway. Always nervous, my mother gave me a whistle to wear around my neck. Fortunately, I had a rapid climb at the AP.

"Since all the young men had gone off to war by 1945, I worked hard and finally got onto the City Desk, which had to be the most exciting job anyone of my age ever had. I did a lot of interviews and went out to Staten Island to meet the incoming troopships. Since the *Baltimore Sun* papers were big AP clients, I would ask the troops where they were from and write about those from Baltimore.... There were also the tiresome things, like interviewing 4-H Club members from Iowa. I can't be thankful enough for the year and a half at AP. The job taught me a lot. Working for a wire service, you learn to cram as much as you can into the smallest space possible. I rarely have to cut anything."

Greene left the Associated Press after she married in 1946 to move to Connecticut and concentrate on raising her family. "It's very difficult to write when you have a bunch of kids around," she revealed to *AAYA*. "With so many interruptions, I found myself putting a lot of things on hold. I wrote short stories because I could do those in one sitting. My mother suggested that I write a book for children, but that was the furthest thing from my mind at that time. I didn't believe that I could sustain the interest of a reader throughout a book, and really wanted, most of all, to write my short stories. I published a series of these one-page short stories in the *Daily News.* I wrote a lot about little kids, especially one named Charlie, but always from an adult's point of view. They were very easy for me."

"When we were living in Connecticut and the children were still growing up," Greene recalled in an article in *50 Plus,* "I joined a short-story writing group at the Darien Community Association. Everyone was very serious about their writing and a few had even been published. I got so tired of the rejection slips that our teacher—who, by the way, was excellent—suggested that I try for the juvenile market. I started writing my first book, *A Girl Called Al,* and it felt right from the beginning. When I showed the teacher the first few chapters, she said, 'This is what you should do.'"

Greene's popular series about a young, spunky New York City nonconformist continues with *Al's Blind Date,* in which Al and her best friend discover romance. (Cover illustration by Tricia Zimic.)

"I should forget all the other stuff, and that my book was good, she told me," Greene continued her story with *AAYA*. "So I sent it to a publisher where a friend's daughter was a reader. The daughter wrote back and said that although they liked my book, they didn't think that it was complete. 'The heck with this,' I decided, and wrote Phyllis McGinley, a friend of my mother's. McGinley had written a lot of children's books and had won a Pulitzer Prize for her poetry. I asked her if there were any agents who handled just children's books. She gave me the name of her agent, Marilyn Marlow, one of the foremost children's book agents in New York. I sent Marilyn my material. She returned my manuscript and said that she also didn't think it was complete, but was interested in my writing. If I finished the book off a little, she would send it out.

"The first publisher to receive it suggested that I make so many changes that I left saying, 'Oh my God, I don't know what to do.' Marilyn advised we try someone else. She sent it to Velma Varner at Viking, who called me in and said, 'You've got the bones, just flesh them out.' That did it for me. I went home absolutely exhilarated to flesh out the bones. It was the best piece of advice I've ever heard. It demonstrated the differences between those two publishers: the first was too wordy and left me discouraged; Velma had the right touch. She said simply, 'Just do this.' It is the same advice that I now give."

A Girl Called Al was published in 1968. Greene discussed the character of Al in her *AAYA* interview: "The special thing about Al is that she describes herself. She has a high I.Q. but doesn't work to capacity. She's also very nonconformist. At the time I invented her, the terminology of a 'latch-key' kid hadn't been created, but that's what Al was. Her mother and father were divorced and she came home every day to an empty place because her mother worked. Those kids, who often have to take care of younger brothers and sisters, have a great weight of responsibility on their shoulders, but Al's nonconformity is what made her different. The narrator of the book is the opposite of Al; she's really the straight man. Her family has a mother, father, and little brother, and she is relatively unsophisticated. Al has traveled to a lot of places and has done all kinds of things like riding on airplanes. The narrator's family can't afford to do all those things, so she and Al make a nice contrast. The

The author's son-in-law, who as a boy could never refuse a dare, provided the inspiration for this novel. (Cover illustration by Peter Catalanotto.)

narrator is about as close to me as anything I've done, or maybe I just remember myself being like that."

Louise Fitzhugh's *Harriet the Spy* provided Greene with the needed inspiration that led to the "Al" series. "I'm almost positive that I started writing *Al* after reading that book," Greene explained to *AAYA*. "It opened doors for me. I set out to write about a city kid because they have such a different life from suburban or country kids, and I enjoyed the idea of moving those two kids around the city.

"Al was thirteen when I started out and after six books, I've reluctantly made her fourteen. Maybe I should not have tampered with her age at all. Although Al and her friend have wandered all over New York City, they have remained relatively unsophisticated. I have always expected somebody to call me out on that fact, but, so far, nobody has."

Throughout the "Al" series, as well as in the rest of her writings, Greene has tried to keep her prose and ideas fresh and enduring. "I read the newspapers and that still gives me a feeling for language," she told *AAYA*. "I also listen to kids." Indeed, "eavesdropping—in the nicest possible way—can be very productive," she wrote in a *Writer* magazine article. Greene admits that while window-shopping she heard one young friend say to another "Have a weird day." She was intrigued by the play on the common "Have a good day" and later used its slangy form in *I Know You, Al* and other "Al" books. Now she receives letters from young fans who sign off with "Have a weird day."

Greene has based many of the ideas for her other books on her own children. For instance, *Leo the Lioness* was inspired by her daughter Lucia. She told *50 Plus:* "[When] our youngest was a teenager, she was an astrology freak. She was always studying the signs and talking about how Leo was the best sign, the lion, the king! So I built a story around it." Other people and events have also inspired her, as well, but Greene interprets those with a writer's eye. The character of Gran in *The Unmaking of Rabbit* is modeled on her own mother-in-law. *Double-Dare O'Toole* was based on a phase in her son-in-law's life when he couldn't resist a dare; as a result he found himself in many dangerous or humorous situations.

Despite Greene's distaste for heavy fiction, one of her most popular books remains *Beat the Turtle Drum,* based on the story of her older sister's death at age thirteen. She wrote the book after the death of her parents. "That is the only book that I have taken directly from my own life," she explained to *AAYA*. "I wrote that story of two sisters many, many years after in order to try and recreate what had happened. I was only eleven at the time and couldn't remember much about how my mother or father felt, or how people reacted. It was difficult in the beginning but, as with most of my books, I started with a real idea and character and then let my imagination take over. *Beat the Turtle Drum* might have been a better story if I'd recited everything

Beat the Turtle Drum, **which was based on the author's own memories of her older sister's early death, was made into the television special "Very Good Friends."**

exactly the way it happened, but oftentimes I don't remember it that way. Though I'm not sure that everything in the story actually happened, writing it did make me feel a little better. When I go to schools, this is the book all kids seem to want to talk about. I would really rather not have it be the one thing that I'm known for."

Beat the Turtle Drum was eventually adapted as "Very Good Friends" for an *ABC Afterschool Special* in 1976. Also in the mid-1970s, Greene moved from Connecticut to Maine, where her husband owned a radio station. The sudden peace and quiet disturbed her concentration, she told *AAYA.* "All my kids were in or through with college and I didn't have any friends. Although I could never understand how anyone could write with little kids around, I could do so once mine were reasonably grown up. Having been used to telephones ringing, people coming and going, and lots of friends, I found that serenity was not really good for me."

Greene and her husband sold their radio station after six years of living in Maine and settled happily in East Hampton, Long Island. "Now we live on North Main Street, smack in the middle of town with the fire engines, the ambulances, and never mind the tourists,"

she informed her *AAYA* interviewer. "I used to be fairly rigid in my writing hours, but either I've changed, or I was doing it wrong all the time. I've found that I work better if I'm not too rigid. I write a little in the afternoon, maybe do something else, and then go back to it.

"I like writing for the middle-grade kids, ages nine to twelve. I think that those kids have changed less from when I or my children were their age than any of the others. The publishers have been wanting funny books for boys that age, so I've been working on that. I've written a couple of books already that have been popular with boys, such as *Double Dare O'Toole. The Love Letters of J. Timothy Owen* was the ideal situation of a lighthearted book with serious overtones.

"I would like to write another adult book. My first was published in 1985 and was called *Other Plans.* It was a story about a boy who didn't get along with his father and although it got some good reviews, it didn't do very well. If I had that one to do all over again, I probably would have written it as a young adult and it probably would have been a heck of a lot more successful. But I have written another adult novel that I started a long time ago that had a very good plot. I used to think that if

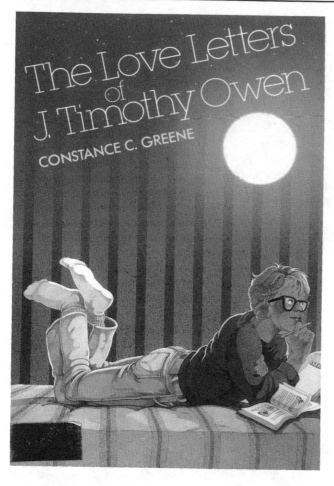

The Love Letters of J. Timothy Owen
CONSTANCE C. GREENE

Greene's work also includes lighthearted comedies, including this novel about a boy's written attempts to win a girl's love. (Cover illustration by Marla Frazee.)

you had a good plot, the rest was easy, but the book didn't turn out to be saleable. I'd like to go back to it, which is sometimes harder than starting afresh, but the book still intrigues me. It is a murder mystery—the sort I like to read, so it might be fun to do. Writing should not be all drudgery."

WORKS CITED:

Greene, Constance C., in an interview with Marc Caplan for *Authors and Artists for Young Adults.*
Greene, Constance C., "What You Can Make Live," *Writer,* August, 1982, pp. 23-26.
Whitcomb, Meg, "Connie Greene's Kids Taught Her Well," *50 Plus,* June, 1981, pp. 74-75.

FOR MORE INFORMATION SEE:

BOOKS

Something about the Author Autobiography Series, Volume 11, Gale, 1991, pp. 129-147.

PERIODICALS

Horn Book, August, 1969; February, 1971; April, 1973; February, 1974; April, 1975.
New York Times Book Review, January 21, 1973; November 15, 1975; February 15, 1981.

Saturday Review, April 19, 1969.
Teacher, April, 1975.

* * *

GROSSMAN, Bill 1948-

PERSONAL: Born April 21, 1948, in Cleveland, OH; son of George (an engineer and company founder) and Phyllis (a homemaker; maiden name, Schmitt) Grossman; married Donna Anischik, May 29, 1977 (divorced, 1992); children: Joshua, Adam, Sally. *Education:* Rensselaer Polytechnic Institute, B.S., 1976, M.B.A., 1977, M.S., 1979; University of Hartford, M.Ed., 1989. *Hobbies and other interests:* Storytelling.

ADDRESSES: Home and office—Windsor, CT. *Agent*—Ginger Knowlton, Curtis Brown Ltd., 10 Astor Place, New York, NY 10003.

CAREER: Computer software engineer and systems analyst in Connecticut, 1977-83; insurance actuary in Hartford, CT, 1983-88; Hebrew Academy of Greater Hartford, Bloomfield, CT, teacher, 1989-90; University of Hartford, West Hartford, CT, adjunct professor of mathematics, 1990—; writer. Worked variously as a "fast food griller, grounds crew laborer, art school model, telephone technician, warehouse worker, grave digger, factory laborer, construction worker, coal shoveler, assembly line worker, patent research assistant, moving and storage flunky, entrepreneur, Fuller Brush salesperson, steelworker, ski equipment salesperson, janitor, and forklift operator," 1968-75. Coach for youth baseball, basketball, and soccer leagues, 1987—. *Military service:* U.S. Marine Corps Reserves, 1969-75.

MEMBER: Society of Children's Book Writers.

AWARDS, HONORS: Publisher's Weekly Editor's Choice Award, 1989, for *Tommy at the Grocery Store; Tommy at the Grocery Store* appeared on the Library of Congress List of Books for Children, 1989; Children's Choice awards, Children's Book Council and International Reading Association, 1989, for *Donna O'Neeshuck Was Chased by Some Cows,* and 1991, for *The Guy Who Was Five Minutes Late;* Georgia Picture Storybook Award Masterlist nominations, 1989, for *Donna O'Neeshuck Was Chased by Some Cows,* and 1990, for *Tommy at the Grocery Store;* California Young Reader Medal Masterlist nomination, 1991, for *Tommy at the Grocery Store;* Colorado Children's Book Award Masterlist nomination, 1992, for *Tommy at the Grocery Store.*

WRITINGS:

Donna O'Neeshuck Was Chased by Some Cows, illustrations by Sue Truesdell, Harper, 1988.
Tommy at the Grocery Store, illustrations by Victoria Chess, Harper, 1989.
The Guy Who Was Five Minutes Late, illustrations by Judy Glasser, Harper, 1990.
Children's Verses, Harper, in press.
The Horrible Singing, Harper, in press.

BILL GROSSMAN

What's Wrong with the Way That I Look?, Harper, in press.
Cowboy Ed, Harper, in press.
Banging Girls, Banging Boys (tentative title), Harper, in press.

Contributor of stories to *Northeast* and *Marlow RFD.*

WORK IN PROGRESS: Rhyming educational and picture books.

SIDELIGHTS: Bill Grossman is the author of humorous rhyming picture books. He published his first book, *Donna O'Neeshuck Was Chased by Some Cows,* in 1988. Donna is a girl who enjoys patting people and animals on the head. But when she does this, the recipient of the pat inevitably runs after her. At first Donna is pursued by a herd of cows. Others try to help her out, but when Donna thanks them with a pat, they join in the chase. In the end Donna is pursued by pigs, dogs, ducks, a cat, a boy, an old woman, a pack horse, a turtle, and a buffalo herd, as well as the cows. She finally turns to the mob, demanding, "What do you want?" What they want, she discovers, is more pats. Donna obligingly pats each one until she collapses from fatigue, and then they all pat each other.

In Grossman's 1989 work, *Tommy at the Grocery Store,* all the characters are pigs. The text is reminiscent of a folksong in that the plot is circular and the verses repeat with slight variations. Like many folktales, *Tommy at the Grocery Store* derives its humor from misapplications of logic. Tommy's mommy accidentally leaves him at the grocery store, and the grocer, mistaking him for a salami, sells Tommy to another customer. She takes Tommy home and is about to slice him when she realizes he has eyes, and therefore must be a potato. The woman returns Tommy to the grocery store, where a doctor buys him and takes him home. The doctor is just about to cook Tommy when she realizes he has a neck, and therefore must be a bottle. The story continues in this manner, and Tommy is mistaken for a banana, a ruler, a corncob, a table, and a chair before regaining his true identity.

Bill Grossman told *SATA:* "I have been telling stories all my life. As the oldest of six children, I frequently told stories to my younger brothers and sisters. In my preschool days, many of my stories centered on a nutty character that I invented called Goofy Guy. Later I regularly took one of my younger brothers on trips to 'Africa.' While leading him blindfolded through the woods, I would describe the elephants and lions and tigers to him, and we would have all sorts of adventures on what he was certain was the dark continent.

"Both my parents were great storytellers. At night my father would tell us bedtime stories, most of which he would make up as he went along. During the day my mother would spontaneously break into stories involving the zany characters that she had invented. Her hands would suddenly turn into Freddy and Dearie, two tiny creatures who were always up to ridiculous antics. Often Glumple, a grumpy, gravelly-voiced little man who lived in my mother's throat, would pipe up to complain about whatever was bothering him. I learned from my parents how easily you can make up a story simply by starting with a character and a setting and letting your imagination take it from there.

"I was fortunate not only to be raised by a family of storytellers but also to have been educated in elementary school by Catholic nuns who drilled the rules of grammar and style into my head using the most effective known technique for teaching writing—torture. At Our Lady of the Angels Elementary School in Cleveland we wrote and wrote and wrote. And we wrote in proper English, no stream-of-consciousness stuff. If your verb did not agree with your subject, a nun, firmly pinching your cheeks between her thumb and forefinger till you looked like a fish, would quietly inform you that unless you wished her to permanently fuse your cheeks together, it would behoove you to rewrite your sentence. If you ever meet a graduate of my elementary school you can be assured that behind that narrow, fish-like mouth with the nunprints all over it is a person who can write the King's English well. Despite being a disorganized person who is not terribly good at following rules, I have always followed the rules of grammar and style that the nuns taught me.

"At my high school, St. Ignatius, the Jesuit priests used torture not for ensuring proper writing, as God had intended it to be used, but for correcting character flaws such as tardiness, laziness, and wittiness in class. Chronically being late, seldom doing homework, and often saying funny things in class, I became a frequent target for such torture, which was mental rather than physical. Persons with character flaws were required to come to school on Saturday morning and were not allowed to leave until they had memorized a lengthy piece of poetry, such as the entire *The Raven* by [nineteenth-century American author Edgar Allan] Poe or the first twenty-one stanzas of *The Rhyme of the Ancient Mariner* by [British poet Samuel Taylor] Coleridge. I was there more than any other kid in the school—just about every Saturday.

"Although those Saturday sessions did not correct my character flaws, they did instill in me a greater appreciation for rhyming verse and showed me enough examples of it to guide me in formulating my own opinions as to how such verse should be written. I am sure that it is no coincidence that the rhyming verse stories I write today are generally similar in structure and length to the poems I had to memorize on Saturdays.

"Rhyming verse has always appealed to me. When I was a kid I wrote many silly little verses. In high school and college, I often made up humorous limericks about people I knew. Later, when I began reading to my own

HARPER
TROPHY

$4.95 US
$6.75 CDN

Tommy at the Grocery Store

GROCERY

by Bill Grossman
illustrated by Victoria Chess

The author's outlandish sense of humor surfaces in this story about being left behind at the supermarket. (Cover illustration by Victoria Chess.)

children, I realized how much children like the sound of rhyming verse and how much fun it is for a parent to read aloud. Today most of my writing is humorous rhyming verse.

"Because I want my rhyming books to be fun to read aloud, I work very hard to give them an unambiguous, rollicking meter, like the meter that makes nursery rhymes so popular. To achieve that kind of meter, I have as many people as possible read the drafts of my books aloud to me, then I rewrite any lines that are not read with the rhythm that I had intended. I also strive to craft my rhymes in an unforced way so that they read as smoothly and as clearly as prose.

"After high school I majored in engineering at Rensselaer Polytechnic Institute (RPI) in Troy, New York, where, after doing almost no academic work for two years, I was dismissed from school with the suggestion that I 'find myself.' Six years later, after having worked as a telephone technician, grave digger, janitor, etc., I somehow convinced RPI that I had been 'found' and was readmitted. I continued to major in engineering because I find mathematical subjects fascinating. Mathematicians are much like writers. To be a good one, you must be able to manipulate the language of mathematics in the same creative ways that an imaginative writer manipulates English. No wonder many mathematicians—Lewis Carroll, to name one—have also been writers. While at RPI, I took as many writing courses as I could from the technical writing department, whose teachers were good for me because of their nunlike insistence on proper grammar and style.

"After finishing college, I got married and took a job as a materials management analyst in Connecticut, primarily because it allowed me to work at the company where my wife worked as an engineer. Normally, the job of materials management analyst is a nice boring one. Unfortunately, I wound up with one of those unusual bosses who makes a job challenging and fun. If you want to be a writer, that's the worst kind of job to have. Many aspiring writers think that they should get exciting jobs like mountain climber, soldier of fortune, or secret agent, but I recommend getting boring ones that do not use up the creativity that could better be used for writing.

"Fortunately, the company eliminated my position and, having no alternative, I took a superbly boring job programming computers. Almost immediately, feeling a desperate need for a creative outlet, I began writing. I wrote in the evenings, on weekends, and even in the bathroom at work.

"After three years of accumulating rejections, I sold a humorous adult short story called 'Attitude Problem' to *Northeast*. A year later, after having had ten previous picture book manuscripts rejected, I sold my first rhyming picture book, *Donna O'Neeshuck Was Chased by Some Cows*, to Harper & Row. In the next few years, Harper & Row (now HarperCollins) bought several more of my books. My editor there seems to share my

He watched every show
From the very last row—
Too late to get a good seat.

When his family ate,
He was five minutes late
And wound up with little to eat.

Grossman credits his clear, rhythmic rhymes to his Catholic school upbringing, where he often memorized poems as punishment for misbehaving. (Illustration by Judy Glasser from *The Guy Who Was Five Minutes Late.*)

enthusiasm for humorous rhyming verses that are fun to read aloud.

"Though I later moved on to less boring jobs, such as mathematician and teacher, I never stopped writing. I am glad that I didn't become a teacher right after college, for teaching is such a fun job that I would never have found the need to write. Although I have taught elementary school, junior high school, and college and have liked teaching all age groups, I think I enjoy teaching little kids the most. Teaching them is like writing a whole new story, whereas teaching older people is more like editing a rough draft. Though I no longer teach full time, I still make many visits to schools to talk to children about writing.

"I don't really have any hobbies other than telling stories to, teaching, and coaching my own three children. When they grow up, I'm sure I'll find other kids to play with."

WORKS CITED:

Grossman, Bill, *Donna O'Neeshuck Was Chased by Some Cows,* Harper, 1988.

FOR MORE INFORMATION SEE:

PERIODICALS

Booklist, November, 1988.
Cleveland Plain Dealer, November 12, 1989.
Hornbook, September, 1988; July 31, 1989.
Kirkus Reviews, November 1, 1988; February 1, 1990.
Los Angeles Times Book Review, November, 1989.
New York Times Book Review, August 6, 1989, p. 29.
Publishers Weekly, October 14, 1988.
School Library Journal, February, 1989; July, 1990.
Wilson Library Bulletin, October, 1988, pp. 76-77; November, 1990.

GRYSKI, Camilla 1948-

PERSONAL: Born March 2, 1948, in Bristol, England; daughter of Denis (a teacher) and Eileen (a homemaker; maiden name, Morgan) Milton; married Chester Gryski (a lawyer), July 29, 1973; children: Mark, Damian. *Education:* University of Toronto, B.A. (with honors), 1971; Toronto Montessori Institute, Primary Teaching Certificate, 1972; University of Toronto, M.L.S., 1976. *Hobbies and other interests:* Juggling.

ADDRESSES: Home—76 Glenholme Ave., Toronto, Ontario, Canada M6H 3B1.

CAREER: Toronto Public Library, Hospital for Sick Children Branch, Toronto, Ontario, Canada, children's librarian, 1977—; writer.

MEMBER: International Board on Books for Young People (councillor, 1984-87), Writers' Union of Canada, Canadian Society of Children's Authors, Illustrators and Performers (treasurer, 1985-87, vice-president, 1991—), Canadian Children's Book Centre, Friends of the Osborne and Lillian H. Smith Collections.

AWARDS, HONORS: American Library Association, notable book citation, 1984, for *Cat's Cradle, Owl's Eyes;* Information Book Award, Children's Literature Roundtables of Canada, 1991, and first runner-up, Toronto Imperial Order of Daughters of the Empire Book Award, both for *Hands On, Thumbs Up.*

CAMILLA GRYSKI

WRITINGS:

Cat's Cradle, Owl's Eyes: A Book of String Games, illustrated by Tom Sankey, Kids Can Press, 1983, Morrow, 1984.
Many Stars and More String Games, illustrated by Sankey, Morrow, 1985.
Super String Games, illustrated by Sankey, Morrow, 1987.
Hands On, Thumbs Up: Secret Handshakes, Fingerprints, Sign Languages and More Handy Ways to Have Fun with Hands, illustrated by Pat Cupples, Addison-Wesley, 1990.
Friendship Bracelets, Morrow, 1992.

WORK IN PROGRESS: Writing several picture book stories; researching other ways to make bracelets.

SIDELIGHTS: Camilla Gryski told *SATA:* "My first major literary work was my autobiography, written as a Grade 8 class project. I began with my birth and worked forward. I described various birthdays and pets; I recounted exciting happenings, the most notable being the emigration of my family from England to Canada, and I ended with a dramatic account of having my tonsils out at the ripe old age of thirteen. My future dreams included university, medical school and work with children in a pediatric hospital. This effort was commented on by a former teacher: 'Although becoming an author hasn't suggested itself to you, I rather think this masterpiece is a good beginning'.

"Somehow, I always knew I could write. In high school, my descriptive paragraphs were read out loud in class, and I also began to write poems. A course I took in college on Frankenstein and the Romantic Narrative in my fourth year introduced me to the works of the writer George Macdonald, and to the Toronto Public Library's Osborne Collection of Early Children's Books. Before I knew it I was hooked on children's literature, past and present. I began to read and to catch up on all the books I had missed.

"In 1980, I had a part-time job as a children's librarian—working for the Toronto Public Library at the Hospital for Sick Children. I was the mother of two small sons, and I thought I was quite busy enough. That summer I volunteered in a children's play area at a folk festival, using my storytelling and puppetry skills. One unforgettable day, the play area was visited by Ken McCuaig, an expert in cat's cradle games, and his 'stringband' of children. Before we knew it, the whole area was filled with kids and adults playing with loops of string. I learned my first two string figures that day and wanted to learn more. I had played cat's cradle as a child, but had no idea that you could make butterflies, fishnets and winking eyes out of a simple loop of string. I began to use string figures at work to illustrate fingerplays in my story times. I bought books, researched string games in anthropology journals, added more string games to my repertoire, and began in a very small way to teach them to children. Then one day, about a year and a half after I had been introduced to

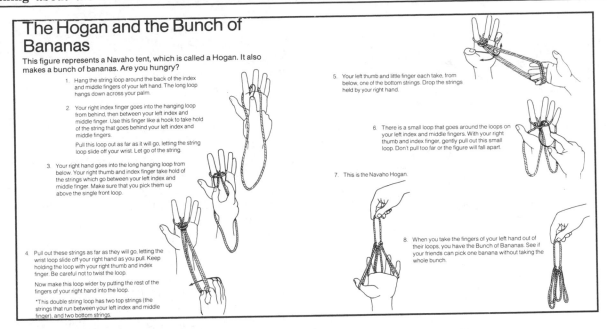

The Hogan and the Bunch of Bananas

This figure represents a Navaho tent, which is called a Hogan. It also makes a bunch of bananas. Are you hungry?

1. Hang the string loop around the back of the index and middle fingers of your left hand. The long loop hangs down across your palm.

2. Your right index finger goes into the hanging loop from behind, then between your left index and middle finger. Use this finger like a hook to take hold of the string that goes behind your left index and middle fingers.

   Pull this loop out as far as it will go, letting the string loop slide off your wrist. Let go of the string.

3. Your right hand goes into the long hanging loop from below. Your right thumb and index finger take hold of the strings which go between your left index and middle finger. Make sure that you pick them up above the single front loop.

4. Pull out these strings as far as they will go, letting the wrist loop slide off your right hand as you pull. Keep holding the loop with your right thumb and index finger. Be careful not to twist the loop.

   Now make this loop wider by putting the rest of the fingers of your right hand into the loop.

   *This double string loop has two top strings (the strings that run between your left index and middle finger), and two bottom strings.

5. Your left thumb and little finger each take, from below, one of the bottom strings. Drop the strings held by your right hand.

6. There is a small loop that goes around the loops on your left index and middle fingers. With your right thumb and index finger, gently pull out this small loop. Don't pull too far or the figure will fall apart.

7. This is the Navaho Hogan.

8. When you take the fingers of your left hand out of their loops, you have the Bunch of Bananas. See if your friends can pick one banana without taking the whole bunch.

Gryski's *Cat's Cradle, Owl's Eyes* details several entertaining games that can be played with just a single string. (Illustration by Tom Sankey.)

string figures, I was showing off my newest string game, the beautiful Inuit 'Little Dog with Big Ears.' Ricky Englander of Kids Can Press happened to see it and about two weeks later I got a phone call. Could I put string games into a book? And that's how it all started.

"I see now that I had been building all the skills I would need. A facility with words, experience with children, expertise at doing research. That first book [*Cat's Cradle, Owl's Eyes: A Book of String Games*] was written in the middle of the night—the only quiet time I could find then with two young children. Tom Sankey was a gem of an illustrator. With the help of his pink-stuffed rubber gloves, he drew detailed and precise pictures of hands and string. My editor Susan Cravit helped to ensure that my descriptions were accurate and unambiguous. I collaborated with Tom and Susan to produce two more books of string games, *Many Stars and More String Games* and *Super String Games.*

"*Hands On, Thumbs Up* presented me with the opportunity to try a different kind of non-fiction writing. The research for this book was done at an academic level. I found myself reading about comparative vertebrate anatomy, about left-handedness, about cave paintings and early humans. I dug up facts. I tracked down allusions. I used almost every library in the city of Toronto. But that was just the beginning of the four-step process. Next came the task of 'translating' the information, making connections in ways that were meaningful and interesting for children. There was much lateral thinking at this level. Then each part of the text was checked for accuracy by an expert. My list of acknowledgements is headed 'Thousands of Thanks'. Lastly, the manuscript must be read by a child. Fortunately, my son Damian, then ten, was willing and interested. He even contributed some silly handshakes and jokes to the book.

"I continue to work as the children's librarian at the Hospital for Sick Children and I continue to write. I'm usually researching one thing or another, and I'm interested in exploring new genres. I still love being with kids (mine and other peoples') and sharing with them all the wonderful figures you can create with a loop of string. In the last year, I've also been talking to children about the amazing world of our hands. And in the last little while, I've taken up juggling as a hobby."

FOR MORE INFORMATION SEE:

PERIODICALS

Quill & Quire, February, 1991, p. 24.
School Library Journal, May, 1984, p. 80; January, 1986, p. 67; August, 1988, p. 103.

*   *   *

GUCCIONE, Leslie Davis 1946-
(Leslie Davis)

PERSONAL: Born December 14, 1946, in Wilmington, DE; daughter of Edward Stowman (a chemical engineer and executive) and Winifred (a homemaker; maiden name, Taylor) Davis; married Joseph Q. Guccione (an accountant), May 3, 1975; children: Christopher J. (stepson), Amy Mendenhall, Taylor Noyes. *Education:* Studied art with Carolyn Wyeth, 1963-65; attended Institute of European Studies, 1968; Queens College, B.A., 1969. *Politics:* Independent. *Religion:* Episcopalian.

ADDRESSES: Office—Box 308, Snug Harbor Station, Duxbury, MA 02331. *Agent*—Denise Marcil, 685 West End Ave., New York, NY 10025.

CAREER: Held various positions in advertising, public relations, and fund raising, 1972-78; Folk Art Antiques,

LESLIE DAVIS GUCCIONE

Duxbury, MA, partner, 1985-86; writer, 1985—. Junior League of Boston, member, 1973-77; Duxbury Art Association, member, 1975—, member of board of directors, 1978-80; St. John's Episcopal Church Altar Guild, member, 1980—, director, 1984-87.

MEMBER: Romance Writers of America, Society of Children's Book Writers, Duxbury Rural and Historical Society, Duxbury Yacht Club (chair).

AWARDS, HONORS: Golden Treasure Award (also known as Rita Award) finalist in young adult division, Romance Writers of America, 1985, for *Something out There; Tell Me How the Wind Sounds* was named an International Readers Association Young Adult Readers' best book of 1991.

WRITINGS:

YOUNG ADULTS

(Under name Leslie Davis) *Something out There,* Pocket Books, 1985.
Tell Me How the Wind Sounds, Scholastic, 1990.
Nobody Listens to Me, Scholastic, 1991.

THE "CHEERLEADER" SERIES BY SCHOLASTIC

Moving Up, 1987.
All or Nothing, 1988.
Pretending, 1988.

ROMANCE NOVELS

A Touch of Scandal, Avon, 1985.
The Splintered Moon, Avon, 1985.
Before the Wind, Silhouette Press, 1986.
Bittersweet Harvest, Silhouette Press, 1986.
Still Waters, Silhouette Press, 1987.
Something in Common, Silhouette Press, 1987.
Branigan's Touch, Silhouette Press, 1989.
Private Practice, Silhouette Press, 1990.
A Gallant Gentleman, Silhouette Press, 1991.
Rough and Ready, Silhouette Press, 1992.
A Rock and a Hard Place, Silhouette Press, 1992.
Major Distractions, Silhouette Press, in press.

WORK IN PROGRESS: Come Morning and *King of the Cafeteria,* both young adult novels.

SIDELIGHTS: Leslie Davis Guccione told *SATA:* "I grew up as the oldest of four children in a very active family. My dad was a chemical engineer, then in the marketing end of the DuPont Company, so we moved around the East Coast about every three years during my school days. I was in Wilmington, Delaware for kindergarten through mid-second grade; Wellesley, Massachusetts for mid-second to mid-fourth grade; back to Wilmington for seventh to twelfth grade; then off to Charlotte, North Carolina for college.

"Moving taught me how to make friends. I was glad to stay put after the seventh grade, but in high school I switched from public to private school and had to develop another batch of friendships at sixteen.

"I've always been what my teachers called 'creatively inclined.' That's to say I was full of imagination. I put on plays in my neighborhoods, drew all the time and wrote pretty awful poetry all through school. I was a terrible speller. My fourth grade teacher told me my spelling was atrocious. When I asked her what that meant and she told me to look it up, I, of course, answered that I couldn't because I didn't know how to spell it! (I work on a computer now and SPELLCHECK has been wonderful.)

"My home in Wilmington during the years 1963 to 1965 was not far from Chadds Ford, Pennsylvania, home of the Wyeth family. When I was sixteen I took my portfolio to Carolyn Wyeth and was accepted as a student in her Saturday class. With the exception of her nieces and nephews, I was the youngest student she had ever accepted. Carolyn is the sister of artist Andrew Wyeth and the daughter of N. C. Wyeth, one of America's best illustrators. She taught in his studio.

"I studied with her for two years and my Saturdays were magic. Not only was I painting, I was listening to constant and countless stories of her childhood as one of five children in an enormously talented family. I was there when celebrities and writers would come and interview her.

"After I graduated from Friends School in 1965, I went off to Queens College to major in art, but I also became involved in all aspects of creative writing. I was a member of the literary fraternity Sigma Upsilon and worked on the college's literary magazine. During the summer of 1968, after my junior year, I studied art history and classical music at the Institute of European Studies in Vienna. I traveled with about thirty other students for five weeks before landing in Austria. It was an incredible summer. Robert Kennedy was assassinated while I was in Portugal; the Vietnam peace talks were taking place in Paris where the Sorbonne riots had closed the university for the first time in history. (We were the first group of tourists let into the city.) Yet another young person was killed trying to escape over the Berlin Wall while I was there and, after a month of studies in Vienna, we took a weekend in Prague just as the Russians invaded! All of these kinds of adventures and experiences shape my stories and my way of looking at life.

"After a few single years in Boston, I married and moved down to a small New England town on the South Shore. Here I fell in love with the sea. Down here much of life revolves around commercial fishing, lobstering, and the cranberry industry. I've gotten to know the lobstermen, harbormaster, cranberry growers, sailors: the people who make up the daily rhythms of my corner of the world.

"I decided since I was home with small children that I really wanted to put my creative energies into works of fiction. My first book for young adult readers, *Something out There,* was a romantic mystery, set right out in our harbor. Because I love sailing and know about it, I made my first heroine a teenage sailing instructor and used our town as a model.

"At the same time, I began to write adult romances using cranberry growers, harbormasters, sailors, and fire fighters as my heroes. These books have paid me a steady income and make possible my career.

"The son of a friend of mine is profoundly deaf and I began to think about a story with a deaf character, one that would appeal to both hearing impaired and hearing readers. The result was *Tell Me How the Wind Sounds,* published in 1990. I set the story on Clark's Island, right out in the bay. It is a simple story about a deaf boy whose life is turned upside down when a hearing teenage girl invades his island for the summer. The International Readers Association Young Adult Readers named it one of their best books of 1991.

"In 1990 my editor at Scholastic read an article about whale watching being harmful to whales in Hawaii and

Many of Guccione's books are set in the coastal towns of her native New England, including *Nobody Listens to Me,* the story of a girl who argues with her father over the fate of local whales.

asked if I might like to develop something with that theme, set in New England. I used the whale topic as the vehicle in *Nobody Listens to Me* and wrote about the conflict of two people, a father and daughter, who love each other, yet get caught up in a disagreement over the issue.

"I'm always working on more ideas, many of which are requests from my own children. Now I'm thinking again about the Delaware area and hope to write some historical fiction set in the black powder yards along the Brandywine River. My interest in painting and visual expression has a noticeable effect on my style. I write colorful stories, full of description and sense of place. Also, I love hearing from my readers and try to answer every letter."

H

HARSH, Fred (T.) 1925-

PERSONAL: Born October 23, 1925, in Denver, CO; son of Fred T., Sr. (an attorney) and Ruth C. (a homemaker; maiden name, Driscoll) Harsh; married Elizabeth Ruedi (a nurse), July 15, 1948 (divorced, 1973); married Natasha Lobunez (an artist), November 11, 1973; children: (first marriage) Susan, Jefferey; (second marriage) Tanya, Amelia, Michael. *Education:* Attended California Polytechnic, 1943-44, Colorado State University, 1945-46, and San Francisco Academy of Art, 1947.

ADDRESSES: Home and office—P.O. Box 156, Greenport, NY 11944.

CAREER: Life magazine, assistant art director, 1953-58; Harsh/Finegold Inc. (graphic design firm), partner, 1959-75; free-lance illustrator, 1976—; author and illustrator of children's books. *Exhibitions:* Work has been shown at Jane Baum Gallery, NY; Hooks Epstein Gallery, Houston, TX; and American Artist Gallery, Taos, NM.

AWARDS, HONORS: Awards of Excellence, American Institute of Graphic Arts (AIGA), 1955 and 1956; two awards of merit, *Communication Arts* magazine, 1967; Gold Mailbox Award, DMMA, 1976, for design of a direct mail piece; Merit Award, New York Art Directors' Club, 1980.

WRITINGS:

SELF-ILLUSTRATED

Mildred, Maude & Mr. Goose, Abingdon, 1988.
Alfie, Abingdon, 1989.

OTHER

Work published in *Art Direction, Graphis Annual, Communication Arts,* and *59th New York Art Directors' Annual.*

WORK IN PROGRESS: Three picture books, tentatively titled *Pin a Rose on Sam, The Red Boots,* and *Punch Buggy Yellow.*

SIDELIGHTS: Fred Harsh told *SATA:* "Although I have been involved with the illustration of children's books and school programs for many years, I just recently discovered (to my immense surprise) that I was also able to write for children. Being both author and illustrator gives me double satisfaction. Good or bad, the responsibility is solely mine.

"My New York studio was in the same building with children's author and illustrator Ezra Jack Keats, and over the years we became good friends. His advice and counsel always stressed the need for complete honesty when writing for children. 'They possess an uncanny ability to see through any show of sham and pomposity. We must keep our own egos and pious judgments from our stories' were his words of advice."

FRED HARSH

A horse learns to appreciate the company of two cantankerous water fowl in Harsh's self-illustrated *Mildred, Maude, and Mr. Goose.*

FOR MORE INFORMATION SEE:

PERIODICALS

School Library Journal, August, 1988, p. 82.

*   *   *

HAYNES, Max 1956-

PERSONAL: Born March 18, 1956, in Mason City, IA; son of William Henry (a materials estimator) and Catherine Ann (a library assistant; maiden name, Pauley) Haynes; married Jane Elizabeth Messenger (a designer), September 6, 1986; children: Madeline Isabel. *Education:* Attended Drake University, 1974-75; University of Iowa, B.A., 1976-82.

CAREER: Free-lance commercial illustrator and writer, 1982—. Illustrator-in-residence for publication *Once Upon a Time.*

MEMBER: Society of Children's Book Writers, Minnesota Cartoonist's League, Minnesota Children's Illustrator's Guild.

WRITINGS:

SELF-ILLUSTRATED

Dinosaur Island, Lothrop, 1991.
Sparky's Rainbow Repair, Lothrop, 1992.

WORK IN PROGRESS: Baxter and Arf and the Red Checkered Scarf, for Lothrop; *Cosmo's Window,* for Lothrop.

SIDELIGHTS: Max Haynes told *SATA:* "My first memorable experience in art was in grade school. Each

Sparky, with the help of his penguin and dog helpers, attempts to solve puzzles that will allow him to fix a broken rainbow in Max Haynes' second book.

spring right before the end of the school year, we had an ice cream social. It was the major event of the season and the teachers put out large boards in the playground to display student projects. Up on the board for all to see was a picture I made of a giraffe. He was made of construction paper with wads of toilet paper as his spots. I was so proud!

"My next art experience was in junior high school when my art teacher locked me in the closet for goofing off. I think she was a bit looney from teaching art to junior high students!

"I was a misfit in school until I reached college and discovered lots of other kids with the same interests I had. I felt like a penguin who had grown up among ducks and then went to college in Antarctica. That realization that I was not alone has given me the strength to believe in my convictions when those around me do not.

"I love picture books, I love to buy them at book signings and meet the author or illustrator, I love to read them to my daughter. I eat, drink, walk, talk, and sleep picture books. I'm so lucky to be able to make them too!"

*   *   *

HEROLD, Ann Bixby 1937-

PERSONAL: Born September 1, 1937, in Essex, England; daughter of Raymond George (a farmer) and Margaret (an artist; maiden name, Fletcher) Bixby; married Horst Herold (a chef), 1968; children: Mattias. *Education:* Took a one-year correspondence course

ANN BIXBY HEROLD

developed by the London School of Journalism. *Religion:* Anglican.

ADDRESSES: Home—223 Bloomfield Ave., Apt. J, Wayne, PA 19087. *Agent*—Barrie Van Dyck, Schlessinger-Van Dyck Agency, 12 South Twelfth St., Philadelphia, PA 19107.

CAREER: Worked in many countries, including Norway, Germany, and Bermuda, in a number of occupations, such as tour guide, colonial police officer, and hotel receptionist. Treasurer of the Friends of Indian Valley Library; member of church vestry.

MEMBER: Society of Children's Book Writers, Philadelphia Children's Reading Round Table.

WRITINGS:

The Helping Day, Coward McCann, 1980.
Aaron's Dark Secret, Bethel Publishing, 1985.
The Mysterious Passover Visitors, Herald Press, 1989.
The Hard Life of Seymour E. Newton, Herald Press, 1990.
The Butterfly Birthday, illustrated by Emily Arnold McCully, Macmillan, 1991.

Contributor to children's magazines, such as *Highlights for Children* and *Hopscotch.*

WORK IN PROGRESS: Ally and Grandpa on the Pirate Ship (tentative title), a humorous picture book; an adventure story set in the 1860s.

SIDELIGHTS: Ann Bixby Herold told *SATA:* "I have wanted to be a writer since the age of eight because I saw my name on the cover of an adult novel. I was only an average student at school because I had two handicaps—I talked too much, and when I wasn't talking, I daydreamed.

"My report card reflected my attitude in class. 'Could do better,' it always said. I graduated at sixteen (British schools graduate a year earlier). Everyone except for my father wanted me to be a teacher. 'See the world!' he urged, and so I did. But all the time, I wrote and read, and wrote. Letters, diaries, etc. Recently a friend returned to me a letter I had written to her thirty years ago while I was crossing Africa, and it is easy to see the budding writer in those letters.

"I was always observant, even as a child, but I had a giant ego that had to be controlled before I could start to *understand* the people I was observing.

Aaron's Dark Secret

Ann Bixby Herold

In Herold's story, a young boy who lies to escape shepherd duty dreads meeting the new Prophet because he fears that he is not worthy of healing. (Cover illustration by Joy Frailey.)

"I wrote light humor for women's magazines after I first 'settled down' with a husband and baby and had to do something with my excess energy. I was successful; and then, when I started to read to my baby, I thought, 'Hey, this looks easy! I'll give it a try!'

"What a fool I was! Almost any profession you can think of is easier than becoming an author of children's books.

"But it is wonderfully rewarding. Children are the world's best audience. I couldn't think of anything I would rather do. Despite the rejections, despite being told I didn't have enough talent to succeed in the 'competitive world of children's books,' I persevered.

"If I can do it, anyone with a love of reading and writing can do it too. It doesn't take a college education. It takes basic skills and a love of life and a thick skin and a sense of humor and a sharp eye.

"I like to write funny stories because there is too much gloom and doom in real life. One of my most popular stories was in *Highlights for Children* in January, 1984. Called 'Beverley's Tall Story,' it is about growing up tall. Children from five to fifteen still laugh out loud when I read that story. My latest book, *The Butterfly Birthday*, is also funny. It's about being teased and how you must be careful whom you tease. Emily Arnold McCully's illustrations really help the story along."

*   *   *

HILL, Kirkpatrick 1938-

PERSONAL: Born April 30, 1938; daughter of William Clifton Hill (a mining engineer) and Isabel Matson Harper (an office worker); divorced; children: Matt, Shannon, Kirk, Crystal, Mike, Sean. *Education:* Attended University of Alaska; Syracuse University, B.S., 1969. *Politics:* Liberal. *Religion:* None.

ADDRESSES: Home—Box 53, Ruby, AK 99768.

CAREER: Elementary school teacher in Alaska, 1969-91.

AWARDS, HONORS: Toughboy and Sister was named a Junior Literary Guild Selection, 1990.

WRITINGS:

Toughboy and Sister, Margaret K. McElderry Books, 1990.

Toughboy and Sister has been translated into German.

WORK IN PROGRESS: A sequel to *Toughboy and Sister*.

SIDELIGHTS: Kirkpatrick Hill told *SATA:* "Having a book published is like dropping a rock in a pond. The ripples—like getting letters from readers and having a listing in *Something about the Author*—continually surprise me. I can't believe that the ripples have spread so far, and for so long. Maybe I'll be getting letters ten,

twenty, thirty years from now. All from the work of a few summer weeks. It's quite amazing. And now *Toughboy and Sister* is going to be translated into German, so there will be German kids reading about my Yukon River kids. That's a trans-Atlantic ripple!

"Unlike a lot of other teachers, I've seen my students grow up. The kids I taught twenty years ago have children now, and I'm teaching some of their kids. They've forgotten most of the stuff I taught them, but there are four things they remember: the songs we sang, the art lessons we had, the plays we put on, and most vividly of all, they remember the books I read out loud. Those books, by people who probably never heard of Athabascan Indians, became an integral part of these children's inner lives. Ripples.

"Children's literature is terribly important, then, isn't it? So I'm glad that I've sort of fallen into writing for children. (I had intended to be the next Willa Cather, but that's another story.)

"It's been a great difficulty finding time to write, and it's a wonder that my first book ever got started, much less finished! I've always thought I was supposed to be a writer, and that I'd get around to it someday, but it's certainly not been a direct line from point A to point B. There were, to begin with, my six children. Well, they weren't exactly there to *begin* with, but I have spent a lot of time raising a lot of children.

"I spent my earliest years in a mining camp outside Fairbanks, Alaska. We moved into Fairbanks so I could go to school. I attended the University of Alaska after I graduated from high school in Fairbanks, and finally, when I already had three kids, I graduated from Syracuse University in 1969. Then I had three more kids. I've been a teacher ever since, mostly in the Alaskan bush.

KIRKPATRICK HILL

"One day, when I'd taken a year off from teaching to be home with my youngest child, I decided that it was the right time to write. I was going to write the Great Alaskan Novel. There are Alaskan novels, of course, but most are romantic cliches, full of absurd situations which could never happen in Alaska. Jack London's stories of Alaska and the Yukon Territory are incredibly popular all over the world. But Jack was only here a year. He got some things right, but he got a whole lot wrong.

"So it was my opinion that the Great Alaskan Novel hadn't been done, and wouldn't be done unless a genuine bona fide and extremely literary Alaskan took the task in hand. Since I answered those qualifications it was obviously a job cut out for me. For the next five months I wrote the Great Alaskan Novel. It was pretty terrible. It was not good. It was definitely not Willa Cather.

"Undaunted—well perhaps a little daunted—I decided that I just needed practice writing in a variety of genres. Two years later during the summer things slacked up a little, so I thought I'd try writing a kid's book. I wanted to write a truly realistic children's book about real Yukon village kids, something especially for the kids I taught. I wanted it to be absolutely authentic, without any romanticizing about Alaskan life.

"I thought about *Boxcar Children,* a book I'd loved. Kids are crazy about stories in which children make do without adults. So I decided to do something like that. There was a true story I'd heard when I was very young about two Indian kids on the Koyukuk river, a boy about three years old and his baby sister, who'd been left alone at their fishcamp for a few days when their mother died. I'd never forgotten that story, so I started to play with that idea a little. The end result pleased me a lot more than the Great Alaskan Novel.

"I'd found that writing children's books was engrossing, demanding, and exhilarating. I felt rather foolish for not having tried it to begin with. After all, I had literally spent my entire life with children. First I *was* a child, and then I had six of my own, and then I began teaching, so it was kids, kids, kids, all day long, all my life long. I thought like a kid, had a kid's point of view, remembered what it felt like to be a kid, and found that in a group of people I always gravitated towards the kids. So of course I like writing for kids.

"I was very fortunate in my editor, Nachama Loeshelle, who pointed out things in the book which would be obscure to a non-Alaskan kid, words we use differently, perhaps, or objects they'd never seen, like a fish-wheel or a kicker. But she let me leave in all the Yukon-ese, all the down-river speech patterns. That was very important to me because the speech has to be right if the book's going to be an authentic picture of our life.

"Nachama and my publisher, Margaret McElderry, didn't shy away from the grim aspects of *Toughboy and Sister.* There are a lot of bad things that happen to the children in this book and they didn't ask me to water it down. Life in Alaskan villages is decidedly rough. We have the highest rate of alcoholism in the United States, the highest accident rate, and the highest infant mortality rate. You probably wouldn't believe some of the things our kids go through on a day-to-day basis. I want to write about those things honestly.

"Kids often write to ask if the things that happen in *Toughboy and Sister* are true. Thinking about that question made me realize how little I make up. Almost all of the events that pop into my head are real and have happened to my family or to someone else I know. Life in the Alaskan bush is very adventurous, and strange things are always happening. My six kids have enough mishaps between them to keep me writing for years!

"For the last twenty years we've lived in a big two-story log house eight miles out of the Yukon village of Ruby. The house is full of dogs and cats and kids and books and music. In between working on the house, starting the light plant, hauling water, cutting wood, baking bread, and all the innumerable bush chores, I keep trying to find the time to write. In the winter we live in the next village downriver where I teach school. Winters are really busy, so there are at least four first drafts sitting around waiting to be polished up. One of these days I'll get around to them."

*   *   *

HOBBS, Will 1947-

PERSONAL: Born August 22, 1947, in Pittsburgh, PA; son of Gregory J. and Mary (Rhodes) Hobbs; married Jean Loftus (a teacher/realtor), December 20, 1972. *Education:* Stanford University, B.A., 1969, M.A., 1971. *Hobbies and other interests:* Hiking in the mountains and canyons, whitewater rafting, archeology and natural history.

ADDRESSES: Office—c/o Atheneum Publishers, 866 Third Avenue, New York, NY 10022.

CAREER: Durango, CO, public schools, taught junior high and high school reading and English, 1973-89; writer, 1990—.

MEMBER: Authors Guild, Authors League of America, Society of Children's Book Writers, Phi Beta Kappa.

AWARDS, HONORS: Notable Book, Children's Book Council, 1989, Best Book for Young Adults Award, American Library Association, 1989, Teachers' Choice Award, International Reading Association, 1990, and Regional Book Award, Mountains and Plains Booksellers Association, 1990, all for *Bearstone; Changes in Latitudes* selected as a runner-up for the 1990 Earthworm Children's Book Award; Best Book for Young Adults and Best Book for Reluctant Young Adult Readers, 1992, American Library Association, Pick of the Lists citation, American Booksellers Association, all for *Downriver.*

WRITINGS:

Changes in Latitudes, Atheneum, 1988.
Bearstone, Atheneum, 1989.
Downriver, Atheneum, 1991.
The Big Wander, Atheneum, 1992.

Also contributed to *Writers in the Classroom,* Gordon, 1990.

SIDELIGHTS: Will Hobbs told *Something About the Author* (*SATA*) he discovered his love of reading "when my fourth grade teacher read *Call It Courage* aloud to the class. After that I went on my own from one book to the next—novels and biographies, mostly—and that's where my urge to write comes from. I'll always be a reader, because it's endlessly fascinating to look at life from someone else's perspective, someone very different from you. You learn so much about other people, other ways of thinking, other creatures, other parts of the world. You learn empathy and open-mindedness as well.

"For me and for almost all writers, it's reading that primes the pump for writing," Hobbs continued. "Your reading is the rain and snow that's absorbed into your language water table. Writing is sinking a well. If you're a reader you can sink a well just about anywhere and find good water ... if you're willing to work at it." As a teacher, Hobbs enjoyed introducing his students to the joys of reading. "I loved putting kids and books

together," he told *SATA,* "and there's nothing that improves reading like reading. About half of my students were reading a book a week or more, the record for a semester was 101! I loved it. Right in my classroom is where I got excited about writing for young people."

Hobbs spent a great deal of time in nature as a youth, and he continues to turn to those topics when choosing themes for his novels. He told *SATA:* "The novel I started first, in the summer of 1980, was originally entitled *The Pride of the West,* after a friend's gold mine. My friend, who was the starting point for the old man in the story, was always talking about reopening his mine. I thought his chances were slim in real life; why not have a go at making it happen in a story? I 'moved' his mine a hundred or more miles to the upper Pine River near the Window, one of the sacred places in the geography of my heart. The ranching I portrayed in the novel I learned helping my friend bring in his hay in the summers. I enlisted a Ute boy to help him, and he became the focus of the story.... My sixth version of that novel was published in 1989 as my second novel, *Bearstone.*"

Hobbs' first published novel, *Changes in Latitudes,* featured an endangered family and endangered sea turtles. "Why turtles? Maybe because I held a box turtle in my hand when I was about four years old; turtles were my first love in the world of nature," he told *SATA.* "I hope the reader hears the subliminal second phrase in the novel's title. It's right from the Jimmy Buffett song, and it's *Changes in Attitudes.*"

Searching for a setting for the novel *Downriver,* Hobbs turned to the Colorado River in the Grand Canyon, where the author himself rowed a white water raft through the canyon's rapids a total of eight times. "In the story," Hobbs told *SATA,* "those seven kids are down there all on their own, discovering the beauty and the excitement and the dangers."

The southwestern setting of Hobbs' novel *The Big Wander* includes Glen Canyon, one of a hundred canyons which were flooded in 1963 to form Lake Powell on the Colorado River. "I wanted to place a character in Glen Canyon in its last summer, and let myself and my readers see through his eyes that which I have only read about and seen in photographs: a marvel unequalled on this planet.

"As I write about the crucial choices facing people today, their struggle for identity, their relations with others, I hope also to be increasing their awareness of their relationship with the natural world. I'd like my readers to be appreciative and to care more about what's happening with wild creatures, wild places, and the diversity of life."

FOR MORE INFORMATION SEE:

PERIODICALS

Center for Children's Books Bulletin, April, 1988.

WILL HOBBS

HOBERMAN, Mary Ann 1930-

PERSONAL: Born August 12, 1930, in Stamford, CT; daughter of Milton and Dorothy (Miller) Freedman; married Norman Hoberman (an architect, a ceramist, and illustrator), February 4, 1951; children: Diane, Perry, Charles, Margaret. *Education:* Smith College, B.A. (magna cum laude), 1951; Yale University, M.A., 1985, postgraduate work in English literature. *Hobbies and other interests:* Biking, gardening, dancing.

ADDRESSES: Home—98 Hunting Ridge Rd., Greenwich, CT 06831. *Agent*—Gina Maccoby Literary Agency, 19 West 21st St., 5th Floor, New York, NY 10010.

CAREER: Speaker, consultant, and artist-in-the-schools, 1955—; author, 1957—; Fairfield University, Fairfield, CT, adjunct professor, 1980-83; C. G. Jung Center, New York City, program coordinator, 1981; former newspaper reporter and editor in a children's book department. Founder and member of The Pocket People (children's theater group), 1968-75; trustee, Greenwich Library, 1986-91.

MEMBER: Authors Guild.

AWARDS, HONORS: Book Week Poem award from Children's Book Council, 1976; American Book Award, 1983, for *A House Is a House for Me; The Looking Book* and *A House Is a House for Me* were both selections of the Junior Literary Guild.

MARY ANN HOBERMAN

WRITINGS:

POETRY FOR CHILDREN

All My Shoes Come in Two's, illustrated by husband, Norman Hoberman, Little, Brown, 1957.
How Do I Go?, illustrated by N. Hoberman, Little, Brown, 1958.
Hello and Good-by, illustrated by N. Hoberman, Little Brown, 1959.
What Jim Knew, illustrated by N. Hoberman, Little, Brown, 1963.
Not Enough Beds for the Babies, illustrated by Helen Spyer, Little, Brown, 1965.
A Little Book of Little Beasts, illustrated by Peter Parnall, Simon & Schuster, 1973.
The Looking Book, illustrated by Jerry Joyner, Viking, 1973.
The Raucous Auk, illustrated by Joseph Low, Viking, 1973.
Nuts to You and Nuts to Me, illustrated by Ronni Solbert, Knopf, 1974.
I Like Old Clothes, illustrated by Jacqueline Chwast, Knopf, 1976.
Bugs, illustrated by Victoria Chess, Viking, 1976.
A House Is a House for Me, illustrated by Betty Fraser, Viking, 1978.
Yellow Butter, Purple Jelly, Red Jam, Black Bread: Poems, illustrated by Chaya Burstein, Viking, 1981.
The Cozy Book, illustrated by Tony Chen, Viking, 1982.
Mr. and Mrs. Muddle, illustrated by Catharine O'Neill, Little, Brown, 1988.
A Fine Fat Pig, and Other Animal Poems, illustrated by Malcah Zeldis, HarperCollins, 1991.
Fathers, Mothers, Sisters, Brothers: A Collection of Family Poems, illustrated by Marilyn Hafner, Joy Street Books, 1991.

Contributor of poems to numerous anthologies, textbooks, and magazines in the United States and abroad, including *The Southern Poetry Review, Small Pond,* and *Harper's.*

OTHER

Contributor of travel articles to the *New York Times* and *Boston Globe.*

SIDELIGHTS: Mary Ann Hoberman is best known for her amusing, colorful poetry for preschool and primary grade readers. By humorously depicting everyday subjects such as animals, insects, clothing, and transportation, Hoberman creates verse that critics deem both entertaining and informative. Hoberman prefers poetry that rhymes and has rhythm, but she recognizes that most "adult" verse does not conform to these rules anymore. "If I want to write poetry th[is] way, writing for children is the last bastion," she told Allen Raymond in *Early Years.* While readers are able to draw lessons from many of her poems, the author does not want her work to seem didactic or dull. "These poems are fun," she told Raymond. "There is no way I want them to be made into chores or into something heavier than what they are!"

Hoberman grew up in Connecticut and decided at an early age—before she even knew how to write—that she wanted to be an author. It was a revelation to her at the age of four that the stories in the books read to her were produced by actual people. "I decided then when I grew up I would write stories, too, that would be printed in books for other people to read," she related in *Sixth Book of Junior Authors.* The goal-oriented child did not wait to learn how to write; instead, she spent her days making up stories, poems, and songs. Often, when she was playing on the swings in her family's backyard, she would use the rhythmic motion to spur her poetic creativity. "As I swung higher and higher and faster and faster, I would sing louder and louder until I was shouting my songs out at the top of my voice and my mother would come out to see what was happening," she wrote. In quieter moments, she would recite her numerous works to her little brother. As Hoberman learned to write, she would transfer her thoughts into scores of notebooks.

It was not until Hoberman was an adult, however, that she met her literary aspirations. She married Norman Hoberman in 1951, shortly before graduating from Smith College. While her four children were young, Hoberman made up poetry and stories to entertain them. When she decided to write down one of the collection of poems, her husband, an architect, illustrated the text, and they mailed the pages to a publisher. "Miraculously they were accepted," she remarked in a *Junior Literary Guild* article, "and so after having been a writer almost all my life, I was at last a *published* writer." The book, titled *All My Shoes Come in Twos,* was praised for its comprehensive discussion of footwear and its melodious rhymes which make it appropriate to read aloud. In the *New York Times Book Review,* C. Elta Van Norman called the work "a happy combination of light verse and humorous, colorful pictures."

Buoyed by the success of *All My Shoes Come in Twos,* Hoberman published a question and answer book the following year entitled *How Do I Go?* This book of verse explores various means of transportation—from elevators to parachutes—with Hoberman's husband, Norman Hoberman, as the illustrator. The pictures are rudimentary, almost child-like in nature, which complements the verse providing a fun way to learn about transportation for a young child. *How Do I Go?* was described as "an effective and well-designed book," according to Alice Low in *New York Times Book Review.*

Five years and three books after the publication of *How Do I Go?,* Hoberman's *A Little Book of Little Beasts* was published. In this work the author describes the habitats of smaller creatures, including frogs, snakes, mice, ants, turtles and more. The verse is humorous and sometimes tongue twisting with the typography varied in select poems to provide a visual interpretation of an animal. In a poem about a worm, the worm is described as a "Squiggly wiggly wriggly jiggly ziggly higgly piggly worm," and the verse is stretched in horizontal fashion for two pages to symbolize the nature of a worm. A

Hoberman frequently uses wordplay and animal characters in her works for younger children, including this story of an argumentative couple who learns to cooperate. (Cover illustration by Catharine O'Neill.)

reviewer for *Kirkus Reviews* praised Hoberman's verse as "smartly put together," and critics agree that the illustrations by Peter Parnell with dark, forest tones will enrich the child's learning experience about the animal kingdom.

Hoberman's next work, *The Looking Book,* was a choice of the Junior Literary Guild and was deemed an original addition to traditional counting books. Ned's cat, Pistachio, is lost on the first page, and the reader must follow Ned through twenty-eight pages to find Pistachio on the last page. The page numbers are a part of the rhyme, providing a new slant on counting books that will appeal to young children. A writer for *Publisher's Weekly* commented that *The Looking Book* is a "good" and "fun" way of learning to count.

Winner of an American Book Award for picture book paperback, *A House Is a House for Me* introduces young children to a plethora of dwellings for humans, animals, insects, and objects. The homes vary from anthills and beehives to cartons for crackers and barrels for pickles, and also include metaphorical images, such as "A mirror's a house for reflections/ A throat is a house for a hum." Hoberman concludes in her final two lines of verse that "Each creature that's known has a house of its own/ And the earth is the house for us all." The illustrator, Betty Fraser, provides an overwhelming amount of drawings with eye-catching colors for Hoberman's verse in *A House Is a House for Me,* and

Publishers Weekly praised the book as a "highly original exploration."

Another of Hoberman's publications, *Mr. and Mrs. Muddle* discusses the art of compromising when horse couple Mr. and Mrs. Muddle disagree over wanting a car for transportation to Aunt Bessie's or the store. Mr. Muddle thinks cars are too noisy and too fast, but Mrs. Muddle loves the sound and swiftness of cars. Since they cannot agree about attaining a vehicle, the Muddles settle on a canoe. Mr. and Mrs. Muddle must rely on each other to paddle, which brings them closer together. Their transportation problem is not resolved, but critics believed the work would foster discussion.

A Fine Fat Pig and Other Animal Poems presents Hoberman's characterizations of animals, including the nature of a giraffe's neck and a pig's sty, in fourteen poems for children. The author incorporates wordplay throughout her verse; when describing the pig's sty, she accentuates how fun it would be to be able to play in mud all day, she writes "To wallow in the mud and muck/ What lucky fun/ What funny luck." *Washington Post Book World* contributor Mary Jo Salter found Hoberman's verse to be "irresistibly memorizable." Another of Hoberman's books of verse, *Fathers, Mothers, Sisters, Brothers: A Collection of Family Poems*, inspects the inner layers of family life through poetry that is humorous yet reflective. Hoberman tries to portray family activities familiar to every type of culture just as Marilyn Hafner's colorful illustrations depict every race. A *Kirkus Reviews* writer described the poems as "wise [and] witty."

Hoberman admits that most of her books of verse started in her head first, not on the page. She wrote in *Sixth Book of Junior Authors*: "[My] poems and songs still begin in the rhythms that I feel when I take my daily walk, kicking up the autumn leaves or crunching through the snow or watching my bare feet make footprints in the sand." Hoberman still feels that writing is a major part of her life, indicating in another *Junior Literary Guild* article that she is constantly writing verse. "*Not* writing a poem would be more difficult. An odd fact or the sound of a name catches my ear or, more likely, its rhythm catches my feet; it irritates me as the grain of sand irritates the oyster. I can't get rid of it . . . . Slowly it accretes words and images until finally it is not a pearl but a poem."

WORKS CITED:

Hoberman, Mary Ann, review of *The Looking Book, Junior Literary Guild*, September 1973, p. 8.

Hoberman, in *Junior Literary Guild*, September, 1978.

Holmes Holtze, Sally, essay in *Sixth Book of Junior Authors*, H. W. Wilson, 1989, pp. 132-133.

Review of *Fathers, Mothers, Sisters, Brothers: A Collection of Family Poems, Kirkus Reviews*, October 1, 1991, p. 1295.

Review of *A House Is a House for Me, Publishers Weekly*, August 28, 1978.

Review of *A Little Book of Little Beasts, Kirkus Reviews*, March 1, 1973, p. 251.

Review of *The Looking Book, Publishers Weekly*, September 3, 1973, pp. 53-54.

Low, Alice, "Getting Around," *New York Times Book Review*, September 28, 1958, p. 48.

Raymond, Allen, "Mary Ann Hoberman: Fun-loving Poet, Student of Literature . . . ," *Early Years*, January, 1985, pp. 23-4.

Salter, Mary Jo, "Peaceable Kingdom," *Washington Post Book World*, May 12, 1991, p. 18.

Van Norman, C. Elta, "Slippers with Zippers," *New York Times Book Review*, May 26, 1957, p. 26.

FOR MORE INFORMATION SEE:

BOOKS

Children's Literature Review, Volume 22, Gale, 1991, pp. 107-115.

PERIODICALS

New York Times Book Review, September 28, 1958; December 10, 1978.

*   *   *

HOFF, Syd(ney) 1912-

PERSONAL: Born September 4, 1912, in New York, NY; son of Benjamin (a salesman) and Mary (Barnow) Hoff; married Dora Berman, 1937. *Education:* Studied fine art at National Academy of Design, New York City.

ADDRESSES: Agent—Scott Meredith Literary Agency, 845 Third Ave., New York, NY 10022.

CAREER: Cartoonist, 1928—. Originator of daily cartoon panels, "Tuffy," William Randolph Hearst Syndicate, 1939-49, and "Laugh It Off," King Features Syndicate, 1958-77. Also star of a series of television

SYD HOFF

shows, *Tales of Hoff,* Columbia Broadcasting System (CBS). National advertising commissions include Standard Oil, Chevrolet, Maxwell House Coffee, and Arrow Shirts.

MEMBER: Authors League of America, Authors Guild, Magazine Cartoonists Guild.

AWARDS, HONORS: Irving and Me was selected as one of the year's ten best children's books by the *New York Times,* 1967.

WRITINGS:

Military Secrets, Hillair, 1943.
It's Fun Learning Cartooning, Stravon, 1952.
Learning to Cartoon, Stravon, 1966.
Irving and Me (young adult novel), Harper, 1967.
Syd Hoff's Joke Book, Putnam, 1972.
The Art of Cartooning, Stravon, 1973.
Jokes to Enjoy, Draw and Tell, Putnam, 1974.
Dinosaur Do's and Don'ts, Windmill, 1975.
Editorial and Political Cartooning: From Earliest Times to the Present..., Stravon, 1976.
Syd Hoff's Best Jokes Ever, Putnam, 1978.
Syd Hoff Shows You How to Draw Cartoons, Scholastic, 1979, reprinted as *How to Draw Cartoons,* 1991.
Mighty Babe Ruth, Scholastic, 1980.
Syd Hoff's How to Draw Dinosaurs, Windmill, 1981.
The Man Who Loved Animals (biography of Henry Bergh), Putnam, 1982.
The Young Cartoonist: The ABC's of Cartooning, Stravon, 1983.
Syd Hoff's Animal Jokes, Lippincott Junior Books, 1985.

Also creator of comic strip, "Tuffy." Contributor of short fiction to *Alfred Hitchcock* and *Ellery Queen.* Also contributor to *Esquire, Look, New Yorker, Saturday Evening Post, Playboy,* and other periodicals.

CARTOON COLLECTIONS

Feeling No Pain: An Album of Cartoons, Dial, 1944.
Mom, I'm Home!, Doubleday, 1945.
Oops! Wrong Party!, Dutton, 1951.
Oops! Wrong Stateroom!, Ives Washburn, 1953.
Out of Gas!, Ives Washburn, 1954.
Okay—You Can Look Now!, Duell, 1955.
The Better Hoff, Holt, 1961.
Upstream, Downstream, and Out of My Mind, Bobbs-Merrill, 1961.
So This Is Matrimony, Pocket Books, 1962.
'Twixt the Cup and the Lipton, Bobbs-Merrill, 1962.
From Bed to Nurse; or, What a Way to Die, Dell, 1963.
Hunting, Anyone?, Bobbs-Merrill, 1963.

SELF-ILLUSTRATED; FOR CHILDREN

Muscles and Brains, Dial, 1940.
Eight Little Artists, Abelard-Schuman, 1954.
Patty's Pet, Abelard-Schuman, 1955.
Danny and the Dinosaur, Harper, 1958.
Julius, Harper, 1959.
Sammy, the Seal, Harper, 1959.
Ogluk, the Eskimo, Holt, 1960.

CHESTER

Story and pictures by
SYD HOFF

An I CAN READ Book

Hoff, who started a cartooning career at age sixteen, has created many enduring animal characters, including Chester, the carousel horse who became real.

Oliver, Harper, 1960.
Where's Prancer?, Harper, 1960.
Who Will Be My Friends?, Harper, 1960.
Albert the Albatross, Harper, 1961.
Chester, Harper, 1961.
Little Chief, Harper, 1961.
Stanley, Harper, 1962.
Grizzwold, Harper, 1963.
Lengthy, Putnam, 1964.
Mrs. Switch, Putnam, 1967.
Wanda's Wand, C. R. Gibson, 1968.
The Witch, the Cat, and the Baseball Bat, Grosset, 1968.
Baseball Mouse, Putnam, 1969.
Herschel the Hero, Putnam, 1969.
Jeffrey at Camp, Putnam, 1969.
Mahatma, Putnam, 1969.
Roberto and the Bull, McGraw, 1969.
The Horse in Harry's Room, Harper, 1970.
The Litter Knight, Putnam, 1970.
Palace Bug, Putnam, 1970.
Siegfried, Dog of the Alps, Grosset, 1970.
Wilfred the Lion, Putnam, 1970.
The Mule Who Struck It Rich, Little, Brown, 1971.
Thunderhoof, Harper, 1971.
Ida the Bareback Rider, Putnam, 1972.
My Aunt Rosie, Harper, 1972.

Pedro and the Bananas, Putnam, 1972.
A Walk Past Ellen's House, McGraw, 1973.
Amy's Dinosaur, Windmill Books, 1974.
Kip Van Wrinkle, Putnam, 1974.
Katy's Kitty, Windmill, 1975.
Pete's Pup, Windmill, 1975.
Barkley, Harper, 1976.
Henrietta Lays Some Eggs, Garrard, 1977.
How to Make Up Jokes, Grosset, 1977.
The Littlest Leaguer, Windmill Books, 1977.
Walpole, Harper, 1977.
Henrietta, Circus Star, Garrard, 1977.
Henrietta, the Early Bird, Garrard, 1978.
Henrietta Goes to the Fair, Garrard, 1979.
Nutty Noodles, Scholastic Inc., 1979.
Santa's Moose, Harper, 1979.
Slugger Sal's Slump, Windmill, 1979.
Henrietta's Halloween, Garrard, 1980.
Merry Christmas, Henrietta, Garrard, 1980.
Scarface Al and His Uncle Sam, Coward, 1980.
Henrietta's Fourth of July, Garrard, 1981.
Soft Skull Sam, Harcourt, 1981.
Happy Birthday, Henrietta!, Garrard, 1983.
Barney's Horse, Harper, 1987.
Mrs. Brice's Mice, Harper, 1988.

ILLUSTRATOR; FOR CHILDREN

Arthur Kober, *Thunder over the Bronc*, Simon & Schuster, 1935.
A. Kober, *Parm Me*, Constable, 1945.
Allan Sherman, *Hello Muddah, Hello Fadduh!*, Harper, 1964.
A. Sherman, *I Can't Dance!*, Harper, 1964.
Joan M. Lexau, *I Should Have Stayed in Bed!*, Harper, 1965.
J. M. Lexau, *The Homework Caper*, Harper, 1966.
J. M. Lexau, *The Rooftop Mystery*, Harper, 1968.
Tom Mac Pherson, editor, *Slithers*, Putnam, 1968.
Jerome Coopersmith, *A Chanukah Fable for Christmas*, Putnam, 1969.
John Peterson, *Mean Max*, Scholastic Inc., 1970.
Mildred Wright, *Henri Goes to Mardi Gras*, Putnam, 1971.
Ruth B. Gross, *A Book about Christopher Columbus*, Scholastic Inc., 1974.
Edward R. Ricciuti, *Donald and the Fish That Walked*, Harper, 1972.
Peggy Bradbury, *The Snake That Couldn't Slither*, Putnam, 1976.
Joan Lowery Nixon, *The Boy Who Could Find Anything*, Harcourt, 1978.
Clare Gault and Frank Gault, *A Super Fullback for the Super Bow*, Scholastic Inc., 1978.
Louise Armstrong, *Arthur Gets What He Spills*, Harcourt, 1979.
J. L. Nixon, *Bigfoot Makes a Movie*, Putnam, 1979.
Al Campanis, *Play Ball with Roger the Dodger*, Putnam, 1980.
J. M. Lexau, *Don't Be My Valentine*, Harper, 1985.
Alvin Schwartz, editor, *I Saw You in the Bathtub, and Other Folk Rhymes*, HarperCollins, 1991.

OTHER

Little Red Riding-Hood (for children), illustrated by Charles Mikolaycak, C. R. Gibson, 1968.
When Will It Snow? (for children), illustrated by Mary Chalmers, Harper, 1971.
Giants and Other Plays for Kids (includes *Lion in the Zoon, Children on the Moon, The Family,* and *Wild Flowers*), Putnam, 1973.
Gentleman Jim and the Great John L., Coward, 1977.
Boss Tweed and the Man Who Drew Him, Coward, 1978.

Hoff's manuscripts are housed at the Kerlan Collection, University of Minnesota, Minneapolis; University of California, Los Angeles; de Grummond Collection, University of Southern Mississippi, Hattiesburg; Syracuse University, New York; and the Library of Congress, Washington, D.C.

ADAPTATIONS: Danny and the Dinosaur was made into a filmstrip by Weston Woods.

SIDELIGHTS: Syd Hoff, who launched his career as a cartoonist in 1928, has become one of the most prolific of contemporary author/illustrator/graphic humorists. Like most artists, he began sketching in childhood, and in *Something about the Author Autobiography Series,* he relates an incident that influenced his desire to become an artist: "I remember one day when we came home from a trolley-car ride; I drew a picture of the conductor, resplendent in his uniform with brass buttons. 'Sydney is the artist of the family,' my mother pro-

"Tell me the story of Goldilocks." (From *Syd Hoff's Animal Jokes.*)

claimed, immediately hammering the picture into the wall with a three-inch nail." Later, when he was a high school student, cartoonist Milt Gross appeared as guest speaker at a student assembly and Hoff was asked to participate on stage as illustrator during another student's presentation. When he finished his illustrations, "Gross leaped to my side and embraced me. 'Kid, someday you'll be a great cartoonist!' he proclaimed, loud enough for the whole school to hear. Later, he made a sketch in my notebook, while everyone was begging him for autographs. It was all like a dream." Although Hoff excelled in drawing, he was less than a stunning student academically and eventually dropped out of school at the age of sixteen. He lied about his age and enrolled in the National Academy of Design in New York City, "in the hope of becoming a fine artist," Hoff once commented, "but a natural comic touch in my work caused my harried instructors to advise me to try something else. I did. At eighteen I sold my first cartoon to the *New Yorker,* and have been a regular contributor to that magazine ever since."

His humorous work is hallmarked by simplicity. Preferring to work in ink, washes, crayon, and watercolor, Hoff draws upon the New York neighborhoods in which he grew up for the characters in his cartoons; however, his humor is not dependent upon cliche or stereotype. Asked in 1939 to create a comic strip for the William Randolph Hearst Syndicate, Hoff worked on "Tuffy," about a little girl, for the next ten years. And in 1958, he began what would become nearly twenty years of work on another comic strip entitled "Laugh It Off." He also starred in a series of television shows called *Tales of Hoff* for CBS, was commissioned by national sponsors for cartoons for their advertisements, and had begun to write short mystery fiction for such publications as *Alfred Hitchcock* and *Ellery Queen.*

By this time, Hoff was married with a family. One of his daughters, though, had been stricken with a physically debilitating condition; and one day he drew some pictures to take her mind off her physical therapy. These pictures formed the basis of *Danny and the Dinosaur,* one of Hoff's earliest books for children. The story tells of a museum dinosaur who takes the day off and spends it with a young boy, playing and exploring the city. Translated into half a dozen languages and having sold more ten million copies, the book has become a classic in children's fare.

Other popular Hoff books and characters include *Albert the Albatross, Sammy the Seal, Julius* (a gorilla), *Stanley* (a caveman), *Chester* (a horse), and *The Horse in Harry's Room.* All are told in a simple, easy-to-read format; the plots "are generally straightforward, dealing positively with concepts familiar to and easily grasped by early elementary audiences," Christine Doyle Francis writes in *Twentieth-Century Children's Writers.* Animals often star in the books, setting off on an adventure in a strange new place before returning home safely. "At his best," Francis concludes, Hoff's "likable" characters "provide the beginning reader with an engaging stimulus to read the easily managed texts."

A children's classic, this tale of a museum dinosaur's day off was inspired by pictures Hoff drew to entertain his sick daughter.

Just as he was once inspired by a visiting author, Hoff now makes trips to schools himself. "Becoming a children's author meant making personal appearances," Hoff indicates in his autobiographical essay. "I traveled all over the country, meeting young people and giving them pointers in the art of cartooning." One of the pointers, the cartoonist relates, is that "the best humor has to do with events that people can identify as having happened to them, or something that has been in the subconscious. As Humor, for some reason, is basically sad. There's some sort of affinity between the sad and the funny that makes it all the funnier."

WORKS CITED:

Francis, Christine Doyle, "Syd Hoff," *Twentieth-Century Children's Writers,* 3rd edition, St. James Press, 1989, pp. 459-460.

Hoff, Syd, essay in *Something about the Author Autobiography Series,* Volume 4, Gale, 1987, pp. 211-31.

FOR MORE INFORMATION SEE:

BOOKS

Contemporary Graphic Artists, Volume 1, Gale, 1986, pp. 138-41.

A little boy keeps an imaginary horse in his house in Hoff's self-illustrated story for beginning readers.

PERIODICALS

Best Sellers, September 1, 1967.
New York Times Book Review, October 8, 1967.
Washington Post, February 8, 1981.
Young Readers' Review, April, 1967.

*   *   *

HOLMES, Martha 1961-

PERSONAL: Born January 22, 1961, in Benghazi, Libya. *Education:* Bristol University, B.Sc. (with honors), 1982; York University, Ph.D., 1988. *Hobbies and other interests:* Mountaineering, skiing, riding, scuba diving, photography.

ADDRESSES: Office—Old Rectory House, Marston Magna, Yeovil, Somerset, England BA22 8DT.

CAREER: British Broadcasting Corporation Natural History Unit, 1988—, presenter of *Reefwatch* and *Great British Birdwatch,* reporter and researcher of *Nature,* presenter and researcher of *Splashdown* and *Sea Trek*; author.

MEMBER: Royal Geographical Society, British Mountaineering Council.

WRITINGS:

Deadly Animals, illustrated by Mike Vaughan, Atheneum, 1991.
Sea Trek, BBC Books, 1991.

SIDELIGHTS: A seasoned traveler even as a child, Martha Holmes was born in Libya, grew up in the Middle East and Africa, and attended English schools, earning her bachelor's degree in zoology from Bristol University. In 1984 she spent three months in the Bahamas studying coral reefs for her Ph.D. in tropical marine biology, and now divides her time between writing and working as a reporter, assistant producer, and presenter for the British Broadcasting Corporation (BBC-TV) Natural History Unit. Her first project for BBC-TV was *Reefwatch,* in which she presented the first-ever live underwater program. Holmes's latest project, *Sea Trek,* was a five-part BBC-TV series which she researched and presented in 1991.

In *Deadly Animals,* Holmes introduces young readers to tigers, hyenas, electric eels, and other predatory animals and fish, using illustrations and boxed collections of facts for each animal.

FOR MORE INFORMATION SEE:

PERIODICALS

Bulletin of the Center for Children's Books, November, 1991, p. 64.
School Library Journal, August, 1991, p. 160.

MARTHA HOLMES

HOWKER, Janni 1957-

PERSONAL: Born on July 6, 1957, in Nicosia, Cyprus; British citizen; daughter of Malcolm (a flight lieutenant in the British Royal Air Force) and Mavis (a schoolteacher) Walker. *Education:* Lancaster University, B.A. (with honors), 1980, M.A., 1984.

ADDRESSES: Agent—c/o Julia MacRae Books, 20 Vauxhall Bridge Road, London SW1V 2SA, England.

CAREER: Writer; creator of writing workshops. Worked variously as hospital aide to mentally ill patients, research assistant in sociology department of Lancaster University, examiner at Open University, census officer, park attendant, tutor, and assistant on an archeological site.

MEMBER: Society of Authors, Northern Association of Writers in Education.

AWARDS, HONORS: International Reading Association children's book award and *Burnley Express* award, both 1985, for *Badger on the Barge,* which also was named Best Book of the Year by the American Library Association, 1984, shortlisted for the Carnegie Medal Award, 1984, commended by the Whitbread Literary Awards, 1985, and listed by *School Library Journal* as a "Best Book of 1985"; Tom-Gallon Trust Award, 1985, for short story "The Egg-Man"; Whitbread Literary Award, children's fiction category, *Young Observer* (now *Observer*) teenage fiction prize, and *Observer*-Rank Organisation prize, all 1985, and Silver Pencil award, 1987, all for *The Nature of the Beast,* which also was named an ALA Notable Book, 1985, highly commended by the Carnegie Medal Awards, 1985, and placed on *Horn Book*'s honor list, 1986; *Boston Globe/Horn Book* fiction honor award and Somerset Maugham award, both 1987, for *Isaac Campion,* which also was highly commended by the Carnegie Medal Awards, 1986, and named Best Book of the Year by the ALA, a *New York Times* Notable Book, and a Best Book for Young Adults by *School Library Journal,* all 1987.

WRITINGS:

FOR YOUNG ADULTS

Badger on the Barge and Other Stories (includes "Badger on the Barge," "Reicker," "Jakey," "The Egg-Man," and "The Topiary Garden"), Greenwillow, 1984.
The Nature of the Beast (novel), Greenwillow, 1985.
Isaac Campion (novel), Greenwillow, 1986.

OTHER

Editor of the poetry magazine, *Brew,* for the Brewery Arts Centre in Kendal, England, 1978-79.

ADAPTATIONS: The story "Badger on the Barge" was adapted for a television film and broadcast on ITV, 1987; *The Nature of the Beast* was adapted for film and released by 4/British Screen, 1988.

WORK IN PROGRESS: Working on a new novel.

SIDELIGHTS: Janni Howker's stories and novels have received international acclaim for their colorful and intelligent portrayals of adolescents encountering issues such as poverty, unemployment, and family crisis in northern England. Reviewers have been impressed with her eye for detail and the intense emotion that fills her work, and have found that Howker's first three books, *Badger on the Barge and Other Stories, The Nature of the Beast,* and *Isaac Campion,* provide stimulating reading for adults as well as children. *Times Literary Supplement* reviewer Neil Philip declared that "Janni Howker is a writer of considerable power: she knows how to sting and how to suggest." Philip also described her as "a writer of real passion."

Howker's father was an officer in the British Royal Air Force, and from the time of her birth in Nicosia, Cyprus, until she was six years old, her family, consisting of Howker, her parents, and an older and younger sister, moved frequently to different military bases. Howker's first memories of a permanent home are the years her family spent living in the Officers' Married Quarters on the Royal Air Force base at Manby in Lincolnshire, England, until she was twelve. In an essay for *Something about the Author Autobiography Series* (*SAAS*), Howker described how at Manby she developed interests and qualities that have shaped her life: "It was there ... among the wheat fields and dykes, small woods and furrows, chalk outcrops and tadpole-wriggling farm ponds that I first fell in love, and nearly became the whole person that love makes of a Self."

Howker was fascinated with nature as a child, and in *SAAS* told of how her explorations of the outdoors affected her way of looking at the world: "What had captured my love at the age of eight? The newts and

JANNI HOWKER

frogs, trees and fish, plants and birds, fossils and feathers, cumuli and constellations, east winds and sea frets which surrounded me. And this was a true and self-discovered passion. It had little to do with school, although I liked the Nature Table best of all things in the classroom. Outside the playground, my life revolved around the wonderful question 'Why?' And the answers were provided by my own curiosity and observations."

This enthusiasm did not carry over to classroom studies. Plagued by a lack of confidence and what she termed a "math phobia," Howker began to have troubles in school. In *SAAS* she explained how "this business with maths troubled my Mum and Dad a great deal. Education was their god. It had proved their salvation. It had taken them from the back streets and cotton mills of Preston [in northern England] to where they were now." In their desire to have their daughter succeed in the same way, her parents put more pressure on her to learn her lessons, inadvertently increasing Howker's distaste for math and school.

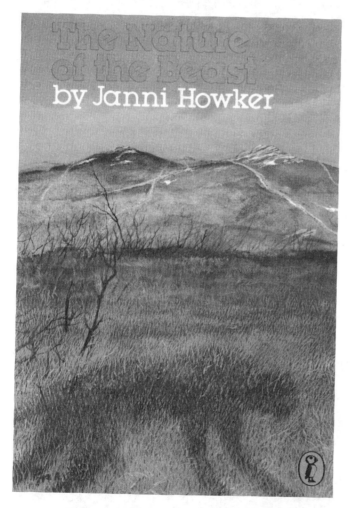

Howker's own difficult school years—which included a math "phobia" and low self-confidence—are reflected in the experiences of Bill Coward, the protagonist of *The Nature of the Beast*. (Cover illustration by Jos. A. Smith.)

The problems at school and the pressure she felt at home to improve her performance drove Howker further into her self-taught outdoor studies. "Another outcome of these events was that I took to reading with a vengeance," she wrote in *SAAS*. "I had always read for pleasure, but now I read to *escape*. [When I went to school] I took books with me. I would sit through lessons with the lid of my desk slightly raised and read and read. *Swallows and Amazons, The Coot Club, The Children Who Lived in a Barn,* and, best of all, *My Side of the Mountain* in which an American or Canadian child went off and lived alone in a hollow tree on the steep forested slopes. What these books chiefly had in common was that the children in them lived, brave, capable, resourceful, in a world where all adults were absent."

When she later was writing as an adult, Howker rediscovered her own childhood emotions in one of her characters. "My hero, Bill Coward, in *The Nature of the Beast,* has much the same kind of problems with teachers and adult truths as I had. Perhaps that is why I found it so easy to write about him. I was only writing about another version of myself. He knows, just as well as I knew, that the really important lessons to be learned about Life did not come to you in the classroom, but came from home, the playground, and the twilight zone of playing out after Tea."

An important change occurred when Howker entered her teen years: her family moved to Kendal, a city near her parents' hometown of Preston in the county of Lancashire. While Howker found the sights and sounds of the manufacturing city difficult to adjust to after her youth in the country, living in Kendal allowed her to become more familiar with her relatives living in the area and to learn about the type of life they and other factory workers had led earlier in the century. Howker stated in *SAAS,* "Some things ... now fell into place—fitted like pieces long missing from a jigsaw puzzle. My parents' attitudes, family sayings, histories did not seem odd or out of place here. Living closer to them, I began to get to know my surviving Lancashire relatives better—not least among them, my Great-Aunt Winifred [who had helped raise Howker's father].... I also came to know my surviving grandfather—my mother's father. He had worked in cotton mills all his life, and, as an old man, was still having splinters extracted from his soles and heels, having worked barefoot among the industrial looms."

It was through correspondence with her grandfather that Howker gained the information and inspiration to write one of her books. Howker described in *SAAS* her reaction to a letter in which her grandfather discussed his difficult childhood in the mills: "Compassion opened in me like a wound. When, four or five years later, I found myself living in the same kind of mill-workers' terraced house as his, and less than twenty miles from the redbrick, soot-grim chimney of Tulketh Mill where he had slaved out his days, I tried to write that book for him. The modern version. *The Nature of the Beast.*"

As a teen Howker moved to Northern England, where the author discovered the countryside of Lancashire, the featured setting for her critically acclaimed collection of short stories. (Cover illustration by Emma Chichester-Clark.)

Learning about her family was an important part of Howker's learning about herself and eventually became a part of her writing; she revealed in *SAAS*: "I began to understand, at last, what had driven them and, perhaps, [in telling their life stories] they too understood more of themselves. For to tell the true story of the meaning of our lives is to break the spells events can cast over us. It is not surprising, in a way, that my first three books share the Northern background which I inherited, and that all the young people in them have one thing in common—they struggle to break spells which family attitudes, social bigotry, or misunderstandings are trying to cast over them."

Howker first began to write seriously as a teenager, initially as another means of escape, and later, as an artistic pursuit; she remembered in *SAAS:* "It was in Kendal that the escape to fantasy and make-believe turned into writing as the isolation of being 'a New Girl' went on forever. I began to make up stories, to write poetry, and, as my reading widened, I began to realise that there were ways of doing this which could make your whole inner self vibrate. It was as if words

themselves were like instruments, cellos and oboes, flutes and trumpets. To hear their music, you had to learn how to play them well and with respect." As Howker continued to write, the activity took on increased meaning for her. In *SAAS* she recalled her discovery "that words need not be used as a form of escape from the real world, but as a means of exploring it" and that "poetry and writing were the most exact record of *how life feels as it is lived.*"

After high school Howker attended Lancaster University, where she earned a bachelor's degree in independent studies in 1980, returning to complete in 1984 a master's degree in creative writing. Around this time Howker wrote a short story entitled "Jakey," the first piece of writing that she felt was good enough to send to a publisher. The publisher not only liked Howker's work, but asked for more, and so Howker wrote a series of short stories that draw on themes from her family's past. The resultant tales, "Badger on the Barge," "Reicker," "The Egg-Man," and "The Topiary Garden," along with "Jakey" became the collection *Badger on the Barge and Other Stories.* All the narratives are set in Howker's home territory of Lancashire, and each deals with a relationship between a child and an elderly person. Reviewers enjoyed her straightforward approach in presenting complex topics and emotions stemming from the problems of individuals and communities in hard times. Ann M. Martin, in a review of *Badger on the Barge* in the *New York Times Book Review,* stated: "Miss Howker's uncanny ability to reach into her past to recall childlike impressions and experiences, to project herself into the minds and bodies of the elderly, and to capture detail and dialogue, give the stories a life and liveliness not often found in children's literature today. The feelings evoked by the stories are at the same time rich, sparse and sharply uncompromising."

Howker's novels, *The Nature of the Beast* and *Isaac Campion,* also received glowing reviews. Both are historical looks at young boys attempting to survive the family, economic, and social difficulties that surround them. Some critics found the books to be surprisingly grim for literature aimed at young adults, although many acknowledged that Howker effectively balanced the darker aspects of the books with humor and warmth. Howker herself avoids labeling her writing as solely for young adults, and told Jaci Stephen in the *Times Educational Supplement,* "My intention is to write good books ... the best I can." Ronald Blythe, reviewing *Isaac Campion* in the *New York Times Book Review,* also commented that "although [the book] is categorized by the publisher as a novel for the over-10's, there is no impediment to this harsh little tale catching the eye of the over-20's. But this is always the hallmark of the best juvenile fiction."

In *SAAS* Howker concluded that being a successful author is a constant struggle between positive and negative influences: "The real truth is that I believe that to become a writer at some point in your life a black 'spell' must be cast on you ... and I would wish this on

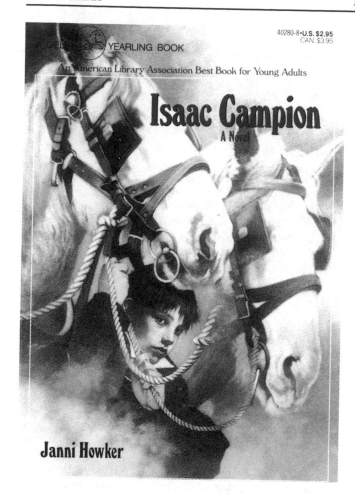

Isaac Campion is the story of the difficulties and joys of growing up in hard times, as told through the memories of a ninety-six year old man. (Cover illustration by Wendy Popp.)

no one. Such spells do not necessarily lead to art but to crippled lives. Enough love must remain intact for you to become your own spell-breaker; enough curiosity and confidence remain for you to stay alive in the world of the *real* as well as in the world of *words.*" The positive reviews and list of major awards that she has received imply that her readers feel Howker has achieved an impressive control over such factors in her writing. *School Library Journal* contributor Sara Miller voiced the opinion of many reviewers when she proclaimed that Howker's "sensitivity to the needs and secret longings of old and young alike make her one of the most exciting young writers working today."

WORKS CITED:

Blythe, Ronald, "A Mouth to Feed," *New York Times Book Review,* May 17, 1987, p. 45.

Howker, Janni, autobiographical essay in *Something about the Author Autobiography Series,* Volume 13, Gale, 1992, pp. 105-19.

Martin, Ann M., review of *Badger on the Barge and Other Stories, New York Times Book Review,* October 6, 1985, p. 41.

Miller, Sara, review of *Isaac Campion, School Library Journal,* June-July 1987, p. 107.

Philip, Neil, "This Business of Remembering," *Times Literary Supplement,* November 14, 1986, p. 1291.

Stephen, Jaci, "Northern Lights," *Times Educational Supplement,* June 7, 1985, p. 51.

FOR MORE INFORMATION SEE:

BOOKS

Children's Literature Review, Volume 14, Gale, 1988, pp. 124-31.

PERIODICALS

Booklist, June 1, 1985, p. 1400; October 15, 1985, p. 328.

Bulletin of the Center for Children's Books, June, 1985; November, 1985; May, 1987.

Horn Book, May/June, 1985, p. 317.

Publishers Weekly, April 26, 1985, p. 82; October 4, 1985, p. 77.

School Library Journal, May, 1985, p. 102; November, 1985, p. 97; September, 1987, p. 137.

I–J

IRVINE, Georgeanne 1955-

PERSONAL: Born October 31, 1955, in San Diego, CA; daughter of George G. and Dorothy E. Irvine. *Education:* San Diego State University, B.A. (summa cum laude), 1977. *Hobbies and other interests:* Travel, photography, music, tennis, laughing, roller skating, walking, animals, practical jokes, kazoo-playing.

ADDRESSES: Office—San Diego Zoo, P.O. Box 551, San Diego, CA 92112-0551; The Gordy Foundation, P.O. Box 3781, San Diego, CA 92163.

CAREER: San Diego Zoo, San Diego, CA, public relations assistant, 1978, public relations coordinator, 1978-88, public relations manager, 1989—; author of books for children, 1982—. The Gordy Foundation, founder and president, 1990.

MEMBER: Society of Children's Book Writers, Writing Women, Public Relations Society of America, Public Relations Club of San Diego.

AWARDS, HONORS: Mark of Excellence, Public Relations Club of San Diego (PRCSD), 1978, 1980, 1985, and 1988, and merit award, PRCSD, 1979, 1981-83, 1986-87, all for *Koala Club News;* Mark of Excellence, PRCSD, 1986, award of merit, San Diego International Association of Business Communicators, and Bronze Anvil award, Public Relations Society of America (PRSA), both 1987, and Silver Cindy film/video award, Association of Visual Communicators (AVC), 1988, all for audio-visual presentation "San Diego Zoo—It's a Wild Life!;" Silver Cindy award, AVC, 1991, and merit award, PRCSD, 1992, both for "A Roarin' Remembrance;" Silver Anvil award, PRSA, 1992, for the San Diego Zoo's Seventy-fifth Birthday campaign.

WRITINGS:

"ZOO BABIES" SERIES; PUBLISHED BY IDEALS PUBLISHING

Alberta the Gorilla, 1982.
Nanuck the Polar Bear, 1982.

GEORGEANNE IRVINE

Sasha the Cheetah, 1982.
Sydney the Koala, 1982.
Wilbur and Orville the Otter Twins, 1982.
Zelda the Zebra, 1982.
Bo the Orangutan, 1983.
Elmer the Elephant, 1983.
Georgie the Giraffe, 1983.
Lindi the Leopard, 1983.
The Nursery Babies, 1983.

Tully the Tree Kangaroo, 1983.

EDITOR OF "SAN DIEGO ZOO SERIES" BOOKS

Families, Heian International, 1983.
Mothers and Babies, Heian International, 1983.
Piggyback and Peek-a-boo, Heian International, 1983.
A Visit to the Zoo, Heian International, 1983.

"ZOO WORLD" SERIES; PUBLISHED BY SIMON & SCHUSTER

Protecting Endangered Species at the San Diego Zoo, 1990.
Raising Gordy Gorilla at the San Diego Zoo, 1990.
The Visit of Two Giant Pandas at the San Diego Zoo, 1991.
The Work of the Zoo Doctors at the San Diego Zoo, 1991.

OTHER

The True Story of Corky the Blind Seal, Scholastic Inc., 1987.
Let's Visit a Super Zoo, Troll, 1990.

Author of articles on animals for the *Lincoln Homework Encyclopedia,* published by Harcourt. Contributor of articles to periodicals, including *Good Housekeeping* and *Zoonooz.* Editor of *Koala Club News,* a zoo publication for children.

WORK IN PROGRESS: A book for children about the plight of koalas in Australia; two more books for the Simon & Schuster *Zoo World* series.

SIDELIGHTS: Georgeanne Irvine is the author and editor of more than twenty nonfiction books about animals. She cites an affection for all animals and lists giant pandas, koalas, gorillas, and "Irving the indigo snake"—named after Irvine herself—among her favorite creatures. Irvine's love for animals not only led her to write about them, it also influenced her decision to take a job where she could be close to them every day. As she described her work to *SATA:* "Since March 1978, I've prowled the San Diego Zoo. As the zoo's public relations manager, I'm a press spokesperson and an advisor to zoo management on media-related zoo and conservation issues. I'm the editor of our award-winning quarterly children's publication, *Koala Club News.* I also work on various publicity topics, which range from baby koalas and tigers to major fundraising events and exhibit debuts to escaped orangutans and bears. All filming and television production at the zoo is under my supervision. In addition, I coordinate in-studio filming and television talk show appearances. I work closely with goodwill ambassador Joan Embery (that 'blonde lady' on the *Tonight Show*) regarding her media appearances. I often handle zoo press conferences, special promotions, and other unusual events. In addition, I write copy for things such as guidebooks, books, and press releases."

In addition to her many duties as a public relations manager, Irvine's work at the San Diego Zoo has provided her with material for her books, offbeat excitement, and opportunities to meet famous people. "I've been chased around hotel rooms by leopards," she recalled, "and I've even slept with a kangaroo at the foot of my bed. I've worked with Brooke Shields, Julie Andrews, Olivia Newton-John, Dudley Moore, Benji the dog, Minnie Mouse, and even the Care Bears."

While Irvine has engaged in these varied activities, she has also devoted her time and energy to protecting animals with her work for the Gordy Foundation. As she explained: "The Gordy Foundation is a nonprofit organization dedicated to the preservation and conservation of endangered animal species and their native habitats. I founded the organization in 1990 to 'put my money where my heart is.' The foundation is funded in part through a percentage of royalties I donate from my children's book proceeds and also from private contributions. Grants from the Gordy Foundation are given to organizations that are actively working to protect animals and their natural homes. The foundation is named after Gordy Gorilla, a real-life gorilla who is featured in my book *Raising Gordy Gorilla at the San Diego Zoo.*"

Irvine summarized her career, stating that "wildlife and wildlife habitat conservation is an important message I convey in my books. Children deserve to inherit a world rich in flora and fauna."

*   *   *

JACKA, Martin 1943-

PERSONAL: Born March 11, 1943, in Newquay, Cornwall, England; son of Tom and Gwendoline (May) Jacka; married, wife's name, Gillian; children: Lisa, Martyn.

ADDRESSES: Home—16 Jervois Road, Semaphore, South Australia, Australia. *Office—Adelaide Advertiser,* Adelaide, South Australia, Australia.

CAREER: News, Ltd., Australia, newspaper photographer for *Adelaide Advertiser.*

WRITINGS:

Waiting for Billy, Omnibus, 1990, Orchard, 1991.

WORK IN PROGRESS: A dolphin book for older children; a dolphin book for adults based on five years of photographic study.

SIDELIGHTS: Photographer Martin Jacka told *SATA:* "Living within two miles of a harbour and open sea, my studies—first as a newspaper photographer and then as a published writer about the local bottlenose dolphin—has led me to start on a series of four related books, all at present unfinished. Five years of shooting pictures so far, with no end in sight."

MARTIN JACKA

JANOSCH
See ECKERT, Horst

*   *   *

JENKINS, Patrick 1955-

PERSONAL: Born March 7, 1955, in Brantford, Ontario, Canada; son of Ivan and Jean (a teacher) Jenkins. *Education:* York University, B.F.A., 1978, M.F.A., 1982; also attended Banff School of Fine Arts and Elliot Lake School of Fine Arts.

ADDRESSES: Home—125 Roxborough St. West, Toronto, Ontario, Canada M5R 1T9. *Office*—c/o Addison-Wesley Publishing Co., Route 128, Reading, MA 01867.

CAREER: Writer, artist, animator, and publisher. York University, Toronto, Ontario, Canada, various teaching and studio positions, 1978-87; Art Gallery of Grant, Brantford, Ontario, Canada, technical assistant, 1978-79, curator for group shows of Canadian Experimental Film, 1983; curator for group shows of Experimental Cinema from Toronto for Media Study, Buffalo, NY, and the Southwestern Alternate Media Program, Houston, TX; Rogers Cable Television System, Toronto, Ontario, Canada, associate producer of *The Amazing Children's Animated Movie Workshop*. Visiting filmmaker at various educational institutions in Ontario; instructor in film animation courses and workshops for high schools and colleges in Ontario. *Exhibitions:* Jenkins's work has been exhibited in Canada, the United States, Britain, New Zealand, Australia, and the People's Republic of China; in addition, his films have been included in group screenings in Canada, Britain, Germany, Japan, Venezuela, and the United States. Jenkins's films and artwork are also represented in collections in Canada and the United States.

AWARDS, HONORS: Grants from the Ontario Arts Council, 1978, 1981, 1983, 1985-88; First Prize, experimental category, Toronto Super-8 Film Festival, 1979, for *Fluster;* Director's Chair Award, experimental category, Toronto Super-8 Film Festival, for *Shadowplay,* Canada Council "B" Grant in visual art/drawing, and Samuel Sarrick Purchase Award, York University, all 1982.

WRITINGS:

SELF-ILLUSTRATED

The Magician's Hat, Patrick Jenkins, 1987.
In the Wink of an Eye, Patrick Jenkins, 1987.
A Fishy Tale, Patrick Jenkins, 1987.
Making Faces, Patrick Jenkins, 1987.
Play Ball, Patrick Jenkins, 1988.
Slap Shot!, Patrick Jenkins, 1991.
Skateboarding, Patrick Jenkins, 1991.
Animation: How to Draw Your Own Flipbooks and Other Fun Ways to Make Cartoons Move, Addison-Wesley, 1991.

Also creator of short films, including *Wedding Before Me, G, Room Film, Isolations, At the Gates, Fluster, A Sense of Spatial Organization, Ruse, Shadowplay, Sign Language, A Matter of Time,* and *Four Short Animated Films.*

WORK IN PROGRESS: New flipbooks.

SIDELIGHTS: Patrick Jenkins told *SATA:* "I can remember drawing at a very early age. I loved to draw. I would fill sketchbooks with hundreds of drawings out of

PATRICK JENKINS

Jenkins translates his cartoon films into "flipbooks" that children can animate by rapidly flipping pages.

my head. In addition to art, I loved to read. I read mainly novels (fantasy, science fiction, mystery) and books on art and history. I was also interested in movies. I remember going to the movies and watching the movie twice. The first time I would enjoy the movie and the second time I would try and figure out how the movie was made.

"At university I studied painting and drawing and took several classes in filmmaking. After I graduated I did several exhibitions of my drawings in galleries in Toronto and created several short movies.

"Around 1985 I began to make animated cartoon movies. Animation brought together my two interests, drawing and movies. About the same time I started doing animation workshops with school children. I work with the children and help them make up stories. Then we turn the story into an animated movie, using the technique of cut-out animation. In cut-out animation you cut the characters and backgrounds out of construction paper. It's like making a flat puppet show. Then we push the characters a little bit at a time and film them with the animation camera. Later, when the movie film has been processed, the children add a soundtrack to their movies.

"My work with children inspired me to make my own animated movies. My first animated movie was entitled *The Magician's Hat.* In this movie a magician tries to pull a rabbit out of his hat. However, he finds that the hat contains more than a rabbit. Over the course of this one-minute movie, the puzzled magician pulls about a hundred different objects out of his hat.

"When I had finished this movie I had lots of drawings of the magician in various poses. I got to wondering, 'What can I do with all these drawings?' I remembered that when I was young I had seen little books called

flipbooks. Flipbooks are books that are made up of a series of drawings. Each drawing is slightly different from the drawings that come before and after it. When the pages of the flipbook are 'flipped,' the drawings come to life in a short animated movie. Flipbooks show our eyes a series of drawings so quickly that our eyes blend all these pictures together and we think that the drawings have come to life. The same thing happens when we watch a movie in a theatre. The movie projector shows our eyes twenty-four pictures a second and our eyes blend all the pictures together.

"I used the drawings of the magician to create my first flipbook, entitled *The Magician's Hat.* Naturally I had to shorten the story of the magician's adventures to create this book. Instead of a hundred different objects, the magician only pulled about twelve different objects out of his hat.

"The second flipbook I created was called *Making Faces.* This book was also created from artwork from one of my animated movies. In the movie *Making Faces* several odd characters play peek-a-boo.

"I love flipbooks because you can really bring your drawings to life. I began to realize that flipbooks were about the enjoyment of movement, watching static drawings magically come to life. I began to think of exciting animated sequences where there was lots of movement. Up to this point I had been making flipbooks based on my animated movies. The flipbooks that I would create from here on in were designed solely as flipbooks.

"The next flipbook I designed was an underwater adventure called *A Fishy Tale.* In this book a cartoon character tries to avoid being eaten by a number of hungry fish. Fish would appear from all sides and the main character would have to dodge to avoid their attacks. To create this book, I had to teach myself how to create flipbooks. I drew stencils of the various fish. Then I would move and retrace these stencils on each successive page of the book. By using a stencil I could keep the characters the same shape and size, allowing me to concentrate on the animation.

"For my next book I decided to experiment with the illusion of depth. I found that if you drew a dot on one page, then drew a small circle on the next page, and then drew a bigger circle on the next page, you could create the illusion that a ball was coming towards you. The new book was called *In the Wink of an Eye.* In this book a man opens his eye and we get closer and see that there is another picture inside his eye. Each successive picture contains another picture within a picture.

"I experimented with the illusion of depth in two other flipbooks, *Play Ball!* and *Slap Shot!* These books show the exciting action of a baseball and a hockey game, with both the baseball and hockey puck hurling straight towards the viewer. The next book, *Skateboarding,* showed a child skateboarder performing some amazing acrobatic stunts.

"My recent book, *Animation, How to Draw Your Own Flipbooks and Other Fun Ways to Make Cartoons Move,* teaches children how to make their own flipbooks and other motion picture devices. I have also created several animated movies including *The Magician's Hat, Making Faces,* and *The Flipbook Movie,* which was screened at the 1991 Chicago International Children's Film Festival. In addition I have produced a video documentary on my work with children, entitled *The Amazing Children's Animated Movie Workshop.*"

*   *   *

JOHNSON, A.
See JOHNSON, Annabell (Jones)

*   *   *

JOHNSON, A. E.
See JOHNSON, Annabell (Jones) and JOHNSON, Edgar Raymond

*   *   *

JOHNSON, Annabel
See JOHNSON, Annabell (Jones)

*   *   *

JOHNSON, Annabell (Jones) 1921-
(A. Johnson; Annabel Johnson; A. E. Johnson, a joint pseudonym)

PERSONAL: Born June 18, 1921, in Kansas City, MO; daughter of Burnam R. and Mary Estelle (Ball) Jones; married Edgar Raymond Johnson (a ceramic artist and writer; died December 2, 1990), September 14, 1949. *Education:* Attended College of William and Mary, 1939-40, and Art Students League. *Hobbies and other*

ANNABEL AND EDGAR JOHNSON

interests: Ceramics, gardening, hand-weaving, trout-fly tying.

ADDRESSES: Home—2925 South Teller, Denver, CO 80227.

CAREER: Worked in publishing houses, as a librarian, legal secretary, and in other secretarial posts prior to 1957; writer, mainly in collaboration with husband, Edgar Raymond Johnson, 1957—.

MEMBER: Gamma Phi Beta.

AWARDS, HONORS: Spring Book Festival Award, 1959, for *The Black Symbol,* and 1960, for *Torrie;* Friends of American Writers Award, 1962, for *The Secret Gift;* Golden Spur Award, Western Writers of America, 1966, for *The Burning Glass;* William Allen White Children's Book Award, 1967, for *The Grizzly.*

WRITINGS:

(Under name A. Johnson) *As a Speckled Bird,* Crowell, 1956.
(Under name Annabel Johnson) *I Am Leaper,* illustrated by Stella Ormai, Galley, 1990.

JUVENILE; WITH HUSBAND, AS ANNABELL AND EDGAR JOHNSON

The Big Rock Candy, Crowell, 1957.
The Black Symbol, illustrated by Brian Saunders, Harper, 1959.
Torrie, illustrated by Pearl Falconer, Harper, 1960.
The Bearcat, Harper, 1960.
The Rescued Heart, Harper, 1961.
Pickpocket Run, Harper, 1961.
Wilderness Bride, Harper, 1962.
A Golden Touch, Harper, 1963.
The Grizzly, illustrated by Gilbert Riswold, Harper, 1964.
A Peculiar Magic, illustrated by Lynd Ward, Houghton, 1965.
The Burning Glass, Harper, 1966.
Count Me Gone, Simon & Schuster, 1968.
The Last Knife (short stories), Simon & Schuster, 1971.
Finders, Keepers, Four Winds, 1981.
An Alien Music, Four Winds, 1982.
The Danger Quotient, Harper, 1984.
Prisoner of Psi, Atheneum, 1985.
A Memory of Dragons, Atheneum, 1986.
Gamebuster, illustrated by Stephen Marchesi, Dutton, 1990.

ADULT FICTION; WITH EDGAR JOHNSON UNDER JOINT PSEUDONYM A. E. JOHNSON

The Secret Gift, Doubleday, 1961.
A Blues I Can Whistle, Four Winds, 1969.

Johnson's manuscripts are included in the Kerlan Collection, University of Minnesota.

SIDELIGHTS: Annabell and Edgar Johnson came from very different backgrounds to form their writing partnership, as Annabell recalled in an autobiographical

essay included in *Third Book of Junior Authors.* Edgar was born in a coal-mining town in Montana and applied himself to a variety of jobs as a young man. He worked as a railroad section hand, tried his luck at a career as a semi-professional baseball player, and even played the fiddle with an old-time country dance band before embarking upon a career as a ceramic artist and author. Annabell was raised in the more conventional surroundings afforded by St. Louis, Missouri, but was drawn to the excitement of New York City when she was old enough to leave home. She lived a rather bohemian existence while she pursued her dream of becoming a writer, and supported herself by holding jobs in several different publishing houses. Their paths merged during the 1940s when Edgar arrived in New York City to study art. They shared a common love of the history and drama of life in the Old West; and after they married, Annabell Johnson was able to make a commitment to becoming a full-time author. The Johnsons fulfilled their desire to communicate this enthusiasm for the West by writing stories for children who lived in urban areas far removed from the rock-strewn landscapes and the independent spirit of frontier life.

The Johnsons began their literary collaborations with several novels whose intent was to bring the Old West to life for children far removed from the country. (Cover illustration by George Salter.)

The Johnsons spent twelve years travelling throughout the majestic panorama of the western United States. They stayed in a small camp-trailer, and worked temporary or part-time jobs for enough money to continue their journey. Annabell and Edgar lived close to the land, camping in the desert in the wintertime, and spending their summer months high up in the Rocky Mountains. They sought out little-known facets of history in the places they visited, gathering ideas for stories from old letters lying inside dusty glass display cases in local historical museums, and collecting personal recollections from the old-timers who frequented the coffee-shops, front stoops, and other local gathering places in the towns they passed through in their travels. The Johnsons compiled accounts of panning for gold, breaking new trails across the land, and other aspects of life unique to the western mountains. Whenever they had accumulated enough material for a story, the couple retreated to the parklands of the national forests to write. Eventually the Johnsons would emerge with novels populated by characters from the era of western expansion, ready to catch the imagination of the young reader wishing to relive the excitement of the gold rush or the early days of the fur trade, experience the hardships of a wagon trek along the Oregon and Mormon trails, or be caught up in a battle to unionize the coal mines.

As time passed, the Johnsons shifted the focus of their writing more toward the present era in an effort to help young adults both examine and come to terms with the changes in today's world. These later writings dealt with such subjects as E.S.P., terrorism, time travel, and other contemporary topics, while still continuing to center around the process of self-discovery and a young person's ability to come to terms with human nature. In *Finders Keepers,* for example, the plot revolves around two teenagers struggling for survival in the aftermath of a disastrous explosion at a nuclear power plant. *A Memory of Dragons* is the story of an eighteen-year-old boy named Paul who, while intellectually brilliant (he is employed by the defense industry), is nonetheless haunted by vivid memories of what seems to be a previous life, dealing with the aftereffects of the death of an abusive father, and meanwhile is involved with a love interest. Paul is sought by two political rivals and becomes embroiled in an international power struggle during the energy crisis of 1991. "That this is not confusing, but stunningly effective in its pace, action, and intricacy, is a testament to the capability of the authors," asserts a contributor to the *Bulletin of the Center for Children's Books.* The Johnsons' books, consistently well-received by both critics and their young adult readership, are noted for their ability to bring to the reader a vivid sense of time and place through an economy of detail. Whether it be their beloved Old West or a modern location, the Johnsons create believable and colorful characters to inhabit their settings, and main characters with whom their young audience can identify. "There are four major elements in a science fiction story: character, background, conflict, and plot," writes Ben Bova in a *Los Angeles Times*

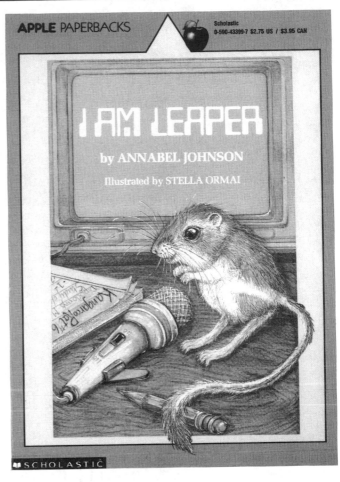

Johnson's later work has included examinations of very modern themes, including this story of a small kangaroo rat who can speak but whose message is ignored. (Cover illustration by Stella Ormai.)

review of *A Memory of Dragons;* "The Johnsons get high grades in all four."

WORKS CITED:

Review of *A Memory of Dragons, Bulletin of the Center for Children's Books,* November, 1985.

Bova, Ben, review of *A Memory of Dragons, Los Angeles Times,* November 8, 1986.

Johnson, Annabell, entry in *Third Book of Junior Authors,* edited by Doris De Montreville and Donna Hill, H. W. Wilson, 1972.

FOR MORE INFORMATION SEE:

BOOKS

Books for Children, 1960-1965, American Library Association, 1966.

Robert G. Carlson, *Books and the Teen-Age Reader,* Harper, 1967.

Child Study Association of America, *The Children's Bookshelf,* Bantam, 1965.

Nancy Larrick, *A Parent's Guide to Children's Reading,* 3rd edition, Doubleday, 1969.

Twentieth-Century Children's Writers, 3rd edition, St. James Press, 1989.

PERIODICALS

Book World, October 13, 1968.
Bulletin of the Center for Children's Books, July-August, 1984; February, 1987.
Library Journal, February 1, 1957.
New York Times Book Review, November 9, 1969; May 2, 1971.
Young Reader's Review, June, 1968.

*   *   *

JOHNSON, Edgar (Raymond) 1912-1990 (A. E. Johnson, a joint pseudonym)

PERSONAL: Born October 24, 1912, in Washoe, MT; died December 2, 1990; son of Oscar and Martha Johnson; married Annabell Jones (a writer), September 14, 1949. *Education:* Studied at Billings Polytechnic Institute; graduated from Kansas City Art Institute; further study at New York State College of Ceramics at Alfred University. *Hobbies and other interests:* Seventeenth-century music, fishing.

ADDRESSES: Home—2925 South Teller, Denver, CO 80227.

CAREER: Ceramic artist and head of ceramics department, Kansas City Art Institute, 1948-49; also model-maker, jeweler, and woodcarver with work exhibited in one-man show in New York City and included in Museum of Modern Art exhibition of American handcrafts; free-lance writer, mainly in collaboration with wife, Annabell Jones Johnson. Sometime restorer of antique musical instruments for Smithsonian Institution, Washington DC.

AWARDS, HONORS: Spring Book Festival Award, 1959, for *The Black Symbol,* and 1960, for *Torrie;* Friends of American Writers Award, 1962, for *The Secret Gift;* Golden Spur Award, Western Writers of America, 1966, for *The Burning Glass;* William Allen White Children's Book Award, 1967, for *The Grizzly.*

WRITINGS:

JUVENILE; WITH WIFE, ANNABELL JOHNSON

The Big Rock Candy, Crowell, 1957.
The Black Symbol, illustrated by Brian Saunders, Harper, 1959.
Torrie, illustrated by Pearl Falconer, Harper, 1960.
The Bearcat, Harper, 1960.
The Rescued Heart, Harper, 1961.
Pickpocket Run, Harper, 1961.
Wilderness Bride, Harper, 1962.
A Golden Touch, Harper, 1963.
The Grizzly, illustrated by Gilbert Riswold, Harper, 1964.
A Peculiar Magic, illustrated by Lynd Ward, Houghton, 1965.
The Burning Glass, Harper, 1966.
Count Me Gone, Simon & Schuster, 1968.
The Last Knife (short stories), Simon & Schuster, 1971.
Finders, Keepers, Four Winds, 1981.

An Alien Music, Four Winds, 1982.
The Danger Quotient, Harper, 1984.
Prisoner of Psi, Atheneum, 1985.
A Memory of Dragons, Atheneum, 1986.
Gamebuster, illustrated by Stephen Marchesi, Dutton, 1990.

ADULT FICTION; WITH ANNABELL JOHNSON UNDER JOINT PSEUDONYM A. E. JOHNSON

The Secret Gift, Doubleday, 1961.
A Blues I Can Whistle, Four Winds, 1969.

Johnson's manuscripts are included in the Kerlan Collection, University of Minnesota.

SIDELIGHTS: Edgar and Annabell Johnson have coauthored many popular works of historical and science fiction for both young adult and adult readers. For more information, see the "Sidelights" section in this volume under Annabell Jones Johnson.

The Johnsons' travels throughout the West in a camp-trailer provided them with the settings for many of their works, including this novel about a boy who leaves home to join a gold-mining camp. (Cover illustration by George Salter.)

FOR MORE INFORMATION SEE:

BOOKS

Books for Children, 1960-1965, American Library Association, 1966.
Carlson, G. Robert, *Books and the Teen-Age Reader,* Harper, 1967.
Child Study Association of America, *The Children's Bookshelf,* Bantam, 1965.
De Montreville, Doris and Donna Hill, editors, *Third Book of Junior Authors,* H. W. Wilson, 1972.
Larrick, Nancy, *A Parent's Guide to Children's Reading,* 3rd edition, Doubleday, 1969.
Twentieth-Century Children's Writers, 3rd edition, St. James Press, 1989.

PERIODICALS

Book World, October 13, 1968.
Bulletin of the Center for Children's Books, July-August, 1984; November, 1985; February, 1987.
Library Journal, February 1, 1957.
Los Angeles Times, November 8, 1986.
New York Times Book Review, November 9, 1969; May 2, 1971.
Young Reader's Review, June, 1968.

[Sketch reviewed by wife, Annabell Johnson]

*   *   *

JONES, Harold 1904-1992

OBITUARY NOTICE—See index for *SATA* sketch: Born February 22, 1904, in London, England; died June 10, 1992. Educator, painter, illustrator, and writer. Jones enjoyed a long career as a critically praised illustrator of children's books. His work is noted for a distinctive, personal style that is simple yet sophisticated. After studying with artistic notables Edmund J. Sullivan, Albert Rutherston, and William Rothenstein, Jones became known for his 1937 illustrations of Walter de la Mare's *This Year: Next Year,* which has been judged one of the best books of its decade. His illustrations for *Lavender's Blue,* a collection of nursery rhymes compiled by Kathleen Lines, have been called his finest. London's Langton Gallery honored Jones, a longtime art teacher, with a one-man show of his oils and illustrations. In addition to writing and illustrating *The Visit to the Farm, There and Back Again, Tales from Aesop,* and *Tales to Tell,* Jones illustrated *The Fairy Stories of Oscar Wilde* and *The Silent Playmate: A Collection of Doll Stories.*

OBITUARIES AND OTHER SOURCES:

PERIODICALS

Junior Bookshelf, August, 1992, pp. 137-139.
Times (London), June 13, 1992, p. 21.

*   *   *

JOYCE, Bill
See JOYCE, WILLIAM

JOYCE, William 1957-
(Bill Joyce)

PERSONAL: Born December 11, 1957; married; wife's name, Elizabeth; children: one. *Education:* Graduated from Southern Methodist University.

ADDRESSES: Home and office—3302 Centenary Blvd., Shreveport, LA 71104.

CAREER: Screenwriter, author, and illustrator. Stoner Art Center, Shreveport, LA, board member, 1987-89.

AWARDS, HONORS: Best Book Award, *School Library Journal,* 1985, for *George Shrinks;* Christopher Award (best illustration), 1987, for *Humphrey's Bear;* Best Illustrated Award, *New York Times,* for *Nicholas Cricket;* Silver Medal, Society of Illustrators, 1992, for *Bently & Egg.*

WRITINGS:

SELF-ILLUSTRATED

George Shrinks, Harper, 1985, special miniature edition, 1985.
Dinosaur Bob and His Adventures with the Family Lazardo, Harper, 1988.
A Day with Wilbur Robinson, HarperCollins, 1990.
Bently & Egg, HarperCollins, 1992.
Santa Calls, HarperCollins, 1993.

ILLUSTRATOR

Catherine and James Gray, *Tammy and the Gigantic Fish,* Harper, 1983.
(Under name Bill Joyce) Marianna Mayer, *My First Book of Nursery Tales: Five Mother Goose Stories,* Random House, 1983.

William Joyce and his lovely wife Elizabeth pose with one of the author's most popular characters, Dinosaur Bob. (Illustration by Joyce.)

Bently Hopperton becomes the loving caretaker of a duck egg in Joyce's gentle-spirited tribute to the works of authors such as Beatrix Potter. (Illustration by the author.)

Bethany Roberts, *Waiting-for-Spring Stories,* Harper, 1984.

Elizabeth Winthrop, *Shoes,* Harper, 1986.

Jan Wahl, *Humphrey's Bear,* Holt, 1987.

Joyce Maxner, *Nicholas Cricket,* Harper, 1989.

Stephen Manes, *Some of the Adventures of Rhode Island Red,* HarperCollins, 1990.

Also contributor of illustrations to periodicals.

ADAPTATIONS: A Day with Wilbur Robinson has been optioned as a feature-length, live-action film by Walt Disney Productions.

SIDELIGHTS: In books such as *Dinosaur Bob* and *Bently & Egg,* author and illustrator William Joyce presents characters and settings that are colorful, magical and slightly wacky. Joyce's whimsical cast of players includes a baseball-playing dinosaur, a frog who can sing and paint, and a little boy who wakes up one morning to find himself becoming very, very small. Drawing on a wide range of influences, ranging from artists Maxfield Parrish and N. C. Wyeth to Technicolor movies, Joyce imbues his illustrations with vivid colors, painstaking detail, and a finely-honed sense of exaggeration. In Joyce's world, it is perfectly normal for a city family to

adopt a friendly dinosaur or a "dull day" at a friend's house to include entertainment by jazz-playing frogs and a robot butler. Malcolm Jones, Jr., writing in *Newsweek,* sums up the author's appeal by noting that "looniness is Joyce's briar patch.... Reading Joyce is like hanging out with that slightly raffish uncle who came to town a couple of times a year, the one who drank martinis ... and always kept a few cherry bombs in the bottom of his suitcase. He was the guy who taught you that fun is the most important thing you can have."

Joyce became interested in drawing and storytelling at an early age. "I loved to draw and I loved to make things up," Joyce says in an interview for *Something about the Author* (*SATA*). "I always took play a little more seriously ... and I always liked to be the guy who got into the story part of the adventure." He received his first artistic kudos for a pictorial rendition of a dog and cat; soon after this success, Joyce moved on to bigger subjects, such as rampaging dinosaurs lopping off the heads and arms of cavemen. Joyce notes that, when sketching these later works, he "always ran out of red crayon and red pen faster than anything because of all the gore and blood."

Joyce wrote his first successful story while still in grade school. *Billy's Booger* chronicles the adventures of a young boy who "sneezes up" a talkative—and very smart—booger. Over the years, Billy's jovial, diminutive, "green and sort of slimy" pal has become a popular part of the author's school visits. Joyce observes in his interview: "Pandemonium ensues when I start drawing him.... [Billy's Booger] appeals to that sense of grotesque kids seem to love."

While he enjoyed reading and watching movies and television, Joyce had ambivalent feelings about school (with the exception of art classes). "I hated [school] and loved it.... I hated getting up in the morning. I hated having to go there every day. I hated having to study. I hated having to sit there and learn mathematics.... I liked the social aspect of school—I mean I had a blast—but I hated the tyranny of learning," he recalls for *SATA*. A self-admitted daydreamer, Joyce spent a lot of time imagining himself as a secret agent, until he realized that "secret agents sometimes get killed *and* kiss girls."

Joyce eventually decided to study filmmaking and illustration at Southern Methodist University. Part of his decision was based on a long-term fascination with movie imagery. "I got into movies," he recounts in his *SATA* exchange. "There were extraordinary things like

Oz, Robin Hood, King Kong.... I was completely swept away.... Picture books and movies have a lot in common in that they both tell their stories visually in color, movement, and composition. Often, when I'm working on my books, it plays as a movie in my head."

Joyce began sending samples of his work to publishers before his graduation from college; within a short time, he received a number of illustration contracts. While happy to gain the practical experience, Joyce eventually found himself becoming a bit frustrated. He notes in his interview: "I began to enjoy it less and less as it went on. I began to work more and more of my own stories into [the assignments]."

Joyce wrote his first self-illustrated book in 1985. *George Shrinks* tells the story of a little boy who wakes up one day to find that he has shrunk several sizes. Instead of panicking, George uses a number of ingenious tricks to get his daily chores done, including feeding his goldfish by diving into their bowl and saddling his baby brother to take out the trash. Writing in the *New York Times Book Review*, Ralph Keyes calls the story "a thoroughly charming piece of work." He adds that the book's minimalist prose is "a perfect foil for Mr. Joyce's whimsical, perceptive illustrations."

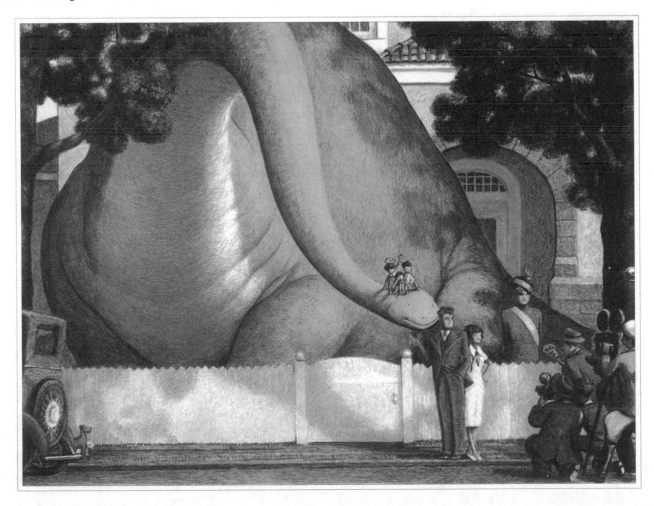

Gentle, fun-loving Dinosaur Bob preens for the press with the Lazardo family in Joyce's self-illustrated *Dinosaur Bob*.

Wild entertainment and wacky characters help make a young boy's visit to his friend's house both strange and memorable in *A Day with Wilbur Robinson.* (Illustration by the author.)

Joyce introduced one of his most popular characters in the follow-up to *George Shrinks,* entitled *Dinosaur Bob.* Bob the dinosaur meets the Lazardos during their annual safari in Africa. The entire family is so taken by the gentle giant that they invite him to live with them in beautiful Pimlico Hills. Once happily settled in his new home, the good-natured dinosaur's baseball-playing skills make him popular with the entire neighborhood; unfortunately, his enthusiasm for chasing cars eventually gets him into trouble with the local police. After a series of adventures-on-the-lam, Bob is reunited with his adopted family and all is well. In a review of *Dinosaur Bob* for the *New York Times Book Review,* Mordecai Richler declares that Bob is "the most adorable of dinos." Richler goes on to note that Joyce "managed the illustrations with considerable panache. His artwork makes it clear why Bob is such a hit with the Lazardos." A *Time* reviewer concurs, noting: "William Joyce's plot and pictures provide laughter, thrills, and most important, a happy ending."

Joyce added to his repertoire of unique characters in *A Day with Wilbur Robinson.* An eye-popping adventure full of music, magic, and mystery, *Wilbur Robinson* centers around a boy's day-long visit with his friend's unorthodox family. Action is the name of the game at the Robinson abode, where Uncle Art regales listeners with tales about his escapades in outer space and giant goldfish mingle with dog-riding frogs. In his commentary on *Wilbur Robinson* for the *New York Times Book Review,* David Leavitt writes: "Painted in such a realistic way, the bizarre events in the pictures seem appealingly plausible.... This is a charming, new-fangled, old-fashioned book."

The drawings in *Bently & Egg* marked a departure for Joyce. Instead of his usual palette of bold colors, Joyce utilizes soft watercolor pastels reminiscent of Beatrix Potter's "Peter Rabbit" tales to tell the story of the frog Bently Hopperton and his efforts to save a duck friend's egg. Whether guarding the egg or sailing in a balloon, Bently's ingenuity never fails him. Jones finds the high-spirited adventures of Joyce's amphibious protagonist highly enjoyable, calling the book "every bit as zestful as its predecessors.... Bently is never at a loss. Jubilantly resourceful, he has a swell time being a hero." And Cathy Collison, writing in the *Detroit Free Press,* praises the illustrations as being "on the Caldecott Medal level."

Joyce admits that many of his story and character ideas come "out of nowhere." "I'll see something that will trigger a series of thoughts or I'll just have some odd phrase words at the back of my mind," he tells *SATA.* "At some point, something strikes my fancy from my past, and ends up being in a book." Joyce often turns to his family for inspiration; in fact, he notes that developing characters is often a family affair: "Elizabeth [his wife] actually posed for a lot of my characters.... My nephews would pose for me, my dad would pose for me, whoever's around. I'll say 'Stand here, put on this cap, do this.'"

Many of Joyce's works, especially *Dinosaur Bob* and *A Day with Wilbur Robinson,* appeal to adults as well as children. Joyce describes the broad-based allure of his books and characters for *SATA* by saying that "they strike a playful chord that grownups remember from their own childhoods.... [The books] ... harken back to the sort of shared popular culture that we all grew up with on television—Flash Gordon from the thirties, the Stooges from the forties, Bugs Bunny from the fifties. Growing up watching television, you would see this constant barrage of cool stuff ... it's become a sort of shared sensibility." Whatever the reasons for his success, Joyce sees his work as having one underlying motivation: "It seems to me that I'm always trying to make and remake my childhood the way it should have been, where's everything's okay.... I like to do stories where everything works out okay."

WORKS CITED:

Collison, Cathy, review of *Bently & Egg, Detroit Free Press,* March 18, 1992.

Review of *Dinosaur Bob, Time,* December 12, 1988, p. 87.

Jones, Malcolm Jr., "Make Room for Bently," *Newsweek,* March 16, 1992, p. 72.

Joyce, William, telephone interview for *Something about the Author,* conducted by Elizabeth A. Des Chenes on June 10, 1992.

Keyes, Ralph, review of *George Shrinks, New York Times Book Review,* December 29, 1985, p. 23.

Leavitt, David, "Can I Go Over to Wilbur's?," *New York Times Book Review,* November 11, 1990, p. 29.

Richler, Mordecai, review of *Dinosaur Bob, New York Times Book Review,* November 13, 1988, p. 60.

FOR MORE INFORMATION SEE:

BOOKS

Sixth Book of Junior Authors, edited by Sally Holmes Holtze, Wilson, 1989.

PERIODICALS

Booklist, January 15, 1986, p. 758; September 15, 1990, p. 171.
Los Angeles Times Book Review, November 25, 1990, p. 24.
Publishers Weekly, January 7, 1990, p. 232; January 4, 1991, p. 38.
School Library Journal, September, 1990, p. 205.

—*Sketch by Elizabeth A. Des Chenes*

*   *   *

JUKES, Mavis 1947-

PERSONAL: Born May 3, 1947, in Nyack, NY; daughter of Thomas H. (a scientist) and Marguerite (a teacher; maiden name, Esposito) Jukes; married Robert II. Hudson (a sculptor and painter), July 24, 1976; children: (daughters) River, Amy; (stepsons) Cannon, Case. *Education:* Attended University of Colorado—Boulder, 1965-67; University of California—Berkeley, B.A., 1969, Elementary Teaching Certificate, 1970; Golden Gate University, D.Jur., 1978.

ADDRESSES: Home—Cotati, CA.

CAREER: Longfellow Elementary School, Berkeley, CA, classroom teacher, 1970-73, art specialist, 1973-75; admitted to the Bar of California, 1979; full-time writer, 1979—.

MEMBER: California Bar Association.

AWARDS, HONORS: Irma Simonton Black Award for Excellence in Children's Literature, Bank Street College of Education, and Parents' Choice Award, Parents' Choice Foundation, both 1983, both for *No One Is Going to Nashville;* Best Books of the Year citations, *School Library Journal,* 1983, for *No One Is Going to Nashville,* and 1984, for *Like Jake and Me;* Children's Literature Award, Bay Area Book Reviewers Association, *Horn Book* Honor List citation, and Newbery Honor citation, all 1985, all for *Like Jake and Me.*

Mavis Jukes with stepsons Cannon and Case.

WRITINGS:

JUVENILE

No One Is Going to Nashville, illustrated by Lloyd
    Bloom, Knopf, 1983.
Like Jake and Me, illustrated by Bloom, Knopf, 1984.
Blackberries in the Dark, illustrated by Thomas B. Allen,
    Knopf, 1985.
Lights around the Palm, illustrated by Stacey Schuett,
    Knopf, 1987.
Getting Even, Knopf, 1988.
Wild Iris Bloom, Knopf, 1991.
I'll See You in My Dreams, Knopf, 1992.

FILM SCRIPTS

Mavis Jukes: A Conversation with the Author, Disney
    Educational Productions, 1989.
(With Patricia McKissack) *Who Owns the Sun* (adapted
    from *Who Owns the Sun* by Stacey Chbosky),
    Disney Educational Productions, 1990.

OTHER

(Contributor) Marlo Thomas and others, editors, *Free to
    Be ... a Family,* Bantam, 1987.

Contributor of a children's story to *Ms.* Also contributor
to various reading textbooks.

**Young Alex and his stepfather, a rough-and-tumble
cowboy, forge a unique relationship in *Like Jake and
Me.*** (Illustration by Lloyd Bloom.)

ADAPTATIONS: Blackberries in the Dark and *Like Jake
and Me* have been adapted as films for Disney Educational Productions; *Like Jake and Me* is available in
both videotape and filmstrip format, Random House,
1984.

SIDELIGHTS: Mavis Jukes is an award-winning author
of children's books, including the Newbery Honor title
Like Jake and Me. In many of her works, Jukes
highlights nontraditional families as well as sensitive
themes such as divorce and child abuse. Noted for their
perception and humor, Jukes's books explore the often
difficult years of adolescence and childhood through
situations that are recognizable to a broad base of young
readers. Jukes once commented: "I am motivated to
write by experience and observations.... I have never
outgrown the urge to make people laugh, and I consider
humor to be a powerful tool for survival and in work."

Jukes was raised in the countryside in New York state.
A tomboy, she was often found in the company of her
older brother Ken. "Ken's expectations of me were
pretty high," Jukes related in an essay for *Something
about the Author Autobiography Series* (*SAAS*), "so he
informally enrolled me in his boot camp. (I was the only
trainee.) Under his spirited command, I learned to jump
out of trees and off roofs, spit, swear, catch and hold a
snake, drive a car, truck (and hearse), chew tobacco—
and test-drive a number of vehicles he designed and
constructed, including a motorcycle made out of a
bicycle and a lawn mower engine."

Jukes's early literary efforts were limited to what she
called writing "really embarrassing poetry" as a seventh
grader. When Jukes was a freshman in high school, her
family moved to Princeton, New Jersey; two years later,
the family moved to California. Jukes eventually attended the University of Colorado—Boulder and the University of California—Berkeley, earning her bachelor's
degree in 1969 and an elementary teaching certificate a
year later. She taught for five years before marrying
painter/sculptor Robert Hudson, who had two sons.

Jukes later aspired to a career in law, but suddenly
changed her mind. "In my third year of law school I had
a baby, and one day I wrote a story for her. When I saw
what I had written, I realized I was a writer," Jukes once
commented. "I never questioned it. I just finished law
school, took the bar and passed it, and then continued
writing."

Jukes found inspiration in other areas of her personal
life. She remarked: "I am a stepmother and also the
mother of two daughters. I am interested in emphasizing
the positive potential of stepfamilies in my work." Her
first books, *No One Is Going to Nashville* and *Like Jake
and Me,* deal directly with the problems of blending two
families. In *Nashville,* a young girl named Sonia asks to
keep a stray dog that she has found. At first her father
refuses, but he relents after the girl's stepmother takes
up her cause. A reviewer for the *Bulletin of the Center
for Children's Books* noted that *Nashville* is an "effective
story" with a lot of "sweetness and warmth."

In *Getting Even,* Maggie and her pal Iris use humor to teach the fifth-grade class bully a lesson. (Cover illustration by Stacey Schuctt.)

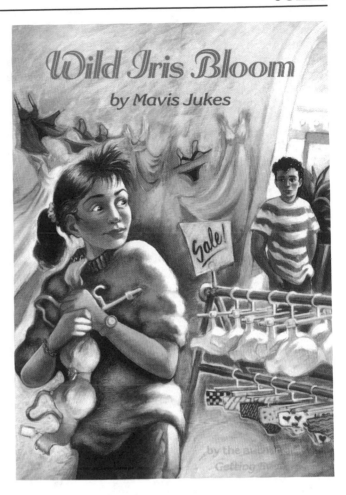

Angry at being left with a babysitter when her parents go out of town, Iris runs away and finds herself in a lot of trouble. (Cover illustration by Schuett.)

In *Like Jake and Me,* young Alex must come to accept and be accepted by his stepfather, a muscular, bearded cowboy. *Like Jake and Me* finds its roots in Jukes's early, difficult relationship with her stepson Cannon. As she recounted in *SAAS:* "One night Cannon, Case, Bob, and I all went to the movies in an old-timey theater that had a stage and curtain in front of the screen. Just before the movie was about to begin, I turned to Cannon [then age nine] and said 'I'll give you five bucks if you go up there and tap dance in front of all these people.' He said, 'I will if you will.' We both jumped up and ran down the aisle and up the stairs to the stage and started tap-dancing like two dopes. I'll never forget it, ever, because it was the first time Cannon had ever held my hand."

Blackberries in the Dark took Jukes three years and many revisions to write. The book describes nine-year-old Austin's first visit to his grandparents' home after the death of his grandfather. For a time, Jukes was concerned with the book's potential impact on its readers. "I had some concerns about whether or not the book would be upsetting to children," she once explained. "As it turns out, the story really doesn't make children cry—only adults! And especially me!"

In a lighter vein, *Lights around the Palm* tells the tale of seven-year-old Emma, who insists that she can talk to the animals on her family's farm. Over time, Emma's previously disdainful ten-year-old brother claims that he, too, can hear the animals talking. While recognizing that *Lights* has many commendable elements, a *Bulletin of the Center for Children's Books* reviewer concluded that the book's ideas "are more intriguing than its execution—the themes and ambiguities crowd out the small and quiet story."

Getting Even and *Wild Iris Bloom* cover the adventures of sensible Maggie and her wild friend Iris. In *Getting Even,* the two pals avenge themselves in humorous ways against the grade-school pest, Corky; in *Wild Iris Bloom,* Iris, angry at being left at home while her parents travel on business, escapes the baby-sitter's supervision and ends up in trouble. *Wild Iris Bloom* "was a very, very difficult book for me to write," Jukes wrote in *SAAS,* "because it involves an episode where Iris is tricked into a car by a stranger and assaulted, something which happened to me. It took me a long time to complete the story because in order to get it right, I had to confront my past and come to terms with it."

In addition to personal experience, Jukes has often listed her education and her children as major influences on her work: "Both teaching and law contributed heavily to my writing," the author once commented.

"Teaching woke me up—it was like taking a crash course in reality; law school taught me how to talk fast and straight, but what it really taught me was to pay attention to my inventive nature." No matter where she gets her ideas, Jukes is always on the lookout for new ways to get her themes across. She remarked: "I'd like to become more involved in filmmaking. I'd especially like to write another script with Pat McKissack. I want to write children's books for as long as I have something to say that interests children. I'd like my work to include a series; I become pretty involved with my characters and hate to give them up after just a book or two."

WORKS CITED:

Jukes, Mavis, essay in *Something about the Author Autobiography Series,* Volume 12, Gale, 1991.
Review of *Lights around the Palm, Bulletin of the Center for Children's Books,* December, 1987.
Review of *No One is Going to Nashville, Bulletin of the Center for Children's Books,* January, 1984.

FOR MORE INFORMATION SEE:

PERIODICALS

Booklist, April 1, 1988.
Bulletin of the Center for Children's Books, May, 1988.
New York Times Book Review, November 18, 1984; December 15, 1985.
Publishers Weekly, January 29, 1988.
Washington Post Book World, February 10, 1985; December 1, 1985; May 8, 1988.

* * *

JURMAIN, Suzanne 1945-

PERSONAL: Born in 1945 in New York, NY; daughter of Paul (an actor and author) and Ruth (an actress; maiden name, Enders) Tripp; married Robert B. Jurmain (a physician), 1966; children: Sara, David. *Education:* University of California, Los Angeles, B.A. (with honors), 1966.

ADDRESSES: Home—Los Angeles, CA. *Agent*—Dorothy Markinko, McIntosh & Otis, Inc., 310 Madison Ave., New York, NY 10017.

CAREER: Television actress, beginning in 1949; *TV Guide,* Los Angeles, CA, assistant editor, 1966; Legal Directories Publishing Co., Los Angeles, editor, 1967; University of California, Los Angeles Museum of Cultural History, editor and public relations coordinator, 1968-77; free-lance writer and editor, 1978—.

MEMBER: Phi Beta Kappa.

AWARDS, HONORS: Once upon a Horse was named an American Library Association Notable Book, 1989; *Once upon a Horse* received the nonfiction award from the Southern California Council on Literature for Children and Young People, 1990.

SUZANNE JURMAIN

WRITINGS:

From Trunk to Tail: Elephants Legendary and Real, Harcourt, 1978.
Once upon a Horse: A History of Horses and How They Shaped Our History, Lothrop, 1989.

WORK IN PROGRESS: A book about "the most successful slave rebellion in United States history."

SIDELIGHTS: Suzanne Jurmain is the author of two nonfiction works, each dealing with an animal and its relationship to humans throughout history. The author's 1978 book *From Trunk to Tail: Elephants Legendary and Real* explores symbolic references to elephants in folklore, as well as their real-life roles as domestic servants, circus performers, and prey. In *Once upon a Horse: A History of Horses and How They Shaped History*—which a *Los Angeles Times* reviewer called "the best horse book to come down the pike in some time"—Jurmain examines the relationship between horses and humans from prehistoric times through the 1980s. The author surveys the use of the animal in transportation and sport, and the ways in which horses have aided (or been exploited by) hunters, warriors, miners, farmers, and mail-carriers. The stories and illustrations—including photographs of ancient coins and cave paintings—reflect the representation of horses in literature, archaeology, and art. Reviewers appreciated the format and illustrations, although some found fault with the writing style and factual information. Charlene Strickland, commenting on *Once upon a Horse* in *School Library Journal,* stated, "The writing style is stilted and wordy, with some awkward phrases," and added that "the text lacks sufficient lore to satisfy curious equestrians." *Kirkus Reviews,* however, praised the book's content as "illuminating far beyond its factual level" and *Booklist* contributor Denise Wilms called *Once upon a Horse* "a handsome history."

Suzanne Jurmain told *SATA:* "When I was little, my parents' apartment had more books than furniture—so it's not surprising that books are practically the first things I remember. My mother read me nursery rhymes, fairy tales, *Oz* books, and A. A. Milne. My father told me stories. And what stories they were! Some came straight from his own imagination; some, from mythology; but many of the best were about real-life heroes, heroines, and villains. As we rode across New York on the subway, he told me about the amazing adventures of Cleopatra, Columbus, Richard Lionheart, Pocahontas—and by kindergarten, I'd already learned that facts could be as exciting as fiction.

"At age four I saw my mother play Maria in a Broadway production of Shakespeare's *Twelfth Night*—and from that moment on, I wanted to be an actress. After making my debut on my father's television show, *Mr. I. Magination,* I wanted to perform as much as possible. My parents, however, felt school was more important than acting experience, and during my childhood, I was only allowed to make occasional television appearances. As a teenager, however, I appeared in several television soap operas and studied acting at New York City's High School of Performing Arts (the school described in the movie and television series, *Fame*) until my parents moved to Los Angeles at the end of my junior year. Still determined to become an actress, I entered the University of California, Los Angeles (UCLA) as a theatre arts major—and then everything changed.

"In college I met my husband, switched my major to English, lost interest in acting, and discovered that I liked writing and telling stories. I began to think that one day I would enjoy writing for young people, but I wasn't sure whether I wanted to write fiction or nonfiction.

"Today, when I visit classrooms, children—who have grown up thinking that facts are about as appealing as fried grasshoppers in library paste—often ask why on earth I chose nonfiction. The answer is very simple: I enjoy it. I love to do research. I love to tell stories. And I hope that—like my father—I'll be able to show others that facts can be just as fascinating as fiction."

WORKS CITED:

Review of *Once upon a Horse, Kirkus Reviews,* November 1, 1989.

Review of *Once upon a Horse, Los Angeles Times,* November 26, 1989.

Strickland, Charlene, review of *Once upon a Horse, School Library Journal,* January, 1990, p. 113.

Wilms, Denise, review of *Once upon a Horse, Booklist,* December 15, 1989, p. 832.

FOR MORE INFORMATION SEE:

PERIODICALS

School Library Journal, September, 1979, pp. 140-141.

Science and Children, September, 1990.

Voice of Youth Advocates, April, 1990, p. 50.

Washington Post Book World, March 11, 1979, p. F5; November 5, 1989, p. 20.

K

KAIZUKI, Kiyonori 1950-

PERSONAL: Born November 8, 1950, in Kushiro, Hokkaido, Japan. *Hobbies and other interests:* "I'm interested in reading books, collecting picture frames, seeing and making picture books and modern art."

ADDRESSES: Home—2-25 Tohya-minami, Kushiro-machi, Kushiro-gun, Hokkaido, Japan. *Office*—Fukutake Publishing Co., Ltd., 2-3-28 Kudanminami, Chiyoda-Ku, Tokyo, Japan.

KIYONORI KAIZUKI

CAREER: Author and illustrator of children's books.

AWARDS, HONORS: Chiba Times Award, 1978; Art of the Country Award, 1983; Graphic Prize, Bologna International Children's Books Fair, 1989; Special Prize, Dosanko TOYP Awards, 1989.

WRITINGS:

SELF-ILLUSTRATED CHILDREN'S BOOKS

A Calf Is Born, translated from the Japanese by Cathy Hirano, Orchard Books, 1990 (originally published by Fukutake Publishing, 1988).

WORK IN PROGRESS: "Undertaking the tale of the farewell of Tancho-crane's child."

SIDELIGHTS: In *A Calf Is Born,* Japanese author and illustrator Kiyonori Kaizuki uses rich, double-page oil paintings to relate a serene tale of the birth of a young calf. Including only a few sentences per page, Kaizuki sets the story in a shadowy barn during a wintry night, and in realistic drawings portrays the calf from its birth, to its first walk and explorations, to its return to its mother at the day's end. *A Calf Is Born* is "a lovely story," decided *School Library Journal* reviewer Eldon Younce, while a critic for the *Bulletin of the Center for Children's Books* concluded that the work offers "a dignified introduction to birth and a quiet statement of respect for animal life."

Kaizuki told *SATA:* "I thought that I wanted to be a painter someday when I was ten years old ... and I am now. I'm making an effort to describe the invisible thing through the visible thing always."

He added: "I like going out to the wild plains near my house to watch the rising and setting sun almost every day."

WORKS CITED:

Review of *A Calf Is Born, Bulletin of the Center for Children's Books,* October, 1990, p. 33.

Younce, Eldon, review of *A Calf Is Born, School Library Journal,* March, 1990, p. 208.

FOR MORE INFORMATION SEE:

PERIODICALS

Horn Book, March/April, 1990, p. 220.

* * *

KERR, Phyllis Forbes 1942-

PERSONAL: Born June 2, 1942, in Beverly, MA; daughter of Robert Bennet and Elizabeth (McKean) Forbes; married Andrew P. Kerr (an investment banker), August 20, 1966 (divorced, 1976; remarried, 1991); children: Adam Forbes. *Education:* Wheelock College, B.S., 1964; Lesley College, M.A., 1977; studied art at DeCordova Museum School and the Cambridge Center for Adult Education.

ADDRESSES: Home—15 Huron Ave., Cambridge, MA 02138. *Office*—36 Bay State Rd., Cambridge, MA 02138. *Agent*—Liza Pulitzer Voges, Kirchoff/Wohlberg, 866 United Nations Plaza, New York, NY 10017.

CAREER: Cambridge Public Schools, Cambridge, MA, kindergarten teacher, 1964-65; Arlington Public Schools, Arlington, MA, kindergarten teacher, 1965-66; Everett School, New York City, kindergarten and first grade teacher, 1966-69; director of and teacher at independent play group and day camp, 1972-73; East Boston Public Schools, Boston, MA, reading specialist, 1978; worked as a teacher, 1978-80; Kristin Elliott Inc.

PHYLLIS FORBES KERR

BUMBLE CAT

How She Came To Be

Phyllis Forbes Kerr

Shy Catherine the kitten acquires superpowers after she is stung by a bumblebee in Kerr's self-illustrated *Bumble Cat.*

(greeting-card company), Beverly, MA, sales representative, 1980-84, designer of the "Phyllis Line" of cards and stationery, 1981—; Cambridge and Brookline Centers for Adult Education, Cambridge and Brookline, MA, teacher of writing and illustration, 1987-89; watercolor artist, writer, illustrator, and sculptor. New York City Public Schools, volunteer teaching assistant, 1969-72; Cambridge Youth Soccer Club, founder, 1978, coordinating manager, 1978-80; Wheelock College Crafter's Show, coordinator, 1981—; employed as a freelance greeting-card artist for the firms D. Forer and Nile Running Studio. *Exhibitions:* Wheelock College Gallery, Boston, MA, solo shows, 1979 and 1984; Sacramento Street Gallery, Sacramento, CA, group show "American Painters in France," 1984; Harvard University Neighbors Gallery, Cambridge, MA, solo show, 1985; Ticknor Library of Harvard University, solo show, 1987; and Waltham Weston Hospital, Waltham, MA, solo show, 1988.

MEMBER: Society of Children's Book Writers, Foundation for Children's Books.

WRITINGS:

SELF-ILLUSTRATED

Bumble Cat: How She Came to Be, Houghton, 1985.
I Tricked You!, Simon & Schuster, 1990.

WORK IN PROGRESS: Three stories about her nurse and grandmothers. Also transcribing and editing the journals of her great-great-grandfather, Robert Bennett Forbes, a China trade merchant from 1838 to 1840, and writing a children's book as told through the eyes of Forbes' dog, Flora, to be published by Mystic Seaport Press.

SIDELIGHTS: Phyllis Forbes Kerr told *SATA:* "I always wanted to write and illustrate children's books. It took me many years and rejection slips to finally get published. As a former teacher I know the influence a book can have on a child. I wrote *Bumble Cat* because I did not think there was a good superhero for little kids. My son Adam was obsessed by comic books about superheroes; Spiderman was his favorite. I was concerned that the stories were sexist, violent, and geared to male adults. I also wanted to create a superhero that little girls could relate to. That's how I thought of Bumble Cat—a shy, timid kitten called Catherine who gets bitten by a bumblebee and changes into the amazing 'Bumble Cat,' endowed with superpowers.

"*I Tricked You!* comes from an idea I developed years ago. I must have revised the story at least three times, and each time it got better. I know that over the years my art work improved and the story line changed so that the main character, a mouse called Morris, is able to control his actions and turns around a bad situation. In my original draft, the teacher gave him the idea for a solution.

"I think my perseverance to get published shows that one must keep trying and never give up. My favorite story to tell my students in the course 'Writing and Illustrating Children's Books' is that Dr. Seuss was rejected twenty-four times before any publisher acknowledged his work.

"I like to use animals for my characters because I think kids can relate to them and often find a situation amusing when otherwise it might be quite heavy. In one of my stories, yet to be published, I write about a boy duck who goes to swimming lessons but doesn't dare swim. By using a duck as the main character it is even more embarrassing and miserable for him not to dare go into the water than if he were a real boy.

"I also love to use humor in my words and often use puns—for instance, in *Bumble Cat* the second part of the title is *How She Came to Be*—often kids don't get puns, but it is fun to use them for the grown-ups who are reading the story so they can have a chuckle as well.

"I have a new golden retriever puppy called Clover and a year-old kitten named Sparkey. I still love dolls, teddy bears, and stuffed animals and am almost fifty! The child in me is still very much alive and helps me think of ideas, delights, and problems of young children."

FOR MORE INFORMATION SEE:

PERIODICALS

Cambridge Chronicle, November 4, 1985.
Publishers Weekly, August 2, 1985, p. 69.
School Library Journal, February, 1986, pp. 75-76; February, 1991, p. 70.

*   *   *

KING, (Maria) Anna 1964-

PERSONAL: Born October 2, 1964, in Upminster, Essex, England; daughter of John James Frederick (a director) and Mavis Esme (a homemaker; maiden name, Clements) King; married Mark Alan Winstanley, March 17, 1990. *Education:* Attended East Ham College, 1983-84; Brighton Polytechnic, B.A., 1987. *Politics:* Green. *Religion:* "None, but I believe in afterlife." *Hobbies and other interests:* "Gardening, baking, reading, walking my dog, and drawing and painting."

ADDRESSES: Home and office—41, Lowerson Rd., West Derby, Liverpool, L11 8LN, England.

ANNA KING

CAREER: Illustrator. Worked variously as a waitress, postal worker, greenhouse assistant, and checkout person. Lecturer on art at secondary schools, volunteer social worker, and member of Brighton Council in 1987.

MEMBER: Association of Illustrators.

ILLUSTRATOR:

Maryann Macdonald, *Little Hippo Starts School,* Aurum, 1990.
Macdonald, *Little Hippo Gets Glasses,* ABC, 1991.

WORK IN PROGRESS: An educational booklet for Kingston Health Authority, wrapping paper, cards, and writing and drawing next book, with a view to a series.

SIDELIGHTS: Anna King told *SATA:* "Although when I first left college, I assumed I'd be rich and famous by now, I'm still as enthusiastic as ever about illustration. I have usually had to do some sort of part-time work at sometime in the year in order to survive financially, but on the whole, my time is dedicated to my artwork. I have total faith that one day I will have my country cottage and pitter about my beautiful garden and bake cakes while I wait for the royalty checks to pop through the letter box! It's a fantastic feeling each time I see a piece of my work published—I can't think of anything more satisfying. Color and bright, happy images are so important and I want children to *really* enjoy their childhood and while, sadly, this is not always the case, at least books and pictures can create a momentary escape, a place of fun and good things, and a safe, cozy environment.

"At the moment, as I wait for fame, I am very happily married to Mark who has just started a degree in South American studies. I spend my days walking my much loved, rather fat dog, 'Spike,' reading and of course drawing, painting, working on existing commissions and drumming up new business."

*   *   *

KIRBY, Margaret
See BINGLEY, Margaret (Jane)

*   *   *

KOIKE, Kay 1940-

PERSONAL: Surname is pronounced "ko-*ee*-kee"; born October 7, 1940, in Waimea, Kauai, HI; daughter of Clarence S. (a civil engineer) and Kakiyo (a nursery school teacher; maiden name, Yamashita) Koike. *Education:* Attended Mid-Pacific Institute, 1956-58; State College of Iowa (now University of Northern Iowa), B.S., 1962. *Religion:* Interdenominational/Protestant.

ADDRESSES: Home—c/o Clarence Koike, P.O. Box 265, Kekaha, Kauai, HI 96752.

CAREER: Dike Elementary School, Dike, IA, elementary school teacher, 1962-65; Department of Defense

KAY KOIKE

Dependent Schools, elementary school teacher in the Azores, 1965-66, Chateaureux, France, 1966, Hahn, Germany, 1966-68, Seville, Spain, 1968-69, Bad Hersfeld, Germany, 1969-70, and Bonn, Germany, 1970—.

MEMBER: Overseas Education Association (president of local affiliate, 1976-78; treasurer of local affiliate, 1988-90).

AWARDS, HONORS: Left or Right? was named a Junior Literary Guild selection.

WRITINGS:

(Coauthor and coillustrator with Karl Rehm) *Left or Right?,* Clarion Books, 1991.

WORK IN PROGRESS: Other photo-concept ideas.

SIDELIGHTS: Kay Koike told *SATA:* "When my brother, Ben, gave me my very first Kodak Brownie camera on my ninth birthday, little did anyone know what it would lead to in the far future. Two years later a new Brownie Hawkeye made it even easier to compose pictures of family and friends as I could look down into the small viewfinder at the top of the camera. I also realized from just observing other casual photographs that a subject should fill up the entire photograph and that it was more effective to move in close to the subject. Always remembering these two 'rules,' I continued to use this camera throughout my teen years and into college life.

"It was an exciting event in 1960 to purchase my first 35mm automatic camera that took excellent photos. It developed a light leak, and I regretfully passed it on to some friends for their use.

The photographs in *Left or Right* help introduce young readers to directional and spatial concepts. (Photograph by Koike and Karl Rehm.)

"By this time I was teaching fourth grade in Dike, Iowa, and had acquired another 35mm camera which I cannot remember at all. But I used it to record my travels which began in earnest with an automobile trip to Phoenix, Arizona, by way of the scenic sights of Colorado in the summer of 1964. I discovered that I really enjoyed composing scenic shots while still taking pictures of my friends from unusual angles and shooting for educational purposes to share with my students.

"Europe beckoned, and in the fall of 1965, I took a flying leap halfway across the Atlantic to the Azores to begin my career as a teacher with the Department of Defense Dependent Schools. From there I went on to France, Germany, Spain, and finally back to Germany again where I presently teach at Bonn American Elementary School. Endless opportunities to travel all over Europe from Great Britain to the Soviet Union and to the Mediterranean countries have provided me with exciting and enriching experiences. Wherever I went, a camera always hung from my shoulder ready to 'point and shoot.'

"While posted to Spain, I finally acquired my first camera with the capability of interchanging lenses. Picture taking also became a frustrating experience at times because I couldn't focus the lens fast enough to get the quick shots that I could previously with a simpler camera. But this didn't hamper my taking hundreds of photographs of this fascinating country. It also began to teach me to compose my pictures even more thoughtfully than before.

"Returning to Germany, I continued to take scenic slides wherever I went but realized that I also wanted 'people' shots to put into an album that could readily be shown to friends. For this purpose I began carrying around a simple camera. But I didn't stop with that. Not content with toting two cameras, I loaded myself down with a third one: a super 8 movie camera. Learning to zoom in and out smoothly and to pan the camera slowly was a new and fun experience.

"Meanwhile, my work with scenic slides began to wane during this concentration on movies and people shots. It took a trip to Prague, Czechoslovakia, a few years ago to renew my interest in shooting with slide film and to learn to see parts of subjects really 'up close.' At the same time, a realization of 29 years of teaching was verbalized in a discussion with Karl Rehm about children: that it has become increasingly common for students, even in the fifth grade, to express confusion in writing letters of the alphabet and in recognizing opposites and left from right. The latter two ideas became book ideas to pursue after a brainstorming session with Karl while driving along the Rhine River." Their conversations resulted in the publication of *Left or Right?*, a book which introduces children to directional and spatial concepts. Concerning the project, Koike further commented: "While photo shooting the medieval town of Andernach, the windows of houses built into the remains of an ancient wall seemed to shout 'left and right.' Being colleagues in Bonn made it easy to collaborate and develop *Left or Right?*, which we hope will be a helpful and an enjoyable learning tool for all young children."

*　　*　　*

KOLLER, Jackie French 1948-

PERSONAL: Born March 8, 1948, in Derby, CT; daughter of Ernest James (an electrical engineer) and Margaret (a homemaker; maiden name, Hayes) French; married George J. Koller (president of a hospital), July 11, 1970; children: Kerri, Ryan, Devin. *Education:* University of Connecticut, B.A., 1970.

ADDRESSES: Home—Westfield, MA.

CAREER: Author. Founder and head, Simsbury Writer's Workshop, Simsbury, CT, 1983-86, and Groton Children's Bookwriters Workshop, Groton, MA, 1986—. Process Writing instructor, Groton Center for the Arts, 1988.

JACKIE FRENCH KOLLER

MEMBER: Society of Children's Book Writers (member of advisory board, New England chapter).

WRITINGS:

FOR CHILDREN

Impy for Always (chapter book), Little, Brown, 1989.
The Dragonling (chapter book), Little, Brown, 1990.
Mole and Shrew (picture book), Atheneum, 1991.
Nothing to Fear (historical novel), Harcourt, 1991.
If I Had One Wish.... (novel), Little, Brown, 1991.
Fish Fry Tonight! (picture book), Crown, 1992.
The Last Voyage of the Misty Day (novel), Atheneum, 1992.
Mole and Shrew Step Out (picture book), Atheneum, 1992.
The Primrose Way (historical novel), Harcourt, 1992.

Also contributor of *What If?* (long poem), to *Cobblestone* magazine. Editor, Swallow Union School News, 1987, and Society of Children's Book Writers New England chapter newsletter, 1988-90.

SIDELIGHTS: Jackie French Koller writes, "*Impy for Always* was inspired by a humorous incident that occurred when my daughter, Kerri, was young. She hadn't seen her cousin, Heather, in some time and she overheard me say on the phone that I couldn't wait to see Heather again because I had heard she'd 'grown another foot.' Kerri suddenly couldn't wait for Heather to visit. On the day she finally arrived, however, Kerri's initial reaction seemed to be one of disappointment. I quickly found out why. Placing her hands on her hips, Kerri gave me an accusing stare and blurted out, 'You lied! She doesn't have three feet. She still only has two!'

"On that note the story began. Then I drew upon a childhood experience of my own to flesh it out. A cousin of mine had once come for a visit, too—a cousin I *used* to get along great with. But something had happened. Since I had seen her last she had changed. She was much taller, and she didn't like to do the same things anymore. Everything I did seemed to irritate her, and everything she did aggravated me. I can still remember my poor mother pulling her hair out over the two of us. Like Impy and Christina we finally made peace, and grew to be good friends again, but thinking back about that awful week still makes me laugh.

"Unlike the rest of my books, *The Dragonling* was not my idea. It was written in answer to a special request from my son Devin, then in third grade. His teacher had suggested that the children do a book report on a chapter book rather than a picture book and had given them two weeks to complete the assignment. Devin wanted a book about dragons because they were his 'second favorite animals next to dogs.' So off we went to the library. Alas, our library didn't have any chapter books about dragons. Not to worry. Devin had a solution—'Write me one, Mom.' And so I did. Each day he would rush in the door after school and ask, 'Did you do another chapter?,' and each day I would hand him the product of my labors. Ten days later, *The Dragonl-*

ing was done. It went through some revisions, of course, before it was published, but Devin did do his dragon book report and even got it in on time!

"*Nothing to Fear* is a very special book to me because it's based on my mother's childhood. My mother grew up in New York City during the Great Depression. She was one of nine children, and her family was very poor. Her father left home at the height of the depression, and all the children had to pitch in to help their mother keep the family together. As a result of the struggles they went through, they grew to be a wonderful, close knit family, full of laughter and love. *Nothing to Fear* is my tribute to my mother and her family and to the whole generation who lived through and managed to overcome the adversities of the Great Depression.

"Writing *Mole and Shrew* was just plain fun. I have always loved little creatures, and even now I like to imagine tiny worlds that exist down beneath the toadstools, among the mosses and the gnarled roots of trees. When I was young I delighted in building wonderful villages in my sandbox, with bark houses, fern trees, little roads, and pie plate ponds. Then I would catch 'hoppy' toads and move them in. They were ungrateful little things, though, and always hopped away again at the first opportunity. Perhaps that's why today I get such a thrill out of creating cozy little imaginary worlds populated by tiny characters that are content to stay. Of course, half the fun is seeing the way a wonderful artist like Stella Ormai brings them to life!

"I'm not just a writer. I'm a mom, too, and my children are a great source of inspiration. A couple of years ago I was having a very typical problem with my two sons. Devin, the little one, was always tagging after Ryan, the older one, and driving him crazy, and Ryan was angry and impatient and constantly threatening to do away with Devin. I was at a loss as to how to bring about a peaceful solution, so I decided to write a book about sibling rivalry: *If I Had One Wish* . . . . Writing the book didn't solve my problem, of course, but I think it helped me understand it better. Oh, and my sons did eventually get beyond that stage. As they grew older they found a common interest—ATVs (four-wheeled motor bikes). Now I don't worry about them killing each other any more. I just worry about them breaking their necks!

"Some books are inspired by characters. *The Last Voyage of the Misty Day* is one, and the character that inspired it is my dad. Dad is a crusty kind of character, but if you scratch his surface you'll find a heart of gold beneath. He's a tool collector and a tinkerer, and there is nothing he won't try to fix or build. When I was a girl he once said to me, 'If someone else put something together, you can take it apart, and if you watch the way it comes apart, you can put it back together.' I tried his theory out one day when my record player wouldn't work, and lo and behold! I fixed it! I've been a bit of a tinkerer myself ever since. Mr. Jones, in the book, is a lot like dad, and Denny, a fourteen year old girl who has just lost her father, finds him fascinating. Mr. Jones is fixing up an old boat and planning to take it to sea. Like

it or not, he soon finds Denny 'tinkering' right alongside him. . . . Boats have always been a special love of dad's—big boats, little boats, sailboats, motorboats, model boats . . . He's built them, fixed them, sailed them, even captained them in the navy. I think in his heart he'd like to find himself an old boat someday and sail off into the sunset, just like Mr. Jones.

"Sometimes I get into silly moods, and *Fish Fry Tonight!* is the result of one of them. One day I just felt like writing something silly and fun. 'Fish' has always struck me as a silly word. I don't know why. Most fish aren't very funny, but when I think of funny names or silly sounds, 'fish' always comes to mind. So I decided my silly book should have something to do with fish. And since it just happened to be a bright, sunny morning in May, the book begins: 'One day, on a bright, sunny morning in May, Mouse left her washing, and all of her dishes, and, dreaming of fishes, ran off to her favorite spot by the brook.' Mouse catches a fish and invites a friend to dinner, who invites a friend to dinner, who invites a friend to dinner, who invites a friend to dinner, and so on, until the situation gets completely out of control. In the end, though, Mouse manages to save the day and everyone gets to share in the fish fry—more or less!

"Mole and Shrew turned out to be such dear little characters that I can't seem to get them out of my mind. I think they're going to have all kinds of adventures together. *Mole and Shrew Step Out* is their second. Shrew invites Mole to attend the ball at Mouse Manor as her guest. But when she tells him he has to wear a black tie and tails, poor Mole is confused. He has only one tail—and a short, stubby thing it is at that! Determined not to disappoint Shrew, Mole sets off in search of some suitable tails to wear, and the outfit he shows up in at the ball causes quite a stir!

"*The Primrose Way:* All of my life I have been fascinated by Native American history and culture, so much so that when I was younger I used to pretend I was part Indian. I think I pretended so long and hard that I eventually came to believe that I was. I even thought I remembered my grandmother telling me of a great grandfather or grandmother who was an Indian. When I asked my father recently, though, he traced all my roots for me—right back to Europe . . . . "As a New Englander I was curious about the Indians who lived here, and I wondered what they thought of the early settlers and how they interacted. A character came to me, a young English girl, traveling to New England to join her Puritan father in the year 1633. She was a fascinating, feisty character, not at all what I expected of a proper young Puritan girl. I liked her immediately, and I decided to travel with her. Together we discovered a New England that I had only glimpsed before, in the silence of the snowy woods, in the sunset by the sea, and in the turning of the seasons in a land that we call new but that the Native American people know is as old as time. Writing the book became a spiritual journey for me, one that deeply affected my life, and now more than ever I know I'm part Indian, if only in my heart."

L

LEEMIS, Ralph B. 1954-

PERSONAL: Born April 28, 1954, in Jacksonville, FL; son of Lloyd Charles (an attorney) and Mary (a housewife; maiden name, Burner) Leemis; married Jeni Bassett (an illustrator), September 20, 1986. *Education:* Attended Farman University, 1972-74; University of Florida, B.A., 1976, J.D., 1979. *Religion:* Christian. *Politics:* Republican.

ADDRESSES: Home—1864 Taylor Ave., Winter Park, FL 32789. *Office*—Neilson and Associates, 1332 West Colonial Dr., Orlando, FL 32804. *Agent*—Dilys Evans, P.O. Box 400, Norfolk, CT 06058.

CAREER: Attorney and author.

WRITINGS:

Mr. Momboo's Hat, illustrated by wife, Jeni Bassett, Cobblehill Books, 1991.
Smart Dog, Boyd Mills Press, in press.

SIDELIGHTS: Ralph B. Leemis told *SATA:* "I acquired my love of reading from my parents, both avid readers. At an early age, I was inspired by my father, Lloyd C. Leemis, who authored the historic *The Record of Senator Claude Pepper.* Through my own writing, I hope to impart some of the joy and wonder of life to children of all ages."

*   *   *

LERANGIS, Peter 1955-
(A. L. Singer; Franklin W. Dixon and Carolyn Keene, collective pseudonyms; M. E. Cooper and Alison Blair, series pseudonyms)

PERSONAL: Born August 19, 1955, in Brooklyn, NY; son of Nicholas P. (a telephone company employee) and Mary (a school secretary; maiden name, Condos) Lerangis; married Cristina L. deVaron (a singer, pianist, and songwriter), September 4, 1983; children: Nicholas James, Joseph Alexander. *Education:* Harvard College,

A.B., 1977. *Hobbies and other interests:* Photography, jogging, paleontology.

ADDRESSES: Home—7 West 96 St., Apt. 4E, New York, NY 10025.

CAREER: Actor and singer, New York City, 1978-86; free-lance copyeditor, 1979-85; free-lance writer, 1986—. Taught copyediting and proofreading course at City University of New York Graduate Center, 1985-86.

MEMBER: Society of Children's Book Writers, National Writers Union, Actors Equity Association, Screen Actors Guild, American Federation of Television and Radio Artists.

WRITINGS:

NOVELIZATIONS; UNDER PSEUDONYM A. L. SINGER, EXCEPT AS NOTED

(Under name Peter Lerangis) *Young Sherlock Holmes,* based on the screenplay by Chris Columbus, Simon & Schuster, 1985.
(Under name Peter Lerangis) *Star Trek IV: The Voyage Home,* based on the screenplay by Steve Meerson, Simon & Schuster, 1986.
License to Drive, based on the screenplay by Neil Tolkin, Scholastic, 1988.
Little Monsters, based on the screenplay by Terry Rossio and Ted Elliott, Scholastic, 1989.
Sing, based on the screenplay by Dean Pitchford, Scholastic, 1989.
Rescuers Down Under, Scholastic, 1990.
Dick Tracy, based on the screenplay by Jim Cash and Jack Epps, Jr., Western, 1990.
Disney's Beauty and the Beast, based on the screenplay by Linda Woolverton, illustrated by Ron Dias and Ric Gonzalez, Disney Press, 1991.
Davy Crockett and the King of the River, based on the Disney television series, Disney Press, 1991.
Davy Crockett and the Pirates at Cave-In Rock, based on the Disney television series, Disney Press, 1991.

Peter Lerangis with sons Joseph and Nicholas.

Bingo, based on the screenplay by Jim Strain, Scholastic, 1991.

Aladdin, Disney Press, 1992.

Home Alone II: Lost in New York, Scholastic, 1992.

Robin Hood, Disney Press, 1992.

Young Indiana Jones Chronicles: Safari Sleuth, based on the teleplay by Matthew Jacobs, Random House, 1992.

Little Mermaid, Disney Press, 1993.

Sleeping Beauty, Disney Press, 1993.

Surf Warriors, based on the screenplay by Dan Gordon, Dell, 1993.

PUZZLE BOOKS; UNDER NAME PETER LERANGIS

Puzzles and Games, Macmillan Educational, 1984.

Mickey's Drill-a-Days: Letters and Words, Simon & Schuster, 1985.

Star Trek Activity Book, Simon & Schuster, 1986.

Star Trek Puzzle Book, Simon & Schuster, 1986.

Super Puzzle #1: Going Batty, Troll, 1988.

Super Puzzle #3: Camp Craziness, Troll, 1988.

ADVENTURE AND MYSTERY SERIES

(Under pseudonym Franklin W. Dixon) *The Genius Thieves,* "Hardy Boys Casefiles" Number 9, Archway, 1987.

(Under pseudonym Franklin W. Dixon) *The Borgia Dagger,* "Hardy Boys Casefiles" Number 13, Archway, 1988.

(Under pseudonym Franklin W. Dixon) *A Killing in the Market,* "Hardy Boys Casefiles" Number 18, Archway, 1988.

(Under pseudonym Carolyn Keene) *A Crime for Christmas,* "Hardy Boys/Nancy Drew Supermystery" Number 2, Archway, 1988.

(Under pseudonym A. L. Singer) *The Sultan's Secret,* "GI Joe" Series Number 6, Ballantine, 1988.

(Under pseudonym Carolyn Keene) *Shock Waves,* "Hardy Boys/Nancy Drew Supermystery" Number 3, Archway, 1989.

(Under pseudonym Franklin W. Dixon) *Danger Zone,* "Hardy Boys Casefiles" Number 37, Archway, 1990.

(Under pseudonym Carolyn Keene) *Buried in Time,* "Hardy Boys/Nancy Drew Supermystery" Number 7, Archway, 1990.

Foul Play (based on characters created by Robert Arthur), "Three Investigators" Number 9, Knopf, 1990.

(Under pseudonym A. L. Singer) *Blaster Master,* "Worlds of Power" Series Number 1, Scholastic, 1990.

(Under pseudonym A. L. Singer) *Ninja Gaiden,* "Worlds of Power" Series Number 3, Scholastic, 1990.

(Under pseudonym A. L. Singer) *Infiltrator,* "Worlds of Power" Series Number 7, Scholastic, 1991.

(Under pseudonym A. L. Singer) *Bases Loaded 2,* "Worlds of Power" Junior Series, Scholastic, 1991.

ROMANCE SERIES

(Under pseudonym M. E. Cooper) *Falling for You,* "Couples" Series Number 30, Scholastic, 1988.

(Under pseudonym Alison Blair) *Campus Fever,* "Roommates" Series Number 14, Ivy/Ballantine, 1988.

Also author of books in the "Sweet Valley High" and "Sweet Valley Twins" series by Francine Pascal.

INTERACTIVE

The Amazing Ben Franklin, "Time Traveler" Series Number 4, Bantam, 1987.

In Search of a Shark, "Explorer" Series Number 3, Scholastic, 1987.

The Last of the Dinosaurs, "Time Machine" Series Number 22, Bantam, 1988.

World War II Codebreakers, "Time Machine" Series Number 25, Bantam, 1989.

(Under pseudonym A. L. Singer) *Dick Tracy Catch-a-Crook Adventure,* Western, 1990.

NONFICTION

A Kid's Guide to New York City, illustrated by Richard E. Brown, Harcourt, 1988.

Teacher Guide to Square One TV Show, Children's Television Workshop, 1989.

(With Peter Dodson) *Dinosaur Bookshelf: Giant Dinosaurs,* illustrated by Alex Nino, Scholastic, 1990.

(With Dodson) *Dinosaur Bookshelf: Baby Dinosaurs,* illustrated by Nino, Scholastic, 1990.

WORK IN PROGRESS: Drivers Dead and *The Yearbook,* young adult thrillers, for Scholastic, 1993.

SIDELIGHTS: Peter Lerangis told *SATA:* "When I was in fourth grade, I used to hide spiral notebooks in my math textbook. My teacher, Ms. Scuderi, thought I was deeply involved in my multiplication tables. I wasn't. I was busy writing stories. (I thought they would be books, but I never seemed to be able to finish them.) My main interest back then was science fiction, and my stories were usually about kids stowing away on rockets to other planets.

"To me, the best thing about writing was this: I could completely escape my house, my town, my family, my body, *everything.* I could fly, burrow, travel in time; I could create people and creatures, tell them what to say, give them powers, kill them off, make them grow old—and when I was done, there'd still be dinner on the table and a nice cozy bed to sleep in. Why did I want to escape? I had a pretty happy, normal life on the outside. *Inside,* though, things weren't so great.

"I grew up in Freeport, New York, a suburb. Until high school I was a pretty fat kid (87 pounds in second grade). I was horrible in gym class. When it came time to pick teams, I tried to be invisible. It never worked. Inevitably someone would say, 'You got *Lerangis,*' as if 'Lerangis' were some kind of annoying condition, like the flu. One time, as I was ducking a fly ball that dropped for a hit, a classmate screamed out, 'Lerangis, you're the worst athleek I ever saw.' At least I knew how to say *athlete.* Even spell it.

"The other problem was clothes. My mom used to choose and buy them for me. I thought she did an okay job, but my schoolmates thought I looked like a dork. One day in eighth grade I took matters into my own hands. I saw a Nehru jacket on sale at Macy's and begged Mom to let me buy it. (Nehru jackets were very hip in 1969. They were tight-fitting, with many buttons up the middle and a priest-like collar.) This one was made of stiff marbled vinyl, like the fabric on a TV-room lounge chair. But it was the one thing I wanted in life. It was going to change my image in school. With a look of compassion and pity, Mom agreed to buy it for me. I was elated. The next day I proudly wore it to John W. Dodd Junior High.

"It did change my image, all right. The hoots of laughter on the playground were heard in the next town. Traffic stopped for miles around at the noise. I felt humiliated. That evening I took it off and hung it in the attic. My mom was wise enough not to ask too much about it. (I wore it only once again, when I played the Fairy Godmother in a comedy version of *Cinderella.*)

"When I was reading or writing, I didn't have to worry about other kids' opinions. Not that my life was so awful. I did have fun as a kid. I could make people laugh. I did good imitations, which sometimes grew into shows (and sometimes got me into big trouble). Between eighth and ninth grade, things changed a lot. I grew about five inches and didn't look so fat anymore. I started getting bad grades on purpose to be cooler (not a great idea, in retrospect). I began playing sports a little and got more involved in drama and music—and girls. My first girlfriend was the sports editor of the high-school newspaper. When she read a poem I'd written (a spoof on 'Casey at Bat,' about a basketball player who stuffs his own team's hoop), she got me a spot on the newspaper right away.

Lerangis, writing as A. L. Singer, tells the story of Belle, her magical friends, and the ferocious Beast in *Disney's Beauty and the Beast.*

"Newspaper writing taught me a lot about organizing my thoughts concisely. But even though fiction writing was my real love, I was hardly doing it at all. I somehow managed to finish first in my high-school class, and a lot of colleges accepted me, so I felt major pressure to do something noble, upstanding, and respectable. Writing was not one of those things. Acting? Forget it. The immigrant ethic was strong in my family. My grandparents had come from Greece with no education or money (my grandfather's last name was Lyrantzis, which means 'lyre player'; the name became 'Lerangis' at Ellis Island). My parents grew up poor and worked hard to rise into the American middle class. Me? I was the first-born in my generation, which was expected to be chock-full of doctors, lawyers, and tycoons.

"Well, I didn't want to be any of those things. But everyone insisted that a life in writing, theater, or music would be full of despair and wasted effort. I went to Harvard College and majored in biochemistry. I guess I thought if I forced the issue, I might magically become interested in medicine after all. Guess what became of that idea?

"In college I did practically no creative writing. (I tried to get into a creative-writing program, but I was rejected.) My main extra activity was singing. I joined a twelve-member a cappella group and became its director. I acted in a play or two. And I didn't do very well in biochemistry.

"After college lots of my friends were going to law school, so I thought I might try that. I applied, got in, sent a deposit, even got a job as a paralegal for a few months. I became pretty miserable and left to be a singing waiter in Nantucket for a summer. That fall I chucked law school and went to New York to try to be an actor. I did *that* for eight years, performing in musical theater. I was even in a Broadway show. In between acting jobs, I waited on tables, but I kept getting fired. In desperation, I tried free-lance copyediting, which means checking authors' manuscripts for grammar, spelling, accuracy. It was flexible work and I could go to auditions and classes. I ended up reading an awful lot of books—some of them *quite* awful! I figured, 'I can do better than that!' So I tried my hand at writing again.

"It had been over ten years since I'd done any creative writing at all, and I was nearly thirty. By 1986 I was writing full-time. I found out that (1) it's never too late to start doing something you love, and (2) *everything* you've done in your life makes your writing rich and unique. My acting experience gave me a good ear for dialogue and an ability to slip in and out of my characters' personalities. My introverted years gave me the patience to sit alone for hours and think and write. Being the oldest in my family, watching sixteen siblings and cousins grow up, gave me insights into kids' ways of thinking. As for the rest—the stories that have nothing to do with life experiences—that's what imagination is for! In writing, the possibilities are endless. If you have a little talent and a lot of passion for it, then the only missing ingredient is discipline. And *that* is something anyone can learn (even a horrendous procrastinator like me).

"I'm thirty-seven now. I live in an apartment in New York City, near Central Park. My wife is a singer and pianist and songwriter. My son Nicholas is in kindergarten. My other son, Joseph, is learning to talk and bite people's shoulders. I've written over sixty books, most under pen names. The name I use most is A. L. Singer, which is an anagram of Lerangis. As a ghost writer, I've written for many series, including 'Hardy Boys' and 'Baby-Sitters Club.'

"A lot of my books are movie novelizations. I love movies, so these are fun for me. I write from a screenplay, long before the movie comes out. This is a mixed blessing. On the one hand, there's no agonizing about plot and characters—they're all there! On the other hand, a screenplay is organized much differently than a novel. In a movie, images are primary; they establish character, rhythm, and mood. A lot can be conveyed by a gesture, a facial expression, a musical score. Points of view can be changed every few minutes by fast cutting. A novel, however, is built on thoughts and dialogue. Too many points of view or physical descriptions can seem choppy. Too much movie dia-

logue makes for shallow reading. The trick is to make a novel that stands on its own—readable and suspenseful, with three-dimensional characters. Often scenes must be rearranged, eliminated, or made up; characters must be given personal histories and motivations. One other problem: sometimes major changes are made in the movie after I've already started writing. The last third of my novelization of *License to Drive* bears no resemblance to the movie. The book had already gone to press when the movie was being reshot. In the original *Beauty and the Beast* screenplay, the 'Be Our Guest' song was sung by Maurice, not Belle. When I got the final draft, I had to throw out everything I'd written and start again.

"For a lot of kids, novelizations are the first books they'll willingly read. I believe that a *good* one will turn kids on to reading in general, which is exciting to me. I have to admit, though, I'm eager to move on to other types of projects. I'm working now on two original young adult horror-thrillers for Scholastic—*Drivers Dead* and *The Yearbook*—which will be very scary and weird. I'm also hatching ideas for other YA, middle-reader, and children's books, screenplays, and a musical comedy."

* * *

LEWIN, Hugh 1939-

PERSONAL: Born December 3, 1939, in Lydenburg, South Africa; son of William (a priest) and Muriel (a nurse; maiden name, Paynter) Lewin; married Patricia Davidson (a lawyer), September 24, 1972; children: Thandi, Tessa. *Education:* Rhodes University, B.A., 1960; University of South Africa, B.A., 1968, Diploma in Library Science, 1970.

ADDRESSES: Home—Box HG236, Highlands, Harare, Zimbabwe. *Office*—Friedrich Naumann Foundation, P.O. Box 1636, Harare, Zimbabwe.

CAREER: Drum, Johannesburg, South Africa, assistant editor, 1963-64; *Observer,* London, England, sub-editor, 1972-73; Nigerian Publications, London, 1974-75; *Guardian,* London, sub-editor, 1976-78; *South,* London, production editor, 1979-81; Friedrich Naumann Foundation, Harare, Zimbabwe, media training officer, 1981—.

WRITINGS:

CHILDREN'S BOOKS

Jafta, illustrated by Lisa Kopper, Evans Brothers, 1981, Carolrhoda, 1983.
Jafta: My Father, illustrated by Kopper, Evans Brothers, 1981, published in the United States as *Jafta's Father,* Carolrhoda, 1983.
Jafta: My Mother, illustrated by Kopper, Evans Brothers, 1981, published in the United States as *Jafta's Mother,* Carolrhoda, 1983.
Jafta: The Wedding, illustrated by Kopper, Evans Brothers, 1981, published in the United States as *Jafta and the Wedding,* Carolrhoda, 1983.

Jafta: The Journey, illustrated by Kopper, Evans Brothers, 1983, Carolrhoda, 1984.

Jafta: The Town, illustrated by Kopper, Evans Brothers, 1983, Carolrhoda, 1984.

(With Tony Namata) *An African Elephant,* Zimbabwe Publishing House, 1984.

An Elephant Came to Swim, illustrated by Kopper, Hamish Hamilton, 1985.

"Second Chance" Series (includes *A Bamboo in the Wind, A Flower in the Forest, A Shell on the Beach,* and *A Well in the Desert*), illustrated by Kopper, Hamish Hamilton, 1989.

OTHER

Bandiet: Seven Years in a South African Prison, Barrie & Jenkins, 1974, Heinemann Educational Books, 1981.

(Editor with Don Rowlands) *Reporting Africa: A Manual for Reporters in Africa,* Thomson Foundation, 1985.

(Compiler) *A Community of Clowns: Testimonies of People in Urban Rural Mission,* WCC Publications (Switzerland), 1987.

Contributor to books, including *Apartheid: Calibrations of Color,* edited by Paul Weinburg, Rosen Publishing, 1991. Work represented in anthologies, including *Poets to the People,* Heinemann, 1980.

ADAPTATIONS: The "Jafta" books were adapted for the Public Broadcasting Service (PBS-TV) *Reading Rainbow* series, 1989.

SIDELIGHTS: Hugh Lewin presents a positive portrait of childhood in contemporary South Africa through his "Jafta" series. The picture books in the series focus on the daily life of Jafta, a lively little boy living in an unspecified village of South Africa. Originally intending to portray Jafta's father as a political prisoner, Lewin decided that the complex subject of life under apartheid was too difficult for his selected audience. The illustrations, however, occasionally supply details not mentioned in the text, such as picturing Jafta's father working behind bars. Using simple, yet lyrical prose, Lewin describes Jafta's feelings about himself and his surroundings, and introduces children of other countries to an unfamiliar culture through his descriptions and use of regional terms. "This is the kind of depicting image children need of cultures other than their own," points out Gillian Klein in the *Times Educational Supplement.* "These are the kind of children's books of which there can never be enough—comprehensible yet enriching, widening horizons, enchanting and delighting."

Lewin spent his own childhood in South Africa, and began the "Jafta" series in an attempt to teach his daughters about his homeland. The son of an Anglican parish priest, Lewin originally intended to pursue the same career. While in college, though, he visited a destitute black community and found himself questioning the contradictory relationship between the laws of apartheid and his Catholic beliefs. Soon after, he

became an active member of the Liberal Party, and in 1962, he joined the National Committee for Liberation (N.C.L.), later renamed the African Resistance Movement. The nonviolent policy of the N.C.L., which called for shocking lawmakers into awareness without using physical force, appealed to Lewin, and he was involved in three subversive acts during his eighteen months with the group.

In 1964, Lewin was arrested and imprisoned when South African police made mass raids on Leftist sympathizers. Because he was a political prisoner, Lewin was considered inferior and received harsher treatment, but managed to earn degrees in both English and librarianship through correspondence courses. Released in 1971, he was given the choice to remain in South Africa under twenty-four hour house arrest, or to leave the country. Moving to London, Lewin remained politically active, worked as a journalist, and wrote his first book, *Bandiet: Seven Years in a South African Prison.* In 1981 he began the "Jafta" series, writing the first four books before moving to Zimbabwe. "I wrote *Bandiet* to give people some idea of the peculiarly nasty way in which political prisoners are treated in South Africa," explains Lewin. "My more recent children's books began as an attempt to explain to my English-born children something about life in Africa. Then I wanted to provide a broad picture of the South African experience for all children."

Interracial Books for Children Bulletin contributor Geraldine L. Wilson criticizes this approach. She maintains that Lewin should identify the society in which Jafta lives, and also sees him as failing to deal with the issue

HUGH LEWIN

of apartheid and its effects on the inhabitants of South Africa. "If books about South Africa cannot reveal some of the realities of life there, perhaps they should not be done at all." Other critics, however, praise the "Jafta" series for introducing children to a new culture, and for including those experiences which are familiar to all children. "That which is different is clearly articulated and explained.... But there are also the common experiences," observes Klein. And Leila Berg writes in the *Times Educational Supplement* that throughout the series there is "a *flavour* of Africa, generalised and idealised, but setting the mind free to wander, to leap, and to reflect."

In the first book of the series, *Jafta,* the young title character expresses his feelings by relating them to the animals living around him. The subsequent books consist of Jafta's descriptions of other aspects of his life, including his mother, his father, his older sister's wedding, and a visit to the town in which his father works. The universal elements of childhood, such as

bedtime stories and the teasing of younger siblings, are a part of Jafta's life, as are elements specific to South Africa, such as living in a one-room village house and having an absent father who must work in a distant town because of apartheid laws. "Knowing South Africa, I welcomed the images of the land so unerringly evoked on every page," comments Klein. "Between them, Hugh Lewin and Lisa Kopper have brought another continent within the grasp of ... children's imaginations."

Lewin explains that the main thrust of the stories in the series "is to describe through the everyday experiences of a child something of his own African environment and what makes it different (e.g., indigenous birds and animals, local village activities and ceremonies, rural and town life in South Africa) as well as what is similar for any child anywhere (e.g., relationships with close family, emotions and responses, youthful enthusiasms and excitements). If the books explain the differences and enliven the similarities, I feel that they will have

Jafta

**Story by Hugh Lewin
Pictures by Lisa Kopper**

Lewin's "Jafta" series recounts the adventures of a young boy living a village in South Africa. (Cover illustration by Lisa Kopper.)

Jafta celebrates a cool rainfall with a friend. (Illustration from *Jafta's Mother* by Kopper.)

achieved something and will incidentally have helped diminish the dearth of decent material on black Africa."

WORKS CITED:

Berg, Leila, "Nourish the Soil," *Times Educational Supplement,* March 12, 1982, p. 38.

Klein, Gillian, "Warm, Brown and Strong," *Times Educational Supplement,* June 5, 1981, p. 37.

Wilson, Geraldine L., review of "Jafta" series, *Interracial Books for Children Bulletin,* Volume 15, numbers 7, 8, pp. 30-31.

FOR MORE INFORMATION SEE:

BOOKS

Chambers, Nancy, editor, *The Signal Review of Children's Books 2: A Selective Guide to Picture Books, Fiction, Plays, Poetry, Information Books Published during 1983,* Thimble Press, 1984, p. 54.

Children's Literature Review, Volume 9, Gale, 1985, pp. 89-92.

PERIODICALS

Booklist, November 1, 1984, p. 370.

Bulletin of the Center for Children's Books, May, 1983, p. 171; January, 1985.

Children's Book Review Service, April, 1983, p. 87.

Curriculum Review, February, 1984, p. 95.

Growing Point, July, 1981, p. 3909.

Language Arts, September, 1983, pp. 771-72.

New Statesman, November 8, 1985, p. 25.

Publishers Weekly, February 4, 1983, p. 70.

School Librarian, December, 1981, p. 333; February, 1990, p. 15.

School Library Journal, May, 1983, p. 63; November, 1984, p. 112.

Times Educational Supplement, October 2, 1981, pp. 20-21.

Times Literary Supplement, October 25, 1985, p. 1218.*

*   *   *

LEWIS, Brenda Ralph 1932-
(Rachel Mark Clifford)

PERSONAL: Born January 3, 1932, in London, England; daughter of Albert (a businessman) and Golda Esther (a housewife; maiden name, Beach) Abulafia; married Percy Sassoon Gourgey (a journalist), July 3, 1954 (divorced); married Harry Ralph Lewis (an estates executive), June 22, 1969; children: Jonathan Lewis. *Education:* Attended North London Collegiate School, 1945-50; attended Trinity College of Music, Cambridge, 1950-58. *Politics:* British Labour Party. *Religion:* Jewish. *Hobbies and other interests:* Playing the piano, tennis, science fiction, astronomy, politics, *Star Trek,*

BRENDA RALPH LEWIS

illuminated manuscripts, the ancient civilizations of Latin America, calligraphy and stamps.

ADDRESSES: Home and office—28 Fair Leas, Chesham, Buckinghamshire, HP5 2QW, England.

CAREER: Writer.

WRITINGS:

Ancient Rome, Transworld, 1974.
The Crusades, Transworld, 1975.
The Vikings, Transworld, 1976.
World History, Lock Ward, 1976.
Arms and Armour, Transworld, 1977.
The Aztecs, Ladybird Books, 1977.
The Incas, Ladybird Books, 1977.
The Vikings, Ladybird Books, 1978.
Hamlyn Book of Great Escapes, Paul Hamlyn, 1978.
Hitler and Nazi Germany, Evans Brothers, 1979.
Islam, Wayland, 1979.
Steam Engines, Wayland, 1979.
Greek Myth and Legend, Wayland, 1979.
Great Names in Music, Wayland, 1979.
Beads, Barter and Bullion, Wayland, 1979.
Growing up in Ancient Rome, B. T. Batsford, 1980.
Growing up in Aztec Times, B. T. Batsford, 1980.
Growing up in Inca Times, B. T. Batsford, 1980.
Growing up in the Dark Ages, B. T. Batsford, 1980.
Timeless Myths, Brimax Books, 1980.
Timeless Legends, Brimax Books, 1980.
Growing up in Samurai Japan, B. T. Batsford, 1981.
World History, Purnell and Sons, 1981.

(Editor) L. Du Garde Peach, *Kings and Queens,* Books 1 and 2, Ladybird Books, 1981.
H.R.H. Princess of Wales, Ladybird Books, 1982.
Chess, Purnell and Sons, 1984.
(Editor) Charles Dickens, *Oliver Twist,* Ladybird Books, 1984, Spanish edition, 1990.
Clothes, Macdonald, 1986.
Your Highway Code Test Made Easy, W. Foulsham & Co., 1986.
(With James Riordan) *Illustrated Treasury of Myths and Legends,* Hamlyn, 1987.
Exploring Clothes, Wayland, 1988.
Stamps! A Young Collector's Guide, Simon and Schuster, 1990.
The Roman Empire, Paul Hamlyn, 1992.

Also author of articles and short stories, some under the pseudonym Rachel Mark Clifford, for adults and children. Also author of numerous books about the British Royal Family. Contributor to radio programs and compiler of resource packets for British museums.

WORK IN PROGRESS: Coins and Currency; historical articles for *Royalty* magazine.

SIDELIGHTS: "I cannot remember the time when I did not want to be a writer," Brenda Ralph Lewis told *SATA.* "I doubt if I sat up in my infant's cot, rusk in hand, and announced the fact to the world, but certainly from the age of eight, in 1940, the idea of being a writer began to take hold. There was no family tradition involved, except for an uncle who wrote Yiddish stories, most of them unpublished.

"In a way, I had no real choice but to be a writer. Use of words, expression, love of words and ideas just came naturally to me. I was an early reader (my father taught me at age two or three) and by age eight, I was ready to start on the usual path of future writers: producing ambitious projects, writing a chapter or two and then abandoning them to start on yet another.

"My name first saw print when I was twelve and had a poem published in *Mickey Mouse* (well, one has to start somewhere!). At fifteen, I won a short story competition in *Strangest Stories* with a rather bloodthirsty mystery story. Later, when I was 21, I had an article published in a British magazine called *Theatre World.* I was theatre-mad at the time, and Shakespeare-mad in particular."

Despite her early start as a reader and writer, Lewis's writing career didn't advance much until she was well into adulthood. She attributed this delay to several causes. "My type of writer, concentrating on nonfiction mainly, needs a long time to mature and gather the background knowledge required. Fiction writing requires less time to mature, though knowledge is needed there, too," Lewis explained.

"More to the point, though, was a distinct lack of encouragement," she continued. "When a careers officer came to my school and I asked her about the prospects of being a journalist, she said one word:

'Don't!' I was about sixteen then. Later, as I approached my twenties, my destiny as far as my parents were concerned was to get married, have children and forget all about being a writer, or indeed anything else.

"It may seem very archaic today, but in 1950, when I left school at the age of eighteen, the idea of girls having careers was not on, except among the professional classes where parents and other children already had them. My mother had vague ideas about my being a professional pianist, but nothing came of it. Getting me married as early as possible seemed to be the most driving ambition of my parents at this time, however, and no one took my writing ambitions at all seriously. I even let them lie fallow myself for quite a time. Eventually, at age 25 (just before I became ancient in the marriage market) I wed my first husband. My parents heaved sighs of relief that I was at last 'parked.'"

Lewis found herself returning to writing, submitting articles to English magazines and finally writing her first book around 1969. She became interested in children's literature when a relative who was a school teacher remarked upon the shortage of intelligent, interesting books for children. After investigating the genre and contacting a publisher, Lewis wrote a series of historical biographies. "In this, I discovered another natural trait in myself, the ability to interest children in historical subjects and to impart to them my own enthusiasm for this type of book," she told *SATA*.

Lewis' interest in the past was initially sparked by a history book at school, she recalled. Growing up in a Jewish family during the Second World War made her particularly conscious of the importance of current events and their role in making history. "The effect all this had on me was to make me acutely aware, long before my time, of events in the world outside, of the terrors and dangers that were occurring not too far away, and of the transitory nature of life itself. In these circumstances, there was a constant sense of living through vital history, real earth-shattering stuff. I remember my childhood vividly and have since transmitted my heightened sense of events to my ongoing studies of history and on to the many historical books and articles I have written."

Although a love for the countryside has helped Lewis envisage Britain as it was in the past—"heavily forested, wild, untracked, laced with rivers and streams"—she acknowledged that a writer "must be able to translate himself or herself into almost any background, environment or time-scale required for producing a book or article. My experience of writing, now nearing the thirty-year mark, has taught me many important principles. Probably the most important is that the writer must be 'whited out' during the production of a book or article. What he or she thinks, believes, feels is not relevant. A writer is simply the conduit by which a story reaches the paper it is written on. Rather, you have to think with your characters, even in a nonfiction book or article, feel what they felt, even experience by one remove what they suffered. A tragic event or historical

Lewis's love of history and stamps is evident in her colorful introduction to stamp collecting entitled *Stamps! A Young Collector's Guide.*

life about which I am writing will always reduce me to tears as I work and somehow that emotion gets into the writing.

"Once a writer has cleared himself or herself out of the way, as it were, the writing of history books and articles becomes straightforward. Coupled with a fascination for other lives and other times, as it is with me, it also becomes a quest for more and more knowledge and learning." Lewis told *SATA* that she considers a constant state of learning to be the greatest benefit of a writing career. "I find it thrilling to know that this time next week, I shall know more than I do now, and that there is still more to learn in subsequent weeks."

Describing herself for *SATA,* Lewis concluded, "I was born hyperactive and have not slowed down since. I am sixty years old, but have yet more plans for further learning experiences far into the future. Sixty, by the way, is the retirement age for women and some men in Britain. Retirement? What retirement?"

*   *   *

LEWIS, Rob 1962-

PERSONAL: Full name, Robert Anthony Lewis; born July 16, 1962, in London, England; son of David Arthur Lewis (university senior lecturer) and Jennifer Ann (Thompson) Sutherland (a teacher); married Tracey Joy, 1984; children: Timothy, Rhydian. *Education:* Bristol Polytechnic, B.A. (graphic design; with honors), 1985.

ROB LEWIS

Politics: Plaid Cymru (Party of Wales). *Religion:* Christian. *Hobbies and other interests:* Walking, caving, organic gardening, and alternative energy sources—wind, water, wave, solar power.

ADDRESSES: Home—6 Sunnyside, Rhayader, Powys, Wales LD6 5ED.

CAREER: Writer and illustrator of children's books. Teacher at Ysgol Feithrin, a Welsh-language nursery school.

WRITINGS:

SELF-ILLUSTRATED

Hello Mr. Scarecrow, Farrar, Straus, 1987.
The Great Granny Robbery, Simon & Schuster, 1987.
Friska: The Sheep That Was Too Small, Farrar, Straus, 1987.
The White Bicycle, Farrar, Straus, 1988.
Come Back Hercules, Simon & Schuster, 1988.
Ollie's Song, Dial, 1990.
Henrietta's First Winter, Farrar, Straus, 1990.
A Scary Story Night, Simon & Schuster, 1990.
Small Change, Bodley Head/Red Fox, 1991.
Mr. Dunfilling and the Toothy Monster, Simon & Schuster, 1991.
Johnny's in Love, Simon & Schuster, 1991.
Jake's Birthday, Bodley Head, 1992.

Tidy up Trevor, Harcourt, in press.

ILLUSTRATOR

Lucille Powney, *You'll Be Late Father Christmas,* Simon & Schuster, 1989.

WORK IN PROGRESS: Developing ideas for picture books to be published in the Welsh language.

SIDELIGHTS: Welsh author-illustrator Rob Lewis remembers wanting to write when he was only nine years old. "I used to fill whole exercise books with stories for my English homework, much to the distress of my poor English teacher who had to spend hours marking them," he told *SATA.* "I used to get [high] marks ... more for endurance than quality of writing!" After graduating from school, Lewis studied graphic design at England's Bristol Polytechnic with the intention of becoming a film editor. "I was first told that my illustration wasn't good enough to make a career from it," he explained. The closing of the school's film department caused Lewis to reevaluate both his plan of study and his career goals. He had recently married fellow student—and soon to be fellow author-illustrator—Tracey Joy and he decided to join her in the school's illustration program. After graduating with honors in 1985, Lewis submitted several of his manuscripts and illustrations to London publishers and the following year several of his books were published. Among these were *Friska: The Sheep that Was Too Small, The Great Granny Robbery,* and *Hello Mr Scarecrow,* a picture book depicting the changing seasons as seen through the eyes of a scarecrow standing guard in a farmer's field.

Lewis uses a variety of mediums such as chalk, gouache, pen-and-ink, acrylics, and wax scrape-and-resist techniques in composing his illustrations. "I guess I tend to concentrate on animal characters mainly because I'm not too good at drawing people!" admitted Lewis. The ideas for the images in his picture books for children come from several areas. "More and more I am using the wonderful landscape of woods, mountains, and moorland around where I live in mid-Wales as inspiration—particularly in *Henrietta's First Winter,*" Lewis told *SATA.* He also draws upon his Christian beliefs in creating his texts and illustrations, saying "I try to make my books warm, reassuring things that children will want to take to bed with them along with teddy."

Working with children remains one of Lewis's greatest joys; he is actively involved in programs for young people in local schools and libraries and teaches at a Welsh nursery school in Rhayader, the small town in the county of Powys where he lives with his wife and young sons Timothy and Rhydian. "Because of my Welsh ancestry I am keen on promoting all things Welsh, especially the Welsh language, although I'm not yet a fluent Welsh speaker myself," admitted Lewis, who is at work on a series of books for pre-readers written in his native Celtic. Although mainly an author-illustrator of picture books, Lewis hopes to extend his talents to writing more story books, and perhaps even novels for the middle grades. "I don't think I would ever be interested in writing for adults," he added.

FOR MORE INFORMATION SEE:

PERIODICALS

Booklist, September 15, 1987, p. 150.
Growing Point, September, 1987, p. 4848.
School Library Journal, March, 1989, pp. 164, 166.

*   *   *

LIESTMAN, Vicki 1961-
(Vicki Revsbech)

PERSONAL: Surname is pronounced "listman"; born August 18, 1961, in Minneapolis, MN; daughter of Peter John (an airline pilot) and Eunice Ann (a dog groomer and trainer; maiden name, McRae) Revsbech; married Timothy Liestman (a salesman), 1985; children: Benjamin Joseph. *Education:* University of Minnesota, B.A., 1983.

ADDRESSES: Office—Carolrhoda Books, Inc., 241 First Ave. N., Minneapolis, MN 55401.

CAREER: Meadowbrook Press, Deephaven, MN, editorial free-lancer, 1982-84; Lerner Publications, Minneapolis, MN, editor, 1984-86; Carolrhoda Books, Minneapolis, editor, 1986-88, senior editor, 1988—.

WRITINGS:

Columbus Day, Carolrhoda Books, 1991.

Editor of children's books for ten years under name Vicki Revsbech.

*   *   *

LIONNI, Leo(nard) 1910-

PERSONAL: Born May 5, 1910, in Amsterdam, Holland; came to the United States, 1939; naturalized citizen, 1945; son of Louis and Elisabeth (a concert soprano; maiden name, Grossouw) Lionni; married Nora Maffi, December, 1931; children: Louis, Paolo. *Education:* Attended schools in Holland, Belgium, the United States, Italy, and Switzerland; University of Genoa, Ph.D. (economics), 1935. *Politics:* "Sometimes on the left—sometimes beyond." *Religion:* None.

ADDRESSES: Home—New York, NY; and Porcignano, 53017 Radda in Chianti, Siena, Italy. *Agent*—Agenzia Letteraria Internazionale, Corso Matteotti 3, Milan, Italy.

CAREER: Free-lance writer, designer, and painter, 1930-39; N. W. Ayer & Sons (advertising agency), Philadelphia, PA, art director, 1939-47; Olivetti Corporation of America, San Francisco, CA, design director, 1949-59; *Fortune* magazine, New York City, art director, 1949-62; Parsons School of Design, New York City, head of graphics design department, 1952-54; author and illustrator of children's books, 1959—. *Exhibitions:*

Has exhibited his paintings and sculpture at numerous individual and group shows in galleries, museums, and at universities throughout the United States and Europe. Individual shows include: Worcester Museum, MA, 1958; Philadelphia Art Alliance, 1959; Naviglio, Milan, 1963; Obelisco, Rome, 1964; Galleria dell'Ariete, Milan, 1966; Galleria del Milione, Milan, 1972; Linea 70, Verona, 1973; Il Vocolo, Genoa, 1973; Baukunst Galerie, Cologne, 1974; Klingspor Museum Offenback, 1974; and Galleria CIAK, Rome, 1975. Group shows include: Museum of Modern Art, New York City, 1954; Bratislava Biennale, 1967; and Venice Biennale, 1972.

MEMBER: Alliance Graphique Internationale, American Institute of Graphic Arts (president, 1956), Society of Typographic Arts (honorary member), Bund Deutscher Buchkunstler (honorary member), Authors League of America, Artists Equity.

AWARDS, HONORS: National Society of Art Directors Award, 1955; Architectural League Gold Medal, 1956; *New York Times* Best Illustrated award, 1959, for *Little Blue and Little Yellow;* Caldecott Honor Book, 1960, Lewis Carroll Shelf Award, 1962, and Children's Book Prize (Germany), 1963, all for *Inch by Inch; New York Times* Best Illustrated award, 1963, Caldecott Honor Book and American Library Association (ALA) Notable Book citation, both 1964, German Government Illustrated Book Award, 1965, and Bratislava Biennale Golden Apple, 1967, all for *Swimmy;* Spring Book Festival picture book honor, 1968, for *The Biggest House in the World; New York Times* Best Illustrated award, 1967, Caldecott Honor Book and ALA Notable Book citation, both 1968, all for *Frederick;* ALA Notable Book citation, 1970, for *Fish Is Fish;* Caldecott Honor Book, ALA Notable Book citation, and Christopher Book Award, all 1970, all for *Alexander and the Wind-Up Mouse;* five major awards at Teheran Film Festival in 1970 for two animated films; elected to Art Directors Hall of Fame, 1974; George G. Stone Center for Children's Books Award for body of work, 1976; American Institute of Graphic Arts Gold Medal, 1984; Jane Addams Children's Book Award, 1988, for *Nicholas, Where Have You Been?*

WRITINGS:

SELF-ILLUSTRATED WORKS FOR CHILDREN

Little Blue and Little Yellow, McDowell Obolensky, 1959.
Inch by Inch, Obolensky, 1960.
On My Beach There Are Many Pebbles, Obolensky, 1961.
Swimmy, Pantheon, 1963.
Tico and the Golden Wings, Pantheon, 1964.
Frederick, Pantheon, 1967.
The Alphabet Tree, Pantheon, 1968.
The Biggest House in the World, Pantheon, 1968.
Alexander and the Wind-Up Mouse, Pantheon, 1969.
Fish Is Fish, Pantheon, 1970.
Theodore and the Talking Mushroom, Pantheon, 1971.
The Greentail Mouse, Pantheon, 1973.

In the Rabbitgarden, Pantheon, 1975.
A Colour of His Own, Abelard, 1975, published as *A Color of His Own,* Pantheon, 1976.
Pezzettino, Pantheon, 1975.
A Flea Story: I Want to Stay Here! I Want to Go There!, Pantheon, 1977.
Geraldine, the Music Mouse, Pantheon, 1979.
Let's Make Rabbits: A Fable, Pantheon, 1982.
Cornelius, Pantheon, 1983.
Frederick's Fables: A Leo Lionni Treasury of Favorite Stories, introduction by Bruno Bettelheim, Pantheon, 1985 (published in England as *Frederick's Tales,* Andersen Press, 1986).
It's Mine!, Pantheon, 1986.
Nicholas, Where Have You Been?, Pantheon, 1987.
Six Crows, Knopf, 1988.
Tillie and the Wall, Knopf, 1989.
Frederick and His Friends, Knopf, 1989.
Matthew's Dream, Knopf, 1991.
A Busy Year, Knopf, 1992.
Mr. McMouse, Knopf, 1992.

"PICTURES TO TALK ABOUT" SERIES

Who?, Pantheon, 1983.
What?, Pantheon, 1983.
Where?, Pantheon, 1983.
When?, Pantheon, 1983.

"COLORS, LETTERS, NUMBERS, AND WORDS TO TALK ABOUT" SERIES

Colors to Talk About, Pantheon, 1985.
Letters to Talk About, Pantheon, 1985.
Numbers to Talk About, Pantheon, 1985.
Words to Talk About, Pantheon, 1985.

OTHER

Design for the Printed Page, Fortune Magazine, 1960.
(And illustrator) *Il Taccuino di Leo Lionni* (title means "Leo Lionni's Notebook"), Electa (Milan), 1972.
La Botanica Parallela (essays), Adelphi (Milan), 1976, translated by Patrick Creagh as *Parallel Botany,* Knopf, 1977.
(Illustrator) Hannah Solomon, *Mouse Days: A Book of Seasons,* Pantheon, 1981.
(Illustrator) Naomi Lewis, *Come With Us,* Andersen Press, 1982.

Also illustrator of *Mouse Days Calendar 1981,* 1980. Contributor to *Fortune, Casabella, Domus, Print, Architecture Plus, Wilson Library Bulletin,* and *Horn Book.* Editor, *Print,* 1955-57, *Panorama* (Italy), 1964-65. All of Lionni's books have been translated into other languages.

ADAPTATIONS: Five Lionni Classics, based on Lionni's stories, was released on videocassette by Random House and was an award winner in the American Film and Video Festival in 1988.

SIDELIGHTS: Born into a creative family, Leo Lionni knew at an early age that he wanted to become an artist and spent much of his adolescence at the art museums of his native Amsterdam teaching himself to draw. And

LEO LIONNI

although his education did not include formal art classes, he did study throughout Europe before earning a doctorate in economics from the University of Genoa in 1935 and simultaneously establishing himself as a painter. Emigrating to the United States in 1939, Lionni became a naturalized citizen in 1945 and was soon recognized as a "dynamic talent in commercial design," notes Lesley S. Potts in the *Dictionary of Literary Biography.* A pioneer in the field of advertising art and design, Lionni also began exhibiting his paintings and sculpture internationally in individual and group shows; and, according to Potts, "reviewers of his work described Lionni as a phenomenon, genuinely versatile, and one of the world's most original designers."

Lionni's career as an author and illustrator of children's books began by chance in the late 1950s. While travelling by train with his grandchildren, he improvised an entertaining story to pass the time and later worked the material into a book—*Little Blue and Little Yellow,* which has since become an acknowledged classic in children's literature. "Among the varied things I have done in my life few have given me more and greater satisfactions than my children's books," states Lionni in his essay, "My Books for Children." Recognized as a master of art and design, Lionni has also succeeded in creating award-winning fables that focus on individuality, self-reliance, and esthetic values. "Artistically and thematically, Lionni's books have developed in ways that reflect his own childhood and its influences, as well as his life as a designer, artist, and thinker," writes Potts, adding that "Lionni's work is further characterized by a deep concern for quality. He believes that children must grow up with a sense of excellence and pride in workmanship."

Little Blue and Little Yellow is a tale about two blobs of color who happen to be close friends but become a single blob of green when they embrace each other too closely. Problems ensue when their parents no longer recognize them, but the story ends happily and the blobs are able to return to their original colors. "Illustrated entirely with torn-paper collage, a dramatically innovative technique for its day, the theme of the book is the unfairness of judging by appearances," writes Potts, who notes that critical reception of the book was "uniformly enthusiastic." Although some critics saw the story as a social commentary on race relations, Lionni denies that this was his intent. However, Potts observes that "it was the first picture book to tell an allegorical tale about human problems and human situations using neither humans nor animals as its protagonists, but merely bits of torn paper distributed across the picture space in such a way as to denote specific actions, purposes, and emotions."

Lionni's next book for children, *Inch by Inch,* was a Caldecott Honor Book and received the Lewis Carroll Shelf Award and the German Children's Book Prize. It tells of a little caterpillar who escapes being eaten by various birds in a clever ploy that involves measuring their tails, necks, and legs for them. Although most birds, whatever their size, present little difficulty for the caterpillar, he must use greater ingenuity when the nightingale asks that his song be measured. "As the little green worm travels across the pages of this book, his ingenuity and that of the artist become more and more apparent," writes Linda Kauffman Peterson in *Newbery and Caldecott Medal and Honor Books.* Illustrated in crayon and textured collage, the book influenced other

artists to use this medium, says Potts, who notes, however, that it "has seldom been equaled in the areas of collage design and technique." Potts relates that, according to Lionni, "*Inch by Inch* reflected his life in advertising. 'When I had to make a living, I had to survive and I really made a living telling people things that they didn't need to know. That's what the inchworm did and he managed, very cleverly, to survive.'"

"If *Inch by Inch* reflects Lionni's pragmatic period of survival in the world of advertising," suggests Potts, *Swimmy,* with its Marxist overtones, "mirrors his increasing involvement in politics." A Caldecott Honor Book and the first picture book by an American illustrator to win the Bratislava Biennale Golden Apple, *Swimmy* is about a little black fish whose family is eaten by a large, ravenous tuna. The sole survivor, Swimmy finds another school of fish and devises a scheme for their safety whereby they all swim in one enormous fish-shaped formation in which Swimmy is the eye. Critics praise the beautifully textured watercolor washes and prints that Lionni used to render the undersea world, as well as the text that accompanies the illustrations. "Though Lionni's text is simple and direct, the economy of words makes the illustrations highly important in extending and embellishing the story," observes Peterson. "The artist's inventive style remains a popular one within the realm of picture books, and the underlying themes have a relevancy that wears well with time."

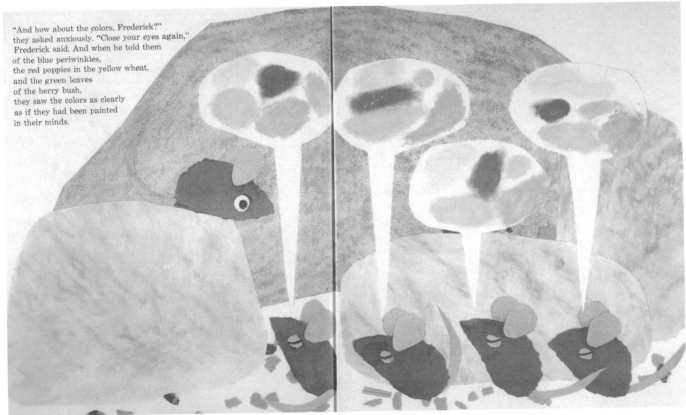

"And how about the colors, Frederick?" they asked anxiously. "Close your eyes again," Frederick said. And when he told them of the blue periwinkles, the red poppies in the yellow wheat, and the green leaves of the berry bush, they saw the colors as clearly as if they had been painted in their minds.

Considered by many critics to be Lionni's best work, *Frederick* relates the story of a young mouse who helps his friends survive a bad winter by telling tales of summertime fun. (Illustration by the author.)

In *Frederick,* which was also named a Caldecott Honor Book and is considered by many critics to be Lionni's best work, the author uses what has since become something of a trademark—a mouse as the main character. In the book, a family of field mice gather food throughout the summer to sustain them during the coming winter. Frederick, on the other hand, spends his time enjoying the sunshine. When winter comes and the stored food is depleted, the other mice fear for their future, but Frederick entertains them with rhymes and stories about summer and gets the entire family through the remainder of winter. Like its predecessors, the story utilizes collage illustrations; and in its stressing of the importance of the artist to society, says Potts, it mirrors Lionni's own concerns at the time of its creation—his questioning of whether the artist's responsibility is to oneself or to one's society. Suggesting that "*Frederick* is one of the most autobiographical of Lionni's fables, going back to his early childhood development as an artist," Potts describes the story as "one of the progression from feelings to images and finally to words—an emergence into literacy—as he experiences the warmth of the sunlight and the colors of nature, then the poetic expression of all that he has felt and seen." Noting that each of Lionni's books is "unique, varied in artistic expression," George A. Woods states in the *New York Times Book Review,* "As Frederick's friends tell him, 'You are a poet'; so is Lionni—with a palette."

Another of Lionni's stories to feature a mouse is *Alexander and the Wind-Up Mouse,* a Caldecott Honor Book and recipient of the Christopher Book Award. Alexander is a mouse whose friend is a toy mechanical mouse named Willy, the favorite toy of the children in the house. Alexander envies the attention his friend receives and wishes that he, too, were mechanical. However, when Willy is broken and tossed into the trash, Alexander asks a magical lizard to make Willy into a real mouse instead. "Alexander's story illustrates the importance of remaining human, of thinking for oneself, and of the transforming power of love," writes Potts. And although Sada Fretz, in a *School Library Journal* review of the book, found that it "lacks the depth and resonance of Lionni's previous mouse fable, *Frederick,*" Mary Hobbs declares in the *Junior Bookshelf* that it "deserves to become a classic among picture books."

Lionni differs from many artists in that he has avoided the development of a consistent style; in "My Books for Children," he remarks that he finds "greater joy and satisfaction in developing a form for each idea." Potts believes that Lionni's books for children reflect his evolving attitude about art and the artist in society: *Little Blue and Little Yellow* expressed his belief that young children could comprehend images devoid of detail; *Inch by Inch* presented his thoughts about his early career in advertising; *Swimmy* asserted his early political position that the artist must also be an activist; *Frederick* demonstrated his later belief that the artist contributes to society apart from any political considerations; and *Alexander and the Wind-Up Mouse* articulat-

One day, when there was no one in the house, Alexander heard a squeak in Annie's room. He sneaked in and what did he see? Another mouse.
But not an ordinary mouse like himself. Instead of legs it had two little wheels, and on its back there was a key.

"Who are you?" asked Alexander.

Alexander the mouse meets Willy, a mechanical rodent, in Lionni's Caldecott Honor and Christopher Award-winning tale of friendship and magic. (Illustration by the author from *Alexander and the Wind-Up Mouse.*)

In Lionni's self-illustrated *Fish Is Fish*, a wise frog tells a small fish about the wonders of the world.

ed the theme that is most important to him—the exercising of personal choice. Potts suggests that this theme "remains Lionni's prime area of concern in his books: 'It's no accident that exactly those books which pose basic problems of choice are my favorite books—*Inch by Inch; Swimmy; Frederick* and *Alexander*. They are the ones which, I find, say the most to me.'"

Lionni explains in "My Children's Books" that his "characters are humans in disguise and their little problems and situations are human problems, human situations." Continuing, Lionni says: "The protagonist of my books is often an individual who is, because of special circumstances, an outcast, a rebel, a victim, or a hero. His story ends happily because of his intelligence..., his vitality and resourcefulness..., his goodness..., or simply because his will and patience turn the laws of averages to his advantage. Often he has to learn through suffering..., but it is always his own vitality, his discovery that life is a positive, exciting fact, that makes him come out on top." And although critics occasionally wonder whether his themes are intended for children, Lionni holds that he is not aware of the age of his readers: "I believe, in fact, that a good children's book should appeal to all people who have not completely lost their original joy and wonder in life.... The fact is that I really don't make books for children at all. I make them for that part of us, of myself and of my friends, which has never changed, which is still child."

WORKS CITED:

Fretz, Sada, review of *Alexander and the Wind-Up Mouse, School Library Journal,* May, 1970, p. 60.

Hobbs, Mary, review of *Alexander and the Wind-Up Mouse, Junior Bookshelf,* December, 1971, p. 364.

Lionni, Leo, "My Books for Children," *Wilson Library Bulletin,* October, 1964, reprinted in *Authors and Illustrators of Children's Books: Writers on Their Lives and Works,* edited by Miriam Hoffman and Eva Samuels, Bowker, 1972, pp. 302-06.

Peterson, Linda Kauffman and Marilyn Leathers Solt, "The Caldecott Medal and Honor Books, 1938-1981," *Newbery and Caldecott Medal and Honor Books: An Annotated Bibliography,* G. K. Hall, 1982, pp. 319-20, pp. 326-27.

Potts, Lesley S., *Dictionary of Literary Biography,* Volume 61: *American Writers for Children since 1960: Poets, Illustrators, and Nonfiction Authors,* Gale, 1987, pp. 139-52.

Woods, George A., review of *Frederick, New York Times Book Review,* June 11, 1967, p. 32.

FOR MORE INFORMATION SEE:

BOOKS

Bader, Barbara, *American Picture Books from Noah's Ark to the Beast Within,* Macmillan, 1976, pp. 525-43.

Children's Literature Review, Volume 7, Gale, 1984.

Hopkins, Lee Bennett, *Books Are by People,* Citation Press, 1969.

McCann, Donnarae, and Olga Richard, *The Child's First Books: A Critical Study of Pictures and Texts,* Wilson, 1973, pp. 58-59.

Twentieth-Century Children's Writers, 3rd edition, edited by Tracy Chevalier, St. James Press, 1989.

PERIODICALS

American Artist, April, 1953, p. 30.

Globe and Mail (Toronto), May 28, 1988.

Library Journal, March 15, 1964, p. 100.

Los Angeles Times Book Review, March 27, 1988; May 22, 1988.

New York Times Book Review, May 29, 1983; December 22, 1985; September 20, 1987.

Time, December 22, 1958, p. 53.

Times Literary Supplement, April 11, 1986.

Top of the News, October, 1962, pp. 65-67.

Tribune Books (Chicago), September 13, 1987.
Washington Post Book World, May 9, 1982.
Wilson Library Bulletin, May, 1970, pp. 947-50; June, 1992, pp. 56-58.

OTHER

Meet Leo Lionni (videocassette), American School Publications, 1992.*

*   *   *

LURIE, Morris 1938-

PERSONAL: Born October 30, 1938, in Melbourne, Victoria, Australia; married; children: two.

ADDRESSES: Home—Hawthorn, Victoria, Australia. *Agent*—c/o Penguin Books, Maroondah Highway, P.O. Box 257, Ringwood, Victoria 4134, Australia.

CAREER: Writer. Worked in advertising.

AWARDS, HONORS: Young Australian's Best Book Award (with Elizabeth Honey), 1986, for *The Twenty-Seventh Annual African Hippopotamus Race.*

WRITINGS:

FOR CHILDREN

The Twenty-Seventh Annual African Hippopotamus Race, illustrated by Richard Sawers, Simon & Schuster, 1969, illustrated by Elizabeth Honey, Penguin, 1977.
Arlo, the Dandy Lion, illustrated by Richard Sawers, McGraw, 1971, illustrated by Brett Colquhoun, Penguin, 1983.
Toby's Millions, illustrated by Arthur Horner, Kestral, 1982, Penguin, 1983.
The Story of Imelda, Who Was Small, illustrated by Terry Denton, Oxford University Press, 1984.
Night-Night! Seven Going-to-Bed Stories—One Wonderful Story for Every Night of the Week, illustrated by Alison Lestis, Oxford University Press, 1986.
What's That Noise? What's That Sound?, Random Century, 1991.

OTHER

Rappaport (novel), Hodder & Stoughton, 1966, Morrow, 1967.
The London Jungle Adventures of Charlie Hope (novel), Hodder & Stoughton, 1968.
Happy Times (short stories), Hodder & Stoughton, 1969.
The English in Heat (essays), illustrated by Michael Leunig, Angus & Robertson, 1972.
Rappaport's Revenge (novel), Angus & Robertson, 1973.
Inside the Wardrobe: Twenty Stories, Outback Press, 1975, Horizon Press, 1978.
Hack Work (essays), Outback Press, 1977.
About Burt Britton, John Cheever, Gordon Lish, William Saroyan, Isaac B. Singer, Kurt Vonnegut, and Other Matters, Horizon Press, 1978.

(Editor and author of introduction) John Hepworth, *John Hepworth: His Book,* Angus & Robertson, 1978.
Flying Home (novel), Outback Press, 1978, Penguin, 1982.
Waterman: Three Plays (includes *Waterman; Jangle, Jangle;* and *A Visit to the Uncle*), Outback Press, 1979.
Running Nicely (short stories), Hamish Hamilton, 1979.
Public Secrets: Blowing the Whistle on Australia, England, France, Japan, the U.S.A., and Places Worse, illustrated by Edward Koren, Sun Books, 1981.
Dirty Friends (short stories), Penguin, 1981.
Seven Books for Grossman (novel), Penguin, 1983.
Outrageous Behavior: Best Stories of Morris Lurie, Penguin, 1984.
The Night We Ate the Sparrow: A Memoir and Fourteen Stories, Penguin, 1985.
Snow Jobs (essays), Pascoe, 1985.
Whole Life (autobiography), McPhee Gribble, 1987, Penguin, 1990.
My Life as a Movie and Other Gross Conceits (essays), McPhee Gribble, 1988.
Two Brothers, Running: Seventeen Stories and a Movie, Penguin, 1990.
Madness (novel), Collins, Angus & Robertson, 1991.

Work represented in anthologies, including *Jewish Writing from Down Under: Australia and New Zealand,* edited by Roberta Kalechofsky and Robert Kalechofsky, Micah, 1984. Contributor to periodicals, including *Antaeus, New Yorker, Penthouse, Transatlantic Review,* and *Virginia Quarterly.*

WORK IN PROGRESS: Two books for children, entitled *Racing the Moon* and *Beyond the Furthest Star.*

SIDELIGHTS: Australian writer Morris Lurie is well known to adult readers for his humor and wit, pointed often at the human condition, and for his incisive insights into family relationships and ethnic roots. Yet he is also recognized among younger readers for his quirky and slightly absurd children's works. These simple, unaffected stories are told through a child's eye and feature appealing, comical characters—both human and animal—caught in challenging situations. For instance, in one story a two-and-a-half ton hippo trains for a swimming race, while in another a tiny girl struggles to make herself grow. By the close of the narratives, many of Lurie's characters have gained a bit of wisdom in how to survive the difficulties of daily life.

Lurie wrote his first book for children in 1969, more than two decades ago. *The Twenty-Seventh Annual African Hippopotamus Race* follows Edward Day, an eight-year-old hippopotamus in training for the annual fourteen-mile swimming competition held on the Zamboola River. Modest, courageous Edward is coached by his one-time champion swimmer grandfather until the day of the meet, when the youngster faces eighty-three competitors—not all of whom swim by the rules (one ill-natured hippo grabs Edward's leg). However, Edward emerges victorious, though he realizes his success will last only a year. Then a new champion hippo will be crowned. *Hippopotamus Race* is "a rare, really funny book for young people," decided a *Horn Book* reviewer.

Arlo, the Dandy Lion features another character drawn from wildlife. An inhabitant of the jungles of Africa, the extremely vain title character is delighted to discover an abandoned trunk stuffed with stylish clothing near his home. Draping himself in red velvet, he swaggers through the jungle spouting fashion tips such as "A gentleman never wears brown after six!," as quoted in the *Times Literary Supplement*. Finally he is captured by local zookeepers, who mistake him for a rare beast. Arlo basks in the limelight for a while but quickly succumbs to loneliness when the weather turns frigid and tourists no longer visit. Sent home with his much-loved clothes in tatters and ruined, Arlo burns them along with the trunk, then happily rejoins his lion family.

Lurie turned to human characters for *The Story of Imelda, Who Was Small,* a tale featuring a well-behaved, though diminutive (six-inch-tall) youngster. Wanting to help their daughter grow to a normal stature, Imelda's parents enlist the aid of Dr. Anderson, an inane physician who advises Imelda to stick with "tall"

In Morris Lurie's *The Story of Imelda, Who Was Small,* six-inch Imelda eats "tall" foods—spaghetti, licorice sticks, and carrots—in the vain hope that they will help her grow. (Illustration by Terry Denton.)

foods—spaghetti, licorice sticks, and carrots. Though Imelda adheres to the strict diet, even making sure she rigorously avoids "short" foods like potatoes and pancakes, she fails to grow. Discouraged, her family unexpectedly receives sound, common-sense advice from a stranger in a neighborhood park. "There is much to look and laugh at in this Australian import," concluded a reviewer for *Booklist.*

The humor found in Lurie's children's works extends into his adult works as well. He has a "lively talent for recording odd encounters," wrote David Wilson in a *Times Literary Supplement* review of *Running Nicely,* one of the author's short story collections. Mixed with Lurie's humor, though, are thoughtful examinations of such subjects as family relationships, loneliness, ethnicity, and human values and behavior. In one of his most well-known works, *Flying Home,* for example, the author focuses on one man's struggle to find his roots and the secret to his "true" self.

Though Lurie has found success writing in numerous genres—short stories, essays, and novels—he once said that he feels most comfortable composing shorter works. "You can spread a short story out (in your mind, or on your table) and see the whole thing, get an idea of the balance, of the way things are developing," he disclosed in *Books and Bookmen.* "I get into trouble if I think too much ... Have I delineated the characters properly? Have I established mood? All I know is that if I'm not bored, if it's moving, if I'm getting down what I want to get down, if I'm having a fine time, then everything is okay. And with a bit of luck, it is for the reader too."

Lurie told *SATA:* "I want a book to put its arms around me. If I can buy it, good. If I can't, then I have to write it. Either way, the essential, vital thing is to get that *hug.*"

WORKS CITED:

Lurie, Morris, "Personal Opinion," *Books and Book-men,* April, 1968.

Review of *The Story of Imelda, Who Was Small, Booklist,* October 1, 1988, p. 323.

Review of *The Twenty-Seventh Annual African Hippopotamus Race, Horn Book,* August, 1970, pp. 381-82.

"When Pigs Have Wings," *Times Literary Supplement,* December 3, 1971, p. 1515.

Wilson, David, "Brief Encounters," *Times Literary Supplement,* December 7, 1979, p. 86.

FOR MORE INFORMATION SEE:

BOOKS

Contemporary Authors, Volume 133, Gale, 1991, pp. 242-43.

PERIODICALS

Horn Book, January/February, 1989, pp. 55-56.
Library Journal, September 15, 1973, p. 2641.
New York Times Book Review, May 24, 1970, p. 32.
Publishers Weekly, October 28, 1988, p. 79.

Saturday Review, May 9, 1970.
School Library Journal, January, 1989, p. 64.

* * *

LUTZEIER, Elizabeth 1952-

PERSONAL: Born November 8, 1952, in Manchester, England; daughter of Denis (a transport manager) and Jane Mary (an administrator; maiden name, Galvin) Byrne; married Peter Rolf Lutzeier (a professor), September 10, 1977; children: Heidi Jane, Thomas Friedrich. *Education:* Leeds University, B.A., 1973, M.A., 1974; Oxford University, P.G.C.E., 1975; University of California, San Diego, certificate in TESL/TEFL, 1987.

ADDRESSES: Home—9 Viscount Dr., Beckton, London E6 4XQ, England.

CAREER: Bishop Grosseteste College, Lincoln, England, lecturer in English, 1975-77; Volkshochschule(n), Berlin, Germany, lecturer in English as a Foreign Language (EFL), 1975-77; University of California, San Diego, visiting scholar, 1986-87; Freie Universitat, West Berlin, Germany, lecturer in EFL, 1980-86 and 1987-88; Newham Education Authority, London, England, English as a Second Language (ESL) advisory teacher, 1988-92; Kent County Council, England, ESL team leader, 1992—; writer.

AWARDS, HONORS: Kathleen Fidler Award, 1984, for *No Shelter;* shortlisted, Guardian Children's Fiction Award, 1992, for *The Wall;* Carnegie Medal nomination, 1992, for *The Coldest Winter.*

WRITINGS:

No Shelter, Blackie's, 1984.
The Coldest Winter, Oxford University Press, 1991.
The Wall, Oxford University Press, 1991.
Lost for Words, Oxford University Press, in press.

WORK IN PROGRESS: A book about a Bangladeshi girl; researching another book.

SIDELIGHTS: Elizabeth Lutzeier told *SATA:* "Studying literature—studying 'great writers'—made me rather inhibited about writing, because only real writers wrote and most of them seemed to have lived a very long time ago. Even after I had published *No Shelter,* I didn't see myself as a 'real writer.' I still don't. But working in Third College Writing Program at the University of California, San Diego made me stop bothering about all that real writer stuff and start to focus on publishing—getting the writing right.

"I wrote *No Shelter* because, having married a German more than thirty years after World War II, I was angry about the way the British media still stereotyped every German as a Nazi. I wanted to show how there were many Germans who didn't want Hitler or the war, so, primed with the stories told to me by friends in Germany—as well as strangers on buses—I wrote about how a young German boy experienced the war. I knew I

ELIZABETH LUTZEIER

had done what I set out to do when one critic described it as 'the best peace book I have ever read.'

"*No Shelter* is dedicated to my husband's aunt who was killed in 1939 in the euthanasia program—aged eighteen—because she had epilepsy.

"*The Coldest Winter* arose partly from my childhood, spent half in England and half in Ireland. A lot of my mother's stories of her own childhood, along with the story of my great-grandfather just walking out one morning—possibly for America—are woven into the research I did about famine times. But I think the strongest motivating force for writing this was seeing, again and again, the pictures of more and more victims of famine—in Sudan, in Eritrea—and not understanding how people could let something like that happen again.

"When the Berlin wall came down, we sat watching the news with tears streaming down our faces, in front of our London T.V. After having lived in Berlin for ten years, we weren't there when the most important event happened. But what struck me, through all the euphoric commentaries, was the sentence, 'It was only seven months ago that the last person was shot trying to cross the wall.' What must the families of the people who had been shot feel like, now that the wall was gone? I wrote *The Wall* to try and find out.

"*Lost for Words,* to be published in 1993, is about a year in the life of a Bangladeshi girl who has just come to England. I am now working on my fifth book, at the same time as researching the sixth, which will be about Romanies. I find it hard to say what the fifth is about—because I'm too busy finding out myself."

M

MACAULAY, David (Alexander) 1946-

PERSONAL: Born December 2, 1946, in Burton-on-Trent, England; came to the United States in 1957; son of James (a textile machine technician) and Joan (Lowe) Macaulay; children: Elizabeth Alexandra, Charlotte Valerie. *Education:* Rhode Island School of Design, B.Arch., 1969.

ADDRESSES: Studio—146 Water St., Warren, RI 02885.

CAREER: Rhode Island School of Design, Providence, instructor in interior design, 1969-73, instructor in two-dimensional design, 1974-76, adjunct faculty, department of illustration, 1976-90, chairman, department of illustration, 1977-79; free-lance illustrator and writer, 1979—. Public school teacher of art in Central Falls, RI, 1969-70, and Newton, MA, 1972-74; designer, Morris Nathanson Design, 1969-72. Visiting lecturer, Yale University, 1978-79, Simmons College, 1989-90; visiting professor of art, Wellesley College, 1985-87; visiting instructor, Brown University, 1982-86. Worked as a consultant and presenter for television shows produced by Unicorn Projects, Washington, DC, including "Castle," 1982, "Cathedral," 1985, and "Pyramid," 1987; presenter of television show "Sense of Place," WJAR-TV, Providence, RI, 1988. Trustee, Partners for Livable Places, Washington, DC, Slater Mill Historic Site, Pawtucket, RI, and Community Preparatory School, Providence, RI. Works are in the permanent collections of Cooper Hewitt Museum, Toledo Museum of Art, and Museum of Art, Rhode Island School of Design.

AWARDS, HONORS: New York Times Ten Best Illustrated Books citation, 1973, American Institute of Graphic Arts Children's Book Show citation, 1973-74, Caldecott Honor Book, American Library Association (ALA), and Children's Book Showcase title, both 1974, Jugendbuchpreis (Germany) and Silver Slate Pencil Award (Holland), both 1975, all for *Cathedral: The Story of Its Construction;* Children's Book Showcase title, 1975, for *City: A Story of Roman Planning and Construction;* Christopher Award, and *New York Times*

DAVID MACAULAY

Outstanding Children's Book of the Year, both 1975, *Boston Globe-Horn Book* honor book, and Children's Book Showcase title, both 1976, all for *Pyramid; New York Times* Outstanding Children's Book of the Year, 1976, Children's Book Showcase title, and *School Library Journal* "Best of the Best 1966-1976" citation, 1978, all for *Underground; New York Times Book Review* Outstanding Book of the Year, 1977, New York Academy of Sciences Children's Science Book Award honorable mention, Caldecott Honor Book, and *Boston Globe-Horn Book* honor book, all 1978, all for *Castle;*

Washington Children's Book Guild Award for a body of work, 1977; American Institute of Architects Medal, 1978, for his contribution as "an outstanding illustrator and recorder of architectural accomplishment"; ALA Best Books for Young Adults and New York Public Library's Books for the Teen Age citations, 1980, both for *Motel of the Mysteries; New York Times* Ten Best Illustrated Books, and Parents' Choice Award for illustration in children's books, both 1980, New York Academy of Sciences Award honorable mention, 1981, and Ambassador of Books-across-the-Sea honor book, English-Speaking Union, 1982, all for *Unbuilding; New York Times Book Review* Notable Book of the Year, 1982, for *Help! Let Me Out!; School Library Journal's* Best Books and New York Public Library's Children's Books citations, both 1983, both for *Mill;* nominated for Hans Christian Andersen Illustrator Medal, 1984; honorary Doctor of Literature, Rhode Island College, 1987; honorary Doctor of Humanities, Savannah College of Art and Design, 1987; *Times Educational Supplement* senior information book award, science book prize for under sixteen, The Science Museum/Copus (London), *Boston Globe-Horn Book* Award for best nonfiction book, all 1989, and American Institute of Physics best science book of the year award, 1990, all for *The Way Things Work;* Caldecott Medal, 1991, for *Black and White.*

WRITINGS:

SELF-ILLUSTRATED

Cathedral: The Story of Its Construction, Houghton, 1973.
City: A Story of Roman Planning and Construction, Houghton, 1974.
Pyramid, Houghton, 1975.
Underground, Houghton, 1976.
Castle, Houghton, 1977.
Great Moments in Architecture, Houghton, 1978.
Motel of the Mysteries, Houghton, 1979.
Unbuilding, Houghton, 1980.
Mill, Houghton, 1983.
BAAA, Houghton, 1985.
Why the Chicken Crossed the Road, Houghton, 1987.
The Way Things Work, Houghton, 1988.
Black and White, Houghton, 1990.

ILLUSTRATOR

David L. Porter, *Help! Let Me Out!,* Houghton, 1982.
Electricity, Tennessee Valley Authority, 1983.
Robert Ornstein and Richard F. Thompson, *The Amazing Brain,* Houghton, 1984.

Contributor of illustrated articles to magazines, including *Washington Post.* Cartoonist for *Architectural Record,* 1990—.

ADAPTATIONS: The following works were adapted and broadcast by PBS-TV: *Castle,* October, 1983; *Cathedral,* 1985; and *Pyramid,* 1987.

SIDELIGHTS: David Macaulay has tackled the daunting subjects of architecture and technology in order to explain to young readers how things are built, how gadgets work, and how abstract ideas become concrete reality. An author-illustrator with a background in architecture, Macaulay has won numerous important awards for such titles as *Cathedral, Castle, Pyramid, Underground,* and *The Way Things Work.* In these and other books, he explains through texts and drawings how complex buildings were put together, or how modern-day underground systems keep city services flowing.

Times Educational Supplement correspondent Valerie Alderson notes that Macaulay "certainly has a gift for putting across the complexities of construction engineering which should be the envy of most of our writers of children's non-fiction. No doubt his training as an architect has contributed much, giving him a thorough understanding of the principles behind the work he describes, but, in addition, he exploits his gifts as an illustrator to underline and expand his text." In *Children's Book Showcase,* Alvin Eisenman calls Macaulay "a born teacher with an interest in things nobody before had the skill or the courage to try to explain."

Macaulay told Joseph O. Holmes of *Publishers Weekly:* "I consider myself first and foremost an illustrator, in the broadest sense, someone who makes things clear through pictures and teaches through pictures." Through his line drawings, readers can ascend into the

Macaulay employs pen-and-ink techniques to depict the workings of a Roman metropolis in *City.*

And something else is
drifting by. Snow?
The boy is thrilled.
He opens the window.
The singing gets louder.

Then they started
marching again and,
by the fourth trip
around the living
room, my brother
was really getting
into it. The little
traitor.

In his self-illustrated Caldecott winner, *Black and White,* Macaulay tells four overlapping stories using a collage format.

heights of a cathedral ceiling and down into the depths of a city sewer system. Little touches of humor lurk in many illustrations, and human characters provide a sense of perspective. In the *Children's Literature Association Quarterly,* Joyce A. Thomas claims that Macaulay's works "exemplify some of the best in non-fiction illustration.... Macaulay's illustrations are often impressive in themselves, always provide an accurate complement to his text, and extend his words in a way that allows the reader-viewer to live the building of that castle or that cathedral. Instead of passively witnessing, one imaginatively participates."

David Macaulay was no passive witness even as a child. In a speech at the acceptance of his 1991 Caldecott Medal for his book *Black and White,* the author lovingly remembered his "problem parents," who used the family kitchen as a workshop for their various projects. "We got used to seeing people make things," Macaulay recalled in the *Horn Book.* "But I'm not just complaining about occasional sawdust or hammering or balls of wool lying around. I'm talking about the *P* word. *Process.*" Macaulay continued: "My siblings and I were systematically and brutally denied mystification of process. We were blatantly encouraged to make things, to understand how things went together and how they came apart. Maybe we didn't know *how* everything was

made, but we knew there was an order to it, and we knew there was a right way to do things. By the time we got out of that kitchen, we actually believed that creativity and craftsmanship were desirable—even normal."

Macaulay was born in England, and he remembers his childhood there as particularly happy. He combined an interest in making things with an active imagination, sometimes constructing string-and-cardboard cable car systems in the family sitting room, and sometimes indulging in solitary adventures in the nearby woods. "One of the great things about Bolton, Lancashire, where I lived, was the twenty-minute walk to school each day through woods past a stream," Macaulay told *SATA.* "I was very familiar with the area, since it was my playground when not in school, and it allowed a chance to let the mind wander. Whenever the opportunity presented itself for me to daydream, I did.... Those experiences of playing alone are remembered as some of the best and happiest times of my childhood."

When Macaulay was eleven, his father took a job in America. The family moved to New Jersey—"an incredible shock," the author told *SATA.* At first Macaulay was uncomfortable with his American contemporaries, who seemed so much more worldly-wise and mature.

THE WHEEL AND AXLE

ON THE GROOMING OF MAMMOTHS

The problem with washing a mammoth, assuming that you can get close enough with the water (a point I will address further on), is the length of time it takes for the creature's hair to dry. The problem is greatly aggravated when steady sunshine is unavailable.

Recalling the incident between the mammoth and the tusk trimmers, and particularly the motion of the free end of the log, I invented a mechanical drier. It was composed of feathers secured to the ends of long spokes which radiated from one end of a sturdy shaft. At the other end of the shaft radiated a set of short boards. The entire machine was powered by a continuous line of sprightly workers who leaped one by one from a raised platform onto the projecting boards. Their weight against the boards turned the shaft. Because the spokes at the opposite end of the shaft were considerably longer than the boards, their feathered ends naturally turned much faster thereby producing the steady wind required for speedy drying.

A colleague once suggested I replace manpower with a constant stream of water. I left him in no doubt as to my views on this ludicrous proposal.

The "wheel and axle" is just one of the machines Macaulay describes in *The Way Things Work,* a lively exploration of how both simple and complex tools operate. (Illustration by the author).

"My childhood came to an end between the sixth and seventh grades, but my imagination never stopped protecting me, coming back into play when I needed it," he told *SATA.*

After five years in New Jersey, the family moved to Rhode Island. There Macaulay discovered his talent for drawing, amusing himself and his classmates by producing pictures of the Beatles. Upon graduation from high school, Macaulay entered the Rhode Island School of Design to study architecture. "It never even entered my mind to study painting or illustration," he told *SATA.* Practical though it may have seemed, the study of architecture did not satisfy the budding artist in Macaulay. "Architecture teaches you how to devise a way of thinking that allows you to believe you can tackle any problem of any scale," he said. "It fueled and educated my desire to understand how things work. Since then, I have realized that what I was learning in architecture—how to break down an immense problem into its smallest parts and put it back together logically with knowledge, expertise, and imagination—could also be applied to making books."

Macaulay taught junior high school art for a year in 1969 and worked in an interior design studio for two years after that. He left the interior design business to work as a free-lance illustrator and began to experiment with books of his own. One that he tried to sell was about a gargoyle beauty pageant, with the ugly beasts flying around a Gothic cathedral. The publishers at Houghton Mifflin did not care for the gargoyle story, but they were intrigued by Macaulay's drawings of the immense church. They commissioned Macaulay to do a picture book about the construction of a cathedral, and sent him off to France to do the research.

The result was the award-winning *Cathedral: The Story of Its Construction,* a work that details the building of a great Gothic cathedral in a fictitious town from the conception of plans to the first service in the finished sanctuary. Published in 1973, *Cathedral* won a Caldecott Honor citation, the Jugendbuchpreis in Germany, and the Silver Slate Pencil Award for best illustrated children's book.

Macaulay followed *Cathedral* with a string of similar titles, all done with his meticulous pen-and-ink illustrations: *City: A Story of Roman Planning and Construction, Pyramid, Castle,* and *Mill. Times Literary Supplement* reviewer Mary Furness claims that the books, with their "beautiful and clear black-and-white line drawings," succeed in making "the most complicated building process comparatively easy to understand." Similarly, in *Children and Books* Zena Sutherland and May Hill Arbuthnot conclude: "David Macaulay's books on architectural landmarks of the past ... have been for many years, and are likely to be for many more, some of the best of their type."

His reputation established, Macaulay tried some more daring projects. In *Underground,* he explained the complicated system of pipes, subway trains, and sewer drains beneath a city street. *Unbuilding* reverses the building process, showing how New York City's Empire State Building might be dismantled piece by piece at the whim of a rich businessman. *Motel of the Mysteries,* one of the author's humorous works, pokes fun at the unfounded generalizations some archaeologists make when confronted with ancient artifacts.

Macaulay's most ambitious book to date is *The Way Things Work,* published in 1988. Using humorous line drawings and silly fictitious scientists, the author explains how many gadgets work, from relatively simple things such as zippers and nail clippers to the automatic transmission in a car. In an interview with *Contemporary Authors New Revision Series,* Macaulay said: "We seem to have developed blind spots, and certainly one of them is towards technology. It's our creation, and here we are becoming intimidated by this thing we've created, theoretically to make life more enjoyable or more satisfying. We create all these things, and then we think of ourselves as being too stupid to understand them. If *The Way Things Work* does anything, I hope it says to readers, You can figure it out. Follow this through and you'll understand how it works."

In 1991 Macaulay received the Caldecott Medal for *Black and White,* a picture book with four stories that overlap in a collage effect. Macaulay told *Horn Book* that recognition of that particular title "tells readers, especially young ones, that it is essential to see, not merely to look; that words and pictures can support each other; that it isn't necessary to think in a straight line to make sense; and finally that risk can be rewarded."

Macaulay's books have been translated into numerous languages. They have also found their way into college classrooms as texts for architecture and design classes. The author told *Publishers Weekly:* "I *want* to communicate.... For me the point is to leave a picture in somebody's mind—not necessarily a sentence or a paragraph—but if you can leave a picture in someone's mind, the chances they'll remember the idea are that much greater."

WORKS CITED:

Alderson, Valerie, "A Sense of Size and Space," *Times Educational Supplement,* September 10, 1976, p. 41.

Contemporary Authors New Revision Series, Volume 34, Gale, 1991, pp. 280-86.

Eisenman, Alvin, *Children's Book Showcase,* Children's Book Council, 1977.

Furness, Mary, "The Art of Building," *Times Literary Supplement,* July 23, 1982, p. 797.

Holmes, Joseph O., "The Way David Macaulay Works," *Publishers Weekly,* October 28, 1988, pp. 30-31.

Macaulay, David, "Caldecott Medal Acceptance," *Horn Book,* July-August, 1991.

Something about the Author, Volume 46, Gale, 1987, pp. 138-51.

Sutherland, Zena, and May Hill Arbuthnot, "Artists and Children's Books: David Macaulay," and "Informational Books: Evaluating Informational Books," *Children and Books,* 7th edition, Scott, Foresman, 1986, pp. 484-87.

Thomas, Joyce A., review of *Cathedral, Castle, City, and Underground, Children's Literature Association Quarterly,* winter, 1981-82, p. 27.

FOR MORE INFORMATION SEE:

BOOKS

Children's Literature Review, Gale, Volume 3, 1978; Volume 14, 1988.
Dictionary of Literary Biography, Volume 61: *American Writers for Children since 1960: Poets, Illustrators, and Nonfiction Authors,* Gale, 1987.

PERIODICALS

New York Times Book Review, September 25, 1983; December 1, 1985; October 18, 1987; June 20, 1988; October 23, 1988; May 20, 1990.
Washington Post Book World, December 12, 1982; December 11, 1983; September 9, 1985.

* * *

MacDONALD, Maryann 1947-

PERSONAL: Born June 28, 1947, in Cleveland, OH; daughter of Harry Lucas (an engineer) and Winifred (Mooney) Vanderwerp; married George Philip MacDonald (a lawyer), May 16, 1970; children: Megan Elisabeth, Alison. *Education:* University of Michigan, B.A., 1969; attended the Sorbonne, University of Paris, 1975-76. *Politics:* Democrat. *Religion:* Catholic. *Hobbies and other interests:* Women's basketball.

ADDRESSES: Home—46 Queen's Grove, London NW8 6HH, England. *Agent*—Gloria Mosesson, 290 West End Ave., New York, NY 10023.

CAREER: Worked as welfare worker and editor, 1970-76; writer. Library volunteer.

MEMBER: Society of Authors (United Kingdom chapter), Society of Children's Book Writers (United States chapter).

WRITINGS:

(Adaptor) *The King Who Learned How to Make Friends,* illustrated by Luis de Horna, Andersen Press, 1979.
No More Nappies, illustrated by Helen Herbert, Dinosaur Publications, 1980.
Moving, Doing, Building, Being, illustrated by Ross Thomson, Andersen Press, 1980.
Peter Gets Angry, illustrated by Ruth Bartlett, Dinosaur Publications, 1981.
Lucy Says No, illustrated by Susie Pritchatt, Dinosaur Publications, 1987.
Fatso Jean, the Ice Cream Queen, illustrated by Selena Tsui, Bantam, 1990.
Little Hippo Starts School, illustrated by Anna King, Dial Books for Young Readers, 1990.

MARYANN MacDONALD

Sam's Worries, illustrated by Judith Riches, Hyperion Press, 1990.
Rosie Runs Away, illustrated by Melissa Sweet, Atheneum, 1990.
Hedgehog Bakes a Cake, illustrated by Lynn Munsinger, Bantam, 1990.
Rosie's Baby Tooth, illustrated by Sweet, Atheneum, 1991.
Ben at the Beach, illustrated by David McTaggart, Viking, 1991.
Little Hippo Gets Glasses, illustrated by King, Dial Books for Young Readers, 1991.
Rabbit's Birthday Kite, illustrated by Munsinger, Bantam, 1991.

WORK IN PROGRESS: Writing *Second Grade Star,* a children's book.

SIDELIGHTS: Maryann MacDonald told *SATA:* "I was raised in a family of ten and have spent a lot of time with children, so I have learned to understand the child's point of view. My father and grandmother told us made-up stories when we were growing up, and I began to enjoy telling my own stories quite young. I published my first story when I was sixteen, but moved away from writing fiction until my own children were born and I rediscovered children's books. I like the spare, poetic quality of picture books best, but I'm learning to enjoy writing longer works."

by Maryann Macdonald
Illustrated by Melissa Sweet

MacDonald focuses on one of the common concerns of young children—losing one's baby teeth—in this amusing tale. (Cover illustration by Melissa Sweet.)

FOR MORE INFORMATION SEE:

PERIODICALS

Publishers Weekly, July 13, 1990, p. 55; August 31, 1990, p. 64; May 31, 1991, p. 74.
School Library Journal, December, 1990, p. 83; January, 1991, p. 95; October, 1991, p. 100.

*   *   *

MacRAOIS, Cormac 1944-

PERSONAL: Surname is pronounced "mac-reesh"; born November 11, 1944, in Belfast, Northern Ireland; son of Proinsias (a breadman) and Hannah (a home-maker; maiden name, Lee) MacRaois; married Doirin Nic Fhinn (a microbiologist), July 24, 1975; children: Niamh, Daire, Ronan. *Education:* Attended St. Mary's Training College, 1963-65; University College of the National University of Ireland, B.A., 1973; Teachers Centre, received certificate in Educational Administration, 1984.

ADDRESSES: Office—St. Patrick's, BNS, Wicklow Town, Ireland.

CAREER: Teacher in Dublin, Ireland, 1965-80, Enniskerry, County Wicklow, Ireland, 1980-88, and Wicklow Town, Ireland, 1988—.

MEMBER: Irish National Teachers' Organization, Children's Literature Association, Irish PEN, Gaelic League.

WRITINGS:

FOR CHILDREN

The Battle below Giltspur, illustrated by Jeanette Dunne, Wolfhound/Dufour, 1988.
Dance of the Midnight Fire, illustrated by Dunne, Wolfhound/Dufour, 1989.
Lightning over Giltspur, illustrated by Dunne, Wolfhound/Dufour, 1991.

OTHER

Contributor to short story anthology *Goodbye and Hello,* Penguin; contributor of short stories and poetry to periodicals, including *Women's Choice, Feasta,* and *An Muinteoir.*

WORK IN PROGRESS: Fantasy novels for children and a serious adult novel; research on the "Druids and their influence on Celtic civilization."

SIDELIGHTS: Cormac MacRaois told *SATA:* "My first novel, *The Battle below Giltspur,* grew out of the mountains, forests, and sea cliffs of the landscape of North Wicklow. It was written in response to the dearth of Irish-based children's books and my experience over many years as a teacher of having to present reading material to my pupils that did not reflect their cultural background or social conditions.

"The story which involved the magically awakened scarecrow, Glasan, and his evil rival, Scarnan, draws on a background of Irish mythology and ancient legend. The children in this story and the subsequent volumes of the Giltspur Trilogy are based on my own daughter Niamh, and my two sons Daire and Ronan, who were delighted not only to find themselves named in a story but to see their own faces faithfully reproduced by the illustrator Jeanette Dunne.

CORMAC MacRAOIS

MacRaois blends adventure with Irish mythology in his "Giltspur" trilogy, in which a magical scarecrow and his young friends battle the forces of evil. (Cover illustration by Jeannette Dunne.)

"Much to my surprise, *The Battle below Giltspur* was very well received, getting very favorable reviews in the national papers and on national television and radio, so that the first edition sold out within three weeks! My young readers as well as my publisher demanded more, so in 1989 *Dance of the Midnight Fire* was published. In this adventure, the children are called out of Ireland into the magical, mythical world of Tir Danann. This is Glasan's country and the adventure includes encounters with the main characters of ancient legend such as the Formorian Giants and The Fir Bolg (credited with being the first residents of Ireland.)

"While *Battle below Giltspur* was set at Bealtaine, the old Celtic festival of summer, *Lightning over Giltspur* is a Halloween story set at Samhain, the Celtic festival of summer's end and a menacingly magical time of year. It is the final volume of the trilogy and brings the epic struggle between good and evil to its dramatic climax.

"My own interest in mythology began at my father's knee in Belfast where he regaled us with tales of Cormac Mac Art, the onetime High King of Ireland after whom he named me. While my stories are not a retelling of the old tales, they are imbued with a sense of the continuity of Irish storytelling down through the centuries. Irish music and culture are a natural part of our everyday life, and both Irish and English are spoken by the family.

"By writing about Glasan and all the other characters in the trilogy something wonderful, magical has entered my life and that of my family, not least the *real* scarecrow who now sits in the place of honor at the head of the dining room table, frightening our unsuspecting visitors!

"Apart from an obvious interest in children's literature and Irish literature in general, I also enjoy oil painting—mainly landscapes and seascapes of my own beautiful County Wicklow. I enjoy listening to music of all types but prefer classical and traditional. I also play piano, guitar and tin whistle.

"My enjoyment of nature takes the form of gardening and going on long walks in the hills and forests and along the sea cliffs near my home. This, along with a twice-weekly swim and workout in the gym, helps to keep my mind clear and sharpen the creative edge of my imagination for future literary adventure."

The epic struggle between good and evil concludes in *Lightning over Giltspur*.

FOR MORE INFORMATION SEE:

PERIODICALS

Derry People Donegal News, January 18, 1992.

*   *   *

MAYBURY, Richard J. 1946-

PERSONAL: Born October 10, 1946, in Hamilton, OH; son of Anthony J. and Ruth M. (Wellinghoff) Maybury; married Marilyn N. Williams (a salesperson), August 7, 1967. *Education:* California State University at Sacramento, B.S. *Politics:* Libertarian. *Religion:* Deist.

ADDRESSES: Office—Henry-Madison Research, Box 1281, Orangevale, CA 95662.

CAREER: Writer. Henry-Madison Research, Orangevale, CA, president, 1982—. Worked as a teacher and building contractor.

WRITINGS:

YOUNG ADULT

Whatever Happened to Penny Candy?, Bluestocking Press, 1989.
Whatever Happened to Justice?, Bluestocking Press, 1992.

OTHER

Precious Metals, Politics, and Paper Money, Bramble, Inc., 1978.
Common Sense for the 1980s, Jefferson Publishing, 1981.
The Jefferson Report, Henry-Madison Research, 1982.
How You Can Strengthen Your Sales and Profits, Henry-Madison Research, 1986.

RICHARD J. MAYBURY

Strengthen Your Sales Fast with the BCM Strategy, Henry-Madison Research, 1990.
The Coming Soviet Civil War, Henry-Madison Research, 1990.
How You Can Find the Best Investment Advice, Henry-Madison Research, 1992.
You Can Profit from the Injection Effect, Henry-Madison Research, 1992.

Also author of *The Injection Effect.* Global affairs editor, *Moneyworld,* 1986-89; editor of monthly newsletter, *Richard Maybury's U.S. and World Early Warning Report.* Contributor to numerous newspapers and magazines, including *Wall Street Journal, USA Today,* and *Sacramento.*

WORK IN PROGRESS: A study of the United States economy.

SIDELIGHTS: Richard J. Maybury told *SATA:* "Aside from my parents, the three most important influences on my thinking were probably Roman Catholic schooling, the television show *Watch Mr. Wizard,* and my Air Force experience. Catholicism taught me that right from wrong are not matters of opinion. They may be difficult to discover but they do exist. *Watch Mr. Wizard,* which is one of my earliest childhood memories, taught me that the world is not chaotic. The world does make sense and we can understand it if we work hard enough at this.

"As a teenager, I devoured Mark Twain's work. The clarity of his writing, the absence of pretense, and finely honed skepticism were examples I've tried to copy. Science fiction has also been a strong influence. I like 'hard' science fiction—stories based on solid scientific reasoning. When I was young, I liked the television show *Science Fiction Theater.* I'm hooked on *Star Trek.* My favorite science fiction writers are Arthur C. Clarke and Robert Heinlein. Heinlein's book *The Moon Is a Harsh Mistress* is my choice for best science fiction book ever."

*   *   *

MAYFIELD, Sue 1963-

PERSONAL: Born March 15, 1963, in North Shields, England; daughter of Alexander William (a merchant naval captain) and Brenda Patricia (a teacher; maiden name, Mobberly) Kinghorn; married Timothy Mayfield (an Anglican clergyman), 1985; children: Frank Alexander, Jonah William. *Education:* Lincoln College, Oxford, B.A. (with honours), 1985; received teaching certificate from University of Bristol, 1986. *Politics:* "Broad left wing—no party involvement." *Religion:* Christian.

CAREER: Teacher of English and drama in secondary school in Bath, England, 1986-87. Involved in church activities.

WRITINGS:

Timeline: Women and Power, Dryad, 1988.
I Carried You on Eagles' Wings, Lothrop, 1991.

SUE MAYFIELD

WORK IN PROGRESS: Hands in Contrary Motion, a novel; *A Time to Be Born,* a sequel to *I Carried You on Eagles' Wings.*

SIDELIGHTS: Sue Mayfield told *SATA:* "Writing fiction is something I have come to gradually and almost accidentally. As a child I was a keen reader and from an early age I loved stories—especially the ones my father made up. I never saw reading as a hobby, though, preferring more active outdoor pursuits such as riding horses and walking. I began to read more seriously from the age of about sixteen onward. Around this time my primary interest was the theatre and I acted a great deal in amateur and school productions. I wrote poems and the odd short story but when I decided to study English literature at Oxford University it was with the intent of becoming an actress rather than a writer.

"At Oxford I discovered how appallingly badly read I was and spent three years trying to catch up and being saturated with literature—most of which had been written well before the twentieth century. It was only when I graduated in 1985 and began training as an English teacher that I started to read much contemporary fiction and to come into contact with novels written specifically for teenagers. Teaching eleven- to eighteen-year-olds in an English school caused me to think a lot about the writing process, and about how stories are constructed. I found that in teaching my students how to improve their writing I inadvertently taught myself a great deal. Teaching also led me to think a lot about teenage life and its pressures, and to be aware of the issues which faced the young people I was teaching.

"I left teaching after only a year when I discovered myself to be pregnant with my first child and fell, providentially, into researching and writing a book for a social history series for schools. The book—entitled

Timeline: Women and Power—was an examination of the role of women in British history with special reference to power and powerlessness. Undertaking this period of research helped me establish a discipline of writing and learn the mechanics of preparing a text for publication. The material I encountered led me deeper than I had previously gone into thinking about feminism and gender. After the publication of *Women and Power* in 1988, I expected to do further journalistic work on women's issues and it was only when a project I was working on fell through the following spring, that I turned my hand, experimentally, to writing fiction.

"*I Carried You on Eagles' Wings* took about nine months from conception to completion and coincided with my second pregnancy. My son Jonah was born within days of the book being finished. The central idea of a teenage boy, Tony, whose mother is dying of multiple sclerosis, came to me one evening in the bath and I sat up, late into the night, making notes about the characters and their situation! The physical aspects of MS and some details of Tony's mother's character and experience came from personal contact with a close friend who was dying of MS at the time I was writing the book. Tony's character is made up but has in it shades of several teenagers I have known, as well as hints of

SUE MAYFIELD
I CARRIED YOU ON EAGLES' WINGS

Tony tries to adjust to his mother's impending death from multiple sclerosis in Mayfield's novel about love and loss. (Cover illustration by Mary Beth Schwark.)

myself. The idea of a teenage boy experiencing, and struggling to express, strong emotions appealed to me partly because it seemed to defy gender stereotyping. I wanted to write a book that would be accessible to most teenagers and which would allow them to empathize with Tony's experience of death and bereavement. It seemed to me, from my own reading of young adult fiction, that few books tackled such issues and that fewer still explored adolescent religious experience. More personally, I wanted to grapple with my own religious confusion in the face of my friend's degeneration and suffering and to express something of my respect for her transcendent Christian faith. I set the book around the town and coastline where I grew up in the Northeast of England and I enjoyed revisiting these places in my imagination as I painted the backdrop to my story.

"My . . . second novel, _Hands in Contrary Motion,_ is set in Yorkshire, where I now live. It concerns a sixteen-year-old girl, Michelle, making the painful transition from childhood to womanhood; coping with the breakdown of her parents' marriage; and, in resisting the pressure to conform to everyone's expectations, discovering a liberating sense of self. It is, I hope—like _Eagles' Wings_—a book that will appeal to teenage readers. I have just begun work on a sequel to _I Carried You on Eagles' Wings_ which picks up the threads of Tony's life a year after his mother's death and will probably be called _A Time to Be Born._

"When that is completed I hope to focus more exclusively on writing fiction for adults. More and more I find myself wanting to make sense of things that happen to me, and to people I know or observe, by writing about them. I keep a journal and a book of 'scribblings' in which I constantly record thoughts and insights as well as observations of places and events. I find that the process of creating characters and describing their inner lives is akin to role playing and that communicating moods and emotions through words is very similar to acting. I enjoy making people laugh and cry and I consider possession of the power to move another human being to be a great privilege."

*   *   *

MEDEARIS, Angela Shelf 1956-

PERSONAL: Last name is pronounced "ma-dare-is"; born November 16, 1956, in Hampton, VA; daughter of Howard Lee (a real estate broker) and Angeline (an interior decorator; maiden name, Davis) Shelf; married Michael Rene Medearis (a funding review specialist), January 25, 1975; children: Deanna Renee. _Education:_ Attended Southwest Texas State University, 1974-1975. _Politics:_ None. _Religion:_ Non-denominational.

ADDRESSES: Home and office—6712 Langston Dr., Austin, TX 78723.

CAREER: Book Boosters, Austin, TX, director, 1989—; Children's Radio Bookmobile, Austin, producer, 1989-92; author. Consultant/writer for Scott, Foresman, Scholastic, and Macmillan.

MEMBER: Society of Children's Book Writers, Austin Writer's League.

AWARDS, HONORS: Dancing with the Indians awarded a special citation, Violet Crown Awards, and named Notable Children's Social Studies Book, American Library Association, 1992; _Zebra Riding Cowboy_ named Pick of the List, American Booksellers Association.

WRITINGS:

Picking Peas for a Penny, State House Press, 1990, revised paperback edition, Scholastic, 1993.
Dancing with the Indians, illustrated by Samuel Byrd, Holiday House, 1991.
The Zebra Riding Cowboy, Holt, 1992.
Annie's Gift, Just Us Books, 1992.
Poppa's New Pants, Holt, 1993.
The Christmas Riddle, Lodestar, 1993.
Treemonisha, Holt, in press.

Also author of articles on African-American art for _Crisis_ magazine, 1987-1990.

WORK IN PROGRESS: Rum A Tum Tum (picture book) for Holiday House; an African-American history for Atheneum/Macmillan; picture book biography series featuring Louis Armstrong and Coretta Scott King for Lodestar; research on Drummer Jackson, an African-American boy who served during the Civil War.

ANGELA SHELF MEDEARIS

SIDELIGHTS: Angela Shelf Medearis told *SATA:* "I love introducing children all over the world to all the different aspects of African-American history, folklore and culture. I love picture books because it's a challenge to convey complex ideas in a simple form for children. I really enjoy factually and vividly presenting history in a thrity-two or forty-eight page book. It's wonderful to be able to hold children's attention and teach them something important.

"Picture books are a child's first step into a lifetime of reading. That's why I feel that my job is important. I want to write in such an interesting and exciting way that the memory of reading my book and the information I've contained about a particular event will linger with a young reader for a lifetime.

"I've always loved history and most of my books are historically based. I enjoy doing research on African-American history because I didn't have the opportunity to study it in school. Most of my books are the result of some wonderful discovery I've made while doing research for something else.

"I remember my teachers commenting on how well I could write ever since I was in elementary school. I didn't think it was any big deal and I didn't realize that writing was a talent until I was thirty and started writing professionally. During the Stone Age when I was growing up, authors didn't visit the schools I attended. That's why I really enjoy visiting schools now. I know how important it is to tell young people that if they can write well, they're just as gifted as any other type of artist. I try real hard to make my school visits as educational and fun as possible.

"My father was a top recruiter in the Air Force and my mother was a housewife. We moved constantly. I used books and reading as a way of constantly adjusting to new surroundings. I knew that my favorite books would be waiting for me at the library in whatever new place we were going. I also knew that there would be a nice librarian there who would be friendly to me. It made a new school and making new friends much easier to deal with.

"I've always loved to read but I can't recall ever reading any books by or about African-Americans when I was in elementary school. My favorite author as a child was Laura Ingalls Wilder. I also enjoyed biographies about famous people in history. My tastes in books haven't changed much since I was a child. I still love biographies and ninety percent of the books I read are children's picture books.

"I've read thousands of books because I love to read and I read all the time. I have to read a lot because sometimes I need special information when I write my own books. My favorite kind of books to read are picture books! I started counting all the books I own one day and I stopped at 500! I still have a bunch more to count but I got tired. I really don't have a favorite book, I just love to read any book that is well written.

"I love children and I like to write books especially for them. I really love writing books. I enjoy that wonderful feeling you get when you have a great idea and can't wait to get started to work on it. I enjoy thinking about all the children that have read my work. I have books in Africa and England and other places I don't even know about. It's fun to think that someone, somewhere is reading one of my books or checking them out of the library.

"Most people think I'm funny. I like to make people laugh. I really, really like to make kids laugh. It's one of the happiest sounds in the world."

FOR MORE INFORMATION SEE:

PERIODICALS

New York Times Book Review, November 24, 1991, p. 31.
Publishers Weekly, October 25, 1991, p. 68.

*   *   *

MEE, Charles L., Jr. 1938-

PERSONAL: Born September 15, 1938, in Evanston, IL; son of Charles Louis and Sarah (Lowe) Mee; married Claire Lu Thomas (an actress), June, 1959 (divorced, 1962); married Suzi Baker (a poet), November, 1962 (divorced); married Kathleen Tolan (a playwright), December, 1983; children: (second marriage) Erin, Charles; (third marriage) Sarah, Alice. *Education:* Harvard University, B.A. (cum laude), 1960.

ADDRESSES: Agent—Lois Wallace, 177 East 70th St., New York, NY 10021.

CAREER: Horizon magazine, New York City, editor in chief, 1971-75; writer.

MEMBER: Urban Institute (member of board of directors), Theatre Communications Group (member of board of directors).

WRITINGS:

FOR CHILDREN

(With editors of *Horizon* magazine) *Lorenzo de'Medici and the Renaissance,* American Heritage Publishing, 1968.
The Horizon Book of Daily Life in Renaissance Italy, American Heritage Publishing, 1975.
(With Ken Munowitz) *Happy Birthday, Baby Jesus,* Harper, 1976.
(With Munowitz) *Moses, Moses,* Harper, 1977.
(With Munowitz) *Noah,* Harper, 1978.

FOR ADULTS

(With Edward L. Greenfield) *Dear Prince: The Unexpurgated Counsels of N. Machiavelli to Richard Milhous Nixon,* American Heritage Publishing, 1969.
(Editor) *Horizon Bedside Reader,* American Heritage Publishing, 1971.
White Robe, Black Robe, Putnam, 1972.
Erasmus: The Eye of the Hurricane, Coward, 1973.

In *Moses, Moses,* Charles L. Mee. Jr., tells the story of the biblical hero by combining easy-to-understand text with Ken Munowitz's dramatic pictures.

Meeting at Potsdam, M. Evans, 1975.
A Visit to Haldeman and Other States of Mind, M. Evans, 1977.
Seizure, M. Evans, 1978.
The End of Order: Versailles, 1919, Dutton, 1980.
The Ohio Gang: The World of Warren G. Harding, M. Evans, 1981.
The Marshall Plan: the Launching of the Pax Americana, Simon & Schuster, 1984.
The Genius of the People, Harper, 1987.
Rembrandt's Portrait: A Biography, Simon & Schuster, 1988.

PLAYS

Players' Repertoire, produced in Cambridge, MA, at Playwright's Theater, August, 1960.
Constantinople Smith (one-act), produced in New York City at Upstairs at the Downstairs, May, 1961.
The Gate (one-act), produced in New York City at the Upstairs at the Downstairs, May, 1961.
Three by Mee, produced in New York City at Fourth Street Theater, November, 1962.
Anyone! Anyone!, produced Off-Broadway, 1964.
Vienna: Lusthaus, produced Off-Broadway, 1986.
The Imperialists at the Club Cave Canem, produced Off-Broadway, 1988.
The Investigation of the Murder in El Salvador, produced Off-Broadway, 1989.
Another Person Is a Foreign Country, produced Off-Broadway, 1991.

Orestes, produced in Cambridge, MA, at the American Repertory Theatre, 1992.

Also author of plays *God Bless Us Everyone, The Life of the Party,* and *Wedding Night.*

WORK IN PROGRESS: Meetings at the Summit, a history book to be published by Simon & Schuster; *The Bacchae,* a play.

SIDELIGHTS: Charles L. Mee, Jr., is a former editor of *Horizon* magazine, a playwright whose plays have been produced throughout the United States, Europe, and Japan, and the author of many celebrated historical works. Although Mee's writing career began with a focus on Renaissance Europe, he quickly branched out to a variety of political and historical interests. One of Mee's most popular books is *Meeting at Potsdam,* his 1975 analysis of the 1945 post-World War II meeting in Potsdam, Germany, between U.S. president Harry Truman, Soviet political leader Joseph Stalin, and British prime minister Sir Winston Churchill. According to Mee, these leaders of the victorious powers of World War II intentionally worked out terms, not of peace, but of cold war. Although some critics found his analysis improbable, many commended the historical accuracy and research behind Mee's political assessments.

Often labelled a "popular historian," Mee frequently presents his own point of reference as an intrinsic part of his historical work. This is most apparent in the autobiographical *A Visit to Haldeman and Other States of Mind,* in which Mee only briefly chronicles his meetings with Watergate conspirator H. R. Haldeman. The author focuses primarily on describing his "other states of mind" during the 1960s and 1970s, including a nearly fatal struggle with polio during his adolescence, his career at Harvard and his indoctrination into extreme intellectualism, the break up of his marriages, and other personal adventures. *Time* magazine writer Lance Morrow, commenting on the many different guises of the book, summarized that "Mee's lively, mordant intelligence is at its best improvising on political ideas—quarreling with Spengler, hallucinating a Socratic dialogue with an Exxon executive."

Mee is also the author of several children's books. His first published book, *Lorenzo de'Medici and the Renaissance,* is a widely praised history for young adults. The book's subject, Lorenzo the Magnificent, was a colorful member of the Medicis, a powerful family of fifteenth-century bankers who fostered Florence's standing as one of the major cultural centers of Renaissance Europe. The book also relates the history of fifteenth-century Florence, highlighting its economic systems, its artistic and philosophical movements, and its power struggles with other nations. A reviewer for the *Bulletin of the Center for Children's Books* called *Lorenzo de'Medici and the Renaissance* "a remarkably fresh and vivid treatment of a familiar figure and of one of the best-known periods in the history of the western world." *New York Times Book Review* contributor Orville Prescott, praising Mee's careful research and effective writing, remarked that "no boy or girl reading this able book could fail to respond to the excitement of the Renaissance and one of its most fascinating characters."

Collaborating with illustrator Ken Munowitz, Mee has also produced several books for younger children which recount stories from the Bible. *Happy Birthday, Baby Jesus* retells the story of the birth of Jesus and the arrival of wise men, shepherds, and animals to wish him a happy birthday. With *Moses, Moses* and *Noah,* Mee and Munowitz continued to present simple and imaginative picture book versions of biblical stories. Although some critics commented that in these adaptations for the very young reader, Mee has lost some of the wonder and beauty of the stories, other reviewers praised the works for their graceful sparseness and simplicity.

WORKS CITED:

Review of *Lorenzo de'Medici, Bulletin of the Center for Children's Books,* June, 1969, p. 159.

Morrow, Lance, "The '60s Trip," *Time,* June 13, 1977, p. 99.

Prescott, Orville, review of *Lorenzo de'Medici, New York Times Book Review,* July 27, 1969, p. 18.

FOR MORE INFORMATION SEE:

PERIODICALS

Bulletin of the Center for Children's Books, September, 1976, p. 14.

Horn Book, August, 1969, p. 422.

New York Times Book Review, March 9, 1975, p. 1; November 13, 1977, p. 36.

Publishers Weekly, December 6, 1976, p. 62.

School Library Journal, October, 1976, p. 85; September, 1977, p. 111; September, 1978, p. 121.

Time, May 5, 1975, p. 78.

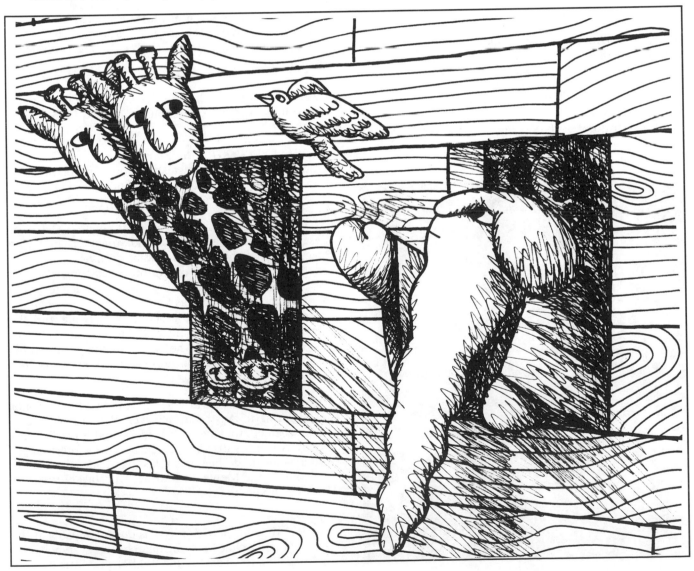

Noah releases the dove to look for land in Mee's retelling of the biblical story. (Illustration from *Noah* by Munowitz.)

MELENDEZ, Francisco 1964-

PERSONAL: Born March 31, 1964, in Zaragoza, Spain; son of Francisco Jose (a manager) and Concepcion (a manager; maiden name, Perez) Melendez. *Religion:* Catholic.

ADDRESSES: Home—San Ignacio de Loyola, 1, Zaragoza, Spain 50008. *Agent*—Howard Morhaim, 175 Fifth Ave., New York, NY 10010.

CAREER: Author and illustrator. Has also worked as a forest ranger. *Military service:* Has served in the merchant marine and as a bugler in the army of Spain.

AWARDS, HONORS: Premio Nacional de Ilustracion, Minister of Culture of Spain, 1987, 1992; Silver Medal, Verliehen fur ausgezeichnete buchkunstlerische Leistungen (Germany), 1991, for *The Mermaid and the Major: The True Story of the Invention of the Submarine;* best published book in the LIBER fair, Madrid, 1991.

WRITINGS:

(Illustrator) Augusto Monterroso, *La oveja negra y demas fabulas,* Ediciones Alfaguara (Spain), 1986.
(And illustrator) *The Mermaid and the Major: The True Story of the Invention of the Submarine,* adapted by Robert Morton from the translation by William Dykes, Abrams, 1991.
(And illustrator) *El Viaje de Colonus,* Aura (Spain), 1991.
(And illustrator) *Leopold,* Abrams, 1993.

FRANCISCO MELENDEZ

Melendez uses whimsical illustrations and humor to depict the story behind the inspiration for the submarine. (Illustration from *The Mermaid and the Major.*)

Also illustrator or author/illustrator of numerous books, chapbooks, and art collections published in Spain.

WORK IN PROGRESS: Tomi-kikansha, a book for children about the first steam locomotive in Japan; a handbook on anthropology for children.

SIDELIGHTS: In a letter to *SATA,* Francisco Melendez described himself as "a frail and romantic child who lagged sorely behind in his studies until he threw them over at fifteen in favour of a military academy where he lasted only a few months. However, he decided to give it another try and enlisted as bugler in the army where he devoted his time to the practice of drawing and the playing of his belligerent bugle, and an occasional trip to the base's library where he could blissfully imbibe his most cherished historical, musical and literary themes.

"It was during this period that he toyed with the idea of immigrating to Australia; however, that country's embassy seemed to have other ideas and squashed his hopes. Not easily discouraged, he became a forest ranger for a while and then tried his hand at sailoring by enlisting in the Merchant Marine. Once again the gods frowned upon him.

"By that time his poor family was understandably at the end of their tether. But fortunately for everybody, in 1983 he illustrated a book for children and little by little worked himself up and was introduced by his brother Alfonso into Madrid's publishing circles."

ELAINE MILLS

MILLS, Elaine (Rosemary) 1941-

PERSONAL: Born December 2, 1941, in Burton-on-Trent, Staffordshire, England; daughter of Eric James (a schoolmaster and managing director) and Dorothy Muriel (a teacher and housewife) Cornes; married Neil Mills, June, 1966 (divorced, 1982). *Education:* St. Martin's School of Art (London), national diploma of art and design; University of London Institute of Education, art teacher certificate. *Politics:* "Liberal attitudes." *Religion:* Agnostic.

ADDRESSES: Home and office—10 Ringmore Rise, Forest Hill, London SE23 3DF, England. *Agent*—Caroline Sheldon, 71 Hillgate Place, Notting Hill, London W8 7SS, England.

CAREER: Artist and illustrator. Worked in advertising studios, Oslo, Derby, London; taught art for five years.

ILLUSTRATOR:

John Gaskin, *Moving,* Watts, 1984.
Gaskin, *Eating,* Watts, 1984.
(With Rob Shone) Peter Eldin, *How to Be Top,* Dragon, 1985.
Primrose Lockwood, *One Winter's Night,* Heinemann, 1991.
Debbie Godbold, *Have You Ever?,* Thornes, 1991.

WORK IN PROGRESS: "A portrait and a children's book about different types of weather (showing children's activities)."

SIDELIGHTS: Elaine Mills told *SATA:* "In the 1960s my husband wrote poetry and did readings around the country with two other writers. My first illustrations were for a children's book that he wrote but which was never published. We read together on an Arts Council record.

"[In 1971], after five years of teaching we left London to live in deepest rural Wales (stunning countryside). I set up a kiln so that I could make a living. I had been making ceramics whilst teaching in London and my work was in demand. I specialized in making figurative clay whistles—they were in the form of mermaids, birds and many species of owl. Some of these had double chambers for playing double notes. During the time in Wales, I opened a store and designed and organized the making of knitware. Although we were always short of money this was a marvelous time—lots of friendship, interest and creative activity.

"We returned to London in 1976. My husband had been building to make a living in Wales. In London he went into advertising and soon after that we split up. This was a difficult time. I worked in animation studios to make a living, and then moved on to assist in an independent graphics studio, working mainly on a series of English language teaching books for Oxford University Press. About 1980, I began to do illustrations for the series of books we were working on. From 1980 up to the present

Mills's artwork often features tranquil settings and colorful scenery.

I have illustrated many nonfiction books for a variety of publishers.

"I have also painted portraits, mostly of children, during this time. In 1987 I painted a portrait of the English 'Miss Pears.' This was unveiled in the Liverpool Tate where it was exhibited beside the well-known Peter Blake Pears portrait executed thirty years ago.

"Fiction offers more opportunity for an imaginative approach to illustration and I have most enjoyed working on the books where I was able to create a complete world from the text .... I plan to work more and more on children's fiction, writing my own text if possible. I am doing some voluntary work in primary schools as I am fascinated by the way a small child sees the world."

*   *   *

MITCHELL, Jay
See ROBERSON, Jennifer

*   *   *

MODRELL, Dolores 1933-

PERSONAL: Born May 8, 1933, in Des Moines, IA; daughter of John (a farmer) and Lucille (Wolcott) Modrell. *Education:* Attended Drake University, 1952-54; Juilliard School of Music (now Juilliard School), B.S., 1963. Studied piano with Adele Marcus, 1964-65. *Politics:* Democrat. *Religion:* Episcopal. *Hobbies and other interests:* Animals, hiking, reading, collecting stamps, hunting for fossils, artifacts, and stones.

ADDRESSES: Home—17 West 82nd St., New York, NY 10024. *Agent*—Joanna Cole, 532 West 114th St., New York, NY 10025.

CAREER: Piano teacher in and around New York City, 1963-67; Brooklyn Conservatory of Music, piano teacher in Flushing, NY, 1967-69 and 1985-91, and in Brooklyn, NY, 1985-91; School of Musical Education, New York City, piano and music study teacher, 1968-72; Harlem School of the Arts, New York City, piano teacher, 1972-75; Manhattan School of Music, New York City, piano teacher in preparatory division, 1975-85; Bloomingdale House of Music, New York City, piano and music theory teacher, 1985—; writer. Member of Musical Education Chamber Players, 1969-72. Has played piano in recitals and as an accompanist.

DOLORES MODRELL

WRITINGS:

Tales of Tiddly, illustrations by Ellen Eagle, Simon & Schuster, 1990.

WORK IN PROGRESS: Another book about Tiddly.

SIDELIGHTS: Dolores Modrell is the author of *Tales of Tiddly,* three stories concerning a real-life kitten whom the author found and adopted. Modrell, a pianist, developed her love for both animals and music as a child living on a farm in Battle Creek, Iowa, where her pets included a tomcat, chickens, a pig, and two sheep. The author began studying piano at the age of seven, and later attended the Juilliard School of Music (now Juilliard School) in New York City. Since then, she has shared her apartment with dogs, cats, and gerbils, as well as her piano. Modrell was inspired to write *Tales of Tiddly* one afternoon as she watched her dog, Meezo, her tomcat, Mr. Bones, and her yellow tabby cat, Tiddly, playing together. In the stories, Tiddly is lost until he meets Meezo and Mr. Bones, who share their home with him. On the subject of *Tales of Tiddly,* the author commented in *Ida County Pioneer Record,* "There aren't any bad guys. Kids need a world without bad guys."

WORKS CITED:

Review of *Tales of Tiddly, Ida County Pioneer Record,* July 11, 1991, p. 8.

N–O

NORTON, Mary 1903-1992

OBITUARY NOTICE—See index for *SATA* sketch: Born December 10, 1903, in London, England; died of a stroke, August 29, 1992, in Hartland, Devonshire, England. Actress and author. Norton is remembered as the author of a popular and critically acclaimed series of children's books based on the Borrowers, a race of minute beings responsible for "borrowing" the small possessions people lose everyday. *The Borrowers,* published in 1952 and awarded England's Carnegie Medal, began the series, which culminated in 1982 with *The Borrowers Avenged.* An actress who performed at the Old Vic Theatre in London for two years, Norton began to write in order to help her family financially after moving to America in 1941. Her first two books, *The Magic Bed-Knob; or, How to Become a Witch in Ten Easy Lessons* and *Bonfires and Broomsticks,* served as the basis for the 1971 Walt Disney film *Bedknobs and Broomsticks.*

OBITUARIES AND OTHER SOURCES:

BOOKS

Who's Who, 144th edition, St. Martin's, 1992.

PERIODICALS

Chicago Tribune, September 7, 1992, section 1, p. 10.
New York Times, September 3, 1992.
Times (London), September 7, 1992, p. 15.

*   *   *

O'GREEN, Jennifer
See ROBERSON, Jennifer

*   *   *

O'GREEN, Jennifer Roberson
See ROBERSON, Jennifer

ODGERS, Sally Farrell 1957-
(Sally Farrell, Sally Darroll)

PERSONAL: Born November 26, 1957, in Latrobe, Tasmania, Australia; daughter of George Lindsay (a dairy farmer) and Patricia Nancie (a teacher and farmer; maiden name, Bonney) Farrell; married Darrel Allan Odgers (a personal assistant), May 26, 1979; children: James Allan, Tegan Maria. *Education:* Graduated from Latrobe Primary School; attended correspondence school, Hobart, Australia, 1970-1974. *Politics:* Green Independent. *Religion:* Church of England. *Hobbies and other interests:* Organic gardening, theatre, kayaking, trivia, games.

ADDRESSES: Home—1 Mill Lane, Latrobe, Tasmania, Australia 7307. *Agent*—Katya Louca, Market Street, Sydney, New South Wales, Australia 2000.

CAREER: Free-lance writer. Speaker at school assemblies; poetry tutor of school students.

MEMBER: Australian Society of Authors, Bookworm Club (secretary, 1991—), Society of Women Writers.

AWARDS, HONORS: International Youth Library Choice designation, 1992, for *Drummond.* Odgers has been the recipient of several prizes for short stories, including an award from *The Writer's News,* 1986.

WRITINGS:

JUVENILE; AS SALLY FARRELL ODGERS

The Bunyip Wakes, Kangaroo Press, 1984.
Dreadful David (picture book), illustrated by Craig Smith, Omnibus Books, 1984.
Winter-Spring Garden, Rigby Education, 1984.
Emma Jane's Zoo (picture book), illustrated by Janet Ayliffe, Omnibus Books, 1986.
Elizabeth, Rigby Education, 1986.
The Haunting of Ace, Rigby Education, 1986.
There Were Cats . . . , Rigby Education, 1987.

SALLY FARRELL ODGERS

How to Handle a Vivid Imagination, Rigby Education, 1987.
Blue Moon Animal Day, Rigby Education, 1987.
What a Day!, Shortland Publications, 1987.
Henry's Ears, Macmillan, 1987.
The Witch, Macmillan, 1987.
Amy Claire and the Legs, Macmillan, 1987.
Show Us!, Macmillan, 1987.
Outside, Macmillan, 1987.
Maria and the Pocket, Macmillan, 1987.
The Powerful Pickle Problem (novel), Angus & Robertson, 1987.
Angie the Brave (picture book), illustrated by Sandra Laroche, Walter McVitty Books, 1987.
The Cat and the King, Shortland Publications, 1988.
The Ghost Collector (novel), Angus & Robertson, 1988.
Rosina and Kate, Hodder & Stoughton, 1988.
The Suitcase, Rigby Education, 1989.
Hey Mum!, Macmillan, 1989.
That's Enough!, Macmillan, 1989.
Dave and Joe, Parteach Books, 1989.
Stick-in-the-Mud, Macmillan, 1989.
My Aunt Agatha, Macmillan, 1989.

Kelly and the Mess, Macmillan, 1989.
Welcome to the Weirdie Club (novel), Kangaroo Press, 1989.
Ex-Spelled (novel), Collins, 1989.
Five Easy Lessons, Collins, 1989.
Drummond, illustrated by Carol Jones, Holiday House, 1990.
The Follow Dog, illustrated by Noela Young, Omnibus Books, 1990.
Wicked Rose (picture book), Margaret Hamilton Books, 1991.
The Magician's Box, Collins/Angus & Robertson, 1991.
Summer Magic, Walter McVitty Books, 1992.
The Window Book, illustrated by Kilmeny Niland, Walter McVitty Books, 1992.
Polly's Party, illustrated by Jenny Clapson, Macmillan, 1992.
Three Loony Months, Collins/Angus & Robertson, 1992.
Just Like Emily, Collins, 1992.
Another Good Friend, Longman Cheshire, 1992.
All the Sea Between, Longman Cheshire, 1992.
Country Girl, Macmillan, 1992.
Kayak, Collins/Angus & Robertson, 1992.
Amy/Amaryllis, Collins/Angus & Robertson, 1992.

JUVENILE; AS SALLY FARRELL

Her Kingdom for a Pony, Hodder & Stoughton, 1977.
The Room Upstairs, Hodder & Stoughton, 1978.
The Day the Cows Slept In, Young Publications, 1979.
Down River, Rigby Education, 1980.
Time Off, Rigby Education, 1980.
Rosina and Her Calf, Hodder & Stoughton, 1983.
Rosina and the Show, Hodder & Stoughton, 1985.

JUVENILE; AS SALLY DARROLL

Dangerous Ride, Collins, 1989.

OTHER

The Bushranger Who Sneezed (play), performed by Ulverstone Repertory Theatre, Ulverstone, Tasmania, 1988.
Under Cole's Rainbow (play), performed by Devonport High School Theatre Group, Devonport, Tasmania, 1988.
Storytrack: A Practical Guide to Writing for Children in Australia and New Zealand, Kangaroo Press, 1989.
Tasmania, a Guide (part of the "Heritage Field Guide" series), Kangaroo Press, 1989.
In Mara's Case (adult romance), Greenhouse Publications, 1989.
Black Lamb (adult romance novella), Australian Consolidated Press, 1990.
Frizzle Sizzle: Sunbusters are Cool (nonfiction), Sunsafe Publications, 1990.

Odgers's poetry has been included in the following anthologies: *Putrid Poems, Vile Verse, Petrifying Poems, Rattling in the Wind, Fractured Fairy Tales and Ruptured Rhymes,* and *Christmas Crackers,* all published by Omnibus Books; *Ten Times Funny,* Houghton Mifflin; and *Macquarie Bedtime Book,* Macquarie, reprinted as *The Puffin Bedtime Book,* Penguin. Short stories published in the following anthologies: *Stories to Share,*

Macmillan, 1987, and *Amazing, A Handful of Ghosts, Before Dawn, Bizarre, Brief Encounters, Stay Loose Mother Goose,* and *State of the Heart,* all published by Omnibus Books. Author of regular columns in periodicals, including *Advocate Weekender, Good Housekeeping, Lucky Magazine, New South Wales School Magazine, Organic Growing,* and *Writer's News.* Author of plays and songs for children.

ADAPTATIONS: Odgers's songs "Up and Down" and "Cost of Living" have been recorded on *A.B.C. Nought to Nine,* Polygram Records.

WORK IN PROGRESS: Anna's Eden, an adult novel; *Motherghosts* and *Sneaking up the Snake,* both for young readers.

SIDELIGHTS: Sally Farrell Odgers is an Australian writer who lives in Latrobe, the rural town in Tasmania where she was born and raised. A prolific author, Odgers has found the time to compose her imaginative poetry and prose between raising two children and maintaining an active involvement in local schools that includes lecturing and teaching writing workshops. Her works range from juvenile picture books to adult romance novels, from stories of farm life to tales of science fiction. Poet, novelist, journalist, and playwright, Odgers is also the author of numerous short stories that employ her characteristic mix of traditional genres within a unique montage. The unifying elements of warmth, friendship, and caring are found within each of her works.

Odgers began writing while a young girl, telling *SATA,* "I was lucky enough to have an old-fashioned Grade Four teacher who believed in the value of times-tables, spelling, and grammar. She encouraged me in my hobby of writing stories and would read and correct those I brought from home. Under her guidance I entered a competition for short story writing and won, earning myself $20.00—my first ever money from writing. I was ten years old." Odgers was a prolific writer even at an early age: "When I was eleven, my parents (bless them forever) gave me a typewriter. I taught myself to type and began writing every weekend. By the time I was fifteen I had sold several stories and written three (unpublished) novels, either fantasy or country stories, based on my own experiences. My Grade Seven and Eight English teacher, another kindly lady, would also correct my unsolicited stories, and she also encouraged me greatly. When my first book, *Her Kingdom for a Pony,* was written and accepted in the mid-1970s, she was delighted."

Odgers is very conscious of the power that children's fiction has over young and impressionable readers. "I grew up very much influenced by the books I read, thus bypassing most of the hassles of teenager-hood. I simply wasn't interested in fashion, rebellion, or keeping up with the Joneses because I was already reading and writing seriously at thirteen." A discriminating as well as a voracious reader, Odgers disliked stories she found too predictable. Ever since she began writing for an

In *Drummond,* Odgers tells the tale of a toy bear determined to be reunited with the little girl who lost him long ago. (Illustration by Carol Jones.)

audience she has tried to do the unexpected. Her plots always present her readers with a surprising twist, sometimes incorporating a mix of fantasy and everyday situations. In *Drummond* a toy teddy-bear who has been "loved to life" is determined to be reunited with the little girl who lost him long ago. Bossy Melinda in *Ghost Collector* collects everything including ghosts, and eventually trouble, when she steps in to help her two uncles solve the problem of their haunted guest-house. And the friendship central to the story in *Five Easy Lessons* is a very uncommon one: eleven-year-old Justin and thirty-two-year-old Mellie become friends despite the fact that they are—mother and son!

Odgers likes to write farm and family stories and draws on memories of the childhood that she spent working on her family's dairy farm. As a professional writer, however, she has found that the market for juvenile literature has shifted away from traditional themes such as farming, and she is versatile enough to make the transition. Willing to explore new genres in children's literature, Odgers still has strong feelings about the characters she brings to life within the pages of her books. Her unconventional approach to accepted "formulas" in creating characters and plots has caused editors to be somewhat hesitant about accepting certain of her manuscripts for publication. "Many editors seem to prefer books which follow the established [genre]

Nicholas and Sarah humor Drummond as he loudly voices his displeasure at having to ride at the bottom of Nicholas's messy schoolbag. (Illustration by Jones.)

pattern," she commented. "[Teenagers] *MUST* be misunderstood or on drugs, heroines of ghost stories *MUST* be downtrodden, kids *MUST* suffer from peer-group pressure and fantasy *MUST* deal with the Clash between Good and Evil." Odgers' unwillingness to sacrifice her characters to such circumstances is reflected by her concern over the direction that children's literature has taken in the past several years. "The self-indulgence displayed by many protagonists of modern children's books worries me. I don't believe it's OK to steal, scream, bash up other kids, or become a hooker just because your mum and dad are fighting or because your best friend has moved away! I know that's simplistic, but all the same—that is the impression some books seem to give.... I am also disappointed to note that many authors seem determined to depict the worse side of life while wholly neglecting the better."

Odgers chooses to portray the world in the manner in which she has experienced it—as a child of a comfortable middle-class family coping with problems universal to all children: learning to grow towards their unique potential and establish their character and individuality through the everyday situations that they encounter. As she told *SATA,* "Perhaps we should give kids more credit—in fiction *and* in real life."

FOR MORE INFORMATION SEE:

PERIODICALS

Publishers Weekly, October 12, 1990, p. 64.
School Library Journal, March, 1991, p. 177.

*   *   *

ORR, Katherine S(helley) 1950-

PERSONAL: Born October 21, 1950, in New York, NY; daughter of William Campbell (a professor and adminis-

trator) and Jean (a housewife; maiden name, Clarin) Orr; married Chuck Hesse, 1974 (divorced, 1980); married Carl J. Berg, Jr. (a marine biologist), April 19, 1985. *Education:* Goucher College, B.A., 1972; University of Connecticut, M.S. (marine zoology), 1976; University of Hawaii, graduate study in seafood science, 1981-82.

ADDRESSES: Home—P.O. Box 769, Kilauea, HI 96754.

CAREER: PRIDE (Caribbean nonprofit foundation promoting research and environmental education), co-founder, researcher, and educator, 1976-1980; U.S. Geological Survey, Woods Hole, MA, biological technician, 1980-81, research associate, 1982-86; East-West Center, Honolulu, HI, aquaculture researcher, 1981-82. Active volunteer in local organizations, including Save-A-Turtle (sea turtle conservation group), Dolphin Research Institute, and Environmental Education Task Force. *Exhibitions:* Mural installed at Meridian Club Hotel, Pine Cay, Turks and Caicos Islands, 1979; oil paintings exhibited at Falmouth Artists Guild, Falmouth, MA, 1982-85; artwork for *My Grandpa and the Sea* included in exhibitions of children's book art at Society of Illustrators' Museum of American Illustration, New York City, The Dairy Barn Gallery, S.E. Ohio Cultural Arts Center, and Olympia and York's Park Avenue Atrium Gallery, New York City, all 1990.

MEMBER: Society of Children's Book Writers.

WRITINGS:

JUVENILE; SELF-ILLUSTRATED

The Natural World of the Turks and Caicos Islands, designed and edited by Jane Allison Halaby, Turks and Caicos Development Trust, 1983.

The Life Story of the Queen Conch, World Wildlife/
    R.A.R.E., 1984.
Shelley, Macmillan Caribbean, 1984.
The Life Story of the Spiny Lobster, World Wildlife/
    R.A.R.E., 1985.
Leroy the Lobster, Macmillan Caribbean, 1985.
(With husband, Carl Berg) *The Queen Conch Book,*
    Windward Publishing, 1987.
Coral Reef Coloring Book, Macmillan Caribbean, 1987.
Wondrous World of the Mangrove Swamps, Florida Flair
    Books, 1989.
*Shells of North American Shores: East Coast Seashells
    from Canada to the Florida Keys* (coloring book;
    part of "The Naturencyclopedia" series), Stemmer
    House, 1989.
My Grandpa and the Sea, Carolrhoda Books, 1990.
Sea Turtles Hatching, Simon & Schuster, 1990.
Story of a Dolphin, Carolrhoda Books, 1993.
Hawaiian Coral Reef Coloring Book, Stemmer House,
    1993.

Orr has contributed articles to professional journals and
periodicals.

ILLUSTRATOR

Key Lime Desert Book, Surfside Publishing, 1987.
Conch Cook Book, Surfside Publishing, 1987.
Key West Woman's Club Cookbook, Surfside Publish-
    ing, 1987.

Orr has designed logos and original artwork for posters,
note cards, and letterheads for various organizations,
including World Wildlife Fund, PRIDE, Turks and
Caicos Development Trust, Turks and Caicos Conservation Association, and the Falmouth Dance Theatre.

WORK IN PROGRESS: The "Discover Hawaii's ..."
series, six illustrated nature books about Hawaii's
unique environments and wildlife, to be published by
Island Heritage Books.

SIDELIGHTS: Katherine S. Orr's love of nature and her
special love of the sea caused her to embark upon a
lifelong exploration of the natural world through scientific study. While in her late twenties Orr began to
realize that science was not able to provide, for her, a
true expression of the forces of nature. As she told
SATA, "[Science's] explanation of the physical world
cannot answer our deepest questions about reality; that
these answers flow from the heart and the mysterious
depths of our own creative expressions." Seeking a
means to integrate scientific knowledge with her love of
the natural world, Orr began writing educational material for local schoolchildren in the Turks and Caicos
Islands of the Bahamas. She has gone on to combine her
talent for writing with her skill as an artist/illustrator.
Orr's books open a porthole for the inquiring eyes of her
young readers through which they can view the wonders
of the sea.

Orr started her "literary career" at an early age. "I began
putting together my first simple books (about Cowboy
Hank and his favorite horse) when I was about four,"

KATHERINE S. ORR

she recalled. "I drew the pictures with big balloons to
enclose dialogue which my mother obligingly printed in
for me. Later, of course, I learned to print it myself. My
father kept my big sister and me stocked with an endless
supply of scrap paper from his office, and with parental
encouragement we happily covered it with drawings and
doodles." While her sister didn't let art disrupt her
schoolwork, Orr covered the pages of her notebooks
with sketches and drawings. "My doodling and daydreaming in class produced very mediocre report cards
which didn't sit well with my teachers and parents. I
began to conclude that my creative and artistic talents,
although praiseworthy, were mere hobby material not
worthy of a career."

Although Orr soon put away the drawing pencils and
applied herself to the studies that enabled her to become
a marine biologist, the creative side of her nature was
eventually to find an outlet when she began composing
books for young people. Her wide-ranging interests have
allowed her to write on a broad range of topics. Orr's
subjects range from the life and times of sea creatures, as
in *Leroy the Lobster,* to a description of tropical
ecosystems in *The Wondrous World of the Mangrove
Swamp.* Diverse though the subjects may be, common
to all Orr's books is her ability to educate her young
readers about the aquatic environment. She researches
each of her books thoroughly by both drawing on her
personal knowledge of animals and habitats and interviewing specialists. In addition, she has the final manuscript reviewed by at least two experts in the field.

My Grandpa and the Sea deals with the worldwide problem of overfishing in coastal waters. Orr's story is set on St. Lucia, an island in the Caribbean. Grandpa has been a fisherman for many years, going out each morning in his small wooden boat. But when men with larger boats, with equipment that can catch many more fish, anchor in the old man's waters, Grandpa's nets soon come up empty. He refuses to join the large boats which "take more than the sea can give," and searches for a new way to earn his livelihood. Using new ideas and simple methods, the old man develops a seamoss farm—seamoss is a staple in the diet of people native to the Caribbean. Through farming seamoss, Grandpa retains his place as a fisherman, and continues to work where he is most happy. Praising Orr's "primitive, brilliantly-hued pictures," a reviewer for *Publishers Weekly* notes that the illustrations in *My Grandpa and the Sea* are "perfectly synchronized with the poignant text."

Orr, like many others, is deeply concerned over the lack of understanding most people have about our ecosystem. "Well-meaning people contribute to ravaging our environment and our fellow non-human inhabitants every day without the slightest awareness of it," she told *SATA.* "Although certain environmental problems are becoming severe enough to thrust themselves before the public eye, the average American still lives with only the dimmest awareness of being an integral and influential part of a vast and wondrous, flowing web of life. So I do what little I can to spark a child's sense of empathy and wonder towards our natural world, because this forms the basis for learning, understanding, and ultimately effecting positive change.

"My goal as an author is to write from the heart those books that will arouse curiosity about nature, kindle a desire to learn, and be shared by children and parents alike. Presenting information through a story line accomplishes this in a way that a mere collection of facts does not. As Rachel Carson [renowned biologist and author of *Silent Spring*] noted, facts are useless in the absence of a desire to learn them. Our desire to learn is aroused by wonder, mystery, and adventure—components of even the simplest story. By presenting facts through a fictional story line I am re-creating those books that I most loved as a child; the ones that nourished my own love of nature and guided my path towards becoming a biologist and environmentalist."

WORKS CITED:

Review of *My Grandpa and the Sea, Publishers Weekly,* August 31, 1990, p. 66.
Orr, Katherine S., *My Grandpa and the Sea,* Carolrhoda Books, 1990.

FOR MORE INFORMATION SEE:

PERIODICALS

Bulletin of the Center for Children's Books, November, 1990, pp. 66-67.
School Library Journal, February, 1991, p. 73.

P

PATON WALSH, Jill
See PATON WALSH, Gillian

* * *

PATON WALSH, Gillian 1937-
(Jill Paton Walsh)

PERSONAL: Born April 29, 1937, in London, England; daughter of John Llewellyn (an engineer) and Patricia (Dubern) Bliss; married Antony Edmund Paton Walsh (a chartered secretary), August 12, 1961; children: Edmund Alexander, Margaret Ann, Helen Clare. *Education:* St. Anne's College, Oxford, Dip. Ed., 1959, M.A. (honours) in English. *Politics:* None. *Religion:* "Skepticism." *Hobbies and other interests:* Photography, gardening, cooking, carpentry, reading.

ADDRESSES: Home—72 Water Lane, Histon, Cambridge CB4 4LR, England.

CAREER: Enfield Girls Grammar School, Middlesex, English teacher, 1959-62; writer, 1962—. Whittall Lecturer, Library of Congress, Washington, DC, 1978. Visiting Faculty Member, Center for the Study of Children's Literature, Simmons College, Boston, 1978-86. Founder, with John Rowe Townsend, of Green Bay Publishers, 1986.

MEMBER: Society of Authors (member of Management Committee), Children's Writers Group.

AWARDS, HONORS: Book World Festival award, 1970, for *Fireweed;* Whitbread Prize (shared with Russell Hoban), 1974, for *The Emperor's Winding Sheet; Boston Globe-Horn Book* Award, 1976, for *Unleaving;* Arts Council Creative Writing Fellowships, 1976-77, and 1977-78; Universe Prize, 1984, for *A Parcel of Patterns;* Smarties Prize Grand Prix, 1984, for *Gaffer Samson's Luck.*

JILL PATON WALSH

WRITINGS:

JUVENILE FICTION; UNDER NAME JILL PATON WALSH

Hengest's Tale, illustrated by Janet Margrie, St. Martin's Press, 1966.
The Dolphin Crossing, St. Martin's Press, 1967.
Fireweed, Macmillan, 1969, Farrar, Straus, 1970.
Goldengrove, Farrar, Straus, 1972.

Toolmaker, illustrated by Jeroo Roy, Heinemann, 1973, Seabury Press, 1974.

The Dawnstone, illustrated by Mary Dinsdale, Hamish Hamilton, 1973.

The Emperor's Winding Sheet, Farrar, Straus, 1974.

The Huffler, Farrar, Straus, 1975 (published in England as *The Butty Boy,* illustrated by Juliette Palmer, Macmillan, 1975).

Unleaving, Farrar, Straus, 1976.

Crossing to Salamis (first novel in trilogy; also see below), illustrated by David Smee, Heinemann, 1977.

The Walls of Athens (second novel in trilogy; also see below), illustrated by Smee, Heinemann, 1977.

Persian Gold (third novel in trilogy; also see below), illustrated by Smee, Heinemann, 1978.

Children of the Fox (contains *Crossing to Salamis, The Walls of Athens,* and *Persian Gold*), Farrar, Straus, 1978.

A Chance Child, Farrar, Straus, 1978.

The Green Book, illustrated by Joanna Stubbs, Macmillan, 1981, illustrated by Lloyd Bloom, Farrar, Straus, 1982, published as *Shine,* Macdonald, 1988.

Babylon, illustrated by Jenny Northway, Deutsch, 1982.

A Parcel of Patterns, Farrar, Straus, 1983.

Lost and Found, illustrated by Mary Rayner, Deutsch, 1984.

Gaffer Samson's Luck, illustrated by Brock Cole, Farrar, Straus, 1984.

Torch, Viking Kestrel, 1987, Farrar, Straus, 1988.

Birdy and the Ghosties, illustrated by Alan Marks, Macdonald, 1989.

Grace, Viking, 1991, Farrar, Straus, 1992.

When Grandma Came (picture book), illustrated by Sophie Williams, Viking, 1992.

OTHER; UNDER NAME JILL PATON WALSH

(With Kevin Crossley-Holland) *Wordhoard: Anglo-Saxon Stories,* Farrar, Straus, 1969.

Farewell, Great King (adult novel), Coward McCann, 1972.

(Editor) *Beowulf* (structural reader), Longman, 1975.

The Island Sunrise: Prehistoric Britain, Deutsch, 1975, published as *The Island Sunrise: Prehistoric Culture in the British Isles,* Seabury Press, 1976.

Five Tides (short stories), Green Bay, 1986.

Lapsing (adult novel), Weidenfeld & Nicolson, 1986, St. Martin's, 1987.

A School for Lovers (adult novel), Weidenfeld & Nicolson, 1989.

Some of Paton Walsh's manuscripts and papers may be found in the Kerlan Collection, University of Minnesota, Minneapolis.

SIDELIGHTS: Jill Paton Walsh is noted for her works which deal realistically with life, death and maturation. Of the many "skilled and sensitive" writers for young people, declares Sheila Egoff in *Thursday's Child,* Paton Walsh "is the most formally literary. Her writing is studded with allusions to poetry, art and philosophy that give it an intellectual framework unmatched in children's literature." Paton Walsh's works examine

eras and topics such as life, death, and honor in Anglo-Saxon England (*Hengest's Tale* and *Wordhoard*), Victorian child labor in England (*A Chance Child*), growing up in World War II England (*The Dolphin Crossing* and *Fireweed*), life in the Early Stone Age (*Toolmaker*), and loyalty in the midst of destruction in fifteenth-century Byzantium (*The Emperor's Winding Sheet*). She has also written several novels that center on the Cornish coast, where she spent part of her young life.

Jill Paton Walsh was born Jill Bliss, a member of a loving family living in suburban London. Her father was an engineer, one of the earliest experimenters with television, and he and his wife actively stimulated their children to enjoy learning. "For the whole of our childhoods," Paton Walsh writes in her *Something about the Author Autobiography Series* (*SAAS*) entry, "I, and my brothers and sister—I am the eldest of four—were surrounded by love and encouragement on a lavish scale.... And to an unusual degree everyone was without prejudices against, or limited ambitions for, girls. As much was expected of me as of my brothers."

"For five crucial years of my childhood—from the year I was three to the year I was eight—the war dominated and shaped everything around me," Paton Walsh explains in *SAAS,* "and then for many years, until well

In *A Chance Child,* young Creep tries to leave his troubled family life behind by sailing away in a small boat. (Cover illustration by Diana Zelvin.)

into my teens, postwar hardships remained." "I do not know if there was a plan of evacuation there when the war began, which my parents did not join in, or if Finchley did not seem a likely target," she continues. Finally her mother's stepfather, upset by a bombing raid, moved the family to his place in Cornwall, in the far west of England. Although Jill's mother soon returned with her younger children to her husband in London, Jill herself remained in Cornwall for the next five years, returning to her family only after her grandmother suffered a fatal heart attack.

"I left St. Ives when I was just eight, and I didn't go back there till I was thirty-six," Paton Walsh explains in *SAAS*. "And it turned out that several people could remember me, and even remember having been in the same class in that little nursery school. A part of me is still rooted on that rocky shore, and it appears again and again in what I write." She stepped out of the comfortable world she had known directly into wartime London. "That first night back," she recalls, "I lay awake listening to the clanging sounds, like dustbins rolling round the night sky, made by German rockets falling somewhere a little distance off."

"The children I talk to nowadays are very interested in the Second World War," Paton Walsh remarks in her *SAAS* essay. "They think it must have been a time of excitement and danger, whereas it was actually dreadfully boring." Wartime restrictions and shortages meant that normal childhood activities—movies, television, radio, and even outdoor play—were severely limited. "I remember, in short, a time of discomfort and gloom, and, above all, upheaval." Part of the upheaval was caused by her mother's relatives, who had been wealthy colonists in Southeast Asia before the war, and who returned to England, newly impoverished, to live with her family. Because they had their own ideas of proper female behavior, Paton Walsh writes, she never knew "whether it was good and clever to give voice to my opinions, or pushy and priggish; not knowing from one day to the next what sort of behaviour would be expected of me." "Yet in the long run," Paton Walsh concludes, "I have benefited greatly from all this. I protected myself. I learned not to care what other people think. I would say what I liked, read what I was interested in, go on my own way, and ignore what the invading hoards of aunts and uncles thought, about me, or about anything else."

Paton Walsh attended a Catholic girl's school in North Finchley, whose environment was quite different from the liberality of her home life. "The nuns who taught me were suspicious of me," she declares in her *SAAS* entry. "They liked girls who worked very hard, not those who found it easy." When Paton Walsh left the school, it was to take a place at Oxford University. "I enjoyed myself vastly at Oxford, made friends, talked late into the night, and even worked sometimes, and work included lectures by both C. S. Lewis and J. R. R. Tolkien. The subject of the lectures and tutorials was always literature or philology—we wouldn't have dared ask those great men about their own work!—but the example they set

Paton Walsh's interest in children, travel, and history is evident in *Lost and Found*. (Cover illustration by Mary Rayner.)

by being both great and serious scholars, and writers of fantasy and books for children was not lost on me."

By the time Paton Walsh completed her degree, she was engaged to a man she had met at school. She obtained a teaching position, but soon discovered that she disliked being a teacher. "I didn't teach long," she explains in her *SAAS* entry. "I got married in my second year as a teacher, and eighteen months later was expecting a child." The life of a housewife, however, did not suit her either: "I was bored frantic. I went nearly crazy, locked up alone with a howling baby all day and all night.... As plants need water and light, as the baby needed milk, I needed something intellectual, cheap, and quiet." So, she says, "I began to write a book. It was a children's book. It never occurred to me to write any other kind."

"Until the moment I began to write I did not know that I was a writer," Paton Walsh explains in *SAAS*. The book she began to work on in those days, she says, "was, unfortunately, a dreadfully bad book. It had twelve chapters of equal length, with a different bit of historical background in each one." Eventually Kevin Crossley-Holland, an editor with Macmillan, explained to Paton Walsh that to publish this particular book might be a bad idea. He then offered her an option on her next work. "I set to work joyfully on *Hengest's Tale*," she recalls, "a gory epic retold out of fragments of *Beowulf*, and I stopped work only for a fortnight—between chapter three and chapter four—when my second child, my daughter Margaret, was born. *Hengest's Tale* was my first published book. And I have never forgotten the difference it made to be able to say, to others, certainly, but above all, to myself, 'I am a writer.'"

"This whole question of where ideas for books come from is very intriguing," Paton Walsh states in her _SAAS_ entry. "I suppose, 'Where do you get your ideas?' is the question most often asked by the children I meet. I think they are hoping for useful guidance on how to get ideas for their English homework, and I am a bit ashamed to be so hopeless at helping. But I don't really know where I get ideas from; each one in turn seems like an accident. It's a question of being on the lookout for the kind of accident that makes the idea for a book . . . . But I can say that a large part of it is giving loving attention to places; not necessarily beautiful places, just anywhere. Most of my books really have begun with thinking about the places they are set in." For example, she continues, "I went to Greece to find the landscapes for a classical historical novel, written for adults, called _Farewell, Great King,_ but when I got there I found Byzantine things, the marvellous mountaintop deserted city of Mistra above all, and the result of that was _The Emperor's Winding Sheet._ And there are more places singing to me . . . ."

Critics celebrate Paton Walsh's ability to evoke both character and setting, and through them to say something meaningful about growing up. She "has an astonishing ability to create appealing personalities," declares

Will James find the Gaffer's luck in time?

James' struggle to be accepted after he moves to a new town leads to confrontation with a vicious gang and the search for an old man's "luck." (Cover illustration by Brock Cole.)

Elizabeth S. Coolidge in the _Washington Post Book World._ In _Unleaving,_ the critic continues, "She has written a book about death, and what this means to a philosopher, a teenager, a grandmother and a very small child. Yet _Unleaving_ is in no way a gloomy book, but one that leaves the reader with a warm and optimistic view of humankind." "[Paton] Walsh doesn't tidy up the blight for which man was born," states Alice Bach in a _New York Times Book Review_ critique of the same book. "She's too wise to attempt answers about growing, living, dying, ethical choices. She exalts the mystery, the unknowing itself." "As time has gone by," Paton Walsh concludes in her _SAAS_ entry, "I have won the friendship of many other writers and readers and book-lovers. I feel lucky in this, beyond my deserts . . . . A writer is what I shall be as long as there is a daydream in my head, and I have strength to sit up and type."

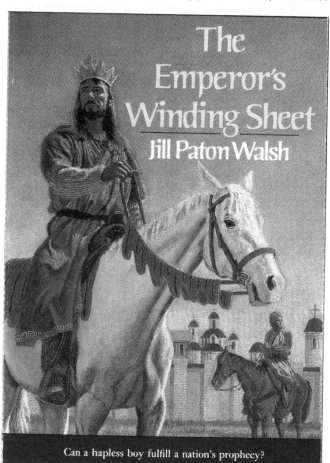

Piers Barber finds adventure and intrigue when he falls out of a tree at the feet of Constantine, Last Despot of Morea. (Cover illustration by Tim Tanner.)

WORKS CITED:

Bach, Alice, review of _Unleaving, New York Times Book Review,_ August 8, 1976, p. 18.

Coolidge, Elizabeth S., "Two Modern English Morality Tales," _Washington Post Book World,_ May 2, 1976, p. L13.

Egoff, Sheila A., "Realistic Fiction," *Thursday's Child: Trends and Patterns in Contemporary Children's Literature,* American Library Association, 1981, pp. 31-65.

Paton Walsh, Jill, "My Life So Far," *Something about the Author Autobiography Series,* Volume 3, Gale, 1987, pp. 189-203.

FOR MORE INFORMATION SEE:

BOOKS

Children's Literature Review, Volume 2, Gale, 1976.
Contemporary Literary Criticism, Volume 35, Gale, 1985.

*   *   *

PATTERSON, Nancy Ruth 1944-

PERSONAL: Born April 27, 1944, in St. Louis, MO; daughter of Jack Hunter, Sr. (a merchant) and Willeyne (a teacher; maiden name, McCune; present surname, Clemens) Patterson. *Education:* University of North Carolina at Chapel Hill, B.A., 1965, M.A.T., 1971. *Religion:* Episcopalian.

ADDRESSES: Home—Roanoke, VA. *Agent*—Christine Tomasino, RLR Associates, 7 West 51st St., New York, NY 10019.

CAREER: Roanoke City Schools, Roanoke, VA, 1966—, began as journalism teacher, became school administrator, currently city school director. Board member, Science Museum of Southwest Virginia, Big Brothers/Big Sisters, and *Artemis* literary magazine.

AWARDS, HONORS: Pioneer Award, National Scholastic Press, for contributions to scholastic journalism; Gold Key Award, Columbia University Scholastic Press Association, for contributions to scholastic journalism; Notable Children's Trade Book in the Field of Social Studies citation, National Council on Social Studies-Children's Book Council, 1990.

WRITINGS:

The Christmas Cup, illustrated by Leslie Bowman, Orchard Books, 1989.
The Shiniest Rock of All, illustrated by Karen A. Jerome, Farrar, Straus, 1991.

WORK IN PROGRESS: A Simple Gift, Just Certain People, and, with Pamela S. Feinour, *I Couldn't Have Done It Without You.*

SIDELIGHTS: Nancy Ruth Patterson told *SATA:* "If anyone had told me five years ago that I would be the author of two novels for children, with two more on the way, I would not have believed it. It's not that I haven't always wanted to be a writer. As long as I can remember, I have loved putting pen to paper. But I became a *published* writer quite by accident.

NANCY RUTH PATTERSON

"I wrote my first novel, *The Christmas Cup,* as a wedding gift for my brother, Jack Hunter Patterson, Jr. He had long wanted me to record the Christmas memory of our childhood in Bowling Green, Missouri, as a legacy of our family, and in particular, our grandmother, whom we called Nannie. Although I altered the plot somewhat and changed the names of all the characters except Nannie, I wrote about the people and the places and the happenings of that Christmas almost exactly as I remember them.

"All I had hoped for was to have my brother like the way I had written the memory. Katie McCabe, a friend of mine who had read the manuscript for me, had a different vision for it. A writer herself, she sent my manuscript to a publisher without my knowledge, knowing I probably would never have the nerve to submit it for publication myself. The manuscript landed in the hands of Ann Beneduce, a respected editor in children's publishing. I will always be grateful for the way she handled my first work—somehow leading me through much-needed and tedious revisions, but always making sure she left my dignity and enthusiasm for writing intact. She and Jeanne Larsen, my professor of creative writing at Hollins College, showed me what it takes to be a master teacher.

"If *The Christmas Cup* was inspired by my family, *The Shiniest Rock of All* was inspired by my own high school students. My twenty-seven years of teaching have introduced me to some of the finest people I know, and I regularly call on these former-students-now-turned-friends for help with my writing. One of my former

The Shiniest Rock of All

NANCY RUTH PATTERSON

Pictures by
Karen A. Jerome

Inspired by one of Patterson's high school students, *The Shiniest Rock of All* **tells the story of shy Robert, who finds out that "you don't have to be perfect to be darned good."** (Cover illustration by Karen A. Jerome.)

students, Pam Feinour, has worked with me on all four of my novels for children, and she always manages to come up with just the right detail or idea when I run out of my own.

"Another student, however, provided the idea for my second novel. Robert told me at a writing workshop that when he was young, he always hated the first day of each school year. Since he had a problem saying his r's, he was often laughed at by other students in his class when he tried to tell the new teacher his name; his 'Robert' always came out 'Wobet.' He had overcome his speech impediment long ago and gone on to become one of the best-liked boys in school, but he still remembered his classmates' teasing. His emotional honesty triggered similar confessions from the other students in the class. I remembered many of their confessions—being afraid of slugs and monsters, trick-or-treating as a fried egg, organizing secret clubs, feeling left out because of some perceived inadequacy—as I wrote about a boy named Robert who found out 'you don't have to be perfect to be darned good.'

"Margaret Ferguson, editor-in-chief of children's books for Farrar, Straus, and Giroux, led me through the revisions of my second book. Her legacies to me are

many, and I am a better writer because she knows how to share 'the shiniest rock of all'—hope. She refuses to let me give up on a story. Even when a book seems to be getting nowhere fast, she makes me believe that the miracle of figuring it all out could be just five minutes away. Her encouragement, and that of my agent, Christine K. Tomasino, have often kept me at the typewriter long after I thought it made more sense for me to give up, drink some hot chocolate, and go to bed.

"I am currently completing *A Simple Gift*, which was inspired by my own brother's death in 1985, shortly after I had written *The Christmas Cup* for him. In the book, ten-year-old Kate McCamity finds a way to give a birthday present to her older brother, who had drowned. I want my lasting gift to my brother to be this book about love that outlasts life. Through Kate and her family and her friends, I want children of all ages to see that people return to us in curious ways, and that the simplest, and very best, gift of all is *remembering*.

"Because I do remember so many people from my own life fondly, I keep on writing, even though it is usually a struggle for me. I do not ever want the goodness I have found in life to be lost. I want the best I know of life—the strength of my mother and the optimism of my father, the goodness of my grandmother and the honesty of my grandfather, the spirit of my brother and the faith of my friends, the gratitude for my students and the encouragement from my editors—to live on through the characters in my books. I want the lives of those I love to live on through my words. That, quite simply, is why I am a writer."

FOR MORE INFORMATION SEE:

PERIODICALS

Horn Book, November/December, 1991, p. 738.
Publishers Weekly, August 16, 1991, p. 58.
School Library Journal, October, 1989, p. 44; November, 1991, p. 122.

* * *

PATTISON, Darcy (S.) 1954-

PERSONAL: Born June 28, 1954, in Albuquerque, NM; daughter of Henry Bonneau Foster (a rancher) and Edith (a nurse; maiden name, Legate) Irvin; married Dwight Pattison (a city planner), August 8, 1975; children: Sara, Jinny, Amy, Luke. *Education:* University of Arkansas, B.A., 1974; Kansas State University, M.A., 1976. *Hobbies and other interests:* Quilting, gardening.

ADDRESSES: Home—3707 Ridgeroad, North Little Rock, AR 72116.

CAREER: Writer of children's books. Instructor of beginning quilting at Arkansas Art Center.

MEMBER: Society of Children's Book Writers, Arkansas Quilters Guild.

DARCY PATTISON

AWARDS, HONORS: The River Dragon was named to the fall, 1991, American Booksellers Association "Pick of the Lists."

WRITINGS:

The River Dragon, illustrated by Jean and Mou-Sien Tseng, Lothrop, 1991.

Contributor of articles to several quilting magazines. *The River Dragon* has been translated into Swedish, Danish, and Norwegian.

WORK IN PROGRESS: Writing a chapter book on dragons; other picture books; researching the Man in the Moon and moon lore, giants, wind.

SIDELIGHTS: Darcy Pattison told *SATA:* "I learned to love reading and stories at a very early age. My family—four boys and three girls—lived on a one-thousand-acre ranch high in the Rocky Mountains of New Mexico. There were no libraries, and books were too expensive. So my mother wrote to the state library in Santa Fe and asked that books be mailed to her. Every night she read to us. We grew up on Dr. Seuss and Pooh Bear.

"While mother read to us, Daddy told stories. When you met him, it wasn't long before he'd clear his throat

and launch into a story. So both written and oral stories became important to us.

"When I was in school, mother arranged for a bookmobile to stop monthly at our house. One month, I asked for a book that wasn't on the bookmobile. 'We'll bring it next time,' they told me. I waited all month for my book and remember the thrill of holding it in my hands when the bookmobile returned the next month.

"I read *Dune,* by Frank Herbert, when I was in sixth grade and was impressed by the creation of another planet and culture. I thought then that I'd like to do that some day. I did no writing though until long after I graduated from college.

"I quit work to stay home with my family and as the children grew, my husband and I decided that we wanted to home school them. One thing I wanted to include in their schooling was creative writing. I began to read about how to teach creative writing, and the books I read said that the teacher should write also to demonstrate how it's done. I dutifully followed their advice. Writing became more and more interesting and I devoured books on how to write. Slowly, I spent more and more time on writing, and then started sending stories to publishing houses.

"The River Dragon, my first book, was the result of research about dragons. I was studying the differences between European and Oriental dragons when I found some interesting information on Oriental dragons. They love pearls and swallows. They can smell very well, and if they smell swallows in a man's belly, they'll eat him to get to the swallows. They are scared of centipedes and five-colored silk scarves. I knew there was a story in

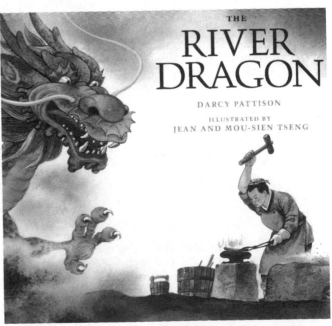

In *The River Dragon,* Pattison uses her knowledge of dragons—including their fear of five-colored scarves—to relate a tale of magic and mystery. (Cover illustration by Jean and Mou-Sien Tseng.)

these facts. It took several months to write, research more details, and revise the story. When I saw the final book, I was impressed with how perfectly Jean and Mou-Sien Tseng had captured the essence of the story. It was the death of one story—the story in my mind—and the birth of another—the book in my hand. And the book in my hand was better than the book I'd imagined. I continue to be awed at what words can do. They convey ideas and images to others that then come back to you richer and fuller than when you sent them out.

"I am working on other picture books, but also on longer stories, including a chapter book on dragons. It will be my first attempt at creating a new world and culture like Frank Herbert did in *Dune*.

"Writing is hard work! It's the hardest thing I've ever tried to do. But it has become the most engrossing, most fun, and most rewarding thing I do."

* * *

PAUSACKER, Jenny 1948-

PERSONAL: Surname pronounced "pow-zack-er"; born November 2, 1948, in Adelaide, Australia; daughter of Kenneth (a university lecturer) and Beryl (a braille transcriber; maiden name, Davies) Pausacker. *Education:* Melbourne University, B.A. (honors), 1970, M.A., 1972; Royal Melbourne Institute of Technology, Dip. Lib., 1974; Flinders University, Ph.D., 1980.

ADDRESSES: Home and office—7 Ivan St., North Fitzroy, Victoria 3068, Australia.

CAREER: Writer and free-lance editor. Teenage fiction reviewer for *Herald*, 1989; tutor and lecturer on children's literature at several universities; judge for writing competitions; speaker, member of committees and judging panels, and performer of readings for various writing festivals. *Exhibitions: What Are Ya?* included in the children's book exhibit *Titles by Noteworthy Authors and Illustrators of Boston and Melbourne*, 1988.

AWARDS, HONORS: General Writers Grant, Australia Council Literature Board, 1981-82; Angus and Robertson Junior Writers' Fellowship, 1985; Category B Fellowship, Australia Council-Literature Board, 1987 and 1990.

WRITINGS:

FOR CHILDREN

Nicky, illustrated by Rae Dale, Sugar and Snails, 1975.
The Three Dragons, illustrated by Dale, Wren, 1975.
Marty Hollitt and the Amazing Game Machine, illustrated by Marina McAllan, Rigby, 1979.
The Go-Cart Kids, illustrated by Tony Oliver, Rigby, 1981.
Fat and Skinny, illustrated by Oliver, Rigby, 1982.
Hunt the Witch, illustrated by David Pearson, Rigby, 1982.
(Editor) *Friday Night, and Other Stories from the West*, Western Region Education Centre, 1983.

What Are Ya?, Angus and Robertson, 1987.
Can You Keep a Secret?, Angus and Robertson, 1989.
Fast Forward, illustrated by Donna Rawlins, Angus and Robertson, 1989, Lothrop, 1991.

NONFICTION

Sugar and Snails: A Countersexist Booklist, Sugar and Snails, 1975.
Role Your Own, Sugar and Snails, 1976.
Women in Maths and Science, Transition Education Girls Project, 1982.
Participation of Girls in Maths and Science, Equal Opportunity Unit, Victorian Education Department, 1983.
That's One of My Talents, Vocational Orientation Centre, 1984.
(Editor) *Just Talking*, Vocational Orientation Centre, 1984.
(Editor) *Questions and Answers*, Vocational Orientation Centre, 1985.
Hands On: Trade and Technical Careers for Girls and Women, Spiral, 1985.

PLAYS

The Carolina Chisel Show, produced at Everyman 16, 1976.
The Redhead's Revenge, produced at Adelaide Festival Centre, 1978.
Chores!, produced at Theatre 62, 1979.
Marty Hollitt and the Amazing Game Machine, produced at Adelaide Come Out Festival, 1981.

SCREENPLAYS

Wipe Out the Jargon, Seven Dimensions, 1981.
Of Primary Importance, Equal Opportunity Resource Centre, 1984.
(Editor) *Preoccupied*, Victorian Women's Film Unit, 1985.

JENNY PAUSACKER

(Editor) *Tango Delta,* Victorian Women's Film Unit, 1985.

OTHER

(With Susan Hawthorne) *Moments of Desire: Feminist Writing about Sex,* Penguin, 1989.

Also author of fifteen teenage romances written under a pseudonym for the Dolly Fiction Series. Contributor to periodicals, including *Primary Education, Readings in Children's Literature, Society for Mass Media and Resource Technology Journal, Gay Information, Looking at Literature, Editions, Australian, Adelaide Advertiser, National Times,* and *Age.*

WORK IN PROGRESS: A sequel to *Fast Forward* and a novel for teenagers; research on women active in the women's liberation movement.

SIDELIGHTS: Jenny Pausacker told *SATA:* "I don't have many specific memories from my early childhood, but among the few is a memory of the first story I ever wrote. I'd snaffled one of those big old ledgers—bound to last for decades, with watermarked edges and interesting blue and red lines running this way and that—and in large laborious letters I scrawled: 'Once there was a dog and a pig and a hen. And they went. And they lived happily ever after. The End.' Not noticeably different from any primary school kid's first story, except for the way that it's stuck in my mind ever since, which seems to indicated that it must've given me a particularly high degree of satisfaction at the time. Certainly, I went on making up stories—telling them to my sister, making them into plays with the kids at school going over my favourite bits before I went to sleep and writing down about one story in every ten.

"Since the youngest author I'd ever heard of was sixteen years old, I was determined to finish my first novel before my seventeenth birthday. I set to work on a long quest-fantasy called *The Ruby of Gna-Vidrir,* and my diary for that year overflows with the belief that, once the book appeared in print, it would change my life. Well, *The Ruby of Gna-Vidrir* was never published undoubtedly because it was a faithful tribute to J. R. R. Tolkien, Alan Garner, and C. S. Lewis, some of my favourite writers at the time. (And I may as well say right now that my life has never been changed by the publication of any of my subsequent books...although I've changed a lot through writing them.)

"Nonetheless, I kept on writing. First another children's book, this time under the influence of H. M. Brinsmead and Eleanor Spence. Then a long novel about university life, begun in Australia, continued in the proverbial garret in London and never finished. Because in London, I finally came across the counterculture. Brought up by scientists, I'd always prided myself on my analytical approach to life, but I soon found out that there were hundreds of things about myself and my society that I'd never even thought to question, and I had to work a lot harder in the discussions around my

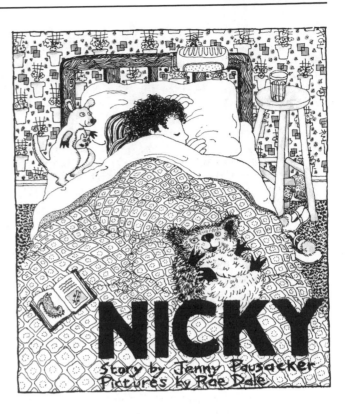

Pausacker focuses on a small boy and his friends in her first book for children. (Cover illustration by Rae Dale.)

household's kitchen table than I'd ever worked in the tutorials at Melbourne University.

"Back in Australia I heard about a Children's Book Group that met at the Melbourne Women's Liberation Centre. Suddenly there was a connection between my new ideas and my old interest in children's fiction. Before long I was part of a group that reflected on the sexism in current children's books, tossed around ideas for positive alternatives, read each other's stories and analyzed them in detail. Some of our books were accepted by a local publisher, and we published others ourselves under the Sugar and Snails imprint, which was to continue for over ten years, producing booklists, kits, picture books and extensive series of career books.

"I'd been in Adelaide for less than a year before I found myself involved in women's theatre. Writing for the stage gave me a much better ear for dialogue. Nothing, but nothing, sharpens your dialogue writing skills so much as seeing an actor struggling to say some tongue-twister of a line that you've landed them with. Eventually I came to the conclusion that I didn't have the same feeling for the theatre as I had for novel writing but, by another piece of good luck, at that point I was asked to write a novel for a new reading scheme.

"Writing for Reading Rigby changed me from an amateur into a professional. I learned to write regularly, rather than when I happened to feel like it. And I learned how to generate ideas, rather than waiting for inspiration to strike. Over the next few years, I wrote four junior novels, finding ideas in all sorts of unusual places. Faced with writing the first book, I went for a walk as a delaying tactic, passed a factory, wondered why its lights were on so late in the evening... and started to develop the idea for *Marty Hollitt and the Amazing Game Machine. The Go-Cart Kids,* about the archetypal moment when boys decide they can't be friends with girls anymore, came directly from a story told to me by a friend. *Fat and Skinny* was brought to life the characters from an old playground rhyme. *Hunt the Witch* was sparked off by feminist research that gave a historical perspective on the storybook witches.

"Then as now, I've never got anywhere by staring at a blank piece of paper. If I'm looking for a new idea or a way to solve some narrative problem, I still go out walking, while other ideas drift into my mind while I'm doing the housework, reading the paper or talking with friends. I used to feel a bit apologetic about the fact that I only work a six-hour day, until I realized that I spend at least two more hours gathering material and turning it over in my mind, so that it will be ready and waiting by the time I sit down at my desk.

"The idea for *Fast Forward,* for example, was the result of my unexpected enthusiasm for video recorders. I'm not very good with technology—I walk so much because I don't own a car, and I still write all my novels in longhand. At the same time I'm quite an impatient person and video cassette recorders offered me the chance to skip all the boring bits in movies. Inevitably I started to wish that I could use the fast forward button on life, as well as on movies, but I had a sneaking suspicion that there would be a catch in it somewhere. So I dreamed up eleven-year-old Kieran—who shares my problem of impatience—and his grandmother—who invents a remote control unit that works on everyday life—and sent them into action, to find out what would happen. My suspicions were correct. Kieran's adventures with the fast forward button got him into all kinds of trouble, including some that I never would have anticipated when I first started the book.

"I've been earning my living as a writer ever since I finished my doctorate, which is over ten years ago now. Up to this point it may sound as though I write mainly for general readers. However, with the assistance of grants from the Literature Board of the Australia Council, I have also published two novels for teenage readers. *What Are Ya?,* for older teenagers, takes two girls in their final year at school through a range of choices about friends and careers and sexuality. By contrast, *Can You Keep a Secret?,* set in the Depression of the 1930s, is a boys' own adventure story, involving secret armies and unemployed workers, spies and mysteries and chases around Melbourne.

"I suspect I will continue to write for both age groups. Since I'm very similar to Kieran in *Fast Forward,* I get a buzz out of trying something different in each new book. Like Kieran, I've found that this can bring its own problems but I like the challenge of continuing to develop new skills.

Eleven-year-old Kieran and his grandmother find themselves in a number of exciting situations when they invent a remote control that works on everyday life. (Cover illustration by Donna Rawlins.)

"Most of all, I appreciate the fact that I have been able to survive and grow and change in a field of work that I've loved ever since I was a kid myself. It's still a thrill to talk to kids who have read my books—and now I have readers in Germany and England and America as well. Now, that's *really* exciting."

*   *   *

PERKINS, Lucy Fitch 1865-1937

PERSONAL: Born July 12, 1865, in Maples, IN; died March 18, 1937, in Flintridge, CA; daughter of Appleton Howe (an educator and manufacturer) and Elizabeth (Bennett) Fitch; married Dwight Heald Perkins (an architect), August 18, 1891; children: Eleanor Ellis, Lawrence Bradford. *Education:* Museum of Fine Arts School, Boston, MA, 1883-86.

CAREER: Writer of children's books and editor. Prang Educational Company, illustrator in Boston, MA, 1886, and Chicago, IL, 1893-1903; Pratt Institute, School of Fine Arts, Brooklyn, NY, teacher, 1887-91.

MEMBER: Chicago Society of Artists, Midland Authors, Woman's Club, Lyceum Club (London).

WRITINGS:

SELF-ILLUSTRATED FICTION FOR CHILDREN; PUBLISHED BY HOUGHTON

The Dutch Twins, 1911.
The Japanese Twins, 1912.
The Irish Twins, 1913.
The Eskimo Twins, 1914.
The Mexican Twins, 1915.
The Cave Twins, 1916.
The Belgian Twins, 1917.
The French Twins, 1918.
The Spartan Twins, 1918.
Cornelia: The Story of a Benevolent Despot, 1919.
The Scotch Twins, 1919.
The Italian Twins, 1920.
The Puritan Twins, 1921.
The Swiss Twins, 1922.
The Filipino Twins, 1923.
The Colonial Twins of Virginia, 1924.
The American Twins of 1812, 1925.
The American Twins of the Revolution, 1926.
Mr. Chick, His Travels and Adventures, 1926.
The Pioneer Twins, 1927.
The Farm Twins, 1928.
Kit and Kat: More Adventures of the Dutch Twins, 1929.
The Indian Twins, 1930.
The Pickaninny Twins, 1931.
The Norwegian Twins, 1933.
The Spanish Twins, 1934.
The Chinese Twins, 1935.
(With daughter, Eleanor Ellis Perkins) *The Dutch Twins and Little Brother,* 1938.

ILLUSTRATOR

Nathaniel Hawthorne, *A Wonder Book,* Stokes, 1908.
Margaret Blanche Pumphrey, *Stories of the Pilgrims,* Rand McNally, 1910.
Maude Warren, *Little Pioneers,* Rand McNally, 1916.
E. E. Perkins, *News from Notown,* Houghton, 1919.
Maude Summers, editor, *The Children's Year Book,* Stoll & Edwards, 1923.
Julia Brown, *The Enchanted Peacock and Other Stories,* Rand McNally, 1925.
Edgar Dubs Shimer, *The Fairyland Reader,* Noble & Noble, 1935.
Verra Xenophontovna, *Folk Tales from the Russian,* Core Collection Books, 1979.

Also illustrator of *Mother Goose Book.*

OTHER

(And illustrator) *The Goose Girl, A Mother's Lap-Book of Rhymes and Pictures* (verse), McClurg, 1906.
(Editor and illustrator) *Robin Hood: His Deeds and Adventures as Recounted in the Old English Ballads,* Stokes, 1906.
(Editor and illustrator) *The Twenty Best Fairy Tales by Hans Andersen, Grimm, and Miss Mulock,* Stokes, 1907.

(Editor and illustrator) *A Midsummer-Night's Dream for Young People* (based on the play by William Shakespeare), Stokes, 1907.
A Book of Joys: The Story of a New England Summer (for adults), McClurg, 1907.
(And illustrator) *Aesop's Fables,* Stokes, 1908.

SIDELIGHTS: Lucy Fitch Perkins was trained in art and began her career as a book illustrator, but she is remembered for her "Twins of the World" series, twenty-six books in which she wrote of the lives of children from more than twenty different countries and cultures.

Perkins was born in rural Indiana, where her family had moved when her father left his job as a school principal in Chicago to enter the lumber business. Perkins and her sister were educated by their parents until the family moved back to their ancestral home in Massachusetts. After graduating from high school, Perkins studied for three years at the Museum of Fine Arts in Boston, worked for a year as an illustrator for the Prang Educational Company, and then went to Brooklyn's Pratt Institute to teach art. Four years later she married Dwight Heald Perkins, a Chicago architect. The couple lived in Evanston, Illinois, and had two children.

In her "Twins of the World" series, Lucy Fitch Perkins explores the lives of children from many different countries, such as *The Filipino Twins.* (Illustration by the author.)

Perkins continued to do illustrations for other people's books for several years after her marriage, and she had two books published for which she wrote text to go with the pictures she had done. But the "real beginning" of her writing, she said in *The Junior Book of Authors*, came when a friend who was also a publisher persuaded her to try writing her own books. She soon presented him with a set of sketches for *The Dutch Twins*, which he accepted and published, thus launching the "Twins of the World" series.

Perkins explained that the series grew out of two ideas: "the necessity for mutual respect and understanding between people of different nationalities if we are ever to live in peace" and the belief that "a really big theme can be comprehended by children if it is presented in a way that holds their interest and engages their sympathies."

She drew her inspiration from two experiences, she related: a visit to Ellis Island, where she saw "the oppressed and depressed of all nations" entering the United States to begin life here; and a visit to a Chicago school in which children from twenty-seven different nationalities were being successfully taught. "It seemed to me," Perkins said, "it might help in the fusing process if these children could be interested in the best qualities they bring to our shores."

In her series, Perkins not only depicted the life of children in the countries and times in which the books are set but also treated social issues that had caused immigration to this country and attempted to show what people from different cultures had contributed to the culture of the United States. In this way she was able to engage her young readers' sympathies and to foster understanding among them.

Bertha E. Mahoney and Elinor Whitney, the compilers of *Realms of Gold*, an annotated list of children's books over five hundred years, commented that several of the Twins books are "notable for the careful study of environment and national traits which characterize them all, combined with an interesting story," and they praised Perkins for having "been able to maintain freshness and life in so long a series." According to the *National Cyclopaedia of American Biography*, in October, 1935, Perkins was honored by her publishers at a ceremony at the Chicago Public Library, during which she was given the two millionth copy of a book from the Twins series.

Throughout her writing career, Perkins worked from a studio at her Evanston home. In addition to writing and illustrating books for children, she enjoyed decorative arts, such as making hand-colored prints and painting murals for public buildings and private homes. When she died on March 18, 1937, the twenty-fifth Twins book had just been published, and she was working on another. With the coauthorship of Perkins's daughter, Eleanor Ellis Perkins, the last book of the series, *The Dutch Twins and Little Brother*, was published in 1938.

WORKS CITED:

Mahoney, Bertha E. and Elinor Whitney, compilers, *Realms of Gold*, Doubleday, 1937, pp. 141-42, 628.

The National Cyclopaedia of American Biography, Volume 33, University Microfilms, 1967.

Perkins, Lucy Fitch, autobiographical essay in *The Junior Book of Authors*, 2nd edition, edited by Stanley J. Kunitz and Howard Haycraft, H. W. Wilson, 1951, pp. 241-43.

FOR MORE INFORMATION SEE:

BOOKS

Twentieth-Century Children's Writers, 3rd edition, St. James Press, 1989.*

*　　*　　*

PERL, Lila

PERSONAL: Born in New York, NY; daughter of Oscar (a printing executive) and Fay (a homemaker; maiden name, Rosenthal) Perl; married Charles Yerkow (a writer and photographer) December 1, 1961; children: two. *Education:* Brooklyn College, B.A.; attended New York University and Columbia University.

ADDRESSES: Home—160-20 Cryders Lane, Beechhurst, NY 11357. *Office*—c/o Clarion, 215 Park Ave. S., New York, NY 10003; and c/o Henry Holt & Co., 115 West 18th St., New York, NY 10011.

CAREER: Writer. Instructor in writing for children; lecturer; Golden Kite Award judge for Society of

LILA PERL

Children's Book Writers; fellow of the MacDowell Colony.

AWARDS, HONORS: American Library Association Notable Book Award, 1965, for *Red-Flannel Hash and Shoo-Fly Pie; Rice, Spice and Bitter Oranges,* illustrated by Stanislao Dino Rigolo, received an American Institute of Graphics Arts Award, 1967; National Science Teachers Association awards, 1973, for *The Hamburger Book,* and 1987, for *Mummies, Tombs, and Treasure;* Notable Children's Tradebook in the Field of Social Studies, National Council for the Social Studies-Children's Book Council, 1975, for *Slumps, Grunts, and Snickerdoodles,* 1977, for *Hunter's Stew and Hangtown Fry,* 1980, for *Junk Food, Fast Food, Health Food,* 1986, for *Blue Monday and Friday the Thirteenth,* 1987, for *Mummies, Tombs, and Treasure,* 1988, for *Don't Sing before Breakfast, Don't Sleep in the Moonlight,* and 1989, for *The Great Ancestor Hunt;* Nonfiction Honor Book, *Boston Globe/Horn Book,* 1981, for *Junk Food, Fast Food, Health Food;* Best Books for the Teen Age, New York Public Library, 1988, for *The Secret Diary of Katie Dinkerhoff;* Parents' Choice Story Book Award, 1991, for *Fat Glenda Turns Fourteen.* Nine of Perl's books have been made Junior Library Guild selections.

WRITINGS:

NONFICTION FOR CHILDREN

Red-Flannel Hash and Shoo-Fly Pie: American Regional Foods and Festivals, illustrated by Eric Carle, World Publishing, 1965.

Rice, Spice and Bitter Oranges: Mediterranean Foods and Festivals, illustrated by Stanislao Dino Rigolo, World Publishing, 1967.

Foods and Festivals of the Danube Lands: Germany, Austria, Czechoslovakia, Hungary, Yugoslavia, Bulgaria, Romania, Russia, illustrated by Leo Glueckselig, World Publishing, 1969.

Yugoslavia, Romania, Bulgaria: New Era in the Balkans, Thomas Nelson, 1970.

Living in Naples, Thomas Nelson, 1970.

Living in Lisbon, Thomas Nelson, 1971.

Ethiopia: Land of the Lion, Morrow, 1972.

East Africa: Kenya, Tanzania, Uganda, Morrow, 1973.

The Hamburger Book: All about Hamburgers and Hamburger Cookery, illustrated by Ragna Tischler Goddard, Seabury, 1973.

America Goes to the Fair: All about State and County Fairs in the U.S.A., Morrow, 1974.

Slumps, Grunts, and Snickerdoodles: What Colonial America Ate and Why, illustrated by Richard Cuffari, Seabury, 1975.

Ghana and Ivory Coast: Spotlight on West Africa, Morrow, 1975.

The Global Food Shortage: Food Scarcity on Our Planet and What We Can Do about It, Morrow, 1976.

Hunter's Stew and Hangtown Fry: What Pioneer America Ate and Why, illustrated by Cuffari, Seabury, 1977.

Egypt: Rebirth on the Nile, Morrow, 1977.

Mexico: Crucible of the Americas, Morrow, 1978.

Puerto Rico: Island between Two Worlds, Morrow, 1979.

BLUE MONDAY AND FRIDAY THE THIRTEENTH
The Stories Behind the Days of the Week

by LILA PERL
illustrated by ERIKA WEIHS

Using a mix of mythology, folklore, and ancient history, Perl explores the stories behind the days of the week in this Notable Children's Trade book. (Cover illustration by Erika Weihs.)

Junk Food, Fast Food, Health Food: What America Eats and Why, Clarion, 1980.

Eating the Vegetarian Way: Good Food from the Earth, Morrow, 1980.

Guatemala: Central America's Living Past, Morrow, 1982.

Pinatas and Paper Flowers: Holidays of the Americas in English and Spanish, illustrated by Victoria de Larrea, Clarion, 1983.

Red Star and Green Dragon: Looking at New China, Morrow, 1983.

Candles, Cakes, and Donkey Tails, illustrated by de Larrea, Houghton, 1984.

Blue Monday and Friday the Thirteenth: The Story Behind the Days of the Week, illustrated by Erika Weihs, Clarion, 1986.

Mummies, Tombs, and Treasure: Secrets of Ancient Egypt, illustrated by Weihs, Clarion, 1987.

Don't Sing before Breakfast, Don't Sleep in the Moonlight, illustrated by Weihs, Clarion, 1988.

The Great Ancestor Hunt, Clarion, 1989.

Molly Picon, A Gift of Laughter, illustrated by Donna Ruff, Jewish Publication Society, 1990.

From Top Hats to Baseball Caps, from Bustles to Blue Jeans, illustrated by Leslie Evans, Clarion, 1990.

It Happened in America: True Stories from the Fifty States, illustrated by Ib Ohlsson, Holt, 1992.

FICTION FOR CHILDREN

No Tears for Rainey, Lippincott, 1969.

Me and Fat Glenda, Seabury, 1972.

That Crazy April, Seabury, 1974.

The Telltale Summer of Tina C., Seabury, 1975.

Dumb Like Me, Olivia Potts, Seabury, 1976.

Don't Ask Miranda, Seabury, 1979.

Pieface and Daphne, Houghton, 1980.

Hey, Remember Fat Glenda?, Clarion, 1981.

Annabelle Starr, E.S.P., Clarion, 1983.

Tybee Trimble's Hard Times, Houghton, 1984.

Marleen, the Horror Queen, Clarion, 1985.

Fat Glenda's Summer Romance, Clarion, 1986.

The Secret Diary of Katie Dinkerhoff, Scholastic, 1987.

Fat Glenda Turns Fourteen, Clarion, 1991.

FOR ADULTS

What Cooks in Suburbia, Dutton, 1961.

The Delights of Apple Cookery, Coward, 1963.

The House You Want: How to Find It, How to Buy It, McKay, 1965.

The Finishing Touch: A Book of Desserts, New American Library, 1970.

WORK IN PROGRESS: Isaac Bashevis Singer: The Life of a Storyteller, illustrated by Donna Ruff, for the Jewish Publication Society.

Perl turned her sights to fiction in this novel about a girl whose dreams—as recorded in her diary—become reality.

SIDELIGHTS: Lila Perl told *SATA:* "I grew up in Brooklyn, New York, and had what I would call a perfectly ordinary childhood, very warm and family-oriented. My parents were achievement-oriented, too, for me and my brother. But I never dreamed that I would become a writer. That seemed very distant for a child who read voraciously but had never met a 'real live writer', as children do nowadays. It also seemed very pretentious in terms of the fact that I had never been anywhere or done anything that seemed exciting enough to write about, nor did I have any perspective on anything.

"I learned later, of course, that everyday experiences and a rich inner emotional life can be the stuff of fiction, and I was glad that I had that introverted childhood to draw on for my novels for the middle-grades and young-adult readers. 'Fat Glenda,' for example, about whom four books have now been written, seems to have touched a nerve in all of us. Although I was never fat, I was able to empathize with her insecurity and vulnerability. (Perhaps all of us are 'fat' on the inside?) Leavened with good humor *and* humor, the stories about Glenda appear to have made her a favorite heroine with readers, who feel they can relate to her.

"The other half of my writing life has been taken up with nonfiction. The desire to 'know more' and to gain the perspective I deemed so important drew me into a great deal of foreign travel, resulting in culture-and-background books set in Africa, China, and Mesoamerica. Journeying into the American past for the 'social-history cookbooks,' *Slumps, Grunts, and Snickerdoodles* and *Hunter's Stew and Hangtown Fry,* was another deeply rewarding adventure.

"Doing research, as one must for nonfiction, is fascinating to me, keeping in mind (as I must) that young readers should find the finished material appealing, accessible, and as exciting as a good work of fiction. *Blue Monday and Friday the Thirteenth* delves into the stories behind the days of the week, a mix of mythology, folklore, and ancient history. *Don't Sing before Breakfast, Don't Sleep in the Moonlight* tells us about the superstitions that have ruled our lives from earliest times, and inquires into their origins. Why *do* we avoid stepping on cracks, walking under ladders, and—yes—singing before breakfast?

"Two books I'm especially happy to have written are *Mummies, Tombs, and Treasure* and *The Great Ancestor Hunt.* One is about the human family as it existed in ancient Egypt; the other is a personal look at our own family histories. Readers are fascinated, as I was, by the many photographs of 'real mummies' that I was able to obtain for the book, by its investigation into why the Egyptians made mummies, how they made them, what their burial customs were, and where all those mummies are today.

"*The Great American Ancestor Hunt* was inspired by my own interest in my origins, and enriched by my wonderful father who, in his mid-nineties, gave me factual information and sharp insights into our family's roots. I wanted to write a book for young readers that would open doors for them, give them a sense of their heritage, offer clues in the form of questions to ask older relatives, teach them how to collect and record memorabilia to pass on to future generations, and above all imbue them with the adventurous activity of finding out who *they* are.

"*Molly Picon, A Gift of Laughter* came about as a result of a request for a junior biography about the petite, vivacious entertainer who delighted audiences in both the Yiddish and American theater, in movies and on television, for a period of eighty years. Even those of us who never saw her on stage 'live' can't help being entranced with this plucky, warmhearted, and talented performer, who made her first appearance at the age of five.

"Most recently published among nonfiction books is *From Top Hats to Baseball Caps, from Bustles to Blue Jeans.* For this social-history book, the world around me was my laboratory—grandmothers in jogging suits, office workers in blue jeans and sneakers. How did this informality in dress come about? How does it differ from the rigid clothing dictates of a hundred years ago?

Molly Picon
A GIFT OF LAUGHTER

by LILA PERL

illustrated by Donna Ruff

Perl's biography of comedienne Molly Picon emphasized the artist's contributions to both Yiddish and American theater. (Cover illustration by Donna Ruff.)

How did this revolution (for youth, on campuses, and for women as well as men) come to be? And what does it tell us about the society in which we live today?"

It Happened in America: True Stories from the Fifty States "has been [a] very challenging project. Imagine searching for a special story for each of our half-hundred states—one that reflects its character, reveals something about its history, its geography, or its multicultural inhabitants in a way that is entertaining, suspenseful, humorous, dramatic, occasionally tragic, but always true. Doing the research for this panoramic presentation was a story in itself!

"Another challenge, currently, is the preparation of the junior biography *Isaac Bashevis Singer: The Life of a Storyteller,* for the Jewish Publication Society. I feel privileged to have been offered this assignment. What a joy to immerse oneself in the life and work of the Nobel laureate who delighted us all with his wit and charm and who was, for both children and adults, one of the greatest storytellers of our time."

Perl's ongoing interest in nonfiction research is evident in this volume that explains the significance of various birthday traditions. (Cover illustration by Victoria de Larrea.)

FOR MORE INFORMATION SEE:

PERIODICALS

Appraisal, fall, 1976; fall, 1987, pp. 45-47.
Bulletin of the Center for Children's Books, June, 1974; April, 1976; September, 1976; December, 1978; October, 1979; April, 1982; September, 1983; Janu-

ary, 1984; December, 1984; January, 1985; June, 1986; June, 1987; November, 1987.

Horn Book, April, 1968; October, 1975; February, 1981; March/April, 1985, pp. 196-97; July/August, 1986; September/October, 1987, p. 632.

Junior Literary Guild Bulletin, March, 1974; September, 1977; September, 1980; April-September, 1986; October 1986-March 1987.

Kirkus Reviews, April 15, 1988, p. 623; October 15, 1989, p. 1535.

Publishers Weekly, April 29, 1988, p. 76; October 13, 1989, p. 55; April 12, 1991, p. 59.

School Library Journal, February, 1985, p. 79; August, 1987, p. 98; November, 1988, p. 121; December, 1989, p. 114; June, 1991, p. 112.

Voice of Youth Advocates, October, 1987; February, 1989; February, 1990; August, 1991.

*   *   *

PETERS, David 1954-

PERSONAL: Born June 25, 1954, in Hastings, NE; son of Robert (in real estate) and Joanne (a homemaker; maiden name, Hoppens) Peters; married Karen Haberl (a homemaker), September 15, 1978; children: Stephanie, Anne. *Education:* University of Missouri at Columbia, B.A., 1976.

ADDRESSES: Home—12812 Wood Valley Ct., St. Louis, MO 63131-2051. *Office*—Dimac Direct, 1 Corporate Woods Dr., Bridgeton, MO 63044.

CAREER: St. Louis Post-Dispatch, St. Louis, MO, artist, 1978-81; Kerlick & Switzer Advertising, St. Louis, art director, 1981-82; David Peters Studio, St. Louis, artist, 1982—; Dimac Direct, Bridgeton, MO, art director, 1991—. Author and illustrator of natural history books and sculptor of prehistoric animals; Peters's sculptures have been purchased by the American Museum of Natural History.

MEMBER: Society of Vertebrate Paleontology, Mid-American Paleontological Society, Eastern Missouri Society for Paleontology (vice president, 1988; secretary, 1990), Fossil Club (vice president, 1988; secretary), Dinosaur Society.

AWARDS, HONORS: Newsweek and the *New York Times* named *GIANTS of Land, Sea, and Air, Past and Present* a best book for Christmas, 1986; *From the Beginning, the Story of Human Evolution* was chosen as one of the best books of the year by New York Public Library, 1991.

WRITINGS:

SELF-ILLUSTRATED

GIANTS of Land, Sea, and Air, Past and Present, Sierra Club Books/Knopf, 1986.

A Gallery of Dinosaurs and Early Reptiles, Knopf, 1989.

From the Beginning, the Story of Human Evolution, Morrow, 1991.

Strange Creatures, Morrow, 1992.

Peters's work has been translated into Japanese, Italian, and French.

SELF-ILLUSTRATED CALENDARS

A Dinosaur Year, 1989 Calendar, Knopf, 1988.

GIANTS, Sierra Club Children's Calendar 1989, Sierra Club Books, 1988.

BIG, The Sierra Club Children's Calendar 1990, Sierra Club Books, 1989.

WORK IN PROGRESS: Researching dinosaur hind limb mechanics.

SIDELIGHTS: David Peters told *SATA:* "I never thought about writing or becoming an author until I had THE BIG IDEA. Out-of-the-blue it hit me. I had never seen a book in which all of the animals in it were drawn to the same scale so that a reader could see just how big animals were in relation to one another and to humans. Perhaps I could design such a book.

"I called it *The Big Book* because it was going to show all of the biggest animals of all time. It even had gatefolds for the biggest critters. Grids were 'hot' then, so each page had a grid of colored squares serving as a background. A local book wholesaler was impressed with the idea enough to act as my agent and submit it to editors he thought might have an interest in it."

DAVID PETERS

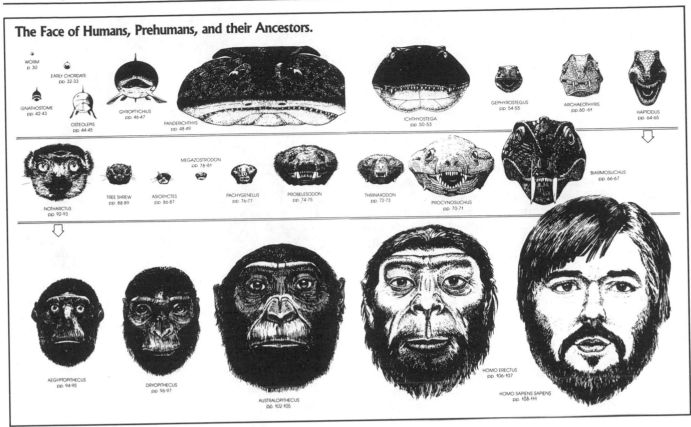

The Face of Humans, Prehumans, and their Ancestors.

Peters explores the history of human development in his self-illustrated *From the Beginning: The Story of Human Evolution.*

Publishers did not share Peters's enthusiasm for the subject, however, and after a number of rejections the author "took a look at the project and decided to revise it. I got rid of the colored backgrounds and made them stark white. I put all of the animals on a line near the bottom of the page that ran from page to page. Since they were all facing left, they looked like they were all on parade. The blue whale and the largest dinosaur were too big to fit on the scale I had chosen for the book, so I inserted something like the map supplement that *National Geographic* includes with many of their magazines, only instead of a map, I drew my creatures. I put a whale on the cover and renamed my book *GIANTS of Land, Sea, and Air, Past and Present.*"

Peters sent the revision to the Sierra Club, which was involved in the fight to save whales. Their publisher, Alfred A. Knopf, agreed to print it; and in 1986 *Newsweek* and the *New York Times* both selected it as one of their ten best books for Christmas. The book sold nearly fifty thousand copies in the United States and later became a successful release in foreign markets.

"I knew very little about animals of any sort before I got the *GIANTS* contract," Peters told *SATA*. "When I realized this was a 'go' project, I began my research. I became fascinated with the subject of prehistoric animals. Unfortunately, I made the same mistake many authors do and relied on the books in the popular press for my research. Many myths are repeated because of lack of proper homework. I didn't realize until much

later how many myths and mistakes crept into my own text. Much of my research into the original scientific literature followed the publication of *GIANTS*. Then the dinosaur renaissance hit and dinosaurs themselves were being redesigned. Soon, much of what I had published was out of date!"

At the request of his publisher, Peters worked on a book that featured prehistoric animals, including the recently discovered Seismosauras—the world's largest dinosaur. *A Gallery of Dinosaurs and Other Early Reptiles,* which was released in 1989, gave Peters an opportunity to draw the dinosaurs with the benefit of new scientific data. "Unfortunately, the market was just too crowded with about a dozen other books on dinosaurs," the author told *SATA*. "Following sales of about fifteen thousand copies, the book was discontinued in 1991. The week it was discontinued an article about dinosaur books came out in the *New York Times* that mentioned my book as one of the few that portrayed dinosaurs accurately.

"In the meantime, I drifted toward the subject of human evolution. In the library and with the help of various scientists (you get to know even the famous ones after you're in this business for a while), I pieced together the chain of animals in our own ancestry back beyond the apes and primates that are usually illustrated as human ancestors. I learned of the fossil mammals, reptiles, amphibians, fish, worms, and microbes that were also vital links in the chain of our ancestry. It was wonderful!

I found out how my body was put together piece by piece. I had to write about it!"

Peters's editor at Knopf thought that the resulting work was too complicated for young children, so the author sent it to William Morrow on the advice of a children's nonfiction reviewer who had seen sketches for the project. According to Peters, "*From the Beginning, the Story of Human Evolution* ... has twice as many pages as my other books, four times as much text, and was illustrated in black and white for a change. I was very excited about the prospect of becoming an author of a 'ground-breaking' book and illustrating something that had never been written about before in such detail. Many of the ancestors I featured had only recently been discovered! I worked hard writing letters to media people and making sure everyone in the evolution business got the book. Unfortunately, the book was ignored by the national media. On the plus side, the New York Public Library chose it as one of the best books for 1991, and it was reviewed favorably in many of the literary journals.

"Evolution is a subject many people are dead set against. When a feature story about my book appeared in the *St. Louis Post-Dispatch,* an editor headlined it: 'Evolutionary Opinions.' That made me angry enough to write a letter telling the editor my book was filled with facts and scientific inferences drawn from facts. What I had written about were not opinions! Other letters also arrived on the editor's desk from readers who felt that evolution was all wrong ... and they had not even bothered to read my book!

"The time I used to spend writing, I now spend with my family or at work or fossil hunting. But I'm still searching for the next great idea that might some day become a great book."

*   *   *

PIRNER, Connie White 1955-

PERSONAL: Born March 23, 1955, in Clarksburg, WV; daughter of Jack (a machinist) and Patricia (Haymond) White; married Bob Pirner (a teacher), August 8, 1981; children: Sara, Jack, Lydia. *Education:* Kent State University, B.A., 1981; attended Kearney State University and West Virginia University. *Politics:* Democrat. *Religion:* Protestant.

ADDRESSES: Home—Route 8, Box 234AA, Fairmont, WV 26554. *Office*—c/o Albert Whitman, 6340 Oakton St., Morton Grove, IL 60053-2723.

CAREER: Valentine Rural High School, Valentine, NE, special education teacher, 1983-89; Marion County Schools, Fairmont, WV, Alternative Learning Center teacher, 1989—. Faculty senate, secretary/treasurer, 1990-91, president, 1991-92; board officer for client rights of developmentally disabled adults.

MEMBER: Kappa Delta Pi.

CONNIE WHITE PIRNER

WRITINGS:

Even Little Kids Get Diabetes, Albert Whitman, 1991.
Even Little Kids Get Asthma, Albert Whitman, in press.

WORK IN PROGRESS: Cover Me with Memories, a story about a quilt and tales of the patches.

SIDELIGHTS: Connie White Pirner told *SATA:* "I grew up in a working class family full of love and support. My parents instilled in me a love of learning from an early age. I was always very curious about everything around me. I grew up believing that anything I wanted was attainable, I just had to figure out how to put all the pieces together.

"My father was an inventor. He could take pieces of things and put them together almost magically and make machines that could do wonderful things. He inspired me to create. Although I'm not able to make machines, the written word has always held wonderment for me."

Although Pirner always loved to read, it was only when she began to travel as a college student that she discovered the joy of writing. While traveling through western Europe and South America, she kept journals of all she saw to share with friends and family back home. "My words shared knowledge about people and places with many people that I cared about," Pirner told *SATA.*

Pirner found that writing helped her a great deal when her young daughter was diagnosed with insulin dependent diabetes in 1987. "It was the first time in my life that I couldn't find all the pieces to put together," Pirner recalled. "I was deeply saddened, very afraid and unable to do anything about it. As I tried to explain diabetes to Lydia and to my other children, Sara and Jack, I put my thoughts into words and out of that came my first book, *Even Little Kids Get Diabetes*. It occurred to me that if my book could help my children, perhaps it could help others. The response from other families has been very warm and rewarding.

"I continue to write and am presently working on several books for children concerning illness and the fears and daily concerns of living with medical difficulties. We all have things in our lives which we must live with. Some bring a greater challenge than others. Hard times can bring unexpected good times. We learn to do things differently and better and get on with our lives. The pieces don't always go together as we'd like but it is very possible to create new and good experiences from them."

*   *   *

POWELL, E. Sandy 1947-

PERSONAL: Born February 12, 1947, in Vancouver, WA; daughter of Kenneth R. (a business manager) and Katharine (a homemaker; maiden name, Chappell) Powell; children: Gisela Powell, Willie Sandry, Elizabeth Powell. *Education:* Western Washington University, B.A. (with honors), 1976. *Politics:* Independent Liberal. *Religion:* New Age Christian.

ADDRESSES: Office—c/o Carolrhoda Books, Inc., 241 First Ave. N., Minneapolis, MN 55401.

CAREER: Writer. Formerly a teacher, child care giver, and daycare director.

MEMBER: Authors Guild, National Association for Education of Young Children.

E. SANDY POWELL

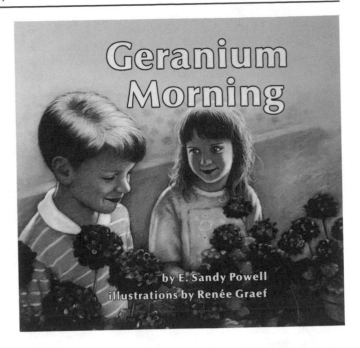

Powell's ability to mix humor with sensitivity is evident in this story of young friendship. (Cover illustration by Renee Graef.)

AWARDS, HONORS: Outstanding Trade Book citation (social studies), National Council of Social Studies/Children's Book Council, 1991, for *Daisy*.

WRITINGS:

JUVENILE

Geranium Morning, Carolrhoda, 1990.
Daisy, Carolrhoda, 1991.
A Chance to Grow, Carolrhoda, 1992.
Washington (volume in "Hello U.S.A." series), Lerner, 1992.

OTHER

Heart to Heart Caregiving, Redleaf Press, 1990.

WORK IN PROGRESS: An activity guide for individualizing preschool studies for Redleaf Press; *Rats* and other books for Lerner science and nature series for beginning readers.

SIDELIGHTS: E. Sandy Powell told *SATA:* "I began to write shortly after I fell in love with reading, which was in the second grade. A dear children's librarian in a public library basement encouraged a friend and I to work our way through the stacks. I'm sure I was also taking after my mom who has always loved to read.... I found a tremendous comfort in books, so by the light of the sweet-smelling electric blanket control, I read under my covers, late into the night."

Powell produced her first work in the seventh grade. According to the author, this play was her "last serious piece of writing as a child." It was not until many years later, at a friend's funeral, that Powell's love for writing became focused. Powell had always loved her work with children, but when someone praised her friend's career as a free lance photographer by saying 'He did what he wanted to do,' she began reassessing her life. "Soul-rankling months later I finally made a clear decision within myself. I wanted to be a writer," she noted.

Despite some financial hardships, Powell persevered: "I was determined to believe in myself, no matter how hard it was.... It hasn't been easy; I've often written until two in the morning.... I write a lot about serious things because there's a lot that bothers me in the world, a lot to care about. I hope that I can make things a little better, through my writing, and with the money I make selling books."

* * *

PRATER, John 1947-

PERSONAL: Born September, 1947, in Reading, Berkshire, England; son of Ronald (a civil servant) and Olive (maiden name, Mears) Prater; children: two daughters, one son. *Education:* Attended Brighton College of Art and Reading University.

ADDRESSES: Office—27 Keydell Ave., Horndean Hants P08 9TA, England.

CAREER: Writer and illustrator. Worked in advertising and taught for twelve years.

AWARDS, HONORS: Mother Goose Award runner-up for *On Friday Something Funny Happened.*

WRITINGS:

On Friday Something Funny Happened, Bodley Head, 1982.
The Party, Bodley Head, 1983.
You Can't Catch Me!, Bodley Head, 1984, published as *Can't Catch Me,* Puffin, 1984.
The Gift, Bodley Head, 1985, Viking, 1986.
The Perfect Day, Bodley Head, 1986, Dutton, 1986.
Gilbert, Bodley Head, 1987, Random House, 1988.
Along Came Tom, Bodley Head, 1990, Red Fox, 1992.
Bear's Bad Mood, Hamish Hamilton, 1990.
Lots to Do, Ideals Children's Books, 1991.
"No," Said Joe, Walker, 1992.
Bear's Den, Hamish Hamilton, 1992.

Once upon a Time, Walker, 1993.
Timid Tim and the Cuggy-Thief, Bodley Head, 1993.

ILLUSTRATOR

Hazel Hutchins, *Anastasia Morningstar,* Annick, 1985.
Paul Rogers, *Lily's Picnic,* Bodley Head, 1988.
P. Rogers, *Me and Alice Go to the Library,* Bodley Head, 1989.
P. Rogers, *Me and Alice Go to the Museum,* Bodley Head, 1989.
Tony Bradman, *Gary and the Magic Cat,* Hodder and Stoughton, 1989.
Gilli Wright, *Green Fingers,* Hamilton Children's, 1989.
Catherine Storr, *The Spy before Yesterday,* Hamish Hamilton, 1990.
Paul Bette, *Unlucky Lucky,* Hodder and Stoughton, 1991.
E. Nesbit, *The Railway Children,* Walker, 1992.

SIDELIGHTS: John Prater is known for his brightly illustrated books for very young children. Kicki Moxon Browne, reviewing *On Friday Something Funny Happened* for *Times Literary Supplement,* notes that Prater's sparse text is paired with "frenzied drawings, capturing wonderfully the built-in slapstick quality of early childhood." Prater details the antic adventures of young children in many of his books. *You Can't Catch Me!* follows the adventures of a small boy as he tries to escape taking a bath, only to fall in a pig-wallow and really need a bath. The short text is "just enough to complement the pictures, which really tell the story," according to *School Library Journal* contributor Denise L. Moll.

WORKS CITED:

Browne, Kicki Moxon, "Romantic and Real," *Times Literary Supplement,* July 23, 1982, p. 793.
Moll, Denise L., review of *You Can't Catch Me!, School Library Journal,* April, 1987, p. 88.

FOR MORE INFORMATION SEE:

PERIODICALS

Junior Bookshelf, August, 1990; October, 1992, p. 193.
Times Literary Supplement, November 25, 1983; November 15, 1985, p. 174; November 28, 1986, p. 1345.

R

RAY, Jane 1960-

PERSONAL: Born June 11, 1960, in London, England; daughter of Donald Edwin (a teacher and musician) and Barbara May (a teacher; maiden name, Rowley) Ray; married David Anthony Temple (a conductor), April 8, 1988; children: Clara Jane, Ellen May. *Education:* Middlesex Polytechnic, B.A. (with honors), 1982. *Politics:* "Left/green/feminist." *Hobbies and other interests:* Music, gardening, green politics, reading, writing.

ADDRESSES: Home—41 Greenham Rd., London N10 1LN, England.

JANE RAY

CAREER: Illustrator. Formerly teacher of art to students with learning difficulties.

MEMBER: Association of Illustrators.

AWARDS, HONORS: The Story of Christmas was shortlisted for the Kate Greenaway Medal, 1992.

ILLUSTRATOR:

Angela Huth, compiler, *Island of the Children,* Orchard Books, 1988.
Nigel Gray, *A Balloon for Grandad,* Orchard Books, 1988.
Suzanna Steele and Morag Styles, compilers, *Mother Gave a Shout,* A. & C. Black, 1989.
Noah's Ark: Words from the Book of Genesis, Dutton, 1990.
Huth, compiler, *Casting a Spell,* Orchard Books, 1991.
The Story of Christmas (based on text from the King James Bible), Orchard Books, 1991.
The Creation (based on text from the King James Bible), 1992.

SIDELIGHTS: Jane Ray told *SATA:* "Drawing and painting have always been my lifeblood, my 'raison d'etre,' nearly as important, now that I have them, as my children! And for me, the best possible use for that drawing and painting is the making of picture books.

"In order to justify the paper and energy used in the production of a book, it must be worthwhile, must add something to the 'sum of human knowledge.' That is quite a tall order—how can I be sure that my books have some sort of value and integrity? I can't. My guidelines are: I want my books to be interesting, to make you want to go back and look again, to keep seeing something different and new every time you look. I want them to inspire, to be remembered in adult life.

"Books have, or should have, a timeless quality that will stand by you and can be referred to and remembered as you grow. The best books encourage your own thoughts and ideas and imagination.... Books don't demand your attention like TV and videos. You can refer to them at your leisure, browse through them at your own pace, linger over favorite pages, and even skip the bits you don't like!

"My last three books have all been Bible stories. I am not a Christian (although I suppose I espouse some Christian values). I wanted to do these books because I think they are wonderful stories and an important part of my heritage. Every culture has its epic stories and legends—these happen to be a part of mine.

"The things that excited me as a child in picture books were the tiny details, the things that appeared new even after six or seven readings, that you didn't notice before—details in corners that only revealed themselves after very careful looking.... Having children of my own has helped me to see something of what appeals to the small child's mind. My three-year-old will often be fascinated by some cheaply designed and illustrated book, one which will certainly win no prizes or be reviewed in the Sunday papers. Yet there is some quality in it, sometimes something sinister or surreal, that enthralls her. One must therefore never feel smug about a good review or a prestigious prize—it doesn't mean that children will actually enjoy your book!

"I've also seen, through sharing picture books with my daughter, the role that they have in the honest and positive representation of different groups of people and situations, and conversely the harm they can do when guilty of negative or damaging images. We must get to the stage where racism and sexism are successfully challenged in this field, but not in a tokenist way. It must become second nature to have black, white, and brown faces in books.

"In the end, what appeals to the imagination, memory, fears, and pleasures of one child will leave another totally unmoved, and I don't think there is any way of changing that. I'm just very, very glad to be in the privileged position of being able to earn my living at the thing I love most of all!"

*   *   *

REHM, Karl M. 1935-

PERSONAL: Born May 8, 1935, in Salem, OR; son of Erwin Martin (a farmer) and Alice (a housewife; maiden name, Wulfemeyer) Rehm; married Marian D. Benson (a nurse), October 4, 1958; children: Sally Kay. *Education:* Oregon College of Education, B.S., 1958, M.S., 1963; attended Oregon State College and University of Hawaii. *Hobbies and other interests:* Photography.

ADDRESSES: Home—c/o American Embassy, Box 390, A.P.O., AE 09080.

CAREER: Salem Public Schools, Salem, OR, teacher, 1958-68, media specialist, 1969-83; counselor in Baumholder, Germany, 1968-69; media specialist in Bonn, Germany, 1984—. Camera technique instructor, Oregon College; instructor, Chemeketa Community Col-

KARL M. REHM

lege, Oregon. Stock photographer for an American photo agency. Librarian, St. Mark's Lutheran Church. *Military service:* Oregon National Guard, 1953-63.

AWARDS, HONORS: Outstanding Children's Book designation, Junior Literary Guild, 1991, for *Left or Right?;* numerous best-of-the-year awards for audio-video productions.

WRITINGS:

Basic Black and White Photography, Amphoto, 1976.
Corso basico de fotografia en blanco y negro, Daimon, 1978.
The Photograph and Its Control, Media Tree, 1983.
(With Kay Koike) *Left or Right?,* illustrated with photographs by the author and Koike, Clarion, 1991.

Also author of *One Hundred Photographs for Teaching About Germany,* 1976, and *One Hundred Photographs for Teaching About the U.S.S.R.,* 1978. Creator of over one hundred sound filmstrips, video tapes, print sets, and computer programs.

WORK IN PROGRESS: Other children's photo concept books.

SIDELIGHTS: Photographer Karl Rehm told *SATA:* "Generally, my audio-visual productions and books have been a result of seeing a need for a specific topic

Karl Rehm and Kay Koike

In *Left or Right?*, Rehm and co-author Kay Koike use a variety of photographic subjects to introduce young readers to directional concepts. (Cover photograph by the authors.)

from my teaching experiences." *Left or Right?*, Rehm's first book for children with coauthor Kay Koike, helps small children grasp the title concept through a series of increasingly detailed photographs. Noting the "clear and attractive" photographic illustrations, Leone McDermott praises the book as a "simple, useful introduction to a difficult concept" in her review for *Booklist*.

WORKS CITED:

McDermott, Leone, review of *Left or Right?*, *Booklist*, October 1, 1991, pp. 333-334.

*   *   *

REVSBECH, Vicki
See LIESTMAN, Vicki

*   *   *

ROBERSON, Jennifer 1953-
(Jennifer O'Green, Jennifer Roberson
O'Green; Jay Mitchell, a pseudonym)

PERSONAL: Surname is pronounced "*robb*-erson"; born October 26, 1953, in Kansas City, MO; daughter of Donald and Shera (a literary agent's reader; maiden name, Hardy) Roberson; married Mark O'Green (a computer game designer), February 16, 1985. *Education:* Northern Arizona University, B.S., 1982. *Religion:* Christian. *Hobbies and other interests:* "Professional dog obedience trainer, exhibitor of Labrador retrievers and Cardigan Welsh corgis in conformation and obedience."

ADDRESSES: Agent—Russell Galen, Scott Meredith Literary Agency, 845 Third Ave., New York, NY 10022.

CAREER: Wyoming Eagle, Cheyenne, WY, investigative reporter, 1976; Farnam Companies, Phoenix, AZ, advertising copywriter, 1977; writer and lecturer, 1982—.

MEMBER: Science Fiction Writers of America, Cardigan Welsh Corgi Club of America, Southern California Cardigan Welsh Corgi Club, Bluebonnet Cardigan Welsh Corgi Club.

AWARDS, HONORS: Best new fantasy author citation, *Romantic Times* magazine, 1984, for *Shapechangers;* Junior Alumni Achievement Award, Northern Arizona University, 1985; best new historical author citation, *Romantic Times,* 1987, for *Royal Captive;* Reviewer's Choice Annual Top Fantasy Novel citations, 1989, for *Sword-Dancer* and *Sword-Singer,* and 1990, for *Sword-Maker;* Jubilee Year Distinguished Alumnus Award, Northern Arizona University, 1990.

WRITINGS:

"CHRONICLES OF THE CHEYSULI" FANTASY SERIES

Shapechangers, DAW, 1984.
The Song of Homana, DAW, 1985.
Legacy of the Sword, DAW, 1986.
Track of the White Wolf, DAW, 1987.
A Pride of Princes, DAW, 1988.
Daughter of the Lion, DAW, 1989.
Flight of the Raven, DAW, 1990.
A Tapestry of Lions, DAW, 1992.

"SWORD-DANCER SAGA" FANTASY SERIES

Sword-Dancer, DAW, 1986.

JENNIFER ROBERSON

Sword-Singer, DAW, 1988.
Sword-Maker, DAW, 1989.
Sword-Breaker, DAW, 1991.

OTHER

Smoketree (romantic suspense), Walker & Co., 1985.
(Under pseudonym Jay Mitchell) *Kansas Blood* (western), Zebra Books, 1986.
(Under name Jennifer O'Green) *Royal Captive* (historical romance), Dell, 1987.
Lady of the Forest, Zebra, 1992.

Work represented in anthologies, including *Sword and Sorceress,* volumes 1-7, edited by Marion Zimmer Bradley, DAW, 1984-90; *Spell Singers,* edited by A. B. Newcomer, DAW, 1988; *Herds of Thunder, Manes of Gold,* edited by Bruce Coville, Doubleday, 1989; and *Horse Fantastic,* edited by Martin Greenberg and Rosalind Greenberg, DAW, 1991. Author of column "Consider This," under name Jennifer Roberson O'Green, for *Corgi Quarterly.* Contributor of short stories and articles to periodicals, including *Aboriginal Science Fiction, Marion Zimmer Bradley's Fantasy Magazine,* and *Writer.*

WORK IN PROGRESS: Prince of Night, 1994, *Queen of Sleep,* 1995, and *King of Dreams,* 1996, all for DAW; *Glen of Sorrows.*

SIDELIGHTS: Jennifer Roberson told *SATA:* "I was fortunate to grow up in a family of readers; our genealogical chart is filled with bookaholics, including the renowned English author Thomas Hardy, of whom I am a direct descendant. An only child of divorced parents, I discovered very young that siblings and best friends were available at all times between the pages of favorite novels. It was not at all unusual for three generations—grandfather, mother, and daughter—to gather in the living room and while away the hours engrossed in our books of the moment.

"We moved to Phoenix, Arizona, when I was four. Throughout elementary school I was a 'daydreamer' who much preferred novels to schoolwork, which was reflected in my grades. It wasn't until my freshman year in high school, when the emphasis on reading and writing skills made education much more enjoyable, that I began to apply myself.

"My world changed that year in 1968, when I was a fourteen-year-old freshman. I protested the Vietnam War, rode my horse in amateur rodeos, sang with the high school choirs—dreaming of someday making a living as a singer—read tons of science fiction and fantasy, and wrote adolescent stories about favorite rock stars and television actors to entertain my friends and myself. I also visited my mother in the bookstore where she worked, reading the wares for free. One day I put down the just-finished typical girl-and-her-horse book, which disappointed me, and said to my mother, '*I* could write a better book than that.' Whereupon she challenged me to try it.

"I did my homework with regard to manuscript preparation, selected the publishing houses I thought might be interested, and, when finished writing the novel some months later, I mailed off my 342-page, typed, double-spaced manuscript to Random House. It was returned with the photocopied form rejection so beloved of all writers: my first novel, and my first official rejection slip, at age fourteen. I was crushed, of course, but not disabused of my new dream: I was completely convinced, in the innocent but robust confidence of youth, that *someday* I would become a published novelist.

"I learned to cope with frequent rejection slips. I wrote three more unsold novels before deciding at last to try the genre I read the most, the fantasy of imaginary worlds, heroic men and women, powerful swords, and sorcery. I attended college sporadically, taking specific classes I felt would help my writing without pursuing a degree, and worked at several jobs, including stints as an advertising copywriter in Phoenix and investigative reporter on a morning daily in Cheyenne, Wyoming. In 1980 I returned to college full time to finally get that

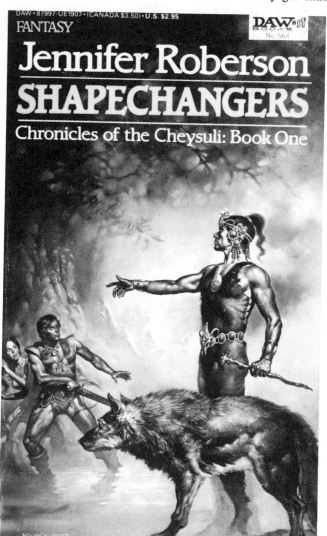

Roberson outlined her first published novel while attending college classes and working at a part-time job. (Cover illustration by Boris Vallejo.)

degree, majoring in journalism at Northern Arizona University in Flagstaff.

"While at Northern Arizona—between classes and a part-time job—I outlined and wrote the first five volumes in what I foresaw as an eight-volume dynastic fantasy series. Determined to write the 'Chronicles of the Cheysuli' for myself even if the series was never published, I managed to procure myself a literary agent via the reading fee system at the Scott Meredith agency. I spent my final semester at the University of London on an American studies program; it was there the telegram from my agent arrived two days after my twenty-ninth birthday, announcing the sale of *Shapechangers* to DAW Books. No more was I a 'wanna-be' but a full-fledged professional novelist—an 'overnight success' fourteen years after I wrote my first manuscript.

"Approximately fifteen months after I signed the contracts, *Shapechangers* was published. The circumstances were somewhat odd: now that I was published, I no longer had to seek out a journalism job but could plan on writing fiction. But I still had to do something to earn a living, and so there I was working in a bookstore, unpacking, pricing, shelving, and selling all kinds of books; and suddenly I was also placing my *own* novel on the shelves—right there next to my favorite authors— and ringing it up at the register. In addition, my personal life also took an upswing: I met Mark O'Green and married him fifteen months later, in February of 1985, one year after the publication of my first novel. The marriage afforded me the chance to quit working part-time and start writing full-time; my husband's emotional support allowed me to believe I could continue to grow as a writer.

"After writing the first three novels in the Cheysuli series, I was struck by inspiration: I wanted to try a serious examination of sexism, but set against an entertaining and intriguing background so readers would not be turned off by the 'message' before it could be delivered. Heroic fantasy such as Robert E. Howard's seminal 'Conan the Barbarian' stories emphasized the man's role and relegated women to mere sex objects. I wanted to write about a man who, in meeting up with a strong, competent woman in the same line of work, has his consciousness raised during a dangerous journey that taxes them physically as well as emotionally. My personal description was 'Conan the Barbarian meets Gloria Steinem.' The true title became *Sword-Dancer,* and it was published in 1986. It became the first of four novels featuring my Spencer Tracy/Katherine Hepburn- like duo.

"With some expert assistance from my agent, Russell Galen, I'd fashioned a solidly successful career in the fantasy genre by 1990. Bowing to my interests in other genres, I'd also published a Louis L'Amour-type western told from a woman's point of view, a contemporary romantic suspense, and a historical romance reflecting my longtime love of British history. But one thing I'd always wanted to try—another 'someday' dream—was a big, sprawling, mainstream historical epic. Russ won me

The escapades of a man and woman addicted to adventure come to a conclusion in the fourth book of the "Sword Dancer" series. (Cover illustration by Corey Wolfe.)

the chance when I submitted an outline and sample chapter package to him in which I proposed to write a reinterpretation of the Robin Hood legend, but with a twist—I wanted to emphasize Marian's point of view and contribution to the legend. Russ auctioned the manuscript and secured me an outstanding mainstream deal. I then spent the next year of my life researching and writing *my* version of the story; in actuality, a 'prequel' to the familiar legend. I wanted very much to write the story of how the legend came to be; the tale of how seven very different people from a rigidly stratified social structure came to join together to fight the inequities of medieval England. To me, the key was *logic*—I interwove historical fact with the fantasy of the classic legend and developed my own interpretation of how things came to be. I wanted to come to know all of these people, to climb inside their heads and learn what motivated them to do what they did. One year later I'd birthed my 'child': a 1,100-page, 257,000-word manuscript titled *Lady of the Forest* that weighed 13 pounds and cost $70 to photocopy and $22 to mail.

"I have learned along the way that a writer, to be successful, must *write;* she cannot be satisfied with what she has already done but must look ahead to what she will do. A writer completely satisfied with her work ceases to grow and stunts her talent. It is far more important to *write* than it is to *have written.*"

FOR MORE INFORMATION SEE:

PERIODICALS

Fantasy Review, August, 1984, p. 22; October, 1985, p. 19; September, 1986, p. 30; June, 1987, p. 40.
Locus, November, 1989, p. 57; July, 1990, p. 55; June, 1991, p. 50.
Science Fiction Chronicle, March, 1986, p. 36; December, 1986, p. 50; January, 1987, p. 40; October, 1987, p. 27; March, 1989, p. 39; December, 1989, p. 39.
Voice of Youth Advocates, October, 1988, p. 196; August, 1989, p. 167; December, 1990, p. 301.

*   *   *

ROSS, Lillian Hammer 1925-

PERSONAL: Born July 16, 1925, in Los Angeles, CA; daughter of David (a merchant) and Frieda (Kamornick) Hammer; married Albert Ellis Ross, August 15, 1948 (died January 7, 1991); children: Stephen Frederick, Susan Ross Peterson, David Paul. *Education:* University of California, Los Angeles, B.A., 1948, English as a Second Language teacher credential, 1974, bilingual Spanish/English teacher credential, 1975.

ADDRESSES: Office—c/o Publicity Director, Jewish Publication Society, 1930 Chestnut St., Philadelphia, PA 19103-4599.

CAREER: Los Angeles Unified School district, kindergarten and primary school teacher, 1948-54 and 1964-80. Author, 1990—.

MEMBER: Society of Children's Book Writers, PEN, Women's National Book Association, Long Beach Authors' Festival.

WRITINGS:

The Little Old Man and His Dreams, Harper, 1990.
Buba Leah and Her Paper Children, Jewish Publication Society, 1991.

Author of unpublished works *David and the Four White Chickens, Hannah, Also Known as Sarah,* and *Papa Is Coming Home for Pesach.* Also contributor of "A Tall Tale" to *Highlights* magazine, 1989.

WORK IN PROGRESS: "Tales my father told me; tales my mother told me."

SIDELIGHTS: Lillian Hammer Ross told *SATA:* "My daughter and son-in-law had set their wedding date for the first night of Hanukkah. Invitations mailed, my ninety-year-old father was hospitalized with heart fail-

LILLIAN HAMMER ROSS

ure. My mother sat by her husband's bed and every time he opened his eyes, she whispered, 'David, you must be well for Susan's wedding.' My mother and father walked down the aisle at their granddaughter's wedding and two months later, my father died. These events were the motivation for my writing the picture/storybook *The Little Old Man and His Dreams.*

"One weekend, I attended the conference of 'Writers of the Pacific Rim' where Charlotte Zolotow, Children's Editor for Harper and Row, was the main speaker. At intermission, I approached her and asked why it was I received complimentary letters about my writing, but no acceptance of my manuscripts. 'You just haven't met the right editor,' was her reply. At home, I sent my manuscript, *The Little Old Man and His Dreams,* with a covering letter. 'Remember me? I'm the woman you met at the writers conference last December.' One month later, I received a call from Charlotte Zolotow's office, and the following month a contract was signed.

"I set the scene of *The Little Old Man* in Europe when people rode in wagons pulled by their horses. My writing has taken me to a past time of Europe in the early 1900s. I have connected with my parents' past life and brought it into the present so that their great-grandchildren will better understand their cultural heritage."

*   *   *

RUCHLIS, Hy(man) 1913-1992

OBITUARY NOTICE—See index for *SATA* sketch: Born April 6, 1913, in Brooklyn, NY; died of kidney failure and a cardiac disorder, June 30, 1992, in West Palm Beach, FL. Educator and author. In addition to coauthoring the book *Atomics for the Millions,* which aimed to explain atomic energy to nonscientists, Ruchlis wrote books and created science kits for children. A physics teacher in New York City schools who retired in 1955, Ruchlis devoted himself to improving the educational system with his writings, which include *How a Rock Came to Be on a Fence on a Road near a Town, Clear Thinking,* and *How Do You Know It's True—Discovering the Difference between Science and Superstition.*

OBITUARIES AND OTHER SOURCES:

BOOKS

Authors of Books for Young People, 3rd edition, Scarecrow, 1990.

PERIODICALS

New York Times, July 2, 1992, p. D19.

S

SAKERS, Don 1958-

PERSONAL: Surname is pronounced "*say*-kers"; born June 16, 1958, in Yokosuka, Japan; son of James Emory (in the U.S. Navy) and Naomi (a homemaker; maiden name, Coates) Sakers. *Education:* Loyola College, B.A., 1980. *Politics:* "Technocrat." *Religion:* Atheist.

ADDRESSES: Home—P.O. Box 265, Linthicum, MD 21090. *Office*—AACPL, 5 Harry S. Truman Pkwy, Annapolis, MD 21401. *Agent*—James Allen, 538 East Harford St., Milford, PA 18337.

CAREER: Anne Arundel County Public Library, Annapolis, MD, library associate, 1980—; writer.

WRITINGS:

Act Well Your Part, Alyson, 1986.
Lucky in Love, Alyson, 1987.
The Leaves of October, Baen Books, 1988.
(Editor) *Carmen Miranda's Ghost Is Haunting Space Station Three,* Baen Books, 1990.

WORK IN PROGRESS: The Paths of the Scattered Worlds, a science fiction novel, completion expected in 1992; *Lightyears,* a television script, completion expected in 1993; researching Western colonialism, Native American history, and the history of the Hope diamond.

SIDELIGHTS: Don Sakers told *SATA:* "I started my first novel in a black-and-white copybook when I was twelve years old. By the third novel, at about age fifteen, I'd learned to type and started submitting stories to science-fiction magazines. My first story was accepted when I was twenty-one, which just goes to show that perseverance is the most valuable quality a beginning writer can have.

"Folks who want to be writers are always asking me for my advice; the best thing I can tell them is to WRITE— that's the only way to learn and get better. Unless you're a very unusual case, you will throw out the first million words you write. Only during the second million will you start to sell.

"Recently I have come to recognize some persistent themes in my writing. However, when I announced my discoveries to some friends, they laughed and told me that they'd known about these themes all along. Just for the record, though, here are some of the things that I've realized I like to write about:

"The perfectibility of mankind. I believe—and have seen plenty of evidence to back up the belief—that human beings are able to surpass and transcend their own limits, whatever those limits may be. Others see Helen Keller as an exceptional type of person; I feel that we are *all* potential Helen Kellers. I regret that many people don't choose to live up to that potential. My novel *The Leaves of October* was (in part) an attempt to show the sort of marvelous future that the human race has before it. I don't claim that mankind *will* develop in the directions I described, only that we *could.* In *Lightyears* I present another—and I hope equally attractive—vision of what mankind could choose to become.

"Immortality. I suspect that I write science fiction because it gives me the opportunity to have characters whose lives are the length of historical eras. The 'Hlutr' characters in *Leaves of October* are tree-like creatures who live anywhere from a few hundred to (in an extreme case) three billion years. The members of the Hoister family each live over ten thousand years—and then they're brought back again later. In *Lightyears* we have the curious case of an occupied planet on which nobody dies anymore.

"Do I think that humans really can live that long? I wouldn't put anything past us. So many things in today's world give promise of longer productive lives: the Human Genome Project, nanotechnology, cryonics, artificial intelligence research.

"The primacy of knowledge. As a librarian and a writer I am convinced that mankind's store of knowledge is the greatest treasure we possess. Two missions that are among the most noble we have ever undertaken are the preservation of the race's knowledge and the effort to make that knowledge as accessible as possible to as many people as possible. Those who are engaged in those missions—librarians, information technologists and theorists, programmers and hardware-makers, the publishing industry—these are the real heroes of the twenty-first century."

*   *   *

SAVITZ, Harriet May 1933-

PERSONAL: Born May 19, 1933, in Newark, NJ; daughter of Samuel and Susan (Trulick) Blatstein; married Ephraim Savitz (a pharmacist); children: Beth, Steven. *Education:* Attended evening classes at Upsala College, one year, and Rutgers University, one year. *Religion:* Jewish.

ADDRESSES: Home—412 Park Place Ave., Bradley Beach, NJ 07720. *Agent*—Curtis Brown Ltd., 10 Astor Place, New York, NY 10003.

CAREER: Writer. Teacher of writing, Philadelphia Writer's Conference; guest lecturer in English literature, University of Pennsylvania. Holds workshops in novel-writing; helped organize workshop at Philadelphia's Free Library for the Blind to sensitize the media to the needs of the disabled.

MEMBER: National League of American Pen Women, National Wheelchair Athletic Association, Disabled in Action, VEEP (Very Exciting Education Program), Pennsylvania Wheelchair Athletic Association, Children's Reading Round Table, Philadelphia (co-founder, 1965; member of steering committee, 1966—).

AWARDS, HONORS: Dorothy Canfield Fisher Memorial Children's Book Award nomination, 1971, for *Fly, Wheels, Fly!*; *The Lionhearted* was listed in University of Iowa's Books for Young Adults, 1975-76, among the most popular books read by teenagers; Outstanding Author Award, Pennsylvania School Library Association, 1981; received recognition for *Wheelchair Champions,* 1981, from the President's Committee for the Handicapped in celebration of the International Year of Disabled Persons; California Young Reader Medal nomination, high school category, 1983-84, for *Run, Don't Walk.*

WRITINGS:

JUVENILE FICTION

(With Maria Caporale Shecktor) *The Moon Is Mine* (short stories), illustrated by Charles Robinson, John Day, 1968.
(With Shecktor) *Peter and Other Stories,* John Day, 1969.
Fly, Wheels, Fly!, John Day, 1970.
On the Move, John Day, 1973.
The Lionhearted, John Day, 1975.
Run, Don't Walk, Watts, 1979.
Wait Until Tomorrow, New American Library, 1981.

HARRIET MAY SAVITZ

If You Can't Be the Sun, Be a Star, New American Library, 1982.
Come Back, Mr. Magic, New American Library, 1983.
Summer's End, New American Library, 1984.
Swimmer, Scholastic Inc., 1986.
The Cats Nobody Wanted, Scholastic Inc., 1989.
(With K. Michael Syring) *The Pail of Nails,* illustrated by Charles Shaw, Abingdon, 1990.
The Bullies & Me, Scholastic Inc., 1991.

NONFICTION

Consider—Understanding Disability as a Way of Life, Sister Kenny Institute, 1975.
Wheelchair Champions: A History of Wheelchair Sports, Crowell, 1978.
The Sweat and the Gold, illustrated by David C. Page, VEEP, 1984.

OTHER

Contributor of short stories to collections, including *Short Story Scene;* contributor to *Encyclopaedia Britannica.* Contributor to magazines and newspapers, including *Philadelphia Inquirer, Denver Post, Scholastic, Boys' Life, Children's Friend,* and *Ranger Rick.*

ADAPTATIONS: Run, Don't Walk was adapted and produced as an American Broadcasting Company "Afterschool Special" by Henry Winkler's production company.

SIDELIGHTS: Caring for others—for the handicapped, the lonely, or the disadvantaged—is a theme that runs through most of Harriet May Savitz's books for young adults. Her motivation may be an unfair law or lack of protection for a significant part of the population. From childhood, she was especially sensitive to the needs of others, as she explained in an essay for *Something about the Author Autobiography Series* (*SAAS*): "I was always looking at life with a third eye, an eye that I sometimes

wished were closed. Why did I have to see the unhap-
piness in someone's face, or hear the pain in his voice?"
But eventually this empathy helped Savitz create believable characters in her fiction: "I learned to use this third
eye .... Dialogue became more than just words. It
became words mixed with movement and expression
and atmosphere. Characters had to be molded like
pieces of clay, only instead of being objects that were set
on a bureau, or shelf, they were meant to move about
and come to life and I had the ability to make them do
so."

Savitz was born in Newark, New Jersey, in 1933. Her
father lost all of his savings during the Depression, so
she spent much of her childhood living in a third-floor
walk-up apartment in Hackensack where the trains on
the railroad below made her bed shake. During these
years, she found a sense of security in books and in her
imagination. She began writing poems at age nine, and
discovered at this early age—when the neighborhood
bully took her scrapbook and was so impressed by her
poetry that he never bothered Savitz again—that she
could touch people with her words.

The family's finances would not allow Savitz to attend a
four-year college, so she tried many types of work, but "I
lost just about every job I acquired after graduating high
school," she explained in *SAAS*. "I always wrote short
stories, poems, and articles on the job." Still not willing
to give up the idea of college, two nights a week after
work she studied poetry, philosophy, and logic at
Rutgers University, but without earning credits. Even
after she married and became a mother, she continued
to write. "I wrote a newsletter for the community where
I lived, a short children's story for a religious organization, and many, many long letters, almost short stories
in themselves, to friends, to politicians, to editors in the
newspaper, to whomever would listen. The words were
fighting their way out," she related in *SAAS*.

After her mother's death Savitz discovered that her
mother had treasured every bit of writing she had done
from the age of nine. About that same time she received
in the mail an advertisement for a creative writing class.
"Always one for believing that fate should not be
denied, I felt it was a sign of what I was to do. I enrolled
in the course and sold the first interview that we were
assigned," she recalled in *SAAS*. "After ten years of
floundering, I had my foot on the first rung of the
ladder. All those years I had felt like a writer. Now I was
being treated like one." She went on to complete
numerous interviews, meeting all kinds of interesting
people, learning her craft, and getting paid for it. Soon
she began collaborating with Maria Caporale Shecktor,
the teacher of her fiction course, on short stories and
poetry for children. Together they published *The Moon
Is Mine* in 1968 and *Peter, and Other Stories* in 1969.

At an autograph party for *Peter, and Other Stories*,
Savitz's editor, Mary Walsh, introduced her to a person
who became very important to the direction of her
writing career: Charles L. Blockson, a black-history
scholar and a promoter of wheelchair sports for the

The life of a handicapped teenager forms the basis for
Fly, Wheels, Fly! (Cover illustration by Charles
Walker.)

disabled. Through their interest in wheelchair sports,
and with the input of quadriplegic Edward A. Davenport, Savitz became deeply involved in making the
public more aware of the disabled—a dynamic but
almost ignored segment of the population. She began by
publishing several fiction books based on the lives of
handicapped teenagers, including *Fly, Wheels, Fly!, On
the Move,* and *The Lionhearted*. After researching the
subject intensively, attending wheelchair sporting events
and traveling with the teams, Savitz wrote her landmark
nonfiction book *Wheelchair Champions*, published in
1978. Besides the compelling stories of champions, the
book also contains a list of goals for the future and a list
of questions for readers to consider under the heading
"If You Were Suddenly Disabled."

One memorable event that served to inspire all who
participated in or witnessed it was Savitz's "incredible
journey," when she accompanied Davenport on a 110-
mile trip at three miles an hour from Norristown to the
capitol in Harrisburg, Pennsylvania—he in his motor-
ized wheelchair and she following in a car. Davenport
organized the journey to call public attention to the
need for Transbus, a low-floored, ramped bus that
handicapped and senior citizens could easily board. On
the way they learned how treacherous the route really
was—especially for Davenport, who braved weather,
insects, traffic, railroad tracks, exhaust fumes, and dust.

In her account for *SAAS,* Savitz noted, "We [also] learned about love, the love of the people waiting for us at the next stop, with food, with lodging, with hope. The disabled followed our route and often would be there on the side of the road, waiting to join Ed for a while." By traveling eleven hours a day they made it to Harrisburg on September 6, 1978. The newspaper headline the next day read "Wheelchair Odyssey Ends With Invitation to Speak," and Davenport concluded his mission by speaking before the State Transportation Commission.

In 1979 Savitz published *Run, Don't Walk,* the story of two teenagers who use wheelchairs, one with a golden retriever as a guide dog. Savitz was pleased when the book was made into an American Broadcasting Company "Afterschool Special" produced by Henry Winkler. A 1990 *Reader's Guide for Parents of Children with Mental, Physical, or Emotional Disabilities* cited the book as "a gripping, contemporary story" about the personal, social, and political barriers that the handicapped must overcome.

Recently Savitz moved to the New Jersey shore, which has been a healing and restoring influence since her family vacationed there during her childhood. But at the time, "I didn't know the ocean would become my next

story. I didn't know that the waves would begin vomiting medical waste upon the beaches—syringes, bottles of blood instead of starfish and sea glass. I didn't know there would be oil slicks and garbage, all kinds of garbage left upon the beaches," she admitted in *SAAS.* "My poor friend was ill and suffering and the human population was responsible and I could not sit silently by while my friend suffered." Savitz addressed this problem by writing a young adult novel about ocean dumping.

Savitz once commented, "I find that the books walk into my life.... Sometimes I just stand somewhere, sit somewhere, walk somewhere, and I feel it. The book. It's around me, and if I look carefully, listen intently, and let myself feel its presence, the book introduces itself. 'How do you do,' I say. 'Let's get on with it,' it answers. From that moment on there is no other world."

WORKS CITED:

Moore, Cory, *A Reader's Guide for Parents of Children with Mental, Physical, or Emotional Disabilities,* Woodbine House, 1990.

Savitz, Harriet May, essay in *Something about the Author Autobiography Series,* Volume 9, Gale, 1990.

Savitz's story about the friendship between two wheelchair-bound teens in *Run, Don't Walk* was adapted as an *ABC Afterschool Special* starring Scott Baio and Toni Kalem.

FOR MORE INFORMATION SEE:

BOOKS

Fifth Book of Junior Authors and Illustrators, pp. 272-74, H. W. Wilson Co., 1983.
Something about the Author, Volume 5, Gale, 1973.

PERIODICALS

Bulletin of the Center for Children's Books, November, 1973; November, 1978.*

*   *   *

SAWYER, (Frederick) Don(ald) 1947-

PERSONAL: Born April 28, 1947, in Ypsilanti, MI; son of Frederick Donald (an engineer) and Carleton (a home economist; maiden name, Farish) Sawyer; married Jan Henig (a literacy instructor), December, 1969; children: Melissa, Farish. *Education:* Michigan State University, B.A. (cum laude), 1969, M.A., 1973; attended University of British Columbia, 1969-70. *Politics:* "Member of New Democratic Party." *Religion:* Humanist. *Hobbies and other interests:* Hiking, cross-country skiing, fitness, swimming, reading, gardening, cultural studies, and international issues.

ADDRESSES: Home—Box 2653, Salmon Arm, British Columbia, Canada V1E 4R5. *Office*—Native Adult Education Resource Centre, Okanagan College, Box 610, Salmon Arm, British Columbia, Canada V1E 4N7.

CAREER: Gill Memorial Central High School, Musgrave Harbour, Newfoundland, teacher, 1970-72; Institute for International Studies in Education, Michigan State University, East Lansing, research assistant, 1972-73; Kumsheen Secondary School, Lytton, British Columbia, teacher, 1973-75; Spallumcheen Indian Band, Enderby, British Columbia, coordinating teacher in Adult Basic Education Program, 1976-78; Simon Fraser University, Burnaby, British Columbia, faculty associate in charge of North Okanagan Native Teacher Education Program, 1978-80, instructor, 1981-82; Okanagan College, Salmon Arm, British Columbia, instructor in adult basic education, 1980-88; Native Adult Education Resource Centre, Salmon Arm, curriculum director, 1988—. Principal of consulting firm, Native Education Services Associates, 1981—; curriculum project leader, Ministry of Advanced Education and Job Training, 1983-84, 1986.

MEMBER: Adult Basic Education Association of British Columbia (president, 1983-85).

WRITINGS:

Tomorrow Is School and I'm Sick to the Heart Thinking About It, Douglas & McIntyre, 1979, reprinted as *Tomorrow Is School,* Goodread, 1984.
(With others) *ABE English and Communications Curriculum Guide,* Ministry of Post-Secondary Education, 1982.
(With Howard Green) *NESA Bibliography for Native Studies,* Tillacum Library, 1983.

(With others) *Native Literacy and Life Skills Curriculum Guidelines,* Ministry of Post-Secondary Education, 1984.
NESA Activities Handbook for Native and Multicultural Classrooms, Tillacum Library, Volume 1, 1984, Volume 3, 1993.
ABE English Resource Kit, Ministry of Advanced Education and Job Training, 1987.
Where the Rivers Meet, Pemmican, 1988.
Donna Meets Coyote, Secwepemc Cultural Education Society, 1988.
(With Art Napoleon) *Native English Curriculum Guidelines,* Ministry of Advanced Education and Job Training, 1991.
Adventures with Miss Flint, Thistledown, 1993.

Also author of curriculum materials and contributor of articles and poems to periodicals, including *B. C. Teacher, Canadian Journal of Native Education, Fiddlehead, Interior Voice, Journal of Reading,* and *Quarry.*

WORK IN PROGRESS: Running, a young adult novel; research on native literacy and learning styles, and writing instruction.

SIDELIGHTS: "I have spent the last twenty years as an educator in areas very different from the flat social topography of Birmingham, Michigan, where I grew up," Don Sawyer once wrote. "Working first as a teacher in rural Newfoundland, and then with Native people in British Columbia, I was exposed to the outrages of poverty and oppression, and the failings of an educational system designed to ignore them. But I also gained entrance into the richness, depth, and resilience of cultures very different from what I had known.

"The intensity of these experiences inspired two of my books, one a nonfiction account of teaching in New-

DON SAWYER

WHERE THE RIVERS MEET

Don Sawyer

"This is a very powerful book...Pemmican brings the Native reality beautifully to the rest of Canada, and I think this is the most powerful book they have done. Really well worth the read."

Cathy Lowinger, CBC's "Morningside"

In Sawyer's sensitive novel, a Native American high school student in British Columbia struggles for a better life in the face overwhelming prejudice. (Cover illustration by Gilbert Freynet.)

foundland, and the other a young adult novel about growing up Indian. I have directed a Native teacher training program, taught adult education for Okanagan College, and presently I direct curriculum for a provincial Native adult education center affiliated with the college. Recent projects range from developing a provincial training program for instructors working with Native adults to organizing a national aboriginal literacy conference."

Sawyer's first book, *Tomorrow Is School and I'm Sick to the Heart Thinking About It,* is a condemnation of Newfoundland's education system, characterized by high dropout rates and widespread illiteracy in the community where Sawyer and his wife were teachers from 1970 to 1972. Sawyer, who taught high school, and his wife, Jan, who instructed the lower grades, found shabby conditions and apathy among students, teachers, and administrators when they took on their positions. Toronto *Globe and Mail* reviewer William French noted, "The [high school] building was badly designed, poorly maintained and almost bereft of even the minimum of necessary equipment. The teachers were demoralized or indifferent, teaching an absurdly irrelevant

curriculum to hostile and sullen students who failed because they were expected to fail." The elementary school building was worse, lacking even indoor plumbing. The principal was responsible for emptying into the ocean the plastic trash bags that served as latrines.

Despite the daunting obstacles, Sawyer found ways to reach his students, including comic books and music. Still, he was no match for the inflexible, old-fashioned system, and found after two years that his efforts had resulted in limited changes. Said W. R. Steur, writing in the *Winnipeg Free Press,* "In the end students respond to [Sawyer's] way of teaching, although they still have to cope with the other teachers and with the school as a whole, an insensitive place that frustrates their originality and ignores their deeper needs."

Lynda Nykor, writing in Ontario's *London Free Press,* found *Tomorrow Is School* an enlightening look at a province still unfamiliar to many Canadians, noting that Sawyer discusses "virtually every aspect of Newfoundland life, the political, the economic, the religious. He also mourns a passing way of life. Newfoundlanders, born and raised to be fishermen and boat builders, are ill-prepared to face a future that's made that untenable. If ever a people were victimized by the mere passage of time, it's these."

Sawyer's novel, based on his experiences with Native education in British Columbia, presents a more optimistic view. In *Where the Rivers Meet,* a high school girl in a British Columbian community struggles to complete her education and secure a better life than most of her Native Canadian relatives have had. She finds comfort and pride in her heritage through a series of ancient rituals, and returns to face her goals with renewed strength. A reviewer for *Children's Book News* noted that the novel is accurate in its portrayal of the problems facing Native youths, but offers a plausible solution as well. "The details of Nancy's story may shock readers," the reviewer stated, "but the strength of her character provides more than a glimmering of hope in the end."

WORKS CITED:

French, William, "Teaching in the outport: an invitation to cultural trauma," *Globe and Mail* (Toronto), August 9, 1979.
Nykor, Lynda, "Account of life in Newfoundland given in brilliant tones of truth," *London Free Press* (Ontario), September 1, 1979.
Steur, W. R., "Two types of education," *Winnipeg Free Press,* February 9, 1980.
Review of *Where the Rivers Meet, Children's Book News,* summer, 1989.

*   *   *

SCOLTOCK, Jack 1942-
(A. Zebra)

PERSONAL: Born August 19, 1942, in Derry, Northern Ireland; son of James Frederick (an engineer) and Kathleen (a homemaker; maiden name, McGuinness)

JACK SCOLTOCK

Scoltock; married Ursula Bridget Bradley (a hairdresser), December 2, 1967; children: Jason, Justine. *Politics:* "Apolitical." *Religion:* Catholic. *Hobbies and other interests:* Scuba diving.

ADDRESSES: Home—27 Caw Park, Waterside, Derry, Northern Ireland BT471LZ. *Office*—Marine Sports, 119 Spencer Rd., Derry, Northern Ireland BT471AE.

CAREER: Worked as a bricklayer in Derry, Northern Ireland and England, 1959-67; Molins Engineering, Maydown, Campsie, Derry, engineering inspector, 1971-85; Marine Sports (a scuba-diving equipment business), Derry, Northern Ireland, owner, 1985—.

AWARDS, HONORS: Best Fiction Award for short story, Downtown Radio (Newtownards, Northern Ireland), 1990, for "County Champion Three Times."

WRITINGS:

Quest of the Royal Twins, illustrated by Jeanette Dunne, Wolfhound Press, 1988.
(Under pseudonym A. Zebra) *A Rumble in the Jungle,* illustrated by Cathy Dineen, Wolfhound Press, 1989.
Badger, Beano and the Magic Mushroom, illustrated by Jeanette Dunne, Wolfhound Press, 1990.
Jeremy's Adventure, illustrated by Aileen Caffrey, Wolfhound Press, 1991.
Seek the Enchanted Antlers, Wolfhound Press, 1992.
Fairy Girl, Wolfhound Press, 1992.
The Magic of Fungie, Wolfhound Press, in press.

Also author of play *Hope in the Derry Workhouse.* Contributor of short stories to the anthologies *Devenish Island,* Western Library Board, 1986, and *Borderlines,* Holiday Projects West, 1988. Also contributor to periodicals, including *Tatler, Fingerpost, Treasure Hunting,*

Writer's Companion, Derry Journal, Belfast Telegraph, Northern Woman, and *Sentinel.*

ADAPTATIONS: The short story, "County Champion Three Times," was performed by local actors on Downtown Radio in Derry, Northern Ireland, in 1990.

WORK IN PROGRESS: Researching the siege of Derry, Northern Ireland, for use in a children's novel.

SIDELIGHTS: Jack Scoltock told *SATA:* "I was born in Derry and grew up in the 'Waterside' part of the city. I had a happy childhood, though when I was very young, my father and mother divorced. I was always an avid reader of comic books, which I still collect and read, though I can't get American or Canadian comics now (too expensive). I firmly believe that reading comics was what developed my imagination. Being the eldest of a family of three I used to pretend I could see things in the light bulb, and I would make up stories for my brother and sister in our bedroom at night. They still remember this. The local cinema, 'The Midland,' was also a great developer of my imagination. Like many other children in Waterside I spent many happy hours there.

Badger—also called the Grey One—and his faithful dog Beano are called into the magical Beyond to help save the population from catastrophe. (Cover illustration by Jeanette Dunne.)

"I joined the Brooke Park Library when I was old enough and my favourite novels were Mark Twain's *Huckleberry Finn, Tom Sawyer,* and, particularly, *A Connecticut Yankee in King Arthur's Court.* These were books I read often. *A Connecticut Yankee,* a story in which the hero is transported to another time, really caught my imagination and some of my children's novels have this theme of being transported to other worlds and times. My favourite modern writer is Terry Brooks.

"I started scribbling when I had an accident to my ankle, which ended my bricklaying career. In 1971 I was one of thirteen Derry divers who found the Spanish Armada wreck of 'La Trinidad Valencera' off the coast of Donegal, Ireland, twenty-five miles away. As an active diver with the Derry Sub-Aqua Club my imagination developed even further. My novel, due out shortly, has a diving theme. At the moment titled *The Magic of Fungie,* it is about twins and their father who drive from Derry to Dingle to dive with the famous dolphin Fungie.

"In Derry most of us were poor, but we were happy. The traumatic experience of the troubles changed all that. Over twenty years ago when the bombing and killing of both Protestant and Catholic sections of the community where I live began, I started to write as a way of relaxation. My writing really began to develop then. Two of my short stories about this situation followed, one an allegory called *A Rumble in the Jungle,* about the animals in the jungle seeking their animal rights (civil rights) and one animal, one say (one man, one vote). My publisher advised me to use the pseudonym A. Zebra because of the touchy subject matter. It was published in 1989. Though life here in Derry is much more peaceful, I am still writing and hope to be able to write for a long time to come.

"During the troubles I wrote quite a few short stories. One of them, called 'Who Killed Bambi?,' received great praise and was published in an anthology of short stories by the Western [Ireland] Library Board. The story is about a small boy, his father who is in the Irish Republican Army (IRA), and a white deer the boy finds injured in the hills above Derry.

"I have read my stories 'Ouija' and 'The Customer Isn't Always Right' on British Broadcasting Service (BBC) radio, and the story 'One Halloween Night in Derry' on Highland radio, and have been interviewed about my writing on other radio stations.

"In 1988 my first novel, *Quest of the Royal Twins,* was published and I have had a novel published every year since. I do produce quite an amount of writing during the winter. My shop does more trade in the summer, so I am lucky enough to have more time for my writing in the slacker winter months.

"My novel *Jeremy's Adventure* is about animal experimentation, which I abhor. I believe that the young should be educated about this so they can be aware that the makeup and shampoo their parents are using are

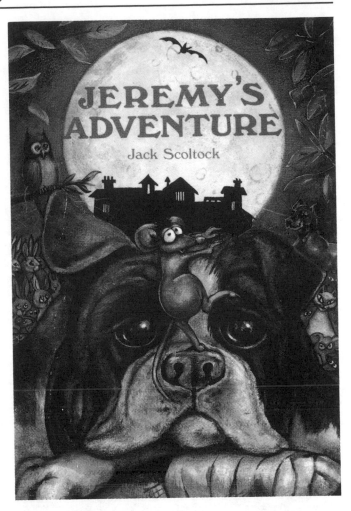

On Christmas Eve, Jeremy the mouse sets out to rescue his friends and family from their imprisonment in the **Black Building.** (Cover illustration by Aileen Caffrey.)

animal experimentation-free. Children don't like to be preached to, but through writing they can be educated in an enjoyable way about animal experimentation.

"Finally, this year I turn fifty and will have been married twenty-five years. I hope to be writing until I die. My hobby is writing, and this plus the feedback I receive from children give me a lot of enjoyment. I have never been particularly concerned about criticism from adults. It is the children's opinions I value most."

*　　*　　*

SINGER, A. L.
See LERANGIS, Peter

*　　*　　*

SINYKIN, Sheri Cooper 1950-

PERSONAL: Legal name, Sheril; surname is pronounced "*sin*-i-kin"; born May 3, 1950, in Chicago, IL; daughter of Norman (an optometrist) and Barbara (an elementary schoolteacher; maiden name, Kresteller) Cooper; married Daniel Sinykin (an attorney and land developer), August 18, 1974; children: Aaron Joel, Rudi

Samuel, Joshua Paul. *Education:* Stanford University, B.A., 1972. *Politics:* Democrat. *Religion:* Jewish. *Hobbies and other interests:* Aerobic dance, collecting dolls from other countries, traveling, speaking foreign languages.

ADDRESSES: Home—26 Lancaster Ct., Madison, WI 53719-1433. *Agent*—Marilyn Marlow, 10 Astor Place, New York, NY 10003.

CAREER: Rockford Newspapers, Rockford, IL, reporter, 1972; Madison General Hospital, Madison, WI, public relations coordinator, 1972-75; Greater Madison Convention and Visitors Bureau, Madison, assistant executive director, 1975-78; children's author.

MEMBER: Society of Children's Book Writers (Wisconsin regional advisor), Children's Reading Round Table, Council for Wisconsin Writers.

AWARDS, HONORS: Ed Press Award, Educational Press Association of America, 1986, for *Humpty Dumpty* story "Mostly I Share ... But Sometimes I Don't."

WRITINGS:

Shrimpboat and Gym Bags, Atheneum, 1990.
Come Out, Come Out, Wherever You Are!, Hazelden, 1990.
Apart at the Seams, Hazelden, 1991.
Next Thing to Strangers, Lothrop, 1991.

SHERI COOPER SINYKIN

The Buddy Trap, Atheneum, 1991.
Slate Blues, Lothrop, in press.

Also author of stories, including "Mostly I Share ... But Sometimes I Don't" and "The Best Thing about Shadows." Work represented in reading textbooks published by C. E. Merrill. Contributor of stories to periodicals, including *Jack and Jill, Humpty Dumpty, Child Life, Children's Playmate, Children's Digest, Redbook, Turtle,* and *Children's Album. Stanford* magazine, "Class of '72" correspondent, 1972—.

WORK IN PROGRESS: Several middle-grade novels, including *Sirens,* a fantasy-thriller, and a fantasy time travel.

SIDELIGHTS: Sheri Cooper Sinykin told *SATA:* "Ever since third grade I knew that I wanted to be a writer. My teacher that year sparked my imagination, and I used to spend recesses working on chapter books that knew no end. My life, however, seemed a boring source for ideas. At the time, I didn't recognize and appreciate my own uniqueness; now, it seems a bottomless mine of potential ideas.

"As the eldest of four children, I spent much of my childhood babysitting, reading, and daydreaming—and trying to fulfill my parents' and my own expectations. A dutiful and high achieving student, I was particularly uncomfortable with expressing negative feelings and found writing, especially poetry, the only way I could permit myself these emotions. From third grade until the present day, my parents have always believed in my dream of becoming a writer and, in fact, surprised me upon high school graduation by publishing a volume of my poetry, entitled *In Shining Amor.*

"An adolescent stint with a junior ballet company in which I danced the only male role, a distorted body image, and my hesitance to express negative feelings conspired to push me into using food as a way to manage my emotions for many years. My resulting eating disorder and my ongoing recovery have played a significant role in both my motivation for writing and in the themes that interest me. *Come Out, Come Out, Wherever You Are!,* my picture book on overeating and self-esteem, and *Apart at the Seams,* my young adult novel about a young dancer's struggle with bulimia, in particular, were born of this pain.

"Because my eating disorder essentially arrested my emotional development at the age of twelve or thirteen, I seem to understand and identify with children in that age group. Their desire to fit in, to be accepted, is one I share, even as an adult. I write hopeful books, the kind I wished I had read in my youth. My goal is not to 'plant messages' but rather to entertain and to connect with the reader's experience. Still, if young readers glean something meaningful that they can use in their lives long after they have closed my books, I will feel gratified.

"My husband and three young sons are a constant source of inspiration, ideas, and encouragement. My

The experiences of Sinykin's son Aaron were the inspiration for this novel about competitive gymnastics.

first book, *Shrimpboat and Gym Bags,* grew out of Aaron's experiences with competitive gymnastics. *The Buddy Trap* was inspired by Rudi's dislike of what were called 'war games' at his summer camp. *Next Thing to Strangers* sprang from our family's visit with my parents at their senior citizens' trailer park in Arizona. Since two of my sons are shorter than other boys their age and I've shared their frustrations, the theme of physical differences influences my work. Because I am fascinated by the interplay between generations, by the similarities and the differences of young readers and their older relatives, I often incorporate such characters in my work."

*　　*　　*

SLOSS, Lesley Lord 1965-

PERSONAL: Born July 9, 1965, in Glasgow, Scotland; daughter of William James (a forensic scientist) and Margaret (a teacher; maiden name, McIntosh) Rodger; married Martyn Sloss (in electronics and computing), October 17, 1986; children: Daniel Jamie. *Education:* Graduated from Edinburgh University (with honours), 1986; CNAA, Ph.D., 1991. *Religion:* Church of Scotland.

ADDRESSES: Home—161 Norbiton Hall, Birkenhead Ave., Kingston, Surrey KT2 2RB, England. *Office*—c/o IEA Coal Research, 10-18 Putney Hill, Putney, London SW15 6AA, England.

CAREER: National Collection of Type Cultures, London, England, research post at central public health labs, 1986-90; IEA Coal Research, London, consultant and technical author in environment group, 1990—. Former Cub Scout leader.

WRITINGS:

Anthony and the Aardvark, Lothrop, 1990.
Freddy Teddy Bear, Gondola, 1990.

Also author of *Freddy Teddy's Eye,* in *My First Story Book,* Brimax Books, 1991; and *The Thing That Lived under the Bed,* in *My Bedtime Storybook,* Brimax Books, 1991. Also author of poems and short stories. Author of numerous scientific papers.

WORK IN PROGRESS: The Mayor of Puddletown Deli and *Running Away,* both children's books; a story for seven- to eleven-year-olds.

SIDELIGHTS: Lesley Lord Sloss told *SATA:* "I started writing in 1986 to pass the time on a twice-daily, one hour thirty minute trip on London transport from my houseboat on the Thames to my Ph.D. research job. I used to type straight into a little lap-top word processor, much to the interest of my co-passengers. Then and even now I find it almost impossible to write longhand, preferring to type directly into a machine. Machines can spell, I cannot. Machines write neatly, I do not. Anyone can read a printout from a computer; no one—not even me—can read my handwriting. The pen doesn't travel fast enough for my brain. It lags behind losing words and joining others together at random until the final

LESLEY LORD SLOSS

Anthony and the Aardvark

Lesley Sloss · Gus Clarke

Humor forms the basis for this story of mistaken identity. (Cover illustration by Gus Clarke.)

product reads like a Chinese menu instead of a children's book.

"I don't read—well, that's not entirely true—I read the labels on tins and the occasional street sign, but that is enough for me. I went through a phase of sitting in the children's department of book shops and reading all the new material to see what was selling (because at that stage it certainly wasn't my stuff), but I then found that I was going home and writing 'new' stories that had been written before. My brain was plagiarizing without telling me. Now I avoid reading children's books completely, apart from those I read to my son. Adult books are beyond me really—too many long descriptive passages and clever between-the-lines writing. I prefer total action stuff, and that's what I write. You won't find any 'deep rolling green plains reflecting golden sunlight' or whatever in any of my material.

"The short stories that I have written are merely the tip of the iceberg. I have written a few longer works—twenty thousand words or more, and my publisher seemed very interested but they take so much longer to write! Now I write full-time about scientific matters. Coming home at night and writing even more is not as much fun as it used to be. Anyway, I now have offspring to rear and they take up a lot of time. So do husbands. Mine has several ideas for full-length bodice-ripping adult books which he reckons will make us our fortune. His writing skills stretch as far as signing his name at the bottom of an occasional cheque, so he says it's up to me to put it all on paper. It's never that easy. He has his ideas of what it should be like and I, of course, write in my own style—it's the only one I've got. It's a big step from 'Freddy Teddy woke up one morning' to 'Abigail found herself being propelled back against the bed, her blouse simultaneously falling around her waist, exposing

her ...' and so on. So don't hold your breath for the name Lesley Sloss to appear next to Jackie Collins in the newsagent.

"By the way, the name is real. It's not a pseudonym or a pen name. Give me some credit! If I was going to make up a name, I would have chosen something far more believable. I don't know where the name comes from—apart from the fact that I obviously got it from my husband."

* * *

SLOTE, Alfred 1926-
(A. H. Garnet)

PERSONAL: Born September 11, 1926, in New York, NY; son of Oscar (an insurance broker) and Sallie (an interior decorator; maiden name, Persky) Slote; married Henrietta Howell (retired assistant to the Dean of the University of Michigan Law School), August 23, 1951; children: John, Elizabeth, Ben. *Education:* University of Michigan, B.A., 1949, M.A., 1950; attended University of Grenoble, 1950. *Hobbies and other interests:* Sports.

ADDRESSES: Home—Ann Arbor, MI.

CAREER: Williams College, Williamstown, MA, instructor in English, 1953-56; University of Michigan Television Center, Ann Arbor, 1956-82, began as producer and writer, became associate director, 1968-73, executive producer, 1973-82; writer. Lecturer on children's literature at University of Michigan and Univer-

ALFRED SLOTE

sity of California, Davis. *Military service:* U.S. Navy, 1944-46.

MEMBER: Authors Guild of America, Phi Beta Kappa.

AWARDS, HONORS: Avery and Jule Hopwood Award in creative writing, University of Michigan, 1949; Fulbright scholar, 1950; Friends of American Writers Award, 1971, for *Jake;* Nene Award, Hawaii Library Association and Hawaii Association of School Librarians, 1981, for *My Robot Buddy;* Edgar Allan Poe runnerup, 1983, for *Clone Catcher.*

WRITINGS:

FOR CHILDREN

The Princess Who Wouldn't Talk, illustrated by Ursula Arndt, Bobbs-Merrill, 1964.
The Moon in Fact and Fancy, World Publishing, 1967, revised edition, 1971.
Air in Fact and Fancy, World Publishing, 1968.
Stranger on the Ball Club, Lippincott, 1970.
Jake, Lippincott, 1971.
The Biggest Victory, Lippincott, 1972.
My Father, the Coach, Lippincott, 1972.
Hang Tough, Paul Mather, Lippincott, 1973.
Tony and Me, Lippincott, 1974.
Matt Gargan's Boy, Lippincott, 1975.
My Robot Buddy, illustrated by Joel Schick, Lippincott, 1975.
The Hot Shot, photographs by William LaCrosse, Watts, 1977.
My Trip to Alpha I, illustrated by Harold Berson, Lippincott, 1978.
Love and Tennis, Macmillan, 1979.
The Devil Rides with Me and Other Fantastic Stories, Methuen, 1980.
C.O.L.A.R.: A Tale of Outer Space, illustrated by Anthony Kramer, Lippincott, 1981.
Clone Catcher, illustrated by Elizabeth Slote, Lippincott, 1982.
Rabbit Ears, Lippincott, 1982.
Omega Station, illustrated by Anthony Kramer, Lippincott, 1983.
The Trouble on Janus, Lippincott, 1985.
Moving In, Lippincott, 1988.
A Friend Like That, Lippincott, 1988.
Make-Believe Ballplayer, illustrated by Tom Newsom, Lippincott, 1989.
The Trading Game, HarperCollins, 1990.
Finding Buck McHenry, HarperCollins, 1991.

Also author of a series of children's television programs titled *The Art of Storytelling.*

FOR ADULTS

Denham Proper (novel), Putnam, 1953.
Lazarus in Vienna (novel), McGraw Hill, 1956.
Strangers and Comrades (novel), Simon & Schuster, 1964.
(With Woodrow W. Hunter) *Preparation for Retirement* (stories), University of Michigan Press, 1968.

Termination: The Closing at Baker Plant (nonfiction), Bobbs-Merrill, 1969.
(Under pseudonym A. H. Garnet; with Garnet Garrison) *The Santa Claus Killer,* Ticknor & Fields, 1981.
(Under pseudonym A. H. Garnet; with Garrison) *Maze,* Ticknor & Fields, 1982.

Also author of television programs, including *Science: Quest and Conquest* and *The Progress of Man.*

ADAPTATIONS: Jake was adapted as an "ABC Afterschool Special" titled *The Rag Tag Champs.*

SIDELIGHTS: Alfred Slote has distinguished himself as a knowledgeable writer of both sports and science-fiction books. A sports enthusiast—with a particular interest in baseball—since childhood, the author later became involved with his sons' little league teams. It was his son John who first suggested that Slote, then an author of novels for adults, write about children's sports. Though his response at the time, according to *Junior Literary Guild,* was "I play ball, John—I don't write about it," he eventually took his son's advice, and became known for his novels about little league baseball players. The author sets most of his works in his own Ann Arbor, Michigan neighborhood, referring to the town as "Arborville." While the protagonists in Slote's

Paul Mather's career as an ace Little League pitcher is put at risk when he discovers that he has leukemia.

books take baseball seriously and tend to be very involved with their teams, the novels are ultimately more concerned with the characters' relationships at home and at school and their growth as people. The novelist once commented, "I don't think of my books as baseball books specifically. Of course, they have a baseball background, but I think of them as books about young people and what happens to them."

Among Slote's better-known works is his 1973 novel, *Hang Tough, Paul Mather.* This story, which concerns a twelve-year-old little league pitcher battling leukemia, focuses on the main character's courage and determination. A *Kirkus Reviews* contributor noted that Slote "handles a sticky subject with finesse." Paul's family moves from California to Arborville so that he can be treated by a specialist there. Although forbidden to play baseball—the thing he loves most in the world—Paul forges his father's signature on a permission slip so that he can pitch in an important game against their rivals, the Ace Appliances. His expert pitching nearly brings the team victory, but Paul injures himself and requires hospitalization. There he meets his new doctor, Tom Kinsella, who—unlike Paul's previous doctors—understands him and treats him like a friend. Tom also lifts Paul's spirits by giving him a tape recorder to document his baseball triumphs. Paul dreams of winning the rematch with the Ace Appliances and convinces his parents and his doctor to let him watch from the sidelines. Although he cannot play, Paul finds a way to help his team win. Recalling that the opposing team's pitcher has trouble shutting out the usual taunting and jeering, Paul calls out a few phrases at opportune moments, causing the pitcher to lose his concentration and his sense of timing. His team's unexpected victory strengthens Paul's resolve to live. Zena Sutherland, writing in *Bulletin of the Center for Children's Books,* praised the novel's "depth and integrity."

Slote further explores the concept of a pitcher whose sensitivity impedes his pitching in his 1982 novel *Rabbit Ears.* Fifteen-year-old Tip O'Hara has a good arm and a sharp ear for music—as well as shouts from the opposing bench. When the other team teases him, he becomes distraught and has difficulty pitching and fielding. Soon the entire league knows of his weakness, and Tip becomes a complete failure on the mound. Tip's coach tries to help him overcome the problem, but finally, despite his talent and love for baseball, Tip quits the team. His bright eleven-year-old brother, Roland, then recruits Tip to play in his rock band. Roland has written a humorous song requiring audience participation. The audience supplies a word and the band integrates it into the song, adding extra syllables so that the word sounds like gibberish. When they perform the song in a contest, the band wins first prize. Roland suggests that Tip apply a similar strategy to his pitching, supplying nonsense responses to the opposing team's comments. Tip rejoins the team and finds this solution effective. He is able to laugh at the situation, regaining his confidence and emerging as his team's hero.

Ace pitcher Tip O'Hara faces some tough going when he develops "rabbit ears" and becomes distracted by the jeers and taunts of the opposing team. (Cover art by Leslie Morrill.)

Although Slote integrates realistic game segments into his plots, his philosophy is similar to that of the main character's father in the author's book *Stranger on the Ball Club,* who tells his son that "baseball is fun, but there's more to life." Rather than focusing directly on the sport, Slote often uses the main character's little league experience as a secondary storyline which enriches both the character and the plot. As in *Hang Tough, Paul Mather,* many of the protagonists' more serious difficulties are unrelated to the game. In the author's 1971 work, *Jake,* the eleven-year-old title character lives with his twenty-four-year-old uncle Lenny, whose career as a musician in the city leaves him little time for his nephew. Jake's lack of supervision causes him to arrive late to school and fall asleep in class, until the school principal threatens to send him to a foster home. While Jake worries about being separated from his uncle, he also has a responsibility to his baseball team. The first-place team has lost its coach and has been unable to find a replacement. Tough and determined, Jake acts as temporary coach until the league prohibits this setup. In a desperate attempt to solve their problem, Jake's teammates look for a nearby practice space for Lenny. When Jake impresses the rival coach with his determination to win, the coach rewards

Robby and his sister Peggy plot to foil the burgeoning romance between their father and his new business partner in Slote's novel about growing up and making difficult adjustments. (Cover illustration by Richard Williams.)

Jake with the use of his warehouse. Lenny agrees to practice there so that he can coach the team and spend more time with Jake.

Although the majority of Slote's sports fiction novels revolve around baseball, he has also written works about young hockey, tennis, and soccer players. *Moving In* incorporates a soccer team into its complex plot, yet the team plays a minor role. Eleven-year-old Robby Miller and his sister Peggy have moved to Arborville with their father following the death of their mother. Their father joins the computer company his friend Ruth Lowenfeld won from her husband in their recent divorce settlement. Robby and Peggy resent both the move and Mrs. Lowenfeld, whom they are convinced is determined to marry their father. Robby finds, however, that he has some interests in common with Mrs. Lowenfeld's daughter Beth, who plays soccer on a team coached by her father. With Beth's help, Robby and Peggy try to prevent the marriage. While Peggy tries to get their father interested in their student housekeeper, Robby becomes involved in a more daring scheme. He copies a valuable computer program written by his father and gives the disk to Mrs. Lowenfeld's ex-husband, hoping to ruin his father's business and end his partnership with Mrs. Lowenfeld. But Mr. Lowenfeld refuses to accept the disk. Eventually, Mrs. Lowenfeld reveals her predetermined plan to marry her boss.

Like many of his sports fiction books, Slote's series of science fiction novels, which follow the adventures of the futuristic Jameson family, also explores relationships. In his 1975 novel *My Robot Buddy,* ten-year-old Jack, a lonely country boy, convinces his parents to have a robot built according to his specifications. Jack's parents agree to buy him the pricey gift, commissioning the scientist Dr. Atkins to build it. Named Danny One, the robot looks very similar to Jack, but is so perfect that the two have little in common. The family has difficulty getting used to the new member of the family, but they eventually grow attached to him. When robot-nappers mistakenly steal Jack, the real robot must come to Jack's rescue. In the 1978 sequel *My Trip to Alpha I,* Jack, wishing to help his aunt prepare to move to Earth, travels to her planet by means of "VOYA-CODE." His body remains behind, but his mind travels by computer to receive a temporary body on Alpha I. When Jack arrives, his wealthy aunt announces her decision to remain on the planet and give her property to two

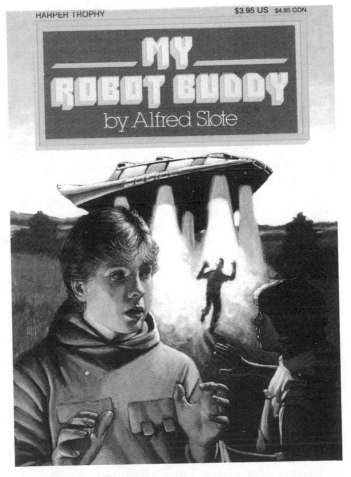

After his parents get him an all-purpose robot for his tenth birthday, Jack stumbles onto a plot to steal his mechanical pal. (Cover illustration by Michael Garland.)

servants. Jack discovers that his aunt is actually in VOYA-CODE and suspects the two servants of foul play.

The Jamesons continue their adventures in *C.O.L.A.R.: A Tale of Outer Space.* While they are traveling, their spaceship runs out of fuel, leaving them stranded on an asteroid which the Colony of Lost Atkins Robots (C.O.L.A.R.) is using as a hideout. The robots hold the family prisoner, but because Jack and his robot are nearly identical, they manage to escape and eventually make peace between the robots and Dr. Atkins, their inventor. In Slote's 1983 book *Omega Station,* the last work of the series, Dr. Atkins informs Danny and Jack that the evil Otto Drago is robot-napping. To figure out why, Jack poses as Danny and is stolen and taken to Omega Station. Here Drago, hoping to create an all-robot world, reprograms robots to make weapons that will destroy the human race. Drago threatens to kill Jack, but Danny and the other robots come to his rescue, destroying Drago and converting Omega Station into a health resort.

Slote returned to his baseball themes in *The Trading Game* and *Finding Buck McHenry,* both of which focus on baseball cards and the history of the game. *The Trading Game,* Slote's 1990 novel, centers on ten-year-old Andy Harris. An avid baseball card collector, Andy desperately wants his friend Tubby's card featuring Andy's grandfather, a former major league player whom Andy idolizes. Tubby offers it to him in exchange for Andy's 1952 Mickey Mantle card, which is worth $2500. While Andy considers this proposition, his grandfather arrives in town and—though ailing—coaches Andy's little league team. When the two quarrel over a rule, Andy learns of his grandfather's competitive streak, which jeopardizes their relationship. Slote's 1991 book, *Finding Buck McHenry,* concerns Jason, an eleven-year-old who cares more about collecting base-ball cards than practicing the game, and has been cut from his little league team. He finds a baseball card displaying a 1930s Negro league star pitcher named Buck McHenry and becomes convinced the player is Mack Henry, a local school custodian. After some hesitation, Mr. Henry confirms Jason's suspicion, but asks him to keep it a secret. Jason asks Mr. Henry to coach a new team that is being formed. Mr. Henry agrees, but then is the subject of a television program about sports which puts the team, Mr. Henry, and Jason in jeopardy.

WORKS CITED:

Junior Literary Guild, March, 1975, p. 32.
Slote, Alfred, *Stranger on the Ball Club,* Lippincott, 1970.
Sutherland, Zena, "New Titles for Children and Young People: 'Hang Tough, Paul Mather,'" *Bulletin of the Center for Children's Books,* June, 1973, p. 162.
"Younger Fiction: 'Hang Tough, Paul Mather'," *Kirkus Reviews,* February 1, 1973, pp. 116-17.

FOR MORE INFORMATION SEE:

BOOKS

Children's Literature Review, Volume 4, Gale, 1982, pp. 198-204.
Something about the Author, Volume 8, Gale, 1976, pp. 192-93.
Twentieth-Century Children's Writers, Third edition, St. James, 1989, pp. 893-94.

—*Sketch by Joanna Brod*

*   *   *

SORENSEN, Virginia 1912-1991

OBITUARY NOTICE—See index for *SATA* sketch: Born February 17, 1912, in Provo, UT; died in 1991. Author. Sorensen is remembered as an acclaimed writer for both children and adults. Her first novel, *A Little Lower Than the Angels,* was praised for its accurate psychological depiction of Mormon women faced with polygamy. Also celebrated was *The Proper Gods,* a novel concerning the Yaqui Indians of the American Southwest; critics cited Sorensen's simple, direct prose and her gift for developing realistic, convincing characters. In the mid-1950s, Sorensen began to write mostly children's novels, which were also met with enthusiasm and recognition. *Miracles on Maple Hill,* for instance, won the John Newbery Medal in 1957. Her other children's books include *Plain Girl* and *Friends of the Road.*

OBITUARIES AND OTHER SOURCES:

Date of death provided by the Kerlan Collection at the University of Minnesota.

BOOKS

Who's Who in America, 46th edition, Marquis, 1990.

*   *   *

SPINKA, Penina Keen 1945-

PERSONAL: Born February 5, 1945, in Brooklyn, NY; daughter of Jack (a shoe-maker) and Yetta (in retail sales) Keen; married Barry A. Spinka (an underwriter), December 23, 1984; children: Rasha Nechama Aberman, Warshaw, Tzivia Leah Aberman Wasserman. *Education:* Attended Queen's Hospital Nursing School, Nassau Community College, NY. *Politics:* "Honesty-Fairness Party (my own)." *Religion:* Jewish-Earthist. *Hobbies and other interests:* Hiking, gardening, sight-seeing, "and of course reading!"

ADDRESSES: Home—4 Glenmont Court, Glenmont, NY 12077.

CAREER: City of Los Angeles Municipal Reference Library, Los Angeles, library clerk; word-processing operator for title insurance reports. Served as a volunteer providing library service to local homebound residents.

PENINA KEEN SPINKA

MEMBER: National Fantasy Fan Federation, Society of Children's Book Writers, Parents of North American Israelis, Woman's American O. R. T., Hudson Valley Writers' Guild.

WRITINGS:

White Hare's Horses, Atheneum, 1991.
Mother's Blessing, Atheneum, 1992.

WORK IN PROGRESS: Blood of a Mohawk and *Mohawk Girl,* a series of books on two Mohawk women. Researching Inuit and lost Greenlandic culture.

SIDELIGHTS: Penina Keen Spinka is noted for the well-researched historical novels about Native Indian culture that she writes for young adults. Drawing her readers into the lives of young Indian people dwelling in pre-colonial North America, Spinka has been praised for her sensitive portrayal of Indian tribes such as the Chumash and the Aztec, and for her attention to detail in her descriptions of Native American culture. "Before it became popular, I wanted to know how the original people of what came to be called America lived," Spinka told *SATA.* First coming into contact with the Chumash culture on hiking trips in the Santa Monica Mountains north of Los Angeles, she was inspired by their peaceful way of life "so 'in harmony' with the Earth's—they had a virtual 'garden of Eden' until they were expelled and enslaved by the Spanish-sent missionaries. My first two books are about them—pre-invasion. I like happy endings. Not much has been happy about their existence since."

White Hare's Horses takes place in 1522 and describes how horses were introduced by the Aztec Indians to the tribes living in what is now southern California. White Hare, a young Chumash girl, bravely faces an invasion of Aztecs who are fleeing through her village on horses that they have stolen from the Spanish Conquistadors. She realizes that the Aztecs are planning to use the strange animals to aid them in conquering and enslaving her people; by bravely setting loose the horses and driving them to freedom over the Santa Monica Mountains the young woman saves her peaceful village.

Mother's Blessing, a prequel to *White Hare's Horses,* recounts the fulfillment of a prophecy which finds a Chumash maiden named Four Cries destined to unite three warring Indian tribes, thus saving many lives and going on to become the leader of her people. "One Dutch reader of my first novel, *White Hare's Horses,* told me the majority of Europeans think 'Indians' dropped into the American West just in time to give the 'calvary' an enemy to fight," Spinka remarked, underscoring the purpose that her novels hold in educating young readers to Indian ways.

Spinka has always placed a high value on imagination, both in her literary tastes and in the subjects she has chosen to write about. "Mrs. Ackerman, my old English literature teacher, told me I ought to be a writer in junior high. I always loved fantasy with creatures that didn't exactly exist (fairies, Peter Pan, Robin Hood) but should have. Then came mythology. Mary Renault was

White Hare bravely faces a threat to her tribe in Spinka's novel about the introduction of horses to Indian tribes in southern California. (Cover art by Ed Martinez from *White Hare's Horses*.)

a major influence: *The King Must Die* made ancient times come alive. *The Long Ships* brought me back to the Denmark of Harold Blue-tooth, adventures and good, sensible Viking thinking. Herman Hesse, Ann Rice, Chelsea Quinn Yarbro (with her wonderful gentleman vampire, St. Germain), Anya Seton Chase. These all influenced my thinking and my writing."

Spinka's personal spirituality also provides her with a motivation for writing for young adults. As she told *SATA,* "Religion ought to be able to lift people to new heights, and to inspire us to care for each other. Much of what entertains the average reader of today does not entertain me. I want to provide an alternative for people who share my feelings."

Spinka has based her next series of books on the Mohawk Indian culture of what is now New York State; her "Mohawk" series will consist of the books *Mohawk Girl* and *Blood of a Mohawk.* "It's a saga of two women, mother and daughter, spanning two generations, the Iroquois culture of the 1300s, the Algonquin, Naskapi, Inuit, and Greenlandic," Spinka told *SATA.* "Journeys and learning about life and cultures are important to the plotting, but the characters of the Mohawk girl, Picture-Maker, and the Viking-Mohawk halfbreed, lngrid, in *Blood of a Mohawk* are what I hope will really make the stories and affect the reader."

FOR MORE INFORMATION SEE:

PERIODICALS

Bulletin of the Center for Children's Books, July, 1992, p. 306.
School Library Journal, April, 1991, p. 124.
Voice of Youth Advocates, April, 1991, p. 36.

*　　*　　*

SPOHN, David 1948-

PERSONAL: Born March 16, 1948, in Dixon, IL; son of Joseph Peter (an editor) and Shirley Jane (a homemaker and teacher; maiden name, Miller) Spohn; married Sandy Jean Barna (a weaver), October 31, 1970; children: Nathan Peter, Matthew Joseph. *Education:* Lovas College, B.A., 1970.

ADDRESSES: Agent—Jonathon Lazear, The Lazear Agency Inc., 430 First Ave. North, Minneapolis, MN 55401.

CAREER: Free-lance illustrator, 1970—; artist-in-residence at public schools in Stillwater, MN, 1976-77; Community Programs in the Arts and Sciences (COMPAS), artist-in-residence, 1978-80; Hazelden Educational Materials, Center City, MN, senior artist, 1981—. Worked variously as factory labor, gypsum mine labor, hog farmer, janitor, and little league baseball coach.

MEMBER: Society for Children's Book Writers.

AWARDS, HONORS: Benjamin Franklin Award, Publishers Marketing Association, 1988, for *The Color of Light;* Bronze Echo Awards, Direct Marketing Association, for educational materials catalog, 1985 and 1987.

WRITINGS:

SELF-ILLUSTRATED

Nate's Treasure, Lothrop, 1991.
Winter Wood, Lothrop, 1991.
Starry Night, Lothrop, 1992.
The Basketmaker, Lothrop, in press.
Home Field, Lothrop, in press.

ILLUSTRATOR

DiGiovanni, Kathe, *My House is Different,* Hazelden Foundation, 1984.
Casey, Karen, *Worthy of Love,* Hazelden Foundation, 1985.

Also illustrator for *Each Day a New Beginning,* Hazelden Foundation, 1982; *The Promise of a New Day,* Hazelden Foundation, 1983; *Today's Gift,* Hazelden Foundation, 1985; *Night Light,* Hazelden Foundation, 1986; *Touchstones,* Hazelden Foundation, 1986; *One More Day,* Hazelden Foundation, 1987; and *The Color of Light,* Hazelden Foundation, 1988.

SIDELIGHTS: David Spohn told *SATA:* "My books are the result of the wish to contribute something lasting and life enhancing to the world of children's literature. My children, our farm, and our experiences together provide settings and stories. My children inspire me in many ways.

"I have done many different kinds of work as well as many art related jobs, and have lived in the Midwest for most of my life, except for a couple of years on the West Coast. Everything we [have] done has been a part of my education as an artist and writer. Although my father, mother, and older brother are all writers and editors, I

DAVID SPOHN

DAVID SPOHN

WINTER WOOD

Spohn's children and his farm helped inspire books like his self-illustrated *Winter Wood*.

have very little training as a writer. In beginning to write, I employed the same basic principles I've always used in my visual art. That is, to choose subjects close to home—things that I care about—and keep the technical aspects simple.

"I like picture books because they are a perfect way to capture and package a warm story or a tiny revelation. I hope that adults benefit from my books as well as children. I have found picture books to be a valuable part of the literature I've experienced as an adult. I feel grateful to my children for all that they teach me, and for all the good books they bring into my life. Some of my favorites are *Natural History* by Brooke Goffstein, *The Tomten* and *Owl Moon* by Jane Yolen, and *Lentil* by Robert McCloskey.

"I grew up in Decatur, Illinois, and Chicago. When I was little, my dad worked at a newspaper and would bring home stacks of newsprint. My older brother and I would devour it. I think he taught me to draw. I imitated what he did and copied all kinds of drawings. My parents always encouraged me, and my teachers did too. I did caricatures and learned a lesson about people in high school this way. I did a caricature of a very handsome, strong teacher who, in turn, wanted to kill me. This was after doing a caricature of a very homely looking, frail man who loved what I did. I studied at the day school of the Chicago Art Institute when I was young, and studied painting with my mother under a private instructor for a while.

"Drawing was always a passion for me and I never really thought of doing anything else when I grew up. I never thought I was capable of writing, but it seems that my children brought my stories to me. I'm still having as much fun as I did as a child."

STEELE, Mary Q(uintard Govan) 1922-1992
(Wilson Gage)

OBITUARY NOTICE—See index for *SATA* sketch: Born May 8, 1922, in Chattanooga, TN; died June 30, 1992. Author. Steele, who wrote the "Mrs. Gaddy" series and other books under the pseudonym Wilson Gage, was the author of many books for young people, one of which, *Journey Outside,* was named a Newbery Honor Book. Her interest in natural history and bird-watching is often evident in her writings, and she has been recognized for creating realistic and respectable characters. Steele's works include *Wish, Come True, The Life (and Death) of Sarah Elizabeth Harwood,* and *Anna's Summer Songs.*

OBITUARIES AND OTHER SOURCES:

BOOKS

Authors of Books for Young People, 3rd edition, Scarecrow, 1990.

PERIODICALS

School Library Journal, August, 1992, p. 23.

*   *   *

STEELSMITH, Shari 1962-

PERSONAL: Born October 10, 1962, in Seattle, WA; daughter of Daniel (an auto industry service manager) and DeMaris (a homemaker; maiden name, Raefield). *Education:* Seattle Pacific University, B.A., 1984. *Religion:* Protestant.

ADDRESSES: Office—c/o Parenting Press, 1106 55th Ave. NE, No. F, Seattle, WA 98125.

CAREER: Author. Parenting Press, Seattle, managing editor, 1983—.

MEMBER: Society of Children's Book Writers, Book Publishers Northwest (co-president, 1990).

AWARDS, HONORS: Alumni Award, Seattle Pacific University, 1991.

WRITINGS:

Elizabeth Blackwell: Story of the First Woman Doctor, Parenting Press, 1987.
(Contributor) *Historical Activity* Parenting Press, 1989.
Juliette Gordon Low: Founder of the Girl Scouts, Parenting Press, 1990.
History Come Alive: 101 Activities. Parenting Press, 1990.

*   *   *

STONES, (Cyril) Anthony 1934-

PERSONAL: Born February 8, 1934, in Glossop, England; son of Arnold (a dyer) and Agnes (a milliner; maiden name, Boyle) Stones; children: Gerrard; other

Anthony Stones, his son Gerrard, and statues of Bougainville, Captain Cook, and Abel Tasman.

sons. *Education:* Attended St. Bede's College, 1945-49; attended Manchester Regional College of Art, 1950-51; attended Auckland Teachers College.

ADDRESSES: Office—c/o Wolfhound Press, 68 Mountjoy Square, Dublin, Ireland; c/o Royal Society of British Sculptors, 108 Old Brompton Rd., South Kensington, London SW7 3RA, United Kingdom.

CAREER: Sculptor, illustrator, author. *Exhibitions:* Portrait bronze of Liam O'Flaherty in National Gallery of Ireland; portrait bronze of Dorothy Hodgkin in Somerville College, Oxford, England; bronze figure of Jean Batten at Auckland International Airport; commissioned by New Zealand Expo '92 to make seven life-size sculptures of Pacific discoverers and explorers for the New Zealand Pavilion at Seville Expo '92. Other sculptures on display in numerous public and private collections in Great Britain, New Zealand, Australia, Ireland, and the United States; drawings and paintings on display in various collections, including Exeter University, Hocken Library, and Auckland City Art Gallery.

MEMBER: Royal Society of British Sculptors (member of council, 1989—).

AWARDS, HONORS: Winston Churchill travelling fellowship, 1992.

WRITINGS:

AUTHOR AND ILLUSTRATOR

Bill and the Ghost of Grimley Grange, Wolfhound Press, 1988.
Bill and the Maze at Grimley Grange, Wolfhound Press, 1990.

EDITOR

Celebration (anthology of New Zealand writing), Penguin, 1985.

WORK IN PROGRESS: A Victorian navvy for British Rail; a posthumous bust of Katherine Tynan for the Irish Writers Museum, Dublin, Ireland.

SIDELIGHTS: Although Anthony Stones is best known as a sculptor of historical figures, he also has used his creative talents to write and illustrate two children's books about the adventures of Bill, a serene child who meets a headless ghost. Stones told *Something About the Author* (*SATA*): "For many years I had from time to time tried to make something out of the cliche ghost who carries his head tucked underneath his arm. In 1984, I suddenly hit on the idea of introducing Bill and the ghost to each other. I drew and wrote the story direct into a sketchbook. I tried the idea out on several publishers to no avail."

Despite the lack of interest from publishers, Stones kept the idea in mind until some years later, when he mentioned his manuscript to a friend at Wolfhound Press, who later arranged to publish it. The book, *Bill and the Ghost of Grimley Grange,* was well-received by critics and Stones decided to write a sequel, *Bill and the Maze at Grimley Grange.* "Both books are conceived of as primarily bedtime stories to be read to a youngster," Stones told *SATA.* "But this does not rule out the hope that they will appeal as 'a good read' to all children from three to ninety-three."

Stones said he "deliberately" created Bill as "an ordinary boy." He told *SATA:* "Too much children's writing in the U.K. has middle-class, goody-goody 'Christopher Robin' types instead of ordinary, believable lads or girls from ordinary, believable backgrounds. If then, as in the 'Bill' stories, the young, ordinary protagonist is placed in a highly unreal situation, his situation is that much more believable to the young reader." Stones added: "I hope that Bill will make further appearances although there is nothing in preparation at present."

In addition to his work in the field of children's literature, Stones is very successful in his main career as a sculptor. One of his most visible projects was the group of sculptures which he created for the New Zealand pavilion at the 1992 Seville Expo. The life-sized sculptures, which represent seven key explorers in New Zealand and Pacific history, gave Stones an opportunity "to think sculpturally about the relations of figures in a group," he told Kevin Ireland of the *Listener & TV Times.* Ireland praised Stones' effort, calling the sculpture "one of [New Zealand's] most ambitious and dramatic sculpture commissions."

WORKS CITED:

Ireland, Kevin, article in *Listener & TV Times,* January 27, 1992, p. 42.

FOR MORE INFORMATION SEE:

PERIODICALS

Center for Children's Books Bulletin, September, 1991, p. 23.
Times Educational Supplement, June 14, 1985, p. 28.

*   *   *

STUCKY, Naomi R. 1922-

PERSONAL: Born December 11, 1922, in Wilson, KS; daughter of John (a minister) and Rose (a homemaker; maiden name, Hampl) Kejr; married Solomon J. Stucky (a minister, teacher, and writer), August 2, 1942 (died, c. 1988); children: Mary Elizabeth Stucky Myers, David Solomon Stucky. *Education:* Attended Midwest Bible Institute; Western Michigan University, B.A., 1954, M.A. (teaching of literature and languages), 1961, M.A. (English), 1971; MacArthur College, Queens University, teaching certificate, 1973. *Religion:* Mennonite.

ADDRESSES: Home—28 Dundas, Brighton, Ontario KOK 1HO, Canada.

CAREER: Board of Education, Lawrence, MI, high school teacher, 1954-60; Board of Education, Kalamazoo, MI, high school teacher, 1960-71, Northumberland and Newcastle Board of Education, Coburg, Ontario, Canada, high school teacher, 1971-85.

WRITINGS:

Sara's Summer, Herald Press, 1990.

Contributor of articles to teachers' magazines, religious magazines, and newspapers.

WORK IN PROGRESS: A sequel to *Sara's Summer,* and a juvenile/young adult work set in central Kansas in 1934-35.

SIDELIGHTS: Naomi R. Stucky told *SATA* that she is the "granddaughter of a Czech Baptist missionary [and] oldest daughter of a Baptist minister." She met her husband while they were both attending Midwest Bible Institute in Salina, Kansas. After graduation, "while my

NAOMI R. STUCKY

husband was in the ministry, I reared our two children, taught Sunday School, Daily Vacation Bible School and taught and chaperoned at summer Bible camps," said the author. "I also furthered my own education." Stucky has taught English, French, and U.S. history in high schools.

Commenting on her writing, Stucky told *SATA:* "I have traveled extensively all over North America with my husband visiting Mennonite and Hutterite communities, resulting in the source material for my novel, *Sara's Summer.*"

T

THALER, Shmuel 1958-

PERSONAL: Born September 20, 1958, in New York, NY; son of Alvin (a television director) and Pat (a university dean; maiden name, Koch) Thaler; married Kathy Cytron (in social work), May 17, 1987; children: Kayla Ariel Cytron-Thaler. *Education:* New York University, B.F.A., 1982. *Religion:* Jewish.

ADDRESSES: Home—3560 North Main St., Soquel, CA 95073. *Office—Santa Cruz Sentinel,* 207 Church St., Santa Cruz, CA 95060.

SHMUEL THALER

CAREER: Freelance photojournalist, 1974—; *Santa Cruz Sentinel,* Santa Cruz, CA, staff photographer, 1988—.

MEMBER: National Press Photographers Association.

AWARDS, HONORS: First place, Kodak/Parade American Woman Photo contest, 1990; first place, Associated Press News Executives Council, 1991.

WRITINGS:

Photography: Take Your Best Shot, Lerner Publications, 1991.

Photographic work published in books, including *Small Inventions that Made a Big Difference,* edited by Donald J. Crump, National Geographic Society, 1984, and in periodicals, including *Time, People, Forbes, USA Today, Los Angeles Times, New York Times, Washington Post, Parade,* and *Landscape Architecture.*

FOR MORE INFORMATION SEE:

PERIODICALS

School Library Journal, November, 1991, p. 142.

* * *

THIELE, Colin (Milton) 1920-

PERSONAL: Surname is pronounced "Tee-lee"; born November 16, 1920, in Eudunda, South Australia; son of Carl Wilhelm (a farmer) and Anna (Wittwer) Thiele; married Rhonda Gill (a teacher and artist), March 17, 1945; children: Janne Louise, Sandra Gwenyth. *Education:* University of Adelaide, B.A., 1941, Diploma of Education, 1947; Adelaide Teachers College, Diploma of Teaching, 1942.

ADDRESSES: Home—24 Woodhouse Crescent, Wattle Park, South Australia 5066, Australia.

CAREER: South Australian Education Department, English teacher and senior master at high school in Port Lincoln, 1946-55, senior master at high school in Brighton, 1956; Wattle Park Teachers College, Wattle Park, Australia, lecturer, 1957-61, senior lecturer in English, 1962-63, vice-principal, 1964, principal, 1965-73; Murray Park College of Advanced Education, director, 1973; Wattle Park Teachers Centre, Wattle Park, principal, 1973-81. Common Wealth Literary Fund lecturer on Australian literature; speaker at conferences on literature and education in Australia and the United States. *Military service:* Royal Australian Air Force, 1942-45.

MEMBER: Australian College of Education (fellow), English Teachers Association (president, 1957), South Australian Fellowship of Writers (president, 1961), Australian Society of Authors (council member, 1965-87; president, 1987-90).

AWARDS, HONORS: W. J. Miles Poetry Prize, 1944, for manuscript of *Progress to Denial;* Commonwealth Jubilee Literary Competitions, first prize in radio play section, for *Edge of Ice,* and first prize in radio feature section, both 1951; South Australian winner in World Short Story Quest, 1952; Fulbright scholar in the United States and Canada, 1959-60; Grace Leven Poetry Prize, 1961, for *Man in a Landscape;* Common Wealth Literary Fund fellowship, 1967-68; *Blue Fin* was placed on the international honours list of the Hans Christian Andersen Award, 1972; Writers Award, 1973, and Edgar Allan Poe Award runner-up, 1974, both for *The Fire in the Stone;* Visual Arts Board Award, 1975, for *Magpie Island;* awarded the Companion of the Order of Australia in the national honours list, 1977; Austrian State Prize for Children's Books, 1979, for *The SKNUKS,* and 1986, for *Pinquo;* Book of the Year Award, Children's Book Council of Australia, for *The Valley Between,* 1982; numerous commendations in Australian Children's Book Council awards.

WRITINGS:

CHILDREN'S FICTION

The Sun on the Stubble, Rigby, 1961, White Lion, 1974.
Storm Boy, illustrations by John Baily, Rigby, 1963, Rand McNally, 1966, new edition with illustrations by Roger Ingpen, Rigby, 1974, film edition with photographs by David Kynoch, Rigby, 1976, new edition with illustrations by John Schoenherr, Harper, 1978.
February Dragon, Rigby, 1965, Harper, 1966.
The Rim of the Morning, Rigby, 1966.
Mrs. Munch and Puffing Billy, illustrations by Nyorie Bungey, Rigby, 1967.
Blue Fin, illustrations by Roger Haldane, Rigby, 1969, Harper, 1974.
Yellow Jacket Jock, illustrations by Clifton Pugh, Cheshire, 1969.
Flash Flood, illustrations by Jean Elder, Rigby, 1970.
Flip-Flop and the Tiger Snake, illustrations by Elder, Rigby, 1970.

COLIN THIELE

The Fire in the Stone, Rigby, 1973, Harper, 1974, film edition, Puffin, 1983.
Albatross Two, Rigby, 1974, published as *The Fight against Albatross Two,* Harper, 1974.
Magpie Island, illustrations by Haldane, Rigby, 1974.
Uncle Gustav's Ghosts, Rigby, 1974.
The Hammerhead Light, Rigby, 1976, Harper, 1976.
Storm Boy Picture Book, photographs by Kynoch, Rigby, 1976.
The Shadow on the Hills, Rigby, 1977, Harper, 1977.
The SKNUKS, illustrations by Mary Milton, Rigby, 1977.
Ballander Boy, photographs by David Simpson, Rigby, 1979.
Chadwick's Chimney, illustrations by Ingpen, Methuen, 1979.
River Murray Mary, illustrations by Ingpen, Rigby, 1979.
The Best of Colin Thiele, Rigby, 1980.
Tanya and Trixie, photographs by Simpson, Rigby, 1980.
Thiele Tales, Rigby, 1980.
Little Tom Little, photographs by Simpson, Rigby, 1981.
The Valley Between, Rigby, 1981.
Patch Comes Home, Reading Rigby, 1982.
The Undercover Secret, Rigby, 1982.
Pinquo, illustrations by Milton, Rigby, 1983.
Pitch the Pony, Reading Rigby, 1984.
Potch Goes Down the Drain, Reading Rigby, 1984.

Coorong Captive, Rigby, 1985.
Seashores and Shadows, McVitty, 1985, published as *Shadow Shark,* Harper, 1988.
Farmer Schultz's Ducks, McVitty, 1986, Harper, 1988.
Skipton's Landing; and River Murray Mary, illustrations by Ingpen, Rigby, 1986.
Shatterbelt, McVitty, 1987.
The Ab-Diver, Horwitz, Grahame, 1988.
Jodie's Journey, McVitty, 1988, Harper, 1990.
Klontarf, Rigby, 1988.
Danny's Egg, Angus & Robertson, 1989.
Stories Short and Tall, Weldon, 1989.
Rotten Egg Paterson to the Rescue, illustrations by Karen Ritz, Harper, 1991.

CHILDREN'S VERSE

Gloop the Gloomy Bunyip, illustrations by Baily, Jacaranda, 1962, revised within *Gloop the Bunyip,* 1970.
Gloop the Bunyip, illustrations by Helen Sallis, Rigby, 1970.
Songs for My Thongs, illustrations by Sandy Burrows, Rigby, 1982.

EDITOR; CHILDREN'S PLAYS

(With Greg Branson) *One-Act Plays for Secondary Schools,* Books 1-2, Rigby, 1962, one-volume edition of Books 1-2, 1963, Book 3, 1964, revised edition of Book 1 published as *Setting the Stage,* Rigby, 1969, revised edition of Book 2 published as *The Living Stage,* Rigby, 1970.
(With Branson) *Beginners, Please* (play anthology), Rigby, 1964.
(With Branson) *Plays for Young Players,* Rigby, 1970.

TEXTBOOKS

The State of Our State, Rigby, 1952.
(Editor and annotator) *Looking at Poetry,* Longmans, Green, 1960.

ADULT FICTION

Labourers in the Vineyard, Rigby, 1970, Hale, 1970.
The Seed's Inheritance, Lutheran Publishing House, 1986.

ADULT VERSE

Progress to Denial, Jindyworobak, 1945.
Splinters and Shards, Jindyworobak, 1945.
The Golden Lightning, Jindyworobak, 1951.
Man in a Landscape, Rigby, 1960.
In Charcoal and Conte, Rigby, 1966.
Selected Verse (1940-1970), Rigby, 1970.
Poems in My Luggage, Omnibus, 1989.

RADIO PLAYS

Burke and Wills (verse), first performed at the Adelaide Radio Drama Festival, 1949, published in *On the Air,* edited by P. R. Smith, Angus & Robertson, 1959.
Edge of Ice (verse), first performed, 1952.
The Shark Fishers (prose), first performed, 1954.
Edward John Eyre (verse), first performed at the Adelaide Radio Drama Festival, 1962.

EDITOR

Jindyworobak Anthology (verse), Jindyworobak, 1953.
(With Ian Munde) *Australian Poets Speak,* Rigby, 1961.
Favourite Australian Stories, Rigby, 1964.
(And author of commentary and notes) *Handbook to Favourite Australian Stories,* Rigby, 1964.

OTHER

Barossa Valley Sketchbook, illustrations by Jeanette McLeod, Rigby, 1968.
Heysen of Hahndorf (biography), Rigby, 1968.
Coorong, photographs by Mike McKelvey, Rigby, 1972, Hale, 1972.
Range without Man: The North Flinders, photographs by McKelvey, Rigby, 1974.
The Little Desert, photographs by Jocelyn Burt, Rigby, 1975.
Grains of Mustard Seed, South Australia Education Department, 1975.
Heysen's Early Hahndorf, Rigby, 1976.
The Bight, Rigby, 1976.
Lincoln's Place, Rigby, 1978.
Maneater Man: The Story of Alf Dean, the World's Greatest Shark Hunter, Rigby, 1979.
The Adelaide Story, Peacock Publications, 1982.
Writing for Children: A Personal View, Oldmeadow, 1983.
South Australia Revisited, Rigby, 1986.
Something to Crow About, Commonwealth Bank, 1986.
Coorong, illustrations by Barbara Leslie, Wakefield, 1986.
A Welcome to Water, Wakefield, 1986.
Ranger's Territory: The Story of Frank Woerle, Angus & Robertson, 1987.

ADAPTATIONS:

Storm Boy (feature film), screenplay by Sonia Borg, South Australian Film Corporation, 1976.
Blue Fin (feature film), South Australian Film Corporation, 1978.
The Fire in the Stone (television film), screenplay by Graeme Koestveld, South Australian Film Corporation, 1983.
Danny's Egg (television film), Channel Nine (Sydney), 1987.
The Water Trolley (television film, adapted from the short story by the same name in *The Rim of the Morning*), Channel Nine (Sydney), 1989.

SIDELIGHTS: One of the most versatile and prolific of living Australian writers, Colin Thiele is responsible for an impressive array of award-winning work. While holding down a succession of positions in teaching and educational administration from the time he left the Royal Australian Air Force at the age of twenty-five at the end of World War II until his professional retirement in 1981, he has produced novels, poetry, and numerous volumes for adults in history, travel, the environment, biography, essay, and anthology. His fiction and verse for children account for more than forty volumes, he has produced several children's textbooks and anthologies, and has written verse plays for radio, television documentaries, children's serials, and school broadcast programs.

Thiele's numerous children's publications are easily described. He once remarked in the *Fifth Book of Junior Authors and Illustrators* that he liked to write about "what I know. That is why most of my books are set in South Australia—on the coastline, the River Murray, the opal fields, the desert, and in the German communities where my ancestors settled. I think the spirit of a place is important, and I think a book should catch that spirit, even though it is often a question of trying to catch the uncatchable. A book should also reveal something about human beings, about the universal things that live in people from generation to generation: happiness and sadness, wisdom and folly, avarice and generosity, cruelty and compassion." As for some critics' charge that his writing is often moralizing, Thiele responds in *Something about the Author Autobiography Series* (*SAAS*) that "if that means I see stories as a teaching instrument I make no apologies for it. I have often argued that all writers for children are teachers whether they are aware or it or not.... But if I teach when I write I sincerely hope that I don't also preach."

Mischief and mayhem form the backdrop for this novel about a very strange friendship. (Cover illustration by Karen Ritz.)

Thiele, the son of first-generation Australians of German parentage, was born in 1920 in the South Australian town of Eudunda. Raised in the German culture, he and his three sisters and brother grew up with the hymns of the Lutheran church, sausages drying in the cellar, and a regular schedule of farm chores. As he put it in *Something about the Author,* his early life was "basically rural—farm and township, fallow and stubble, week-day and Sunday ... yabby creek and red-gum hillock, candlelight and oven bread, mealtime grace and family Bible, Christening font and graveside coffin." Thiele ranged far and wide about the countryside in his leisure time, a factor to which he attributes his lifelong interest in the environment. Much of his children's fiction deals with environmentalist or conservationist themes.

Thiele began primary school in the town of Julia at the age of four, and he recalled in *SAAS* that the school affected him "profoundly." By the time he was ten he had read all twenty-five books in the library, and by the age of eleven he had written "a massive pirate novel called 'Blackbeard.'" He went on to higher primary school in Eudunda, high school in Kapunda, and, beginning in 1936, the University of Adelaide. By then, he told *SAAS,* he knew "the writing virus" was in his blood. While at the university Thiele met and worked with other writers, read extensively, and worked as a junior teacher in the education department to help pay his expenses. He also began to publish poetry. In 1941 he went on to teachers college and earned certification for high school teaching.

The onset of World War II interrupted Thiele's career, and as a member of the Royal Australian Air Force he served in New Guinea and the islands north of Australia until the end of the war. During his military service he produced an unpublished novel called "Of Few Days." He married in March 1945, left the service in October, and a few weeks later took a position as an English teacher at Port Lincoln High School. He moved on to Wattle Park College in 1957, became principal there in 1965, and in 1973 became principal at Wattle Park Teachers Centre.

By the time his first children's novel, *The Sun on the Stubble,* was published in 1961, Thiele had already published four volumes of poetry for adults. The novel, written while Thiele was a Fulbright scholar in the United States studying teacher education, was about the German-Australian communities of his youth. Calling it "episodic in form—a series of related pictures and incidents held together by a simple plot with a boy in the centre," he described it further in *SAAS* as "partly a book of boyhood, partly of adulthood." *The Sun on the Stubble* has remained in print from the date of its publication and has sold, in Thiele's words, "hundreds of thousands of copies."

Thiele's next work for children, *Storm Boy,* is the story of an isolated rural boy in South Australia who moves to the city when a hunter shoots his pet pelican. In the words of a 1979 reviewer for the *Bulletin of the Center for Children's Books,* the book carried the "perennial

Thiele received many letters from young readers who were moved by this tale about a boy from rural Australia who moves to the city when a hunter shoots his pet pelican. (Illustration from *Storm Boy* by John Schoenherr.)

appeal of a tender, if sad, pet story" with an "appeal to young conservationists." Made into a feature film in 1976 by the South Australian film corporation, the story in Thiele's words in *SAAS* was "unbelievably successful" and helped typecast him as an "environmental writer." The author received thousands of letters of praise for the book from children, epitomized by one that he remembered read: "Dear Mr. Thiele, I will never, never, NEVER kill a pelican, Yours sincerely . . . . "

Thiele continues to produce many well-received books for children. *February Dragon* is the story of the destruction of a New South Wales farm family's home and miles of surrounding bush country by fire. *Blue Fin,* also made into a feature film, is about a seemingly hopelessly untalented boy who finds his niche as a tuna fisherman. *The Fire in the Stone* is about the struggles of a boy living among the Australian opal fields at Cooper Pedy, where, Thiele remembered in *SAAS,* "the country-side looked like a moon landscape—dusty, waterless,

and pock-marked with mines and mullock heaps." *The Fire in the Stone* was made into a television film in 1983.

Partly because of advancing rheumatoid arthritis, Thiele changed jobs in 1973 to one that required less administrative responsibility. Consequently he found he had more time to write. *Ballander Boy, Tanya and Trixie,* and *The SKNUKS* were intended for very young readers, while other novels were aimed at older readers. *Albatross Two* is about the dangers inherent in offshore oil drilling, *The Hammerhead Light* deals with the relationship between a young girl and an elderly seaman, and *River Murray Mary,* a historical novel, concerns the establishment of irrigation settlements by Australian soldiers coming home from World War I. Books such as *Uncle Gustav's Ghosts, The Shadow on the Hills,* and *The Valley Between* are, like *The Sun on the Stubble,* about Thiele's German-Australian origins.

Retired from his day job in early 1981, Thiele has continued to write, both for adults and children, despite the fact that his arthritis makes it increasingly difficult for him to move around. He has also managed to continue a vigorous schedule of speaking engagements at schools and colleges, clubs, parent groups, and conferences and has continued to broadcast on radio what he calls "hundreds of little historical cameos that ... set the telephone ringing with requests from listeners who have become absorbed in this issue or that." He added in his *SAAS* essay that he still has "a few unwritten books dancing about inside my head. I don't know whether they'll ever get out."

WORKS CITED:

Bulletin of the Center for Children's Books, April, 1979.
Thiele, Colin, *Fifth Book of Junior Authors and Illustrators,* edited by Sally Holmes Holtze, H. W. Wilson, 1983, pp. 310-312.
Something about the Author, Volume 14, Gale, 1978, pp. 201-205.
Something about the Author Autobiography Series, Volume 2, Gale, 1986, pp. 251-270.

FOR MORE INFORMATION SEE:

BOOKS

Contemporary Literary Criticism, Volume 17, Gale, 1981.
McVitty, Walter, *Innocence and Experience,* Nelson, 1981.
Prentice, Jeffery, and Bettina Bird, *Dromkeen: A Journey into Children's Literature,* J. M. Dent, 1987.
Twentieth-Century Children's Writers, 3rd edition, St. James, 1989, pp. 957-959.

PERIODICALS

Australian Book Review, Children's Supplement, 1964, 1967, 1969.
Books and Bookmen, July, 1968.
Bulletin of the Center for Children's Books, November, 1966.
Childhood Education, December, 1966; April, 1967.
Publishers Weekly, March 24, 1989.
Variety, December 29, 1976; September 28, 1983.

*   *   *

TUSA, Tricia 1960-

PERSONAL: Surname is pronounced "too-sa"; born July 19, 1960, in Houston, TX; daughter of Theodore S., Jr., and Francese (Moran) Tusa. *Education:* Attended University of California, Santa Cruz, summer, 1978; studied art in Paris, spring, 1981; University of Texas at Austin, B.F.A., 1982; New York University, masters in art therapy, 1989. *Hobbies and other interests:* Horseback riding, oil painting, reading.

ADDRESSES: Home—1357 Santa Rosa, Santa Fe, NM 87501. *Office*—c/o Farrar, Straus & Giroux, Inc., 19 Union Square W., New York, NY 10003.

CAREER: Author and illustrator of children's books. Art therapist with learning disabled and emotionally disturbed children, Acquired Immune Deficiency Syndrome (AIDS) patients, and psychiatric care patients at various institutions, including Mount Sinai Hospital, New York City, 1988, Kingsboro Hospital, Brooklyn, NY, 1988, and Reece School, New York City, 1989. Art instructor at numerous institutions, including Houston Retarded Center, Houston, TX, 1980, Children's Museum, Houston, 1984, and Post Oak Montessori School, Houston, 1989-90. Designer and illustrator for Estee Lauder, 1982, DC Comics, 1983, and Cooper Hewitt Museum. Head chef at soup kitchen in Santa Fe, NM.

MEMBER: American Art Therapy Association, Southwest Writers.

AWARDS, HONORS: Miranda was named a children's choice selection by the International Reading Association and the Children's Book Council, 1986; *Maebelle's Suitcase* was chosen as an American Bookseller "Pick of the List," 1987; *Miranda, Maebelle's Suitcase,* and *Stay Away from the Junkyard!* were chosen as Reading Rainbow selections, 1989.

WRITINGS:

SELF-ILLUSTRATED

Libby's New Glasses, Holiday House, 1984.
Miranda, Macmillan, 1985.
Chicken, Macmillan, 1986.
Maebelle's Suitcase, Macmillan, 1987.
Stay Away from the Junkyard!, Macmillan, 1988.
Sherman and Pearl, Macmillan, 1989.
Camilla's New Hairdo, Farrar, Straus, 1991.
The Family Reunion, Farrar, Straus, in press.

ILLUSTRATOR

Steven Kroll, *Loose Tooth,* Holiday House, 1984.
William H. Hooks, *Lo-Jack and the Pirates,* Bantam, 1991.

Also contributes illustrations to several children's magazines.

WORK IN PROGRESS: "Carefully studying my family, friends, and cousins! Their quirks, mannerisms, shoes, hairdos ...."

SIDELIGHTS: Tricia Tusa told *SATA:* "I think I do what I do because I am endlessly fascinated by children—how they think and feel, what delights them, what scares them, how they wonder about things. I often wonder if children aren't here as complex gifts for us to learn by. I admire the uncanny ability to cut to the truth. They often can be the most honest reflection you may have around of yourself.

"I am also aware of and am concerned about children's vulnerability. There are so many outside influences interfering with the child doing what comes so very naturally—discovering and developing into and becoming who they are. Quite unconsciously, my books seem

Some wave back.

Tricia Tusa's close inspection of the people she meets, as well as friends and family, helps form the design of characters like those in _Sherman and Pearl._

to repeatedly reflect this idea of becoming who you are—and that it's okay to be different. Also, my books are embarrassingly autobiographical. Again, quite unconsciously, they inevitably reflect whatever feelings, issues, struggles I am dealing with at the time. And, strangely enough, they are usually the same issues I wondered about as a child—yet, now with older eyes and ears.

"For inspiration I study people's faces down the aisles at the grocery store, at the laundromat. I eavesdrop at the hardware store. One unusual face or some innocuous comment from a stranger can spark or complete an idea. However, my luxuriously endless conversations in the kitchen with my three older sisters are often the best form of creative outpouring—as well as therapy.

"And, I can't forget to mention my pet rabbit, Mrs. Stewart—named after my first-grade art teacher. With great concentration, she thump, thump, thumps around my house and occasionally pauses long enough for us to have an in-depth discussion about the meaning of life, the weather, and what it's like to have a nose that is constantly moving."

FOR MORE INFORMATION SEE:

PERIODICALS

Bulletin of the Center for Children's Books, November, 1984; April, 1985; June, 1986; July-August, 1987.

U–W

UCHIDA, Yoshiko 1921-1992

OBITUARY NOTICE—See index for *SATA* sketch: Born November 24, 1921, in Alameda, CA; died after a stroke, June 21, 1992, in Berkeley, CA. Educator, secretary, and author. Uchida is the author of widely recommended children's books that deal with the Japanese-American experience and are noted for their elaborate plots and fleshed-out characters. She taught schoolchildren while she and her family were confined to a internment camp for Japanese Americans in the Utah desert during World War II. Later, she worked as a secretary in order to have time to write after work. Her first book, *The Dancing Kettle and Other Japanese Folk Tales*, consists of stories she adapted for American children. Uchida's nonfiction includes *Desert Exile: The Uprooting of a Japanese-American Family*, a memoir, and *The Invisible Thread*, an autobiography aimed at teenagers. She is also the author of *A Jar of Dreams* and *The Happiest Ending*.

OBITUARIES AND OTHER SOURCES:

BOOKS

Twentieth-Century Children's Writers, 3rd edition, St. James Press, 1989.

PERIODICALS

Chicago Tribune, June 28, 1992, section 2, p. 6.
Los Angeles Times, June 27, 1992, p. A26.
New York Times, June 24, 1992, p. A18.
School Library Journal, August, 1992, p. 23.

*   *   *

VALENTINE, Johnny [a pseudonym]

ADDRESSES: Agent—c/o Alyson Publications, 40 Plimpton St., Boston, MA 02118.

WRITINGS:

The Duke Who Outlawed Jellybeans, Alyson Wonderland, 1991.
The Daddy Machine, Alyson Wonderland, 1992.

WORK IN PROGRESS: A book of fairy tales.

SIDELIGHTS: In a recent interview, Johnny Valentine said: "My goal was to write stories so good that they'd be enjoyed by kids from all types of families—stories that both gay and straight parents would want to buy for their kids.... Fairy tales break the world into black and white, heroes and villains. On the other hand, I think the real essence—and the most interesting aspect—of the world is that there is no black and white, only infinite shades of grey."

JOHNNY VALENTINE

WORKS CITED:

Valentine, Johnny, publicity interview conducted for Alyson Publications, 1991.

*   *   *

WALSH, Jill Paton
    See PATON WALSH, Gillian

*   *   *

WARD, Helen 1962-

PERSONAL: Born November 9, 1962, in Gloucester-shire, England; daughter of Gordon (an artist) and Maureen (an artist) Ward. *Education:* Attended Glou-cestershire College of Art, 1981-82; Brighton Polytech-nic, B.A. (honours), 1985.

ADDRESSES: Office—c/o Templar Publishing Company, Pippbrook Mill, London Rd., Dorking, Surrey RH4 IJE, England.

CAREER: Author and illustrator.

AWARDS, HONORS: Walker Books student prize, illustration, 1985.

WRITINGS:

SELF-ILLUSTRATED

The Moonrat and the White Turtle, Ideals, 1990.

The characters in Helen Ward's self-illustrated *The Moonrat and the White Turtle* exist in an invented landscape inspired by the author's geological studies.

The Golden Pear, Ideals, 1991.

*ILLUSTRATOR; "JUNGLE HIDEAWAYS" SERIES
  WRITTEN BY A. J. WOOD*

Animal Families, Price, Stern, 1989.
Animal Food, Price, Stern, 1989.
Animal Friends, Price, Stern, 1989.
Animal Homes, Price, Stern, 1989.

Also illustrator of *Animal Colours, Animal Counting, Animal Opposites,* and *Animal Sounds,* all for Price, Stern.

*ILLUSTRATOR; "CURIOUS CREATURES" SERIES
  WRITTEN BY JOYCE POPE*

(With Stella Stilwell) *Living Fossils,* Steck-Vaughn Library, 1991.
(With Stilwell) *On the Move,* Steck-Vaughn Library, 1991.
(With Adam Hook) *Making Contact,* Steck-Vaughn Library, 1992.
(With Hook) *Strange Nature,* Steck-Vaughn Library, 1992.
(With Stilwell) *Two Lives,* Steck-Vaughn Library, 1992.

ILLUSTRATOR

Andrew Lang, *Sinbad the Sailor and Other Stories,* Longman, 1986.
Geraldine McCaughrean, *The Story of Christmas,* Ideals, 1989.
McCaughrean, *The Story of Noah and the Ark,* Ideals, 1989.
Wood, *Helen Ward's Amazing Animals,* Bell Books, 1991.
Wood, *Helen Ward's Beautiful Birds,* Bell Books, 1991.

WORK IN PROGRESS: Illustrations for a treasury of nursery rhymes; a novel "currently called 'Brydge' and unlikely to be finished."

SIDELIGHTS: Helen Ward told *SATA:* "To me as an illustrator and author, the pictures in my books are at least as important as the text. The plots and pictures develop together usually from one or two images—real or imagined. Photographs of the peculiar and magical limestone towers of China and East Asia first caught my imagination years ago whilst I was studying geology. *The Moonrat and the White Turtle* was written around an invented landscape. *The Golden Pear* was written some years after I watched a crow take a small pear from a tree. The near silhouette of the bird's wings and the pear held delicately by the stalk in its beak was an impressive image.

"I determined to be an illustrator as soon as I became aware that there was such a profession; this would have been at about the age of nine. I soon added writing to this ambition. Most of my writing however has been for my own pleasure; in consequence, I find writing for publication difficult. The biggest challenge seems to be knowing when to stop reworking the text. With illustration this stage is obvious."

WIESNER, David 1956-

PERSONAL: Surname is pronounced "*weez*-ner"; born February 5, 1956, in Bridgewater, NJ; son of George (a research manager at a chemical plant) and Julia (a homemaker; maiden name, Collins) Wiesner; married Kim Kahng (a surgeon), May 21, 1983; children: Kevin. *Education:* Rhode Island School of Design, B.F.A., 1978.

ADDRESSES: Home—700 Westview, Philadelphia, PA 19119. *Agent*—Dilys Evans, P.O. Box 400, Norfolk, CT 06058.

CAREER: Author and illustrator of children's books. Has appeared as a guest on the *Today* show, NBC-TV, 1992. *Exhibitions:* Wiesner's paintings have been displayed in the Metropolitan Museum of Art, New York City, 1982, as well as in various galleries, including Master Eagle Gallery, New York City, 1980-89, Academy of Natural Sciences, Philadelphia, PA, 1986— (permanent exhibit), Museum of Art at Rhode Island School of Design, Providence, RI, 1989, Brooklyn Public Library, Brooklyn, NY, 1990, Muscarele Museum of Art, College of William and Mary, Williamsburg, VA, 1990, Society of Illustrators, New York City, 1991 and 1992, and Greenwich Public Library, Greenwich, CT.

AWARDS, HONORS: The Loathsome Dragon was granted a Children's Picturebook Award by *Redbook,* 1987; *Free Fall* was named a Caldecott Honor Book by the American Library Association (ALA), 1989; *Hurricane* was named a "Pick of the List" by *American Bookseller,* and one of the "Best Books of 1990" by *School Library Journal; Tuesday* was awarded the Caldecott Medal by ALA, 1992, and was named a 1991 notable children's book by ALA, a 1991 Reviewer's Choice by *Sesame Street Parents' Guide,* one of the "Ten Best Books of 1991" by *Parenting Magazine,* a "Pick of the List" by *American Bookseller,* and one of the "Best Books of the Year" by *School Library Journal* and *Publishers Weekly;* Parents' Choice citation, 1992, for *June 29, 1999.*

WRITINGS:

SELF-ILLUSTRATED

(Reteller with wife, Kim Kahng) *The Loathsome Dragon,* Putnam, 1987.
Free Fall (picture book), Lothrop, 1988.
Hurricane (picture book), Clarion Books, 1990.
Tuesday (picture book), Clarion Books, 1991.
June 29, 1999 (picture book), Clarion Books, 1992.

ILLUSTRATOR

Gloria Skurzynski, *Honest Andrew,* Harcourt, 1980.
Avi, *Man from the Sky,* Knopf, 1980.
Nancy Luenn, *The Ugly Princess,* Little, Brown, 1981.
David R. Collins, *The One Bad Thing about Birthdays,* Harcourt, 1981.
Jane Yolen, *The Boy Who Spoke Chimp,* Knopf, 1981.

Yolen, *Neptune Rising: Songs and Tales of the Undersea Folk,* Philomel Books, 1982.

Mike Thaler, *Owly,* Harper, 1982.

Vera Chapman, *Miranty and the Alchemist,* Avon, 1983.

Allan W. Eckert, *The Dark Green Tunnel,* Little, Brown, 1984.

William Kotzwinkle, *E. T.: The Storybook of the Green Planet* (based on a story by Steven Spielberg), Putnam, 1985.

Eckert, *The Wand: The Return to Mesmeria,* Little, Brown, 1985.

Dennis Haseley, *Kite Flier,* Four Winds, 1986.

Nancy Willard, *Firebrat,* Knopf, 1988.

The Sorcerer's Apprentice: A Greek Fable, retold by Marianna Mayer, Bantam, 1989.

Laurence Yep, *The Rainbow People,* HarperCollins, 1989.

Tongues of Jade (Chinese American folk tales), retold by Yep, HarperCollins, 1991.

ADAPTATIONS: Free Fall has been adapted into a videocassette with teacher's guide, distributed by American School Publications, 1990; *Tuesday* has also been adapted into a videocassette, distributed by American School Publications, 1992.

DAVID WIESNER

SIDELIGHTS: "I create books I think I would have liked to have seen when I was a kid," David Wiesner remarked in an interview with *Something about the Author* (*SATA*). "I loved being able to get lost in paintings and to get involved in all the details." Winner of the 1992 Caldecott Medal for his picture book *Tuesday,* Wiesner combines his imaginative powers with his talent for illustration, producing award-winning works like *Free Fall, Hurricane,* and *The Loathsome Dragon.* He was born into a creatively inclined family— art and music number among his siblings' interests— and grew up in an environment that encouraged his own flair for drawing. "I never had the sense that I had to rebel at home so my parents would let me be an artist," he recalled in his interview. "They made my love of drawing seem like something natural—I thought it was the norm." Eventually, his love of drawing fused with his fascination for storytelling, and he found his niche in children's literature, particularly in picture books. He works primarily in watercolors, and expresses his passion for creativity in humorous and inventive tales. "What I really find interesting is that opportunity to take a normal, everyday situation and somehow turn it on its end, or slightly shift it. I love to introduce a 'what if?,' or juxtapose things that aren't normally together. Those just happen to be the kind of ideas I generate."

Born in 1956 to George and Julia Wiesner, David found the diverse landscape of his Bridgewater, New Jersey, hometown well-suited to his active imagination. Making use of the local cemetery, the river that bordered it (which neighborhood kids called a swamp), the nearby woods, and the town dump, Wiesner and his friends concocted all sorts of games, among which "army" was a particular favorite. "We had very specific rules when we played army," Wiesner remembered in his interview, "that said if you were chasing someone and came to a road in the cemetery (which was to us a river), you had to shuffle your feet and hold your hands over your head to keep your gun dry (which was usually a stick). As soon as you got to the other side you could run again because you'd be on dry land." Ordinary objects were also transformed by the young Wiesner's creativity: wire hangers and plastic bags formed homemade hot-air balloons for a pastime called UFO, and a simple tree and some sticks made wonderful tree forts. "There was that constant ability to transform the everyday world into the pretend. We continually reinvented the world around us when we played."

Even though neighborhood companions in Bridgewater were in abundance, Wiesner enjoyed spending long stretches of time by himself, so much so, he laughingly admitted to *SATA,* that "there were times my parents were probably worried that, somehow, I didn't have any friends." During these periods of solitude, Wiesner often found himself drawing. "Art has always been a part of my life. I can't pinpoint the exact time when I began drawing; it was something I was always doing, and it became part of how I was perceived. It also defined my personality to a certain extent: clearly when relatives were aware of my interest in art, I would get various art supplies on Christmas and birthdays, and a lot of hand-me-downs—boxes of pastels, watercolors—from Carol, my oldest sister, and George, my brother, who are both pretty artistically inclined. I loved to watch them draw things."

Wiesner's penchant for drawing was fueled further by a television show he watched when he was about six or seven years old. Hosted by artist Jon Gnagy and originally aired in the late 1940s, *You Are an Artist* marked one of TV's first forays into instructional programming. Wiesner, who caught the telecast in reruns, was fascinated with Gnagy's work, particularly with the artist's attention to perspective, light, and scale. The youngster bought Gnagy's instruction books and earnestly practiced drawing all the pictures first in charcoal in black and white, then in color. "The books and program probably provided my first formal exposure to techniques and ideas about drawing," Wiesner recalled in his *SATA* interview. "Gnagy could stand there and in fifteen or twenty minutes turn out these drawings. I thought it was just miraculous. I still keep a framed picture of him on my wall."

By junior high school Wiesner had discovered the Renaissance and Surrealism, two creative movements that helped shape his artistic style. The Renaissance artists of the late fifteenth and early sixteenth centuries appealed to the youngster because of their sensitivity to space and perspective. He found himself particularly enchanted by the works of Michelangelo, Leonardo da Vinci, Albrecht Duerer, and Pieter Brueghel the Elder—"the real draftsmen," he declared in an interview for *Clarionews*. "[I] could sit and look at those paintings for hours. There was so much happening in them, from the foreground back to the very, very far distance. You could follow things back to deep space." Surrealism, a twentieth-century art movement committed to the distorted portrayal of reality, also captured Wiesner's attention. "When I finally came across the surrealists," he told *SATA*, "it was like all hell broke loose—not only because they were painting with a similar quality that I saw in the Renaissance painters, but because the subject matter was just unbelievable. I really responded to it. Conceptually, I was really taken with the imagery, the bizarreness, that other-worldliness, that weirdness—it was really very appealing."

That love of the fantastic found its way into Wiesner's creative outlets throughout his teenage years. Horror movies and sci-fi films provided favorite forms of entertainment, and one film in particular, Stanley Kubrick's *2001: A Space Odyssey,* even helped inspire his enthusiasm for wordless storytelling. "I remember going to see *2001* in 1968," Wiesner recalled in *Clarionews*. "I don't want to be too dramatic, but I remember coming out of the theater a changed person. It was unlike anything I'd ever seen. It's almost a silent film; there's very little dialogue. It's all pictures, which tell a remarkably complex story and set of ideas, up there for the viewer to decipher."

Drawing continued to engage Wiesner's interest throughout high school, and he especially enjoyed

The young apprentice looks in awe as his master conjures a new spell. (Illustration by Wiesner from *The Sorcerer's Apprentice,* written by Marianna Meyer.)

sketching "sort of odd subjects," he recalled to *SATA*. "I would conjure up images that usually got some very strange responses. It was really a direct response to the surrealist work that I saw—lots of weird, creepy, floating and flying things which have always been part of the work I do." His own anti-hero super-hero creation, Slop the Wonderpig, grew out of his love of comic books, and his own film, *The Saga of Butchula,* about a milquetoast-turned-vampire who avenges an attack by young thugs, grew out of his desire to experiment with the storytelling process. "Showing *Butchula* at the senior talent show at Bridgewater Raritan East was one of the high points of high school," Wiesner exclaimed to *SATA,* "because the audience reacted at all the right points. I experienced this incredible feeling. It was great!"

High school provided Wiesner with one other strong creative influence: his art teacher Robert Bernabe. "In Mr. Bernabe I finally found someone I could talk to about art," Wiesner revealed in his *SATA* interview. "He essentially encouraged me to follow whatever inclinations I had and was willing to do what he could to facilitate that. This was the first time something like that had happened. He became a sort of confidant for me—I think that to a large degree art is this very personal thing, and Mr. Bernabe was someone with whom I could share my work. He didn't so much

Caldecott Honor-winning *Free Fall* is an imaginative, wordless picture book that follows a boy through the fantastic journey he experiences during one of his dreams. (Illustration by the author.)

influence the projects I was pursuing as he provided me with a sense of encouragement."

However strong an interest art was for Wiesner, he scarcely entertained the idea of turning his craft into a career, until a student from the Rhode Island School of Design (RISD; pronounced "*riz*-dee") visited his art class. "He gave this presentation to the class," Wiesner explained to *SATA,* "and brought along these eight millimeter films of some of the projects he had completed at RISD—interactive sorts of things that were set up in the middle of school. He brought some little contraptions he had made as well as a commercial he had developed for one of his classes. I was just amazed at all the wonderfully creative stuff. I thought, 'Here's a place where everybody is doing art all the time, as opposed to once a week,' and it finally dawned on me that I could actually keep doing this and go to school and study it and make this my living. I kept expecting someone to say, 'okay, now you have to figure out what

you want to do before you go to college for four years.' It finally became clear that I could in fact be an artist."

With encouragement from his parents, Wiesner applied to five art schools in 1973, including New York's Pratt Institute, the Philadelphia College of Art, the Cleveland Institute of Art, and RISD. Accepted by all five, there was no question as to which one he would attend: "I was totally ready for RISD and ready to immerse myself in what the school had to offer," Wiesner told *SATA.* The aspiring artist was greeted with a "pretty intense first year"—one in which he had unlearn many old habits and absorb new ideas and ways of thinking about art. "I remember going to my life-drawing class and noticing that while the teacher didn't really respond to my work, he would look at another student's work and say, 'this is really terrific,' or something like that. I would look at the same work and wonder, 'why is he saying that? He doesn't understand.' Yet by the end of the year I was able to look at that same work and realize 'that's great

stuff.' RISD helped me reorient myself and helped me get rid of some of my preconceived notions."

In short, though Wiesner's experience at RISD was an active one, it was hardly a painful one. In fact, when asked to describe just one highlight he recalls from the school, he is at a loss for words; there were too many, he explained. However, one project does stand out in his memory with particular fondness. The assignment was simply the word "metamorphosis"—a vague suggestion that Wiesner finds challenging; a ten-foot-long, forty-inch-tall painting was the result. "I had this big piece of paper I'd been waiting to use," Wiesner explained to *SATA*, "and I started to play around with these images that began to change and metamorphosize. I suppose it also relates to Dutch artist M. C. Escher (whose work I admire), who tended to focus on flat, graphic objects that shift and change from one to the other. I began the painting with images of oranges, then drew the orange sections falling away and turning into sailing ships. The ground then turned into water, and the ships changed and mutated into giant fish swimming out in the ocean.

When I finished I knew I was on to something—the response in class was really good and I just kept thinking about it. Clearly there was more I could do with this."

The thought of expanding the painting into a narrative—either with words or without—fascinated Wiesner, and his assignments at RISD began to reflect this interest. At first he directed his talent toward adult-fantasy, short, wordless sequences done in oils. As he gained experience, he began developing his own style, primarily using watercolors, and experimenting with characters, settings, and storylines of a lengthier nature. By his senior year he completed a forty-page wordless picture book for adults based on the short story "Gonna Roll the Bones" by Fritz Leiber. "The idea of wordless storytelling was really appealing to me," Wiesner told *SATA*. "I was learning how to compress information as well as how to convey that information visually."

As graduation loomed, Wiesner tossed around the idea of working as an illustrator in some kind of published format, possibly for adult fantasy magazines. Pursuing a career in children's literature hardly crossed his mind. "If you looked at the work I was doing, though," he admitted in his *SATA* interview, "it was obvious I should be going into children's books." Evidently Lester Abrams, one of his instructors at RISD, thought the same thing, for he encouraged his pupil to show his work to noted children's author and illustrator (and later Caldecott Medalist) Trina Schart Hyman, who happened to be speaking at RISD. Hyman, who in 1978 was art director for *Cricket,* a children's magazine recognized for its exceptional illustrations, took one look at Wiesner's work and promptly offered the young artist a magazine cover. Wiesner was both surprised and pleased to discover an audience for his work in children's literature. "I realized," he related to *SATA,* "that there really is this remarkable range in children's literature open to very different personal visions of books. Not all illustrations are fuzzy bunnies and little cute things."

In children's literature Wiesner found his artistic niche. After graduating with his bachelor of fine arts in illustration in the spring of that same year, he procured work illustrating textbooks, which allowed him to compile a professional portfolio and compelled him to work under a variety of constraints involving size, medium, and content. "It's funny," he pointed out to *SATA.* "One of the harder things to resolve coming out of school was moving from a situation in which I wasn't working with too many restrictions into an environment where someone would say, 'Okay, down here in these couple inches along the bottom and maybe partly up the side we want to see Robin Hood, his band of men, the archery contest, the bleachers in the back, the king, and the sheriff of Nottingham.' It's a very difficult thing to adapt to without losing some of your spontaneity. It took me a while to reconcile these different ways of working. Early on, it was somewhat intimidating."

Intimidating or not, Wiesner persevered, and in 1980 secured contracts (with the help of agent Dilys Evans) to illustrate two children's books: Gloria Skurzynski's *Honest Andrew* and Avi's *Man from the Sky.* By this time he had moved to New York City with Kim Kahng, who would later become his wife, and during the next few years he kept busy illustrating a variety of children's books. He also used the time to experiment with and fine-tune his own technique and form. At first, as he candidly admitted to *SATA,* his work appeared a bit unpolished—due in part to his inexperience in the field and in part to having to work with preseparated art, in which color is added only at the printing stage. However, with experience came the development of his own distinctive style as well as the ever-increasing desire to pursue his own book ideas. (The idea for *Free Fall,* inspired by the ten-foot-long painting he had completed at RISD, was already forming in his mind.) However, in 1983 his career was unexpectedly put on hold. The apartment building housing himself and his wife, Kahng, burned to the ground, destroying everything the newly married couple owned.

By the time the Wiesners rebuilt their lives, David faced pressing deadlines for illustrations that had been contracted for a year or two years down the road. Consequently, he was compelled to work on *Free Fall* only in pieces—he would complete a picture or two for the book, then be forced to stop and work on other titles. The pattern continued throughout the 1980s, during which time he illustrated such works as William Kotzwinkle's *E. T.: The Storybook of the Green Planet,* Allan W. Eckert's *Wand: The Return to Mesmeria,* and Dennis Haseley's *Kite Flier.* In 1987 he tackled another self-illustrated project—*The Loathsome Dragon,* retold with Kahng and based on the English fairy tale *The Laidly Worm of Spindleston Huegh.* The narrative relates the story of the beautiful Princess Margaret, who becomes trapped inside the body of an enormous dragon through the sorcery of her evil, jealous stepmother. Only three kisses from Margaret's brother, Childe Wynd, who is traveling in a far-off land, will free the princess from the spell. Wiesner captured *The Loathsome Dragon*'s medieval setting with double-page watercolor paintings, which portray detailed landscapes and seascapes, sprawling castles, elaborate robes, jewelry, and armor, and the frightful, yet gentle dragon. Reviewers applauded Wiesner's carefully crafted and attractive scenes as well as his regard for historical accuracy. "Few artists depict the medieval world or labyrinthine castles ... as well," judged a *Publishers Weekly* reviewer. Wiesner's artwork is "delicate, misty, and enchanting, extending and harmonizing with the traditional motifs of this fairy tale," noted *School Library Journal* contributor Constance A. Mellon. Perhaps the most flattering remarks came from 1991 Caldecott Medalist and RISD department head David Macaulay, who wrote in *Horn Book:* "Take a look at the watercolor landscapes [*The Loathsome Dragon*] contains and tell me you don't see a little Da Vinci in there."

By the time *The Loathsome Dragon* was completed, Wiesner was at the point of finishing *Free Fall.* "It had taken me longer than I had hoped to get to the point of completing *Free Fall,*" he revealed to *SATA,* "and the breaks in working on it were hard. But it was better than rushing it. Throughout that time I was focusing on the RISD assignment about metamorphosis—the continuous picture that tells a story. It was when I came up with the idea of the dream, using sleeping and then waking as a framework, that *Free Fall* really began to come together and make sense. The structure of the dream afforded me the opportunity to have the book be less a strict narrative and more a sort of free floating imagery—more impressionistic than a straight storyline."

Released in 1988, *Free Fall* is an imaginative, wordless picture book that follows a young boy through the fantastic journey he experiences during one of his dreams. Featuring images that continually transform into other images, the narrative opens as the youngster falls asleep while studying a book of maps. Reality fades as his bedspread metamorphosizes into a landscape, and he is transported along with exotic companions onto a chessboard with live pieces, to a medieval castle housing knights and a dragon, to rocky cliffs that merge into a

Based on an old English fairy tale, *The Loathsome Dragon* relates the story of a beautiful princess trapped by an evil witch inside the body of a huge lizard. (Illustration by the author from the book by Wiesner and Kim Kahng.)

city skyline, and to a larger-than-life breakfast table. Finally he floats among swans, fishes, and leaves back to his starting place. Especially characteristic of Wiesner's creative ingenuity are the many events and characters the young boy encounters during his dream; most of them correspond to objects in the youngster's bedroom—from the goldfish next to his bed, to the chess pieces stashed in his nightstand, to the pigeons hovering near his window, to the leaves sketched on his wallpaper.

"When I finished *Free Fall*," Wiesner emphasized to *SATA,* "I realized that this was the type of work I really wanted to do. A lot of the sample pieces I had shown to publishers were geared toward typical fairy tale/folk tale kind of works, but there were also these other illustrations in the back of my portfolio that were just weird—editors would usually look at them and go 'oh, this is very interesting....' I would ask if they had any manuscripts to fit the drawings, and they'd invariably say 'no.' So I knew that ultimately I would have to invent my own ideas for books. *Free Fall* was the first true expression of the kind of work that I wanted to be doing."

Critical reaction to *Free Fall* was decidedly mixed. On one hand, reviewers admired the author's technical skill, his attention to architectural detail and form, and his visual creativity. The book is "an excellent replication

of a dream," decided one *Bulletin of the Center for Children's Books* critic. On the other hand, some commentators found the book too complex to be readily understood by a young audience, and they criticized what they perceived as a murky narrative sequence. "The nameless protagonist's ... adventures are confusing, complicated, and illogical," assessed Julie Corsaro in *School Library Journal.* Instead of being upset by the critical response to his first book, Wiesner was amused: "I sort of enjoyed the fact that some reviewers got it," he confessed to *SATA.* "Some of the reviews were absolutely right on and connecting with everything, and others seemed not at all there. It was actually kind of interesting to get that very mixed reaction."

The mixed reaction did not extend to the committee selecting the Caldecott Honor Books in that year, for "the phone rang one Monday morning," Wiesner related to *SATA,* "and the chair of the committee said they had chosen *Free Fall* as an honor book. I experienced the classic reaction: I was left speechless—I just hung up the phone." After some time passed, Wiesner was able to verbalize his reaction: "Having *Free Fall* named a Caldecott Honor Book was a wonderful confirmation that 'yes, this does seem to be the way to go.' It felt really, really satisfying because all along I had the feeling I had been going in the right direction with the pieces I had done and conceived on my own. It was really encouraging that they [the committee] chose a work that isn't in the strict mold of the usual picture book—one that was even perceived by a lot of reviewers as difficult and something that kids wouldn't even relate to."

The same year *Free Fall* was named an honor book, Wiesner was asked by *Cricket* to design another cover (ironically, ten years from the time he illustrated his first *Cricket* cover). Given the artistic freedom to draw whatever he wished—the folks at *Cricket* told him only that the March issue would feature articles on St. Patrick's Day, frogs, and the like—Wiesner responded enthusiastically. "St. Patrick's Day didn't strike a chord—but frogs, they had potential," he said in his Caldecott acceptance speech, as reprinted in *Horn Book.* "I got out my sketchbook and some old *National Geographic*s for reference. Frogs were great fun to draw—soft, round, lumpy, and really goofy-looking. But what could I do with them?" The rhetorical question was no sooner asked by Wiesner, than it was answered. As he recounted to *SATA:* "I envisioned a frog on a lily pad, which reminded me of a flying saucer in a 1950s B movie. As soon as I saw that frog on the lily pad fly, the cover was pretty much right there—this whole bunch of frogs flying out of the swamp."

But a simple cover didn't satisfy the storyteller in Wiesner, who was already envisioning a narrative featuring the frogs. "I was sitting in an airplane, looking through my sketchbook," he continued in his Caldecott acceptance speech, "and I thought, Okay, if I were a frog, and I had discovered I could fly, where would I go? What would I do? Images quickly began to appear to me, and for fear of losing them I hastily scribbled barely legible shapes onto the page: a startled man at a kitchen

In his self-illustrated *Tuesday,* Wiesner tells the whimsical tale of flying frogs who zoom through a small town, creating havoc in their wake.

table; a terrified dog under attack; a roomful of frogs bathed in the glow of a television. A chronology began to take shape, and within an hour I had worked out a complete layout, which remained essentially unchanged through to the finished book. Everything was there: the story, the use of the panels, the times of day, and the title." *Tuesday,* Wiesner's almost wordless 1991 picture book, was created.

Winner of the 1992 Caldecott Medal, *Tuesday* is a whimsical tale about a night when a crowd of frogs ascend to the sky on lily pads and soar over the surrounding neighborhood. Zooming past startled birds and an incredulous resident indulging in a late-night snack, the frogs speed through a clothesline (causing some minor entanglements), and spook Rusty, a sizable dog. They even sneak into a living room housing a sleepy elderly lady and watch some TV (one member of the assemblage operates the remote control with his spindly tongue). "I really felt good when I finished *Tuesday,*" Wiesner admitted in his *SATA* interview,

"and the response was immediate from everyone who saw it." But winning the Caldecott was something Wiesner hardly imagined. His astonishment was yet apparent when he was asked by *SATA* to describe his reaction: "I couldn't quite really believe it had happened ... My reaction is hard to explain ... The Children's Book Council puts out little bookmarks that list all the Caldecott winners back to 1938, and each year they just add the new winner. Looking at that list and seeing my name at the end of it as part of that tradition ... whatever else happens, that's there forever. It really felt good to be included in that."

In addition to *Tuesday, Free Fall,* and *The Loathsome Dragon,* Wiesner has also produced 1990's *Hurricane,* as well as his latest work, 1992's *June 29, 1999.* The former is a well-received picture book drawn from an incident in Wiesner's youth. Depicting the warmth of a family gathered together to wait out a storm, the book also describes the fantastic explorations David and George (two youngsters appropriately named after the Wiesner

brothers) imagine themselves undertaking after the hurricane downs a large elm on their neighbor's front lawn. The latter, *June 29, 1999,* is an amusing, innovative picture book that revolves around young Holly Evans, who sends an assortment of vegetable seedlings into the atmosphere as part of a science experiment for school. A little more than a month later, gigantic rutabagas, avocados, lima beans, artichokes, cucumbers, peas, and all sorts of other vegetables begin falling to the earth. Amazement, anxiety, and confusion overcome citizens. In addition, rumors spread ("4000 lb. Radish Has Face of ELVIS!" screams one tabloid headline); business opportunities in real estate flourish ("Gourd Estates" quickly sprouts in North Carolina); and at least one Iowa farmer is ecstatic ("At last, the blue ribbon at the state fair is mine!" he announces upon finding a gargantuan head of cabbage on his property).

If there is one common thread running through Wiesner's works, it is that his books are entertaining. "I'm hoping kids have fun when they read my books," he expressed in his *SATA* interview. Wiesner has fun

creating them—the abundance of innovative, imaginative, and fantastic events and characters in his works attest to that—yet he also enjoys the challenge of expressing his ideas in a visual format. "I have found that wordless picture books are as enriching and as involving as a book with words in it. In a wordless book, each reader really completes the story; there is no author's voice narrating the story. In books like *Free Fall* or *Tuesday,* there is a lot going on there, and you really need to *read* the picture. A reader can't just flip through the book; all the details add up to more fully tell the story. It's exciting to me to develop that visual literacy."

WORKS CITED:

Corsaro, Julie, review of *Free Fall, School Library Journal,* June-July, 1988, p. 95.
Review of *Free Fall, Bulletin of the Center for Children's Books,* May, 1988, p. 193.
"An Interview with David Wiesner," *Clarionews,* spring, 1992.

A month after Holly Evans sends seedlings into space as part of a science experiment, large vegetables begin falling to Earth. (Illustration from *June 29, 1999,* written and illustrated by Wiesner.)

Review of *The Loathsome Dragon, Publishers Weekly,* October 30, 1987, p. 70.

Macaulay, David, "David Wiesner," *Horn Book,* July-August, 1992, pp. 423-28.

Mellon, Constance A., review of *The Loathsome Dragon, School Library Journal,* March, 1988, p. 178.

Wiesner, David, "Caldecott Acceptance Speech," *Horn Book,* July-August, 1992, pp. 416-22.

Wiesner, David, *June 29, 1999,* Clarion Books, 1992.

Wiesner, David, telephone interview with Denise E. Kasinec for *Something about the Author,* conducted August 27, 1992.

FOR MORE INFORMATION SEE:

PERIODICALS

Bulletin of the Center for Children's Books, November, 1990, p. 74; November, 1992, pp. 93-94.

Horn Book, January-February, 1991, pp. 61-62; January-February, 1992, p. 84.

New York Times Book Review, September 25, 1988, p. 51; August, 1988, p. 99.

Publishers Weekly, July 25, 1986, pp. 187-88; May 12, 1989, p. 294; September 20, 1991, p. 134.

Giant potatoes become an artist's canvas in *June 29, 1999.* (Illustration by the author.)

School Library Journal, January, 1986, p. 66; November, 1986, p. 78; August, 1988, p. 99; May, 1990, pp. 107-08; October, 1990, p. 104; December, 1990, p. 25; January, 1991, p. 56; May, 1991, p. 86; December, 1991, p. 132.

—Sketch by Denise E. Kasinec

*   *   *

WILCOX, Charlotte 1948-

PERSONAL: Born May 2, 1948, in Harris, MN; daughter of Donald (a farmer) and Alice (a homemaker; maiden name, Farmer) Wilcox. *Religion:* Baptist.

ADDRESSES: Home—RR 2, Box 35, Harris, MN 55032.

CAREER: Fingerhut Corporation, Minneapolis, MN, keyliner and copywriter, 1967-69; *Post,* Rush City, MN, typesetter/keyliner/reporter, 1970-75; free-lance writer and graphic designer, 1976—; Rush Printing, Rush City, MN, owner, 1978-81.

WRITINGS:

Trash!, illustrated by Jerry Boucher, Carolrhoda, 1988.
A Skyscraper Story, illustrated by Boucher, Carolrhoda, 1990.
Mummies and Their Mysteries, illustrated by Boucher, Carolrhoda, 1992.

Contributor to Minnesota periodicals.

WORK IN PROGRESS: A "Nature Watch" book on bald eagles for Carolrhoda; research for two books on energy.

SIDELIGHTS: Charlotte Wilcox told *SATA:* "My career as a writer is the sum of two early influences in my life: a love of reading and my desire to become an artist. I took my first bite of classical literature at age six, when I [was] determined to read the King James Bible from beginning to end. Although I did not reach that goal for over fifteen years, my introduction to the Bible's Elizabethan-style prose gave me a head start in learning to read styles beyond those provided in my school textbooks. At age ten I read my first Victorian novel, *Jane Eyre* by Charlotte Brontë—and became a book lover for life. Since I love horses even more than I love books, my favorite reading in elementary school included *The Black Stallion* by Walter Farley and *Black Beauty* by Anna Sewell. Reading aloud also helped me become a better reader. I read *Charlotte's Web* by E. B. White many times over to my brothers and sisters when we were growing up on our farm in Minnesota in the 1950s.

CHARLOTTE WILCOX

"As a teenager I learned to appreciate other literature styles—like the plays of William Shakespeare. After years of reading the King James Bible, I found Shakespeare easy to understand because the style is similar. I especially enjoyed the writings of William Blake, because he combined writing and art in his works. I had always wanted to become an artist, and I liked the way Blake used art engravings to enhance his poems.

"When I entered the world of commercial art as a graphics assistant in 1967, I discovered that the graphic artist's medium is primarily typography—the art of placing words on a page in a manner that says in a visual way what the words themselves say through language. My early career in graphic design provided a natural incubator for a parallel vocation in writing.

"A free-lancer in a rural area is a little like the country doctor who must be physician, veterinarian, dentist, and midwife all in one. A free-lance writer in an outlying area has to balance many hats on one head—technical writer, journalist, script writer, photographer, ad executive, editor, and typographer. Writing nonfiction for children requires some of the same juggling: translating technical information into everyday language, condensing it into bite-size pieces, and framing it in a context that makes sense to the young reader. My goals in writing for children are to present detailed concepts in a linear structure, so that one detail builds on another rather than confusing it; and to provide meaningful comparisons between technical information and familiar ideas or objects, giving the reader a framework for translating the information into his own experience."

Y–Z

YANG, Mingyi 1943-

PERSONAL: Born July 15, 1943, in Suzhou, Jiangsu, China (now People's Republic of China); son of Yang Zhengguan and Wu Qiuying; married Zhu Qian; children: Yang Huan. *Education:* Attended Suzhou Arts and Crafts Institute, 1958-62, and Central Fine Arts Institute, 1981-82; has been studying in the United States since 1987.

ADDRESSES: Home—143-43 41st Ave., number 7G, Flushing, NY 11355. *Agent*—Amelia L. Carling, 375 Hudson St., New York, NY 10014.

CAREER: Suzhou Arts and Crafts Research Institute, designer, 1962-63; Suzhou Arts and Crafts Institute, teacher, 1963-72; Suzhou Traditional Painting House, artist, 1972-87. *Exhibitions:* Yang's work has been displayed at various national exhibits in Beijing, People's Republic of China, as well as in exhibitions in Hong Kong, Japan, Taiwan, India, France, and the United States.

MEMBER: Chinese Painting Association, Jiangsu Woodcuts Academy, Suzhou Painting Academy, Suzhou Woodcuts Arts Research Association.

AWARDS, HONORS: Prize for Excellence, Eighth National Woodcuts Exhibition (Beijing, People's Republic of China), 1983; Bronze Medal, Sixth National Art Exhibition (Beijing), 1984; Prize for Excellence, Eighteenth Selected Contemporary Ink and Brush Painting Exhibition of Japan, 1985; Second Prize, Chinese National Woodcuts Invitation Exhibition, 1985. Stamp design chosen as winner of national competition sponsored by the Chinese Postal Service, issued fall, 1989.

WRITINGS:

The Matching-Selling Girl (fairy tales), Jiangsu Province Publishing House, 1980.
Classmates, Beijing Children Publishing House, 1981.
Water Town, Beijing Peoples' Art Publishing House, 1985.

MINGYI YANG

Dreamland of Hometown, Xing Yuan Art Gallery, 1991.
Yang Ming-Yi Painting Anthology, Great Master Art Center, 1991.
The World of Yang Ming-Yi, Carolyn Hill Art Gallery, 1991.
The Journey of Meng, Dial, 1991.

SIDELIGHTS: Mingyi Yang told *SATA:* "The influence of the traditional Chinese opera and the living [conditions] of my childhood stimulated my rich imagination and deep love for art. My father was a great fan of the traditional Chinese opera. He was not only an expert in playing the two-string violin—a Chinese musical instrument used especially in Chinese opera—but also an opera actor.

"Chinese opera is an exquisite art of singing and acting. It conveys the most expressive inner feelings and thoughts of the human being. And the rich-colored costumes the performers wore increased the charm and beauty of their performance. It stimulated my imagination and gave me an impulse to draw what I was thinking as I was watching. This started my life of painting. At that period, I could stay at home, thinking and drawing and making my home the place for exhibiting my 'production.'

"I still remember the piece of wall located outside my bedroom. I saw it everyday through the window of my bedroom. It was a piece of very plain, old, and variegated wall. But for me, it was everything. I could find different scenes from the wall every time I looked at it: forest, mountain, sea or plain, city or field, animals and flowers—everything. I was always eager to draw on paper the inspiration I got from the wall. For me, drawing is just like play, full of fun. This made me a constant winner [of] schools' art contests.

"My native city is Suzhou, the 'Oriental Venice.' The rivers stretch everywhere in the city. There are many artistically built gardens around or along the rivers, decorated with houses, pavilions, bridges, artificial hills, trees and bushes, flowers and fences, so poetic and beautiful. I had spent countless days there, drawing and painting. These wonderful days not only became my precious memory but also made it possible for me to devote myself to painting as a career.

"Lately, Chinese painters are [no longer] satisfied with their traditional art only. They wish to broaden their view with the achievements of artists outside of China. They wish to share their experiences with foreign artists. They go [into] the world. That's why I came to New York. I believe this is the beginning of a new era in art, the era of modern Chinese art.

"Since I arrived [in] New York, I [have been] overwhelmed by the rich treasure of the art of the Western World. Besides going to school, I spent almost all my time visiting museums and art galleries. I still do. I wish to create a special art style, based on traditional Chinese painting conceptions, combined with Western painting methods and techniques, and with new painting materials. Now I am working on water-color and water-ink paintings. I also create a series of water-color pictures for ancient Chinese tales. These books are designed for young readers. I [hope] this series of books will open a new world for readers, especially young readers here. The first book of this series is *The Journey of Meng.*"

YOUNG, Judy (Elaine) Dockrey 1949-

PERSONAL: Middle name is pronounced "dock-*reh*," born June 25, 1949, in Muskogee, OK; daughter of Lewin Haden (a farmer) and Iola Fern (a housewife; maiden name, Peterson) Dockrey; married Richard Alan Young (a teacher), March 27, 1982. *Education:* Southwest Missouri State College, B.A., 1972; attended Dallas Theatre Center at Trinity University, 1972-74. *Politics:* Democrat. *Religion:* Presbyterian.

ADDRESSES: Office—c/o Publicity Director, August House Inc. Publishers, P.O. Box 3223, Little Rock, AR 72203.

CAREER: Republic High School, Republic, MO, secondary speech and English teacher, 1976-78; Silver Dollar City, Branson, MO, storyteller, 1978—.

MEMBER: National Storytelling Organization.

WRITINGS:

WITH HUSBAND, RICHARD ALAN YOUNG

Ozark Tall Tales: Collected from the Oral Tradition, August House, 1989.
Favorite Scary Stories of American Children, August House, 1990.
Ghost Stories from the American Southwest, August House, 1991.
Stories from the Days of Christopher Columbus, August House, 1992.
Outlaw Tales of the Middle Border, August House, 1992.

ADAPTATIONS: The Youngs have recorded *Ozark Ghost Stories* and *Ozark Tall Tales* on cassette for August House, 1992.

WORK IN PROGRESS: Editing a volume of African-American stories, researching stories of free Baltic States.

SIDELIGHTS: Raised on a farm in Oklahoma, Judy Dockrey Young told *Something About the Author* (*SATA*) that "reading became my magic carpet early in life. Town was a place we went once a week, maybe. Friends were an impossible bicycle pump up a dirt and gravel road. There was little time available for amusing the kid sister."

"But books were always there," Young recalled for *SATA*. "We *owned* few, but a Carnegie Library was inexhaustible. Recently I returned to my hometown for a visit, and had a thrill. I found some books I wanted at that old friendly library, and they suggested I use a family card. While digging for my mother's card, they unearthed *mine,* signed by me, dated 1956. Books are and always have been my magic. To *make* books, with my husband and co-author, is my joy, because I know what books meant to me."

RICHARD AND JUDY DOCKERY YOUNG

YOUNG, Richard Alan 1946-

PERSONAL: Born March 1, 1946, in Huntsville, TX; son of Morgan Martin (a college professor) and Gertrude (Farine) Young; married Judy Elaine Dockrey (a storyteller), March 27, 1982. *Education:* University of Arkansas at Fayetteville, B.A., M.A. *Religion:* Baptist.

CAREER: Harrison, AR, public schools, social studies and foreign language teacher, 1968-92; Silver Dollar City, Branson, MO, character actor, summer seasons, 1980—, storyteller, 1983—.

MEMBER: National Association for the Preservation and Perpetuation of Storytelling, National Education Association, American Association of Teachers of Spanish and Portuguese, Sons of Confederate Veterans.

WRITINGS:

WITH WIFE, JUDY DOCKREY YOUNG

Ozark Tall Tales: Collected from the Oral Tradition, August House, 1989.
Favorite Scary Stories of American Children, August House, 1990.
Ghost Stories from the American Southwest, August House, 1991.

Stories from the Days of Christopher Columbus, August House, 1992.
Outlaw Tales of the Middle Border, August House, 1992.

Also a professional writer for theme parks and community theaters.

ADAPTATIONS: The Youngs have recorded *Ozark Ghost Stories* and *Ozark Tall Tales* on cassette for August House, 1992.

WORK IN PROGRESS: Working on volumes of African American and Native American stories; researching oral stories from American mining history, particularly Colorado during the 1880s.

SIDELIGHTS: Richard Alan Young's interest in writing was sparked by his father and grandfather, who were both educators and writers. Encouraged to write in grade school, Young continued through high school and college, writing skits, monologues and plays as well as contributing to newspapers.

Young began collecting and telling legends, urban legends, folktales and ghost stories as early as 1954. Interested in reaching a wider audience with his collection of tales, Young collaborated with his wife to produce several books. Together, the Youngs have "traveled to, lived in, or studied in, seventeen foreign nations, especially Ecuador, Mexico, and Germany," the author told *SATA*. He went on to say that he hopes their books will "build bridges between cultures, help people from one area or ethnic group preserve their heritage and be proud of their stories, and share these stories with people of other regions and cultural backgrounds."

* * *

ZEBRA, A.
  See SCOLTOCK, Jack